Advances in Educational Technologies and Instructional Design (AETID) Book Series

ISSN:2326-8905
EISSN:2326-8913

Editor-in-Chief: Lawrence A. Tomei Robert Morris University, USA

MISSION

Education has undergone, and continues to undergo, immense changes in the way it is enacted and distributed to both child and adult learners. In modern education, the traditional classroom learning experience has evolved to include technological resources and to provide online classroom opportunities to students of all ages regardless of their geographical locations. From distance education, Massive-Open-Online-Courses (MOOCs), and electronic tablets in the classroom, technology is now an integral part of learning and is also affecting the way educators communicate information to students.

The **Advances in Educational Technologies & Instructional Design (AETID) Book Series** explores new research and theories for facilitating learning and improving educational performance utilizing technological processes and resources. The series examines technologies that can be integrated into K-12 classrooms to improve skills and learning abilities in all subjects including STEM education and language learning. Additionally, it studies the emergence of fully online classrooms for young and adult learners alike, and the communication and accountability challenges that can arise. Trending topics that are covered include adaptive learning, game-based learning, virtual school environments, and social media effects. School administrators, educators, academicians, researchers, and students will find this series to be an excellent resource for the effective design and implementation of learning technologies in their classes.

COVERAGE

- Bring-Your-Own-Device
- Curriculum Development
- K-12 Educational Technologies
- Hybrid Learning
- Digital Divide in Education
- Instructional Design
- Instructional Design Models
- Game-Based Learning
- Social Media Effects on Education
- Educational Telecommunications

IGI Global is currently accepting manuscripts for publication within this series. To submit a proposal for a volume in this series, please contact our Acquisition Editors at Acquisitions@igi-global.com or visit: http://www.igi-global.com/publish/.

The Advances in Educational Technologies and Instructional Design (AETID) Book Series (ISSN 2326-8905) is published by IGI Global, 701 E. Chocolate Avenue, Hershey, PA 17033-1240, USA, www.igi-global.com. This series is composed of titles available for purchase individually; each title is edited to be contextually exclusive from any other title within the series. For pricing and ordering information please visit http://www.igi-global.com/book-series/advances-educational-technologies-instructional-design/73678. Postmaster: Send all address changes to above address.

Titles in this Series

For a list of additional titles in this series, please visit:
www.igi-global.com/book-series/advances-educational-technologies-instructional-design/73678

Practical Perspectives on Educational Theory and Game Development
Fabio Perez Marzullo (Federal University of Rio de Janeiro, Brazil) and Felipe Antonio de Oliveira (Arco Labs, Brazil)
Information Science Reference • © 2021 • 252pp • H/C (ISBN: 9781799850212) • US $185.00

Handbook of Research on Developing a Post-Pandemic Paradigm for Virtual Technologies in Higher Education
Sandra Maria Correia Loureiro (ISCTE, BRU, Universitário de Lisboa, Portugal) and João Guerreiro (ISCTE, BRU, Universitário de Lisboa, Portugal)
Information Science Reference • © 2021 • 420pp • H/C (ISBN: 9781799869634) • US $245.00

Handbook of Research on Barriers for Teaching 21st-Century Competencies and the Impact of Digitalization
Harpreet Kaur Dhir (Hacienda La Puente Unified School District, USA)
Information Science Reference • © 2021 • 468pp • H/C (ISBN: 9781799869672) • US $245.00

Strategies for Student Support During a Global Crisis
Jeffrey D. Herron (Campbellsville University, USA) and Taurean Douglas (Indiana University Bloomington, USA)
Information Science Reference • © 2021 • 283pp • H/C (ISBN: 9781799870005) • US $195.00

Handbook of Research on Supporting Social and Emotional Development Through Literacy Education
Jill Tussey (Buena Vista University, USA) and Leslie Haas (Buena Vista University, USA)
Information Science Reference • © 2021 • 571pp • H/C (ISBN: 9781799874645) • US $245.00

For an entire list of titles in this series, please visit:
www.igi-global.com/book-series/advances-educational-technologies-instructional-design/73678

IGI Global
PUBLISHER of TIMELY KNOWLEDGE

701 East Chocolate Avenue, Hershey, PA 17033, USA
Tel: 717-533-8845 x100 • Fax: 717-533-8661
E-Mail: cust@igi-global.com • www.igi-global.com

Table of Contents

Detailed Table of Contents

Choosing the right technologies to match student learning outcomes in today's technology-integrated classrooms presents educators with multiple instructional design challenges including selecting appropriate technologies to match desired student learning outcomes. As students continue to have broad access to information from a variety of web-based platforms, teachers are increasingly tasked with ensuring the information used to complete key assignments is authentic and from a verifiable resource. As such, the era of deep fakes in images, audio, videos, and digital texts is more prevalent than ever as numerous programs using artificial intelligence (AI) can significantly alter original content to fundamentally change the intent of original content. A discussion of educational and pedagogic responsibility in the era of deep fakes will serve as the primer for reform of the TPACK construct with recommendations for remediating student work in which deep fake resources were utilized.

The use of existing and emerging technologies in teaching and learning provides the opportunity to present subject-area content using devices, programs, and venues in ways that promote higher-order thinking and long-term retention. In the last decade, advances in artificial intelligence (AI) have resulted in the development of virtual

Today, adolescent learners are exposed to deepfakes from online news to social media. They need data literacy—being able to pose questions about data, extract relevant information, and evaluate claims about data—to retrieve factual information and take informed actions. However, not many students in the U.S. are equipped with data literacy to detect deepfakes. This chapter examines existing practices for teaching and assessing data literacy and suggests best practices for supporting adolescent learners in attaining data literacy. This chapter also discusses the future steps needed to implement these best practices in the classroom so that young learners can mitigate the impacts of deepfakes in their lives.

Artificial intelligence technologies are beneficial for individuals' lives, but those technologies are also sources of mass and chaos. Due to hyper-realistic videos based on artificial intelligence, deepfakes have effects on the public and individuals in terms of manipulation. Researchers try to warn the public and individuals about the threats and harms of these technologies. Moreover, users cannot distinguish whether it is real and fake. As it is known, children and youths are vulnerable to the dark side of technology. So, for risks and harms of technology, digital citizenship is advised as a protection method. In this chapter, the long-term effects of digital citizenship in terms of protecting children and youths from the dangers and threats of deepfakes will be discussed in depth.

Globally, no country has been spared by the spectre of the COVID-19 pandemic and infodemic that continues to wreak havoc on the socio-economic and political stability of governments and communities. The oxymoronic nature of fake news raises many questions with regards to the issues of authenticity because the concept of news is underpinned by verifiability. While fake news lacks variability, it is surprising that its digital imprint on the social media platforms continues to leave indelible marks that will undermine democracy, responsible journalism, and the benefits of the digital media. It is against this background that this chapter seeks to find strategies to flatten the curve of fake news in the epoch of the COVID-19 pandemic and infodemic, an epistemic challenge. The chapter is based on a positivist research methodology that sought to gather views from the study respondents on their epistemic experiences with fake news amidst the COVID-19 pandemic and infodemic. It seeks to gather views to counter the upsurge of fake news amidst the COVID-19 pandemic.

Deepfakes have become an emerging threat to media. Many authors have identified social and digital media as a multimodal artifact. Others have identified the weaponization of that same digital media. At times when media was weaponized before, students were taught persuasive techniques, not as an incentive to use them, but as a guard against those persuasive techniques taking advantage of the students. In this new age of digital, multimodal propaganda, adapting persuasive techniques will help to combat the dangers our society faces. This chapter will examine three different anti-propaganda interventions and examine their implementation against a deepfaked video.

Social media is one of the topmost communications in the present world and some discomforts are also hidden in this. Social media is one of the platforms for cyberbullying. Teenagers who are not under the guidance of their parents are the major victims of cyberstalking and cyber abuses. Forensic image processing enhances the digital image using different computer techniques. Deep fake uses the technology to superimpose more than one image, video, and audio with other images, videos, and audios with the well-known artificial intelligence and generative adversarial networks (GANs). This technology raises the curtain to create many fake images, fake videos, especially porn videos and fake audios of celebrities, especially actors and politicians. This chapter explains the impacts of deep fakes in social media, especially Facebook and Twitter. This chapter proposed a new framework called the extended-RACYBDD to detect the deep attacks.

Preface

The distribution of altered or false information is certainly not a new concept in advertisement, news reporting, and politics. One does not have to venture too far in the immediate past to find examples of how advertising executives, news anchors, field reporters, and politicians have intentionally manipulated data, facts, and events to promote one agenda or viewpoint over another. With the continued rise in the use of social media, online media, and mass communication outlets to distribute information and news, a new type of disinformation has emerged known as the "deep fake". Deep fakes can assume many forms, but the basic definition is that of manipulating audio, images, or video using some form of Artificial Intelligence. For educators and researchers, particularly those in higher education, deep fakes are problematic in terms of ensuring students are receiving accurate information in terms of completing key assignments, tasks, and research.

Choosing the right technologies to match student learning outcomes in today's technology-integrated classrooms presents educators and instructional designers with multiple curricula and instructional design challenges including selecting appropriate technologies to match desired student learning outcomes. As students continue to have broad access to information from a variety of web-based platforms, educators and educational professionals are increasingly tasked with ensuring the information used to complete key assignments or tasks is authentic and from a verifiable resource. As such, the era of deep fakes in images, audios, videos, and digital texts is more prevalent than ever as numerous programs using Artificial Intelligence (AI) can significantly alter original content to fundamentally change the intent of original content. Because many of these AI-based programs are more user-friendly and easily accessible on the internet or mobile devices in a free or relatively inexpensive app, an increase in deep fake content is particularly noticeable within the last decade. Accordingly, educators and educational professionals are now tasked with employing best practices to not only teach basic digital literacy and citizenship skills but also recognize how technology immersed learning environments interact with deep fakes while equipping students with the tools necessary to recognize authentic and altered content.

One of the hallmarks of public education is access to relevant materials and resources that accurately reflect instructional content and anticipated student learning outcomes. For teaching faculty, it is of critical importance that the information students have access to and use to complete content-related tasks is sourced from legitimate, vetted resources accurately reflecting the desired information the student means to convey. However, a growing trend across the Internet is the deliberate misrepresentation of otherwise factual information to sway an end-user to adopt a position or line of thinking that may support their position or act in counter thereof. Manipulating images and text to deliberately misinform or mislead the intended audience, or the rising phenomenon known as deep fakes, has definitely impacted areas such as advertisement, politics, and social media. As research about the effects of deep fakes in these areas has risen significantly over the past few years, especially noted during their intense saturation during the 2016 election cycle, understanding how deep fakes have the potential of negatively affecting the fields of teaching and learning presents as an investigative area in need of significant exploration. Accordingly, the purpose of the query here is to understand the history of deep fakes, their proliferation across mainstream and social media outlets, and the extent of their permeation in classrooms and curricula across educational settings. The intended audience for this work includes curriculum designers, cybersecurity specialists, educational professionals, historians, instructional designers, librarians, media specialists, political scientists, psychologists, sociologists, social media managers, and the like.

The contributors in this volume provide a variety of different perspectives on the impact of deepfakes in teaching and learning. While the topics primarily focus on the educational aspect of deepfakes, their conclusions can inform other disciplines as well. In Chapter 1, author Rebecca Blankenship, in her chapter entitled "Educational Responsibility in the Deepfake Era: A Primer for TPACK Reform" explores techniques teaching professionals can use to mitigate deepfakes by reforming the Technological, Pedagogical, and Content Knowledge (TPACK) framework. She posits that adding additional types of scaffolding to the original model has the potential of increasing digital literacy skills that will facilitate self-regulatory cognition such that end-users can recognize deepfakes in subject-area content.

In Chapter 2, author Rebecca Blankenship suggests a primer to mitigate deepfake and malinformation using the TPACK and Levels of Use (LoU) frameworks filtered through the Vygotskian object/other to self-regulation sociocultural (SCT) lens. The use of existing and emerging technologies in teaching and learning provides the opportunity to present subject-area content using devices, programs, and venues in ways that promote higher-order thinking and long-term retention. In the last decade, advances in Artificial Intelligence (AI) have resulted in the development of virtual reality programs that enable end-users to interact with content in third and fourth-dimensional interactive spaces (i.e., Extended Reality or XR). The transformation beyond traditional face-to-face or two-dimensional teaching and learning has resulted in an unforeseen digital side effect. The digital side effect presents in the form of deepfakes or the deliberate alteration of audio and visual content to advance a specific point of view. The premise of this chapter, then, is to present a primer using the Technological, Pedagogical, and Content Knowledge (TPACK) and Levels of Use construct to mitigate the presence of deepfake and malinformation in subject-area content when working in XR environments.

Authors David Ross and Gina Peyton, in Chapter 3 entitled "The Never-Ending Intellectual Theft of Truth: How the Mainstream Media Cartel Dismembers the Facts," discuss the importance of digital citizenship and literacy among educators and learners to combat deepfake and fake news content. The purpose of this chapter is to examine how the Fake News originated. This term by many who feel it just started in 2016, has been in existence for decades since the evolution of the printing press, which also disseminated false information. The mainstream media and non-mainstream media or just individuals in general have their own biases and agendas, so misinformation, disinformation, exaggerations, and deceptions will exist. This chapter provides individuals from any political perspective or other beliefs evidence to make their own judgements. Digital citizenship and literacy are explored using various examples of obtaining information and use of devices. In addition, this chapter considers how researchers should take risks to explore controversial topics such as fake news to inform an audience using research.

Chapter 4's author Adebowale Adetayo discusses how the role of librarians and media specialists can add another educational scaffold to help teachers and learners better navigate deepfakes in the big data and social media eras. In his chapter entitled "Fake News and Social Media Censorship: Examining the Librarian's Role," he suggests that overconsumption of information, especially as end-users filter content through the lens of their own personal truths and worldviews, actually perpetuates the dissemination of misinformation. Adetayo suggests that librarians and media specialists can provide teachers and learners with the analytic and branching literacy skills needed to filter through the vast amounts of online information to hone in on sources that are accurate and reliable to support cognitive growth in the subject area.

For Chapter 5, author Semi Yeom addresses best practices for supporting adolescent learners to attain digital citizenship and civic participation using enhanced digital literacy skills. By using these skills, she suggests teachers and learners can be empowered with the skills to critique data-based arguments and recognize data representations that are manipulated with biased intentions. Yeom asserts that data and digitally literate students can responsibly communicate using communication and information technologies through a scaffolded, holistic iterative learning cycle scaffolded by effective digital literacy teaching strategies. Her piece, "Teaching and

Assessing Data Literacy for Adolescent Learners," focuses on the interplay among digital resources and literacy skills to combat deepfake content.

Seda Gökçe Turan, in Chapter 6, suggests a long-term solution for facilitating young learners' digital citizenship and literacy skills to prevent misinformation having the potential of polarizing cognitive processes. "Deepfake and Digital Citizenship: A Long-Term Protection Method for Children and Youth" serves as a primer for exploring the importance of teaching digital citizenship at an early age to palliate exposure to disinformation, misinformation, and polarization. As such, the author explores the cognitive competencies needed to combat deepfakes by offering solutions and suggestions designed for scaffolding younger learners through the digital learning plane.

Oluwole Durodolu, Collence Chisita, and Tinyiko Dube, in Chapter 7 denoted "Flattening the Curve of Fake News in the Epoch of Infodemic: An Epistemic Challenge," discuss the challenges associated with the prominence of fake news and deepfakes across digital communication platforms. Specifically, they address the noted increase of fake news and deepfakes during the height of the COVID-19 pandemic across social media platforms resulting in what would ordinarily be trustworthy information skewed to fit a particular political or social narrative. Thus, combating the influence of disinformation and misinformation has resulted in an epistemic challenge resulting in the need to provide enhanced strategies to attenuate the potential negative impacts of deepfakes on teaching and learning.

In Chapter 8, author Paul Siegel takes a novel approach to recognizing and ameliorating deepfakes. In his piece entitled "Schrodinger's Deepfake: Multimodal Analysis to Combat Deepfakes," Siegel suggests it is not a matter the existence of deepfakes but rather the impact they cause across teaching and learning platforms. To palliate the effects of deepfake on instructional content, he explores three different models to minimize or eliminate deepfakes particularly from existing educational practices and subject-area content.

Finally, Bhimavarapu Usharani's Chapter 9 piece entitled "A Novel Extended Ripple and Cyberbullies Data Detection (E-RACYBDD) Framework to Mitigate Deepfake Attacks on Social Media" provides the readers a glimpse into potential deepfake detection software to prevent teenage cyberbullying. Cyberbullying is particularly egregious among teenagers as it can occur internal and external to an educational setting and can be an almost 24/7 phenomenon. Frequently, parents and teachers are unaware of cyberbullying particularly when it is created using deepfakes which can amplify the already false information being posted and shared. Here, a framework is provided to help teachers and learners recognize and eliminate deepfake content on social media platforms to stop the spread of misinformation that contributes to the devastating effects of cyberbullying on teenagers particularly as it relates to their higher-order cognitive processing skills.

Chapter 1
Educational Responsibility in the Deepfake Era:
A Primer for TPACK Reform

Rebecca J. Blankenship
https://orcid.org/0000-0002-1142-0487
Florida Agricultural and Mechanical University, USA

ABSTRACT

Choosing the right technologies to match student learning outcomes in today's technology-integrated classrooms presents educators with multiple instructional design challenges including selecting appropriate technologies to match desired student learning outcomes. As students continue to have broad access to information from a variety of web-based platforms, teachers are increasingly tasked with ensuring the information used to complete key assignments is authentic and from a verifiable resource. As such, the era of deep fakes in images, audio, videos, and digital texts is more prevalent than ever as numerous programs using artificial intelligence (AI) can significantly alter original content to fundamentally change the intent of original content. A discussion of educational and pedagogic responsibility in the era of deep fakes will serve as the primer for reform of the TPACK construct with recommendations for remediating student work in which deep fake resources were utilized.

INTRODUCTION

Choosing the right technologies to match student learning outcomes in today's technology-integrated classrooms presents educators with multiple instructional

DOI: 10.4018/978-1-7998-6474-5.ch001

design challenges including selecting appropriate technologies to match desired student learning outcomes. As students continue to have broad access to information from a variety of web-based platforms, teachers are increasingly tasked with ensuring the information used to complete key assignments is authentic and from a verifiable resource. As such, the era of deepfakes in images, audios, videos, and digital texts is more prevalent than ever as numerous programs using Artificial Intelligence (AI) can significantly alter original content to fundamentally change the intent of original content. Because many of these AI-based programs are more user-friendly and easily accessible on the internet or mobile devices in a free or relatively inexpensive app, an increase in deepfake content is particularly noticeable within the last decade. Accordingly, educators are now tasked with employing best practices to not only teach basic digital literacy and citizenship skills, but also recognize how technology immersed learning environments interacts with deepfakes while equipping students with the tools necessary to recognize authentic and altered content. Thus, the purpose of this chapter is to explore techniques educators can use to mitigate deepfakes in key assignments and learning outcomes. Readers will explore the impact of using deepfake imagery, on teaching and learning as well as higher-cognitive processes leading to student learning outcomes. Further exploration of debunking deepfake content through guided techniques such as cross-referencing with non-digital resources will be discussed. An exploration of how deepfakes affect teacher and learners' trust in common search and information resources such as Google, social media, and the like will be undertaken. Discussion of educational and pedagogic responsibility in the era of deepfakes will serve as the primer for reform of the TPACK construct filtered through the scaffolded lens of Vygotskian (1978) sociocultural theory as interpreted by Lantolf and Thorne (2006). Specifically, the notions of object, other, and self-regulation using three distinct scaffolding techniques aligned with TPACK subdomain dyads will be discussed as a potential remediation of deepfake content.

Canned messaging, stylized imagery, and visual manipulation of content are hallmarks of several image-driven industries including advertising agencies, news programs, and social media outlets. Image manipulation is one method used to advance a desired narrative. The distribution of altered or false information is certainly not a new concept. One does not have to venture too far in the immediate past to find examples of how advertising executives, news anchors, field reporters, and politicians have intentionally manipulated data, facts, and events to promote one agenda or viewpoint over another. With the continued rise in use of social media, online media, and mass communication outlets to distribute information and news, a new type of disinformation has emerged known as the "deepfake". Deepfakes can assume many forms, but the basic definition is that of manipulating audio, images, or video using some form of Artificial Intelligence (AI) housed within audio and video editing software. For educators and researchers, particularly those in higher education, deepfakes are problematic in terms of ensuring learners are receiving accurate information to complete key assignments and achieve desired learning outcomes.

One of the hallmarks of education is access to relevant materials and resources that accurately reflect instructional content and anticipated student learning outcomes. For teachers, it is of critical importance that the information learners have access to and use to complete content-related tasks is sourced from legitimate, vetted resources accurately reflecting the desired information the student means to convey. However, a growing trend across the Internet is the deliberate misrepresentation of otherwise factual information to sway an end-user to adopt a position or line of thinking that may support a particular position or act in counter thereof. Manipulating images and text to deliberately misinform or mislead the intended audience, or the rising phenomenon known as deepfakes, has definitely impacted areas such as advertisement, politics, and social media. As research about the effects of deepfakes in these areas has risen significantly over the past few years, especially noted during their intense saturation during the 2016 election cycle, understanding how deepfakes have the potential of negatively affecting the fields of teaching and learning presents as an area in need of significant exploration.

Understanding the Technological, Pedagogical, and Content Knowledge (TPACK) Construct in Teaching and Learning Methodologies

A Brief History of TPACK

The Technological, Pedagogical, and Content Knowledge (TPACK) framework was first conceptualized by Punya Mishra and Matthew Koehler in their 2006 article entitled *Technological Pedagogical Content Knowledge: A new framework for teacher knowledge*. The underlying purpose of developing the initial TPACK framework was to bridge the noticeable theoretical gap in explaining how the use of technology in teaching and learning informs pedagogic practice and content knowledge acquisition. Specifically, the framework built on Lee Shulman's (1986) existing work explicating knowledge growth by focusing on pedagogical content. Mishra and Koehler advanced the initial framework by including the technology component not included in Shulman's initial concept. The inclusion of technology was a natural progression of the original framework as, particularly at the turn of the 21st century, the use of technology as the method or venue for instructional delivery shifted significantly teaching and learning modalities in the modern classroom. As such, traditional teacher-centered classrooms in brick-and-mortar settings were slowly reimagined to allow more flexibility in terms of method, space, and time.

Accordingly, teaching and learning became unfettered by conventional instructional hours and spaces. Thus, teachers were uniquely positioned to reimagine content delivery using existing and emerging technologies to encourage higher order thinking while promoting long-term knowledge retention. Further, the introduction of virtual environments powered by artificial intelligence enabled teachers to redesign key assignments aligned with student learning outcomes to facilitate authentic learning while enabling students to make deeper connections to content.

Figure 1. Graphic representation of the original TPACK model as conceptualized in 2006

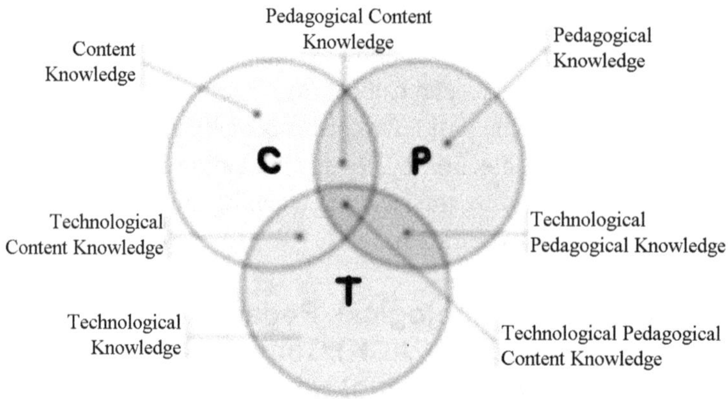

Deconstructing TPACK Domains and Subdomains

The TPACK framework is subdivided into three (3) main domains further delineated into three (3) subdomains. The three subdomains are: 1. Technology Knowledge (TK); 2. Pedagogical Knowledge (PK); and 3. Content Knowledge (CK). According to Mishra and Koehler (2009), Technology Knowledge (TK) is a way of thinking about working with technology and its concomitant resources to inform the broader goals of teaching and learning. TK also informs how technology can be used to enhance productivity in an effort to actualize teaching and learning outcomes within more authentic contexts. Pedagogical Knowledge (PK) encompasses the knowledge a teacher has about the general processes of the teaching and learning cycle. PK includes an overall understanding regarding the goals, objectives, and values of education. Content Knowledge (CK) represents the teacher's knowledge of the subject matter being taught. Through CK, teachers are able to demonstrate their command of subject and ability to engage students using proven methodologies that promote long-term retention of key content. The TPACK model informs teaching and learning in such a way that promotes instructional malleability as teachers move among the main domains as they modify teaching practices and student learning outcomes as technology, content, and instruction change and diversify according to circumstance.

Figure 2. Graphic representation of the three TPACK main domains and subdomains

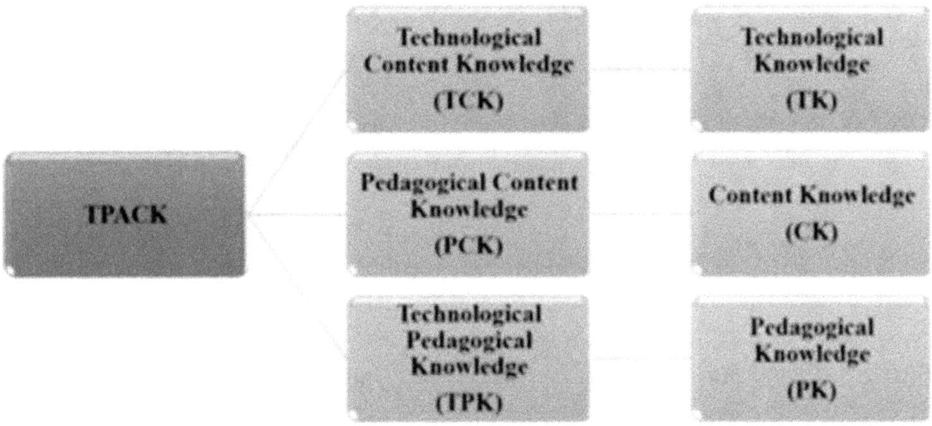

There is an anticipated and natural interplay among the main domains that generates certain subdomains. These subdomains include the following: 1. Technological Pedagogical Knowledge (TPK); 2. Technological Content Knowledge (TCK); and 3. Pedagogical Content Knowledge (PCK). Of note, the subdomains focus primarily on how technology informs pedagogic and content knowledge. Technological Pedagogical Knowledge (TPK) explains how instructional strategies change based on the technologies used as either the vehicle of instruction or instructional venue. TPK facilitates a teacher's understanding of how to match the right technologies to support teaching and student learning outcomes. Similarly, Technological Content Knowledge (TCK) informs how technology can advance or hinder the advancement of content. Again, teachers must commit, under TCK, to strategically select technologies that support teaching subject matter and reciprocally, how content can affect the technologies used. Finally, Pedagogical Content Knowledge (PCK) informs how teachers use a variety of instructional strategies that supports deeper understanding and long-term retention of subject matter influenced by such factors as assessment, curriculum, conceptions/misconceptions, prior knowledge, and reporting.

Figure 3. Representation of the Technological Pedagogical Knowledge (TPK) dyad

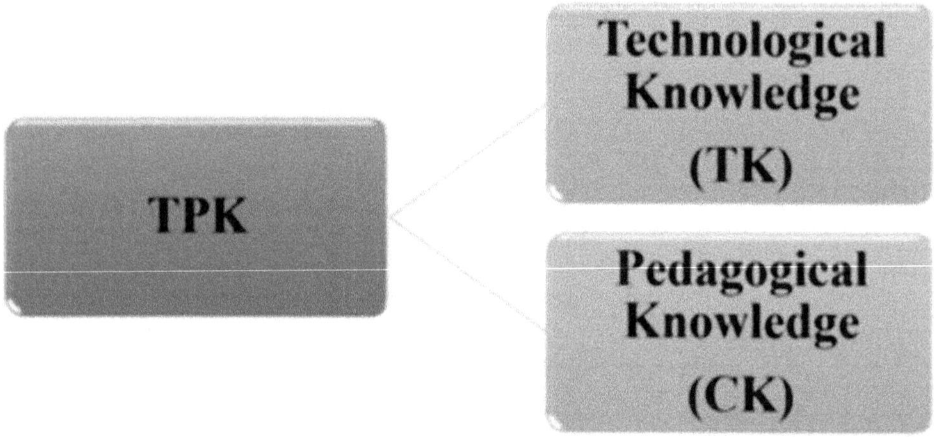

Figure 4. Representation of the Technological Content Knowledge (TCK) dyad

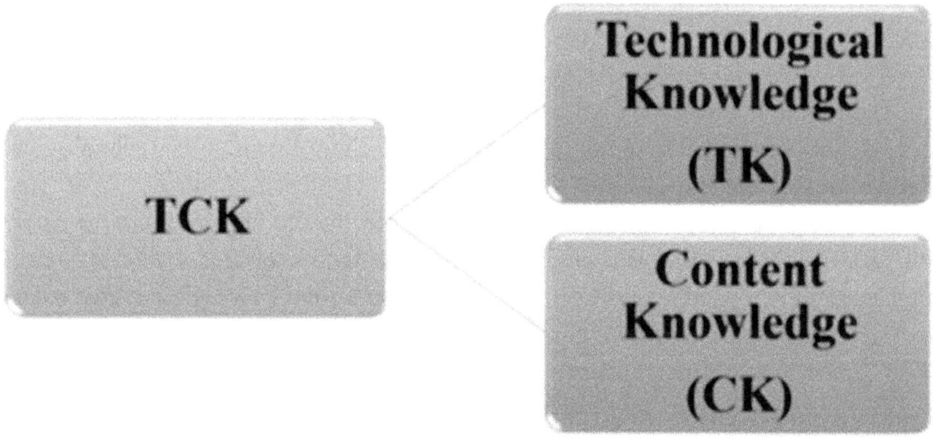

Direct Application in Teaching and Learning Methodologies through Dyadic Relationships

The interplay among the TPACK domains and subdomains is further explicated through the dyadic relationships within the subdomains. Subdomain Technological Content Knowledge (TCK) is subdivided into Technological Knowledge (TK) and Content Knowledge (CK). Subdomain Pedagogical Content Knowledge (PCK) is subdivided Pedagogical Knowledge (PK) and Content Knowledge (CK). Finally, Technological Pedagogical Knowledge (TPK) is subdivided into Technological Knowledge (TK)

Figure 5. Representation of the Pedagogical Content Knowledge (PCK) dyad

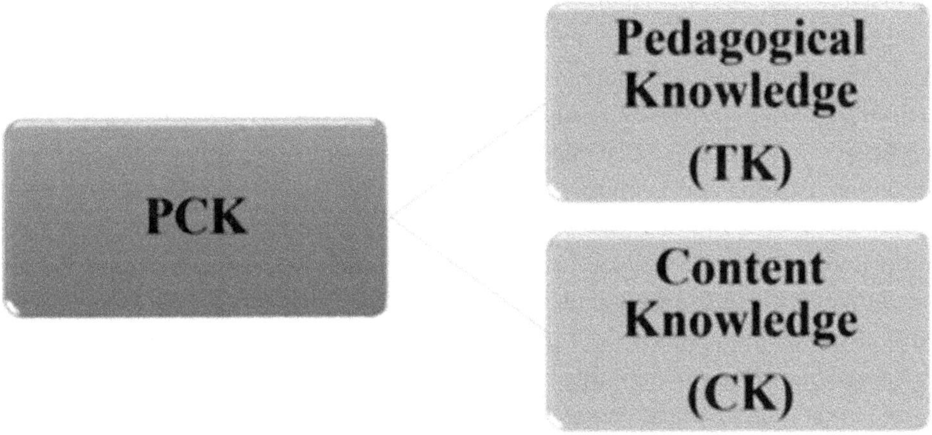

and Pedagogical Knowledge (PK). The subdomain dyadic relationship between TK and CK explains how teachers teach content either using technology directly to engage in the subject matter or use technology as the instructional venue. Selecting the right technology to teach content is an important first step in mitigating deepfake influence over content. Here, it is incumbent upon the teacher to vet any technologies used during instruction to ensure the intended content messaging is not altered by the technology itself. For example, if a social media platform is used as the direct instructional vehicle, the teacher must thoroughly cross-check any images, videos, writings, and the like against non-social media sources to ensure the content is being accurately portrayed. Concurrently, if technology is used as the venue of instruction, i.e. Microsoft Teams, Zoom, and the like, the teacher is charged with securing those virtual settings to ensure content cannot be manipulated during instruction.

Next, the subdomains PK and CK explain how teachers use various instructional strategies to teach subject related content. To combat deepfakes, teachers are charged with selecting instructional best practices free from internal and external biases. Identifying if bias has adversely affected content can be revealed by using a variety of formative and summative assessments to evaluate if students are demonstrating content knowledge as intended. Finally, subdomains TK and PK explicate how teachers can advance pedagogic best practices by selecting technologies free from potential exposure to deepfakes. Understanding the subdomain dyadic relationships further unpacks the overall framework into its component parts such that a deeper understanding is garnered as a result of the iterative interchanging cycles between teaching practices and learning outcomes. Reducing TPACK to its dyadic subdomains also provides a more directed theoretical lens through which the effects of deepfakes in teaching and learning can be further explained.

Best practices in teaching and learning using different technologies in virtual learning spaces is certainly not a new concept in TPACK. However, creating effective activities to elicit higher-order student learning outcomes has presented educational professionals with unique challenges in the deepfake-era, especially with the increase of online teaching and learning during the 2020-2021 COVID-era academic year. These challenges implicate every aspect of educational processes making it even more imperative that all stakeholders including administrators, teachers, and college and university faculty are equipped with best practices in matching technologies and virtual pedagogic practices to engage learners at deeper cognitive levels through enhanced preparation of digital pedagogy and concomitant student learning outcomes while mitigating misinformation resulting from deepfake content.

TPACK in the 21st Century – Teaching with Context

In 2019, Mishra and Koehler revisited the original TPACK model to include an outer layer that addresses teaching within the TPACK framework according to Contextual Knowledge (XK). Adding the XK layer helped explain the organizational and situational contexts within which teachers work that could directly impact content if not considered within the proper context. Context is directly affected by deepfakes as the original source of any media must be central to instructional decisions, learning outcomes, and selected technologies. Adding this additional layer to the TPACK framework has the potential of mitigating deepfakes in instructional content by focusing on their contextual origins.

Guess, et al., (2020) characterized this in terms of a significant gap in digital literacy skills that continues to go unmitigated and under-researched. As such, the ability to recognize deepfake content before it skews the end-users' perceptions can be mitigated if they receive interventive training on how to spot a deepfake. While Guess, et al.'s piece focused primarily on recognizing deepfakes in media outlets, the principles can be transferred to teaching and learning best practices. Pennycook, et.al, (2021) noted there is a disconnect between what end users share versus the accuracy of the content. The authors suggested, based on the results of their study, one possible explanation of the intentional sharing of misinformation was that of a type of virtue signaling to please family or members of particular political or social groups. Further, sharing misinformation was not found to be a deliberate or intentional act based on the former assumption. Kozyreva, et al., (2020) recommended a model focused on enhancing cognitive interventions to counteract the nonrecognition and dissemination of deepfakes. The primary cognitive tool they recommend is a "boost" meant to enhance an end-user's digital agency as well as digital reasoning skills.

Figure 6. Revised model of TPACK framework including the outer context layer

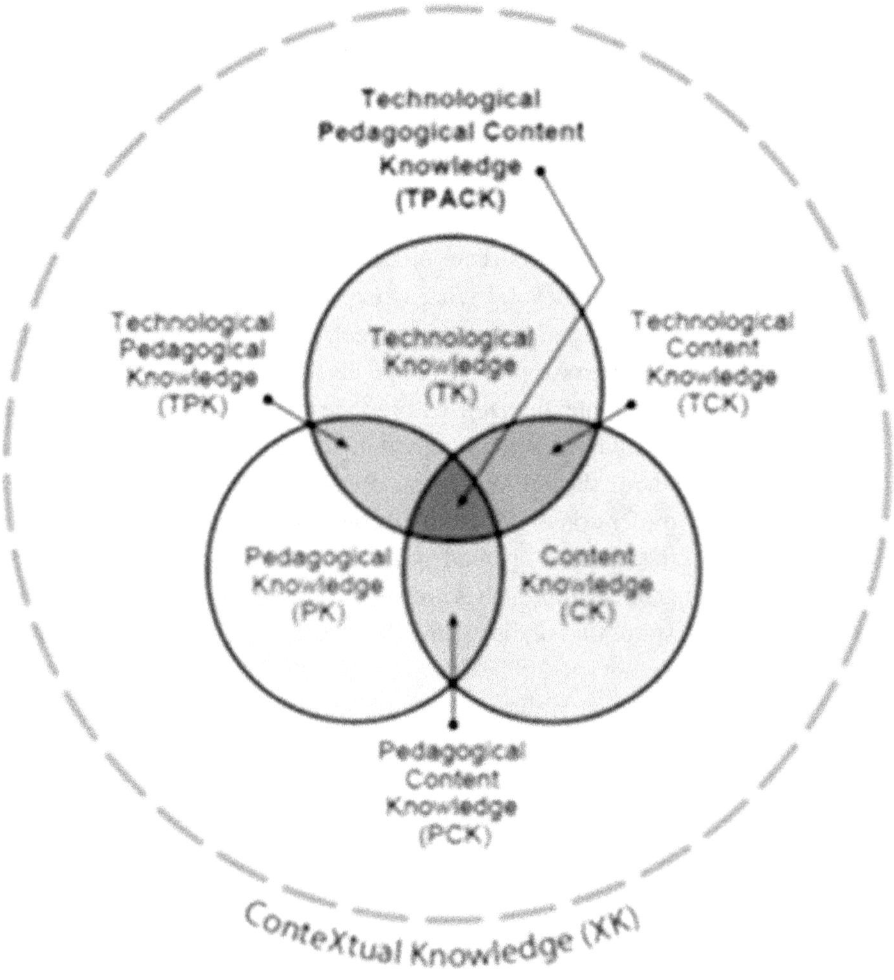

Further, Van Bavel, et al. (2021) suggested that exposure combined with existing belief structures directly contribute to the sharing of misinformation including deepfakes which further be explained according to cognitive style. Accordingly, using guided cognitive techniques aligned with enhanced, contextualized digital literacy skills have the potential of providing end users with the tools necessary to recognize deepfakes before they affect student learning outcomes.

Combating Deepfakes With the Enhanced Digital Literacy Skills

Guided Techniques

The current ethos in teaching and learning positions the teacher and learner as subservient to institutional constraints – constraints which may be fiscal or logistical. However, in order for 21st century teachers and learners to acquire the necessary skills to effectively teach and learn in today's highly immersive digital teaching environments, these constraints must be lifted such that the institution does not impede their ability to grow beyond what is expected to what is instructionally transformational. Accordingly, the bulk of research has primarily focused on (and accepted) teachers and learners as passive recipients of perceived roles and learning norms that are typically contextualized within face-to-face instructional settings. These roles and norms are perceived as something done to the teacher and learner rather than done with them; they ultimately become noticeably absent from training and is then seen as professionally "tamed" through this process (Lingard, et al. 2003; Hayes, et al., 2020). Teaching and learning practices that are considered as a more process-outcome linear approach is favored by most educational institutions in order to maintain the status quo of distancing the instructional relationship between teacher and student (Zembylas, 2003; Granjo, et al., 2021). Teaching and learning have become almost scripted to follow exactly idealized professional standards with no real accommodations for individual teacher and student differences especially in the digital era.

Operating in an industrial, marketplace mentality, current teaching and learning practices reflect institutional desires to simply reproduce the existing face-to-face system, emphasizing current policy rather than promoting cognitive development. Notably scarce from the educational research and related literature is the deconstruction of traditional notions of the teacher and learner as passive in favor of exploring how the same experiences offered in a different environment – such as a virtual setting - might actually contribute to authentic cognitive growth. Traditional face-to-face instruction, then, is characterized by the noted cognitive distancing between teacher and learner. This distancing results in the situational removal of the teacher from instruction which can contribute to contextual disconnects.

Although much has been written about the need to harmonize teaching with authentic learning examples, current practices certainly reflect the opposite (Albion & Maddux, 2007; Blankenship, 2013; Rios, 2017). The lack of authentic and real-world simulated practice is most likely the result of ends-oriented development standards. Colleges and universities in the United States have been characterized by their notable use of business-type, cognitively distanced instructional models. Rather than consider them as microecosystems reflective of the diversity that exists among the larger teacher and student population, a more controllable, assembly-line managerial standard is applied to control content. Albion and Maddux (2007) noted that this approach is entirely reflective of the industrial movement of the early 20th century as well as the behaviorist psychology movement of the 1950s and 1960s (Skinner, 1967). Atwell (2007) characterized this as a dysfunctional relationship between institutional expectations and cognitive development which can implicate the recognition and remediation of deepfake content.

As the sociocultural and economic status of the United States changed and became more global in perspective, the need for teachers and learners to change their cognitive approaches to subject-specific content. Teachers and students are more digitally aware as technologies changed to become more user-friendly and interactive providing alternative methods to demonstrate competencies in subject areas. This is particularly noted with the rise in use, especially in the last decade, of the personal computer/tablet, cell phones, and social media outlets (Prensky, 2010; Prensky, 2013). As Prensky noted, the technology-driven brain functions within a different cognitive plane resulting in the need to reimagine the relationships among teachers and learners as they think and create in digital spaces. Here, he posits a new way of demonstrating content acquisition using higher-order, problem-based solutions to real-world issues. By so doing, cognitive distancing between teachers and learners could be significantly reduced which would facilitate the type of digital-cognitive skill set needed to combat deepfakes.

Since 2002, The New Media Consortium (NMC) has partnered with the EDUCAUSE Learning Initiative to generate an annual report highlighting what practitioners in the fields of education and technology project to be the current technology trends that will be potentially adopted into higher education pedagogy. The Horizon Report (2021), as it is denoted, identifies key trends and predicts the time from recognition to exploration to adoption. With each annual iteration of what is trending in educational technology, the NMC is careful to point out that, even though many trends have ultimately been adopted into and are actively used in higher education curricula, understanding the long-term impact on teaching and learning is in its relative infancy particularly with the marked increase in the use of social media for sharing content and information. As noted in the 2021 report, social media now plays a ubiquitous role in terms of how and where teachers and learners choose to interact within digital learning spaces. While the technical skill set among teachers and learners is relatively competent (i.e., creating posts, commenting/liking, uploading media, and the like), there is an increasingly noticeable gap in content sharing. In other words, the sharing of relevant and salient information has not kept pace with accuracy. Of the six key technologies and practices identified in the report, the evolution of artificial intelligence (AI) is one of the driving forces behind the emergence of deepfakes in teaching and learning. AI has enabled content developers to use sophisticated editing software to alter, manipulate, or completely change images and video some to the extent that recognizing the difference between the original and edited versions are almost indistinguishable. Creating a deepfake involves four step process: 1. Identify the source image or video; 2. Identify the target image or video; 3. Identify facial landmarks; and 4. Import into software and generate results. Accordingly, as noted in the TPACK framework revision, providing appropriate context combined with Guess, et al.'s (2020) digital literacy skill intervention as well as Prensky's call for higher-order, problem-solving tasks has the potential of becoming a model framework to mitigate deepfake content.

Figure 7. Deepfake examples in politics and pop culture
<<Source – CNET from https://www.cnet.com/tags/deepfake/ >>

Types of Digital Literacy Skills Needed to Mitigate Deepfake Content

Understanding the connection between teaching and learning and digital literacy skills is particularly important in recognizing why deepfakes are such a prevalent concern in the 21st century. Understanding the importance of teaching digital literacy skills in addition to content is particularly relevant for teachers when conceptualizing courses that include the use of existing and emerging technologies to introduce and evaluate subject-specific content. Accordingly, teachers are not only charged with instruction but also ensuring learners possess skills essential to demonstrating knowledge acquisition through higher-order tasks which include the ability, as Prensky (2013) advocated, to analyze and evaluate content to solve authentic, real-world scenarios. Here, teachers can mitigate gaps in digital literacy skills by using the TPACK framework specifically aligned with key assignments and higher-order student learning outcomes. In the following sections, different types of digital literacy are explored and paralleled to the TPACK framework in an effort to advance the construct to accommodate for technology changes that can increase the exposure to misinformation such as a deepfake. Here, and of most important note, equipping learners with digital and non-digital resources in order to cross-reference the accuracy of subject-related content becomes a scaffolded essential in the teaching and learning process. As Lee (2021) asserted, scaffolding learners' epistemic cognition while working across different virtual document modalities is essential to ensure disinformation does not impact student learning outcomes and key assignment goals.

Branching Literacy

The advent of and advancement in artificial intelligence and hypermedia technologies has enabled end-users interact with content that is almost unbounded by traditional linear thinking. Web browsers such as Google Chrome and Microsoft Edge (formerly Explorer) have provided search platforms which have liberated teachers and learners in their search for the most pertinent information available on a given topic. By extension, social media platforms such as Facebook Instagram, and Twitter are additional search venues that have gained particular prevalence in the late 2010s as alternatives to traditional web-based content searchers. Web browsers and social media platforms are driven by embedded algorithms that key on certain search terms to customize the browsing experience. Rather than just receiving the information provided on one search engine or social media page, teachers and learners are able to explore (i.e., *branch*) many more related topics in a non-linear method through these algorithms and embedded links. Eshet-Alkali (2004) explains that branching literacy provides teachers and learners with opportunities to seek knowledge through non-linear means thus challenging them to bring together information collected in a different way to create new thoughts and concepts about a particular subject. Branching literacy requires teachers and learners to "step outside of the thinking box" to explore new areas of information without losing their focus on the subject matter at hand. In terms of the TPACK construct, this would impact the Technological Content Knowledge (TCK) subdomain dyad as it explicates the cyclical movements teachers and learners experience as they work through content-related tasks using different technologies.

Information Literacy

Eshet-Alkalai (2004) defines information literacy as, "the cognitive skills that consumers use to evaluate information in an educated and effective manner" (p 101). Since this article was published ten years ago, the amount of information

Figure 8. Relationship between branching literacy and Technological Content Knowledge (TCK)

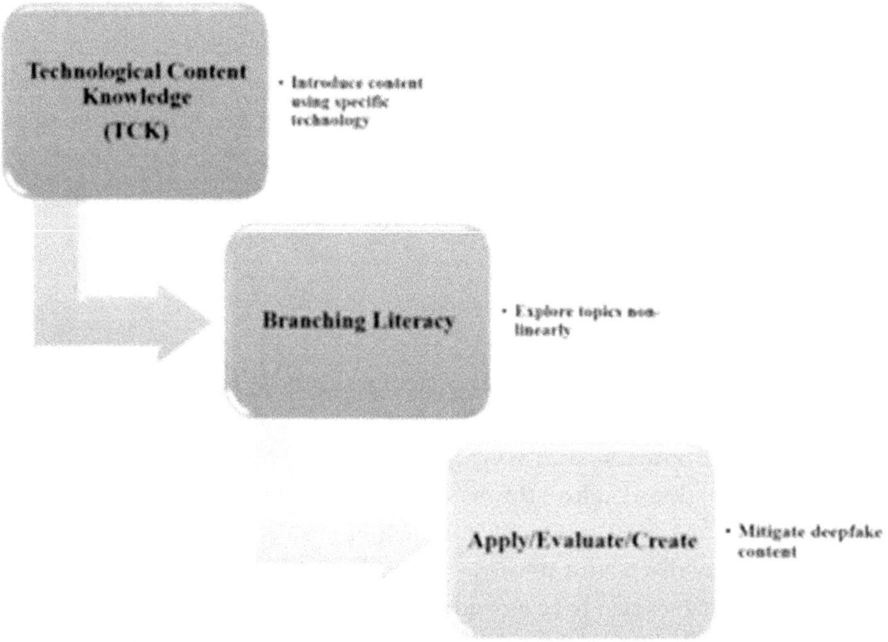

available from different digital platforms and resources has grown and changed exponentially. This growth is especially apparent as personal computing experienced a significant transformation from the traditional notions of a PC or laptop to cell phones and tablets. As end-users became more mobile, so did their ability to interact with information in an anytime/anywhere on-the-go format having literally 24/7 access to information. It is even more pertinent today that teachers and learners have digital literacy competencies and well-developed understandings of information literacies to combat the dissemination of misinformation and deepfakes. Further, Eshet-Alkalai and Amichai-Hamburger (2004) explained that those who possess the information literacy skill are ones that, "have the ability to make educated, smart information assessments" (p. 423). Here, teachers would scaffold learners using the Technological Pedagogical Knowledge (TPK) dyad as direct modelling to deepen cognitive skills to evaluate effectively the accuracy of information used to complete key assignments while actualizing student learning outcomes.

Figure 9. Relationship between information literacy and Technological Pedagogical Knowledge (TPK)

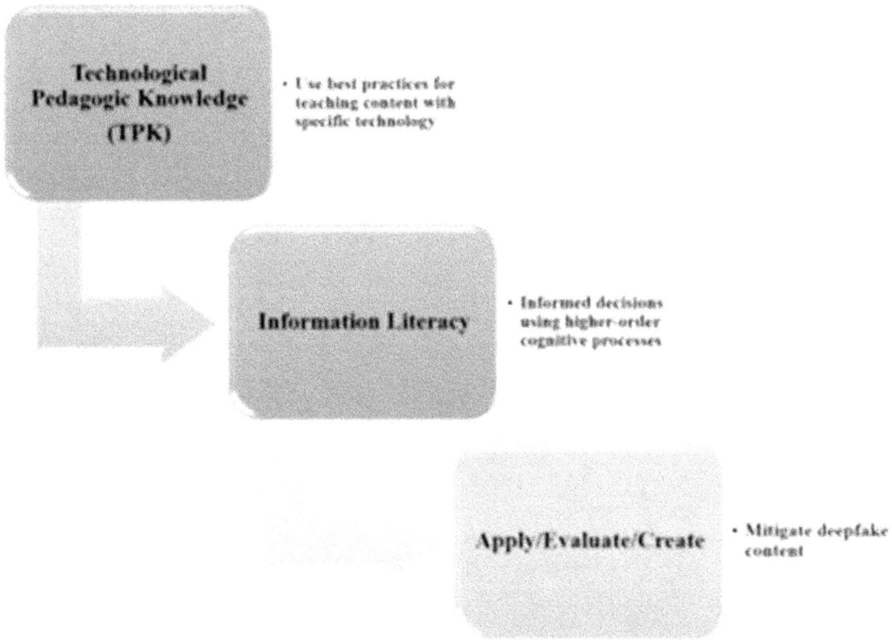

Photo-Visual and Reproduction Literacy

As a culture, most of the civilized world have been highly visual in teaching and learning (Emanuel & Challons-Lipton, 2013). "Visual literacy is essential for 21st century learners. Across the higher education curriculum, students are being asked to use and produce images and visual media in their academic work, and they must be prepared to do so" (Hattwig, Bussert, Medaille, & Burgess, 2013, p.1). End-users rely more on images as a means of conveying information or self-expression, drawings, graphs charts and the like to interpret and make sense of different stimuli (Baker, 2008). These stimuli can be in the forms as advertisements, social media posts, web-based searches and the like. Similarly, reproduction literacy implicates what the end-user does with the information retrieved from photo/digital stimuli (Jones-Kavalier, & Flannigan, 2006). In education, it can be problematic in terms of using information obtained from digital sources through a critical lens as there is a creative element that can skew content accuracy – thus enters the deepfake (Emanuel & Challons-Lipton, 2013). Additionally, interpretation of digital information can be indiscriminate between teacher and learner depending on how it is filtered through the TPACK framework (Head & Eisenberg, 2011). Here, the Pedagogical

Content Knowledge (PCK) dyad provides the structure around which teachers can use their preexisting pedagogic knowledges to present content in such a way that will enable learners to filter through accurate and misinformation presented in the form of deepfakes.

Figure 10. Relationship between photo-visual and reproduction literacy and Pedagogical Content Knowledge (PCK)

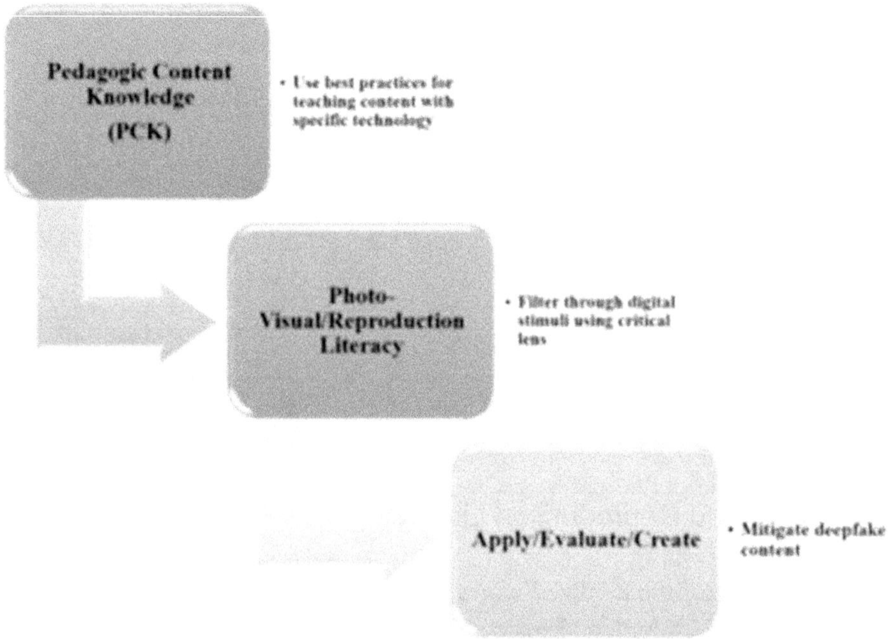

Educational Responsibility in the Era of Deepfakes

Reforming the TPACK Construct – The New Scaffolded Self-Regulated Model to Mitigate Deepfakes and Misinformation in Teaching and Learning

Here, a new model to mitigate deepfakes in teaching and learning around the existing TPACK framework is proffered using three types of scaffolding techniques. This enhanced scaffolded TPACK model was conceptualized the Vygotskian (1978) recognition of cognitive processes that can lead to higher-order self-regulation. Vygotsky suggested that learners possess an internal self-regulatory cognitive control that, through scaffolded instruction between a master (teacher) and novice (learner), can be opened to allow for self-regulation over their learning. Denoted the Zone of Proximal Development (ZPD), the technique is conceptualized in terms of what a learner can do with assistance of another person, what the learner can do assistance from some object such as a mobile app or textbook, and what the learner can do unassisted. Lantolf and Thorne (2006; 2007) took Vygotsky's concept, branding it as the cognitive processes of "other", "object", and "self" regulation. The ultimate goal among teachers and learners is for the learner to eventually achieve self-regulation such that they are able to engage in higher-order activities with subject-specific content such that performing deeper and more complex cognitive processes such as evaluating and creating around a particular concept. In order for this type of scaffolding to occur, especially in digitally rich learning environments, teachers must employ instructional best practices guided by a research-driven best practices pedagogic framework. In the case here to mitigate deepfakes in teaching and learning, the TPACK framework was selected as the focus.

As noted previously, while the TPACK framework can be used to guide teachers and learners through the iterative contextual interplay among content, learning, and technology knowledges informed by certain digital literacy skills, what tends to be missing from the narrative is which scaffolded techniques will lead to learner self-regulation. Here, three (3) types of cognitive and instructional scaffolds are used to support the TPACK domains and subdomains such that the learner's ZPD can fully open and self-regulation within a subject area can be actualized at higher-order cognitive levels. In common construction, there are different types of scaffolds used to support structures as they are being built. Each scaffold serves a distinct purpose, aligned directly with the type of building or structure under construction. These scaffolds include the following: 1. Supported scaffold; 2. Suspended scaffold; and 3. Ariel or Mobile scaffold. A supported scaffold typically consists of a series of interconnected platforms supported by rigid, load-bearing items such as poles or beams. A suspended scaffold is supported by overhead roped support. Ariel or mobile scaffolds are characterized by personal hoists or some type of vehicle or other machinery. It is here that the three TPACK subdomain dyads can be reconceptualized around the scaffold types to reframe the original framework to include teaching discrete higher order, self-regulated digital literacy skills to mitigate the dissemination of misinformation and deepfakes in teaching and learning. Accordingly, it is suggested that each scaffold type would mirror a point of cognitively regulated behavior with the end result being that of ensuring self-regulating higher-order cognitive behavior. Thus, it is through such self-regulation that learners will be able to differentiate between accurate and misinformation embedded within deepfakes. As such, these parallels emerge with a more distinct model to follow:

- Supported Scaffold ------------------------→Object Regulated - TCK
- Suspended Scaffold------------------------→Other Regulated - TPK

• Arial Scaffold------------------------------→Self-Regulated - PCK

Figure 11. Reimagining the TPACK Model using a 3-Point scaffolded cognitive concept to mitigate deepfakes

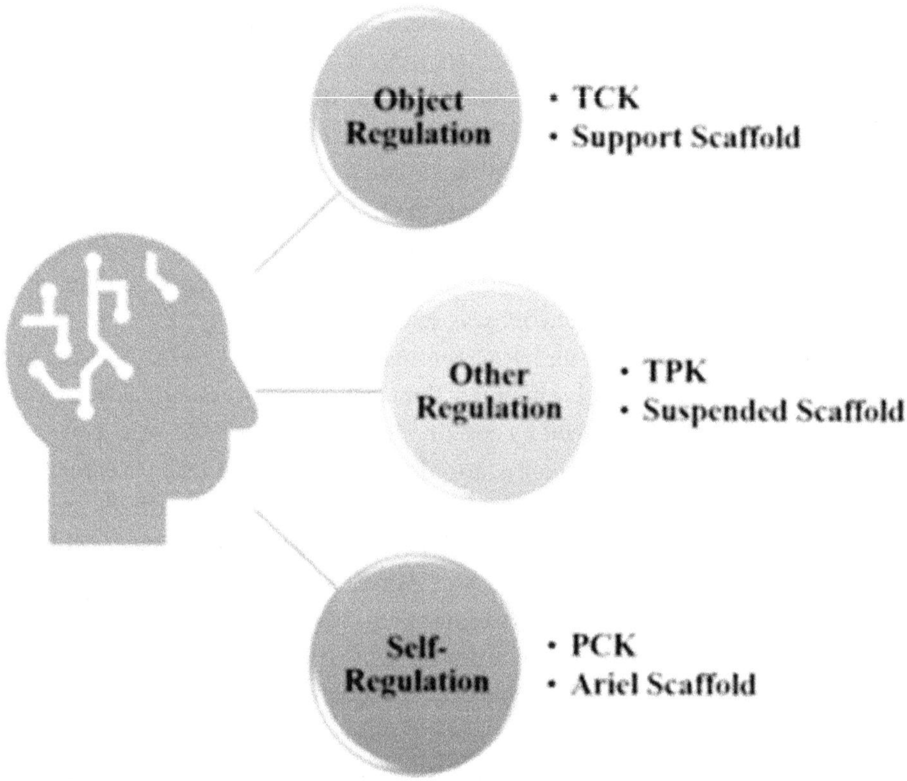

Finally, the following 10 best practice suggestions aligned with the proposed scaffolded TPACK self-regulation model act as a roadmap to facilitate teachers and learners as they navigate digitally sourced content to mitigate deepfakes:

1. Combine digital and non-digital content-specific resources.
2. Use a variety of digital and non-digital content-specific resources.
3. Do not saturate the learning environment with too many digital resources.
4. Marry "old" and "new" digital resources to inform content.
5. Match higher-order learning outcomes with existing technologies.
6. Consider the digital instructional venue – technology may not be the best choice for the desired student learning outcome.

7. Identify technology that can be paired with a specific content-based key assessment aligned with higher-order student learning outcomes.
8. Ensure that the selected technologies and resultant content are secure especially when working within social media platforms.
9. Align selected resources with a specific digital literacy skill or skill.
10. Enhance collaboration between teachers and learners to ensure clear and open communication to prevent breakdowns in the scaffolded constructs.

REFERENCES

Albion, P., & Maddux, C. D. (2007). Networked knowledge: Challenges for teacher education. *Journal of Technology and Teacher Education, 15*(3), 303–310.

Alkali, Y. E., & Amichai-Hamburger, Y. (2004). Experiments with digital literacy. *Cyberpsychology (Brno)*, *7*(4), 425–434. doi:10.1089/cpb.2004.7.421

Atwell, N. (2007). *The reading zone*. Scholastic.

Baker, F. (2008). *Visual literacy defined & other related quotes*. Visual Literacy. Retrieved from https://www.frankwbaker.com/vl_defined.htm

Blankenship, R. J. (2013). Teacher as object to teacher as subject: A critical perspective of teacher training in the 21st century. *International Journal of University Teaching and Faculty Development*, *4*(1), 27–43.

Emanuel, R., & Challons-Lipton, C. (2013). Visual literacy and the digital native: Another look. *Journal of Visual Literacy*, *32*(1), 1. doi:10.1080/23796529.2013.11674703

Eshet-Alkalai, Y. (2004). Digital literacy: A conceptual framework for survival skills in the digital era. *Journal of Educational Multimedia and Hypermedia, 13*(1), 93–106. doi:10.4018/978-1-60566-198-8.ch154

Granjo, M., Castro Silva, J., & Peixoto, F. (2021). Teacher identity: Can ethical orientation be related to perceived competence, psychological needs satisfaction, commitment and global self-esteem? *European Journal of Teacher Education, 44*(2), 158–179. doi:10.1080/02619768.2020.1748004

Guess, A. M., Lerner, M., Lyons, B., Montgomery, J. M., Nyhan, B., Reifler, J., & Sircar, N. (2020). A digital media literacy intervention increases discernment between mainstream and false news in the United States and India. *Proceedings of the National Academy of Sciences of the United States of America, 117*(27), 15536–15545. doi:10.1073/pnas.1920498117 PMID:32571950

Hattwig, D., Bussert, K., Medaille, A., & Burgess, J. (2013). Visual literacy standards in higher education: New opportunities for libraries and student learning. *Portal (Baltimore, Md.), 13*(1), 61–89. doi:10.1353/pla.2013.0008

Hayes, D., Christie, P., Mills, M., & Lingard, B. (2020). *Teachers and schooling making a difference: Productive pedagogies, assessment and performance*. Routledge., doi:10.4324/9781003117643

Head, A., & Eisenberg, M. (2011). How college students use the web for everyday life research. *First Monday, 16*(4). Advance online publication. doi:10.5210/fm.v16i4.3484

Jones-Kavalier, B., & Flannigan, S. (2006). Connecting the digital dots: literacy of the 21st century. *Educause Review*. Retrieved from: http://www.educause.edu/ero/article/connecting-digital-dots-literacy-21st-century

Koehler, M. J., & Mishra, P. (2009). What is technological pedagogical content knowledge? *Contemporary Issues in Technology & Teacher Education, 9*(1), 60–70. doi:10.4324/9781315771328

Kozyreva, A., Lewandowsky, S., & Hertwig, R. (2020). Citizens versus the internet: Confronting digital challenges with cognitive tools. *Psychological Science in the Public Interest, 21*(3), 103–156. doi:10.1177/1529100620946707 PMID:33325331

Lantolf, J. P., & Thorne, S. L. (2006). *Sociocultural theory and the genesis of second language development*. Oxford University Press. doi:10.1093/applin/amm027

Lantolf, J. P., & Thorne, S. L. (2007). Sociocultural theory and second language learning. In B. VanPatten & J. Williams (Eds.), *Theories in second language acquisition* (pp. 201–224). Lawrence Erlbaum.

Lee, Y. H. (2021). Scaffolding university students' epistemic cognition during multimodal multiple-document reading: The effects of the epistemic prompting and the automated reflection report. *The Internet and Higher Education, 49*, 100777. doi:10.1016/j.iheduc.2020.100777

Lingard, B., Hayes, D., & Mills, M. (2003). *Leading learning: Making hope practical in schools: Making hope practical in schools*. McGraw-Hill Education.

Mishra, P., & Koehler, M. J. (2006). Technological Pedagogical Content Knowledge: A new framework for teacher knowledge. *Teachers College Record*, *108*(6), 1017–1054. doi:10.1111/j.1467-9620.2006.00684.x

Pennycook, G., Epstein, Z., Mosleh, M., Arechar, A. A., Eckles, D., & Rand, D. G. (2021). Shifting attention to accuracy can reduce misinformation online. *Nature*, *592*(7855), 590–595. doi:10.103841586-021-03344-2 PMID:33731933

Prensky, M. (2013). Our brains extended. *Educational Leadership*, *70*(6), 22–27.

Prensky, M. R. (2010). *Teaching digital natives: Partnering for real learning*. Corwin press.

Report, H. (2021). *The New Media Consortium*. Retrieved from https://library.educause.edu/resources/2021/4/2021-educause-horizon-report-teaching-and-learning-edition

Ríos, R. (2017). *Teacher Agency for Equity: A Framework for Conscientious Engagement*. Taylor & Francis., doi:10.4324/9781315178646

Shulman, L. S. (1986). Those who understand: A conception of teacher knowledge. *American Educator*, *10*(1). Advance online publication. doi:10.3102/0013189X015002004

Van Bavel, J. J., Harris, E. A., Pärnamets, P., Rathje, S., Doell, K. C., & Tucker, J. A. (2021). Political psychology in the digital (mis) information age: A model of news belief and sharing. *Social Issues and Policy Review*, *15*(1), 84–113. doi:10.1111ipr.12077

Vygotsky, L. S. (1978). Socio-cultural theory. *Mind & Society*, *6*, 52–58. doi:10.5040/9781472541437.ch-003

Zembylas, M. (2003). Emotions and teacher identity: A poststructural perspective. *Teachers and Teaching*, *9*(3), 213–238. doi:10.1080/13540600309378

ADDITIONAL READING

Campbell, C., Plangger, K., Sands, S., & Kietzmann, J. (2021). Preparing for an era of deepfakes and AI-generated ads: A framework for understanding responses to manipulated advertising. *Journal of Advertising*, 1–17. doi:10.1080/00913367.2021.1909515

Fallis, D. (2020). The Epistemic Threat of Deepfakes. *Philosophy & Technology*, 1–21. PMID:32837868

Fraga-Lamas, P., & Fernández-Caramés, T. M. (2020). Fake news, disinformation, and deepfakes: Leveraging distributed ledger technologies and blockchain to combat digital deception and counterfeit reality. *IT Professional*, *22*(2), 53–59. doi:10.1109/MITP.2020.2977589

Kietzmann, J., Lee, L. W., McCarthy, I. P., & Kietzmann, T. C. (2020). Deepfakes: Trick or treat? *Business Horizons*, *63*(2), 135–146. doi:10.1016/j.bushor.2019.11.006

Krishna, D. (2021). Deepfakes, online platforms, and a novel proposal for transparency, collaboration, and education. *Richmond Journal of Law & Technology, 27*(3).

Liv, N., & Greenbaum, D. (2020). Deep fakes and memory malleability: False memories in the service of fake news. *AJOB Neuroscience*, *11*(2), 96–104. doi:10.1080/21507740.2020.1740351 PMID:32228386

Tolosana, R., Vera-Rodriguez, R., Fierrez, J., Morales, A., & Ortega-Garcia, J. (2020). Deepfakes and beyond: A survey of face manipulation and fake detection. *Information Fusion*, *64*, 131–148. doi:10.1016/j.inffus.2020.06.014

Vaccari, C., & Chadwick, A. (2020). Deepfakes and disinformation: Exploring the impact of synthetic political video on deception, uncertainty, and trust in news. *Social Media + Society*, *6*(1), 2056305120903408. doi:10.1177/2056305120903408

Vizoso, Á., Vaz-Álvarez, M., & López-García, X. (2021). Fighting Deepfakes: Media and Internet Giants' Converging and Diverging Strategies Against Hi-Tech Misinformation. *Media and Communication*, *9*(1), 291–300. doi:10.17645/mac.v9i1.3494

Whyte, C. (2020). Deepfake news: AI-enabled disinformation as a multi-level public policy challenge. *Journal of Cyber Policy*, *5*(2), 199–217. doi:10.1080/23738871.2020.1797135

KEY TERMS AND DEFINITIONS

Arial Scaffold: Defined as a scaffold that provides mobile support in the form of freely moving mechanism.

Branching Literacy: Defined as the ability to contextualize information using a nonlinear, multidimensional approach.

Information Literacy: Defined as the ability to gather information from multiple resources to provide context for particular content.

Deepfake: Defined as the deliberate manipulation of media using AI driven software to skew the context of audio, images, or video in an effort to promote a particular point of view.

Digital Literacy: Defined as the set of skills needed for an end-user to learn, live, and work in a society that depends on technologies for access and communication.

Object Regulation: Defined as a learner being instructionally scaffolded using some object such as an app, computer, textbook, and the like.

Other Regulation: Defined as a learner being instructionally scaffolded by another individual such as a teacher or peer mentor.

Photo-Visual Literacy: Defined as how a learner interprets and applies meaning of photos and video to related content.

Reproduction Literacy: Defined as the ability to create meaningful content based on curated digital resources.

Scaffolding: Defined as the educational concept in which a learner receives additional instructional support around particular content.

Self-Regulation: Defined as a learner negotiating content without object or other scaffolding.

Sociocultural Theory: Defined as a theory in psychology in which learners cognitively develop based on their personal and cultural interactions.

Supported Scaffold: Defined as a scaffold that is fixed using rods, platforms, and the like.

Suspended Scaffold: Defined as a scaffold that is suspended using ropes, pullies, and the like.

Technological, Pedagogical, and Content Knowledge (TPACK): Defined as a framework that explicates the interrelated skill sets a teacher needs to teach content using technology.

Zone of Proximal Development: Defined as a theory in psychology identifying a learner's ability level based on what s/he can or cannot do with scaffolded instruction.

Chapter 2
Extended Reality (XR) Teaching in the Era of Deepfakes:
A TPACK and LOU Primer for Filtering Deepfakes and Malinformation in Subject-Area Content

Rebecca J. Blankenship
https://orcid.org/0000-0002-1142-0487
Florida Agricultural and Mechanical University, USA

ABSTRACT

The use of existing and emerging technologies in teaching and learning provides the opportunity to present subject-area content using devices, programs, and venues in ways that promote higher-order thinking and long-term retention. In the last decade, advances in artificial intelligence (AI) have resulted in the development of virtual reality programs that enable end-users to interact with content in third and fourth-dimensional interactive spaces (i.e., extended reality or XR). The transformation beyond traditional face-to-face or two-dimensional teaching and learning has resulted in an unforeseen digital side effect. The digital side effect presents in the form of deepfakes or the deliberate alteration of audio and visual content to advance a specific point of view. The premise of this chapter is to present a primer using the technological, pedagogical, and content knowledge (TPACK) and levels of use construct to mitigate the presence of deepfake and malinformation in subject-area content when working in XR environments.

DOI: 10.4018/978-1-7998-6474-5.ch002

INTRODUCTION

The use of existing and emerging technologies in teaching and learning provides the opportunity to present subject-area content using devices, programs, and venues in ways that promote higher-order thinking and long-term retention. In the last decade, advances in Artificial Intelligence (AI) have resulted in the development of virtual reality programs that enable end-users to interact with content in third and fourth dimensional interactive spaces (i.e. Extended Reality or XR). The transformation beyond traditional face-to-face or two-dimensional teaching and learning, while it has provided unique modalities to not only deliver instructional content but also actualize student learning outcomes, has resulted in an unforeseen digital side effect. The digital side effect presents in the form of deepfakes or the deliberate alteration of audio and visual content to advance a specific point of view. Typically, deepfake content is characterized by the dissemination of malinformation in teaching and learning which can negatively impact desired student learning outcomes. Thus, the premise of this chapter is to present a primer using the Technological, Pedagogical, and Content Knowledge (TPACK, Mishra & Koehler, 2006) and Levels of Use (Hall, et al., 1978) construct contextualized within Vygotskian (1978) object/other to self-regulation Sociocultural Theory (SCT) to mitigate the presence of deepfake and malinformation in subject-area content when working in XR environments.

Teaching and learning methods and modalities in the 21st century continue to evolve as technologies change. As such, today's learner expects their learning environment to reflect the technologies they have adopted in their everyday lives. Educators, then, are charged with ensuring that subject-area content is delivered using a variety of technology-infused and content-relevant instructional strategies that will keep learners engaged while ensuring learning outcomes produce higher-order thinking and long-term retention. As more digitally literate learners enter colleges, schools, and universities, they expect teaching faculty and content-related programing to reflect a digitally rich environment as the technologies they use evolve and change. These digitally native learners crave interactions and simulations that mirror activities in daily life, and this is evinced by the increase in the use of Extended Reality programs that allow educators to reimagine teaching content in virtual spaces. This is particularly noted with the rise in use, especially in the last decade of programs driven by artificial intelligence (AI) that have cross-platform operability (Prensky, 2010; Horizon Report, 2021). As Rosen (2010) pointed out, there has not been a study conducted to suggest if or how teachers are using virtually based programs, such as popular social media sites, to supplement their training that they perceive as non-responsive to their preferred "anytime, anywhere" learning preferences. Therefore, in considering the technical skill set of the 21st-century teacher, teacher education faculty must respond in kind by filtering their existing face-to-face models through a model such as the Technological, Pedagogical, and Content Knowledge (TPACK) and Levels of Use (LoU) framework (Mishra & Koehler, 2006) to enable the Zone of Proximal Development (ZPD) to open and salient, higher-order learning can occur among learners (Vygotsky, 1978). External to the educational setting, many learners are regular users of XR platforms to enrich their learning experiences beyond traditional teaching and learning modalities, especially those that are technology-driven. If the efficacy of using XR is filtered through the TPACK and LoU filtered through an SCT lens, not only will this facilitate digital competency and literacy among educators but also provide additional support structures to mitigate deepfake and malinformation from negatively impacting content.

As businesses, education systems, and industries increase their digital footprints, digital skill sets among stakeholders must align with both the content and technical competencies expected in the 21st century. Accordingly, educators and learners are becoming more digitally literate as technologies evolve and become more user-friendly and interactive, almost mirroring activities in daily life as evinced by the increase in the use XR platforms to deliver content. This is particularly noted with the rise in use, especially in the last decade, of the personal computer, mobile devices, and the Internet in schools as they relate to XR realities and digital learning platforms (Prensky, 2013; Horizon Report, 2021). During this time, the technological expectations of educators and learners has significantly changed; it is expected that 21st-century educators and educational entities will not only be able to deliver content knowledge through effective pedagogy but be technically flexible enough to provide the same content using some technology during the lesson especially as it relates to solving authentic, real-world issues (Prensky, 2013). Thus, for the 21st century educator and learner, it is not enough just to have a set of fixed, predetermined content knowledges and technical skills such that there is little to no room for continued, emergent growth within the content area. As the geopolitical landscape changed at the end of the 20th century and technologies have significantly advanced, educators and learners were faced with multiple challenges, requiring the adaptation and mailability to align better with the rapidly changing curricular and technical needs of the modern educational landscapes. However, many of these changes have not been implemented due to a variety of reasons including lack of infrastructure to support XR learning spaces, lack of changes to existing content-area teaching and standards to reflect new technologies and learning spaces, and lack of training among educators on effective content delivery and instructional strategies using existing and emerging technologies. These lack of supporting infrastructure have resulted directly in deepfake and malinformation content negatively impacting higher-order content acquisition thus prompting the call for an SCT driven TPACK and LoU primer to mitigate the same.

Current Models for Conceptualizing Digital Literacy Skills

Understanding the Combination of Cognitive and Technical Awareness within the SCT Powered TPACK and LoU Frameworks

Before arriving at a model for teaching content-responsive digital literacy skills to 21st century learners, it is prescriptive to examine how the existing literature arrives at a working definition of what it means to be considered *digitally literate*. Eshet (2004) suggested that a digitally literate person possesses a complex skill set that involves more than just interacting with software or operating some digital device which, necessarily, aligns with the notion that the decision to use certain technologies is a complex act. In reality, a digitally literate person possesses a sophisticated set of skills that include the digital negotiation of cognitive, cultural, emotional, motor, and social competencies (p. 93). Further, within these competencies, there is a subset of literacy skills that the end-user varies according to the type of digital media being used. As an example, the literacy skill set for gathering information from different digital media sources about learning the Spanish language is different from the skill set needed to actually interacting across digital platforms using the Spanish language. Even among these digital informational and interactive platforms, there is a yet another subset of skills needed to negotiate how content knowledge is interpreted across digital interactive planes. Following the example, an end-user may react differently to the information gathered from a wiki site that teaches Spanish vocabulary than from a language learning website like *Don Quijote*; similarly, the end-user may respond differently to a tweet in Spanish on Twitter than a posting written in Spanish on Facebook. It is within these negotiated movements across digital platforms that deepfakes and malinformation can negatively impact content-knowledge and communication.

Accordingly, Hall, Loucks, Rutherford, & Newlove (1975) suggested a model to explain how an end-user behaves at different stages of interaction with a particular technology which explicates filtering out deepfakes and malinformation (p. 52). Specifically, they identified 6 levels of use (LoU). These levels included: (a) Level 0 - non-use; (b) Level I - orientation; (c) Level II - preparation; (d) Level III - mechanical use; (e) Level IV A & B - routine and refinement; (f) Level V - integration; and (g) Level VI - renewal. Here, it can be suggested that digital literacy is developed as the end-user interacts with different technologies across the varying levels. The challenge faced in today's digitally enhanced learning environments is ensuring that the saliency of the technology in relation to student learning outcomes facilitates a learner's growth across the LoU (Horizon Report, 2021). Hall, et al. also asserted that "strategies must then be developed that deal with the user's present LoU and facilitate growth" (p. 56). They further suggested that facilitation must extend across several iterative cycles - this necessarily implicates the cognitive connections that the user (learner) associates while interacting with a specific technology. What educators must avoid, especially when dealing with today's learner, is what Hall, et.al. referred to as a "hit-and-run" type of training (p. 52). As Hall and Loucks (1978) pointed out, it is the individual that should be the primary focus of whatever technology is implemented such that the personal interactions with selected technologies facilitates digital literacy through a personal experience of self-regulation and pedagogic transformation. With the complexities that exist across the increasingly vast landscape of technology innovations, how, then, can a primer be proposed that can both explicate and inform how a learner forms a digital literacy skill set responsive to deepfakes and malinformation?

Aviram and Eshet-Alkalai (2006) suggest two schools of thought. First, there is the conservative notion that takes the concept of a *digital literacy* at its face value. Accordingly, digital literacy is conceptualized as a finite set of discrete skills employed by the end-user using different technologies as the vehicles to activate a particular skill. Eshet-Alkalai (2004; 2005) proposed a framework identifying five specific types of digital literacy skills: (a) photo-visual literacy; (b) reproduction literacy; (c) information literacy; (d) branching literacy; and (e) socio-emotional literacy. However, the skeptical position posits that these "skills" are simply enumerations of existing larger learning concepts and different learning styles and can be explained as extensions of present-day learning theory that is simply filtered through some technology. For our purposes here, the conservative approach is proposed to explain how a learner arrives at responsive digital literacy skills, especially when faced with educators who exhibit low digital literacy skills and defer to traditional face-to-face models as definitive of best teaching practices (Horizon Report, 2021).

Much of what is known about how learners receive and integrate knowledge comes from the literature on face-to-face teaching and learning. The bulk of research dealing with professional development has primarily focused on (and accepted) the learner as passive recipient of education typically conceptualized around industry standards and professional requirements. Learners, then, view traditional face-to-face teaching and learning as something done to them rather than done with them; the learner, then, becomes cognitively distant, and in some cases, absent from the learning environment and is then seen as cognitively "tamed" through this directed process (Lingard, 2003). Alternative teaching and learning practices that are considered as a more process-outcome linear approach is favored in order to maintain the status quo of distancing the instructional relationship between educators and learners (Johnson, 1997; Zembylas, 2003). Teaching and learning are almost prescripted to follow exactly idealized industry and professional standards with no real accommodations for individual learner differences in cognitive ability and digital learning skills. As more digital adept learners are entering the workforce, the need to provide more technologically integrated learning environments that provide opportunities for real-world learning scenarios is a pervasive issue that many educators are, at present, ill-equipped to implement based on either their own lack of knowledge or lack of resources (Horizon Report, 2021). This is especially important as learners entering the workforce will need to navigate content using different digital literacy skills, especially in XR environments, to mitigate deepfake and malinformation from negatively impacting workplace outcomes.

Operating in an industrial, marketplace mentality, current teaching and learning environments reflect the desire among universities simply to reproduce the existing system, emphasizing current policy rather than promoting learner cognitive development and professional identity growth (Chalmers & Keown, 2006). Notably scarce from the educational research and related literature is the deconstruction of traditional notions of the learner as a passive training recipient in favor of exploring how the same education offered in a different environment – such as a virtual XR setting - might actually contribute to a learner's authentic cognitive development and ultimately, self-regulation (Vygotsky, 1978). Traditional face-to-face education, then, is characterized by the noted digitally cognitive distancing between teachers and learners. This distancing results in the situational removal of the learner from the actual educational context. Such distancing is of particular concern when considering the real-world needs of the 21st century digitally literate learner when entering a problem-based and solving workforce (Prensky, 2013).

Although much has been written about the need to harmonize teaching and learning with authentic, real-world examples, educational programs certainly reflect the opposite practice (Albion & Maddux, 2007). The lack of authentic and real-world simulated XR practice during is most likely the result of ends-oriented industry required professional development standards. Educational systems in the United States have been characterized by their notable use of business-type administrative and instructional models. Rather than consider learning environments as microecosystems reflective of the diversity that exists among the larger population of learners, a more controllable, assembly-line managerial standard is applied to. Albion and Maddux noted that this approach is entirely reflective of the industrial movement of the early 20th century as well as the behaviorist psychology movement of the 1960s (Skinner, 1967). One of the most observable indicators of these standards is seen not only in the type of education a learner receives but also in later, more formal content-based problem solving. Atwell (2007) characterized this as a dysfunctional relationship between professional expectations and the learner's longer-term cognitive development tooled to address real-world problems.

Many educational programs in the 1980s and 1990s have been characterized by the efforts of educators and industry professionals to realign professional standards using a predetermined, fixed set of benchmark teaching and learning criteria. These decades also evinced changes in how and when learners received content-based learning as well as which programs best suited their immediate and long-term career goals. Also, as the world's cultural, economic, social, and technical landscape has changed, the need for better educated and more globally conscious educators and learners has prompted many universities to explore and offer nontraditional professional training. As more digitally literate learners enter these programs, they expect their educators and learning environments to reflect digitally rich venues as the technologies they use are in a constant state of change. These learners crave interactions and XR simulations that mirror activities in daily life, and this is evinced by the increase in the use of XR learning platforms as alternatives to traditional face-to-face instruction. This is particularly noted with the rise in use, especially in the last decade, of AI and XR (Horizon Report, 2021). As such, the risk of deepfake and malinformation tainting otherwise legitimate content directly affects the ability of learners to apply practically what they have learned in solving authentic problems in real-time professional settings.

Since the late 20th century, the digital literacy and technological expectations of leaners has significantly changed; it is expected that 21st-century learners will be technically flexible and capable of solving content-based problems using a hybrid model driven by face-to-face and XR virtual interactions (Prensky, 2013; Rosen, 2010). Thus, for the 21st century learner, it is not enough just to have an institutionally pre-determined set of knowledge and technical skills, especially if those skills mirror digitally weak learning environments (Chan & Pang, 2006). As the geopolitical landscape changed at the end of the 20th century and technologies advanced, educational stakeholders were faced with multiple challenges, requiring the adaptation of teaching and learning modalities to align better with the rapidly changing practical and technical workplace needs. To address the needs of providing educators and learners with the digital literacy skill set needed to mitigate deepfakes and malinformation when working in XR and other technology enhanced learning spaces, the following two disparities have been identified in the current literature around the TPACK and LoU frameworks that must be addressed: 1. The efficacy of continuing traditional face-to-face learning modalities with today's digitally literate learner; and 2. How the lack of response to digital learners' needs results in limitations on applying practically content to solving real-world problems in addition to recognizing deepfake and malinformation that could potentially affect content-based outcomes.

Teaching and learning in the 21st century present an especially unique challenge when considering redesigning existing face-to-face and hybrid instructional modalities to emerging technology trends, especially those using AI and XR platforms. In its 2021 higher education edition, the Horizon Report suggests that implementing hybrid and XR virtual learning programs encourages more effective collaboration among teachers and learners. Emerging technologies have led to additional interest among educational stakeholders regarding the influence of these technologies on how they can potentially affect intended learning outcomes. The Horizon Report recognized early on the significant impact that AI and XR technologies would potentially have on teaching and learning. Specifically, the 2021 report identified four technology trends that have ultimately materialized as the game changers in terms of which technologies are used as today's preferred modalities. These modalities include the following: (a) the widespread acceptance of social networking and dynamic knowledge creation; (b) the recognition that personal and mobile technologies (especially AI and XR platforms) are being used increasingly as platforms to engage services (educational and otherwise) of all kinds; (c) the expectation among education stakeholders that the technologies will be personalized to their specific needs; and (d) the acknowledgement that multi-institutional collaboration, both internal and external to the institution, is critical to advancing the consistent use of these technologies. Within the context of these trends, the report identified six specific technologies that were having a significant impact on educational venues in the United States: (a) social computing; (b) personal broadcasting; (c) mobile phones and personal digital assistants (PDAs); (d) augmented realities; (e) context-aware environments; (f) educational gaming; and (g) digital badging and microcredentialing. The acknowledgement of these multidimensional communicative and learning platforms is of particular interest to informing the redesign teaching and learning programs, especially with the noted and recent attention being given to the advantages of hybrid AI and XR platforms.

Another important consideration is what learners – by way of technologies – cognitively receive out of their coursework at higher-order levels. For the multitasking digitally literate learner, the traditional lecture format or assignment of a PowerPoint does not address the individual learning needs that learners expect from respective programs. AI and XR powered blended or hybrid learning models enable educators and learners to transform the traditional face-to-face content learning into a network of synergistic collaborative movements from what a learner learns in the classroom to what is put into actual practice for real-world problem solving. Waycott, et al. (2010) characterized this notion as a distinction between technologies that educators and learners use for "living" and those they use for "learning" and how the two can be seamlessly blended to provide the most optimal learning platform. In his 2013 piece for *The Chronicle of Higher Education*, Helfand asserts that hybrid or blended learning environments are a progressive method for producing university graduates who are highly skilled both in collaboration and communication. Professional collaborations and effective communication are definitely two skills that industry and professionals expect learners to have a working mastery of upon graduation and entrance into their respective careers, especially as it applies to engaging with content to solve real-world problems. Of course, complicating the implementation of these skills is taking into consideration not only the digital literacy skills of all educational stakeholders but also equitable access to different technologies. As noted in the 2021 Horizon Report, the 2020 academic year certainly bore out the digital inequalities among educators and learners as face-to-face instruction was relocated to virtual platforms due to the change from face-to-face to online, remote instruction as educational venues were shuttered based on CDC social distancing guidelines around the COVID outbreak. A noticeable digital literacy gap, which included lack of access and inexperience, or no knowledge of the new technologies being used to deliver content, emerged which directly, and in some cases, negatively impacted content-delivery and associated student learning outcomes. As a result, and due to the lack of skill set needed to recognize legitimate versus illegitimate content, deepfakes and malinformation tainted instructional delivery such that teachers and learners were not capable of distinguishing between the two. Here, it is imperative that the SCT focused TPACK and LoU frameworks be actively implemented to mitigate the negative impacts on learning ecosystems.

To arrive at salient digital literacy, educators and learners must be organized as cognitive-based social units within a dynamic learning ecosystem given the fact that technology use has become a complex interaction of inherently cognitive and social activities. If educational programs are re-conceptualized following the principles a cognitive-based learning theory such as sociocultural theory (SCT), it is anticipated that intrapsychological development can potentially occur among learners across the socially interactive plane expected as part of the overall deeper cognitive learning experience (Wertsch, 1985). One of the underlying tenets of SCT is the understanding that learning (and hence cognitive development) is enabled through the scaffolded interactions between the novice and expert learners (Vygotsky, 1978) – in the case of teaching and learning here, these would reference the interactions between the educator (as the master) and the learner (as the novice). This internalization is facilitated by the mediated communicative system used among interlocutors and knowledge is viewed as transferred when the novice becomes self- rather than other- or object-regulated (Luria, 1976; Smagorinsky, 1995). Upon successful completion of student learning acquisition and by association cognitive development within the content area, the learner, based on this tenet, should be able to self-regulate when adapting to the technology changes that characterize the modern instructional settings and thusly, more adept and recognizing fake versus real content.

In terms of teaching the 21st century learner, the objective is for the educator and learner to interact in such a way that the learner internalizes knowledge and can become more cognitively independent. Vygotsky (1978) suggested that higher mental functioning is a socially constructed process, where the "social dimension of consciousness is primary in time and in fact" (p. 30). The individual's awareness is considered by Vygotsky to be a secondary by-product of these interactions. Knowledge, then, is based on the associations between the knower and the known (Kanuka & Anderson, 1998). Kanuka and Anderson (1999) pointed out "that knowledge is constructed as a social process rather than an individual process," and it necessarily follows that "constructing the knowledge [involves] examining and understanding the experience where the process occurred" (p. 5). However, existing teaching practices resemble those of bank transactions—the educator deposits knowledge into the learner that is ultimately left unaltered and withdrawn at a later time making it much more susceptible to deepfake and malinformation content. This notion must be recognized and challenged if educators and learners are to appropriately respond to today's digitally saturated learning environments, especially those that use AI and XR as the learning platform. Educators with high digital literacy skills, then, must be attuned to their learners' cognitive needs using techniques that differentiate between learner digital literacy skills and cognitive position; therefore, teaching and learning best practices must be realigned to reflect current and emerging technology use balanced within the TPACK and LoU constructs framed around they Vygotskian postulates of object/other to self-regulation.

As further suggested in the 2021 Horizon Report, one of the significant challenges faced in teaching and learning in adapting and adopting new technologies to meet AI and XR enhanced learning spaces is the low digital fluency among educators and learners which can directly and negatively impact the ability of educators and learners to distinguish between authentic and manipulated content. The recognition of this deficiency is noted in the marked absence of trending technologies integrated into current instructional models, most notably in terms of AI and XR learning spaces implemented using the SCT self-regulatory construct within the TPACK and LoU frameworks. At present, there is a significant disconnect between acceptance of new technologies among educators, available (and salient) training on new modalities, relevant technology integrated curriculum, and stakeholder support for necessary hardware and software upgrades to match new learning realities. Even though the current trend among many educational entities is the requirement that all educators must teach at least one course as a hybrid or completely on-line course, there is little incentive or sparse support to move a face-to-face classroom to a virtual format, even after the return to face-to-face instruction post-COVID (Stoltz-Loike, 2014). While learners have begun to embrace and integrate new technologies into their course work as the new realities of their learning ecosystems, for the most part, teaching and learning modalities still lag behind. The problem is exacerbated by the fact that programs so often minimalize the importance of digital literacy and marginalize its integration into existing curriculum going back to the original assertion that programming still is centered around a linear means-ends model rather than a recognized instructional framework, such as TPACK and LoU.

CONCLUSION AND FUTURE RECOMMENDATIONS

The purpose of this chapter was to begin a dialogue towards recognizing the immediate need for change in reconceptualizing teaching and learning modalities in response to the increasing digitalization of learning ecosystems. Thus, a primer was recommended using the Technological, Pedagogical, and Content Knowledge (TPACK) and Levels of Use construct embedded within Vygotskian sociocultural object/other to self-regulation to mitigate the presence of deepfake and malinformation in subject-area content when working in AI and XR environments to produce desired student learning outcomes. The use of existing and emerging technologies in teaching and learning provides the opportunity to present subject-area content using devices, programs, and venues in ways that promote higher-order thinking and long-term retention. In the last decade, advances in AI have resulted in the development of virtual reality programs that enable end-users to interact with content in third and fourth dimensional interactive spaces (i.e. XR). The transformation beyond traditional face-to-face or two-dimensional teaching and learning, while it has provided unique modalities to not only deliver instructional content but also actualize student learning outcomes, has resulted in an unforeseen digital side effect. The digital side effect presents in the form of deepfakes or the deliberate alteration of audio and visual content to advance a specific point of view. Typically, deepfake content is characterized by the dissemination of deepfake and malinformation; in teaching and learning, this can negatively impact desired student learning outcomes. Teaching and learning modalities must be reimagined to include contingencies for mitigating digital literacy inequalities that may result in the inability of teachers and learners to recognize and mitigate for deepfakes and malinformation as they interact in virtual instructional venues, especially those that are powered by AI and XR platforms. Educational programs are at the precipice of understanding the impact that these new digital platforms have on content delivery and student learning outcomes especially if they are not fully conceptualized around a research-driven and proven framework such as TPACK or LoU. As noted in the Horizon Report (2021), due to the low digital literacy among many educators and learners, notable inequalities related to access and technology-related skills has contributed to the increase of deepfake and malinformation content.

REFERENCES

Albion, P. R., & Maddux, C. (2007). Editorial: Networked knowledge: Challenges for teacher education. *Journal of Technology and Teacher Education*, *15*, 303–310.

Atwell, G. (2007, January). Personal learning environments: The future of elearning? *eLearning Papers, 2*, 1-7. Retrieved March 4, 2008, from, http://www.elearningeuropa.info/files/media/media11561.pdf

Aviram, A. & Eshet-Alkalai. (2006). Towards a theory of digital literacy: Three scenarios for the next steps. *European Journal of Open, Distance, and E-Learning.* at www.eurodl.org/materials/contrib/2006/Aharon_Aviram.htm

Chalmers, L., & Keown, P. (2006). Communities of practice and professional development. *International Journal of Lifelong Education, 25*(2), 139–156. doi:10.1080/02601370500510793

Chan, C. K., & Pang, M. F. (2006). Teacher collaboration in learning communities. *Teaching Education, 17*(1), 1–5. doi:10.1080/10476210500527899

Eshet, Y., & Chaiut, E. (2005). Living books: On the acquisition of digital skills in multimedia environments. In *Learning in the Technology Era. Proceedings of the Chais Conference.* The Open University of Israel.

Eshet-Alkalai. (2005). Thinking skills in the digital era. In Encyclopaedia of Distance Learning (vol. 1). Idea Group Inc.

Eshet-Alkalai, Y. (2004). Digital literacy: A conceptual framework for survival skills in the digital era. *Journal of Educational Multimedia and Hypermedia, 13*(1), 93–106.

Eshet-Alkalai & Amichai-Hamburger. (2004). Experiments with digital literacy. *Cyberpsychology (Brno), 7*(4), 425–434.

Hall, G., & Loucks, S. (1978). Teacher concerns as a basis for facilitating and personalizing staff development. *Teachers College Record, 80*(1), 36–53.

Hall, G., Loucks, S., Rutherford, W., & Newlove, B. (1975). Levels of use of the innovation: A framework for analyzing innovation adoption. *Journal of Teacher Education, 26*(1), 52–56. doi:10.1177/002248717502600114

Helfand, D. (2013). Watering the roots of knowledge through collaborative learning. *The Chronicle of Higher Education.* Retrieved from October 28, 2014, from http://chronicle.com/article/Watering-the-Roots-of/140135/

Johnson, K. E. (1997). Comments on Karen E. Johnson's "The role of theory in L2 teacher education": The author responds. *TESOL Quarterly, 31*(4), 779–782. doi:10.2307/3587761

Kanuka, H., & Anderson, T. (1999). Using constructivism in technology-mediated learning: Constructing order out of the chaos in the literature. *Radical Pedagogy*, *1*, 1–12. Retrieved March 4, 2008, from https://radicalpedagogy.icaap.org/content/issue1_2/02kanuka1_2.html

Kaplan, A. (1997). Work, leisure, and the tasks of schooling. *Curriculum Inquiry*, *27*(4), 423–451. doi:10.1080/03626784.1997.11075501

Lingard, B. (2003). Where to in gender policy in education after recuperative masculinity politics? *International Journal of Inclusive Education*, *7*(1), 33–56. doi:10.1080/13603110210143626

Luria, A. R. (1976). *Cognitive development: Its cultural and social foundations*. Harvard University Press.

Mishra, P., & Koehler, M. J. (2006). Technological pedagogical content knowledge: A framework for teacher knowledge. *Teachers College Record*, *108*(6), 1017–1054. doi:10.1111/j.1467-9620.2006.00684.x

Prensky, M. (2010). *Teaching digital natives: Partnering for real learning*. Corwin Press.

Prensky, M. (2013). Our brains extended. *Educational Leadership*, *70*(6), 22–27.

Report, H. (2021). *The New Media Consortium*. Retrieved from https://library.educause.edu/resources/2021/4/2021-educause-horizon-report-teaching-and-learning-edition

Rosen, L. (2010). *Rewired: Understanding the igeneration and the way we learn*. Palgrave Macmillan.

Rosenblatt, L. M. (1976). *Literature as exploration* (3rd ed.). Noble and Noble. (Original work published 1938)

Smagorinsky, P. (1995). The social construction of data: Methodological problems of investigating learning in the zone of proximal development. *Review of Educational Research*, *65*(3), 191–212. doi:10.3102/00346543065003191

Stoltz-Loike, M. (2013). Incentives and training. *Inside Higher Ed*. Retrieved October 28, 2014 from https://www.insidehighered.com/advice/2013/12/18/essay-incentives-and-training-teaching-online

Vygostky, L. S. (1978). Interaction between learning and development. In L. S. Vygotsky, M. Cole, V. John-Steiner, S. Scribner, & E. Souberman (Eds.), *Mind in Society: The development of higher psychological processes* (pp. 79–91). Harvard University Press.

Waycott, J., Bennett, S., Kennedy, G., Dalgarno, B., & Gray, K. (2010). Digital divides? Student and staff perceptions of information and communication technologies. *Computers & Education, 54*(4), 1202–1211. doi:10.1016/j.compedu.2009.11.006

Wertsch, J. V. (1985). *Vygotsky and the social formation of mind.* Harvard University Press.

Zembylas, M. (2003). Emotions and teacher identity: A poststructural perspective. *Teachers and Teaching Theories and Practice, 9*(3), 213–238. doi:10.1080/13540600309378

ADDITIONAL READING

Ahmed, S. (2021). Fooled by the fakes: Cognitive differences in perceived claim accuracy and sharing intention of non-political deepfakes. *Personality and Individual Differences, 182*, 111074. doi:10.1016/j.paid.2021.111074

Almars, A. M. (2021). Deepfakes Detection Techniques Using Deep Learning: A Survey. *Journal of Computer and Communications, 9*(5), 20–35. doi:10.4236/jcc.2021.95003

Cochran, J. D., & Napshin, S. A. (2021). Deepfakes: Awareness, concerns, and platform accountability. *Cyberpsychology, Behavior, and Social Networking, 24*(3), 164–172. doi:10.1089/cyber.2020.0100 PMID:33760667

Godulla, A., Hoffmann, C. P., & Seibert, D. (2021). Dealing with deepfakes–an interdisciplinary examination of the state of research and implications for communication studies. *SCM Studies in Communication and Media, 10*(1), 72–96. doi:10.5771/2192-4007-2021-1-72

Johnson, D. G., & Diakopoulos, N. (2021). What to do about deepfakes. *Communications of the ACM, 64*(3), 33–35. doi:10.1145/3447255

Khalil, H. A., & Maged, S. A. (2021, May). Deepfakes Creation and Detection Using Deep Learning. In 2021 International Mobile, Intelligent, and Ubiquitous Computing Conference (MIUCC) (pp. 1-4). IEEE.

Krishna, D. (2021). Deepfakes, online platforms, and a novel proposal for transparency, collaboration, and education. *Richmond Journal of Law & Technology, 27*(3).

Meckel, M., & Steinacker, L. (2021). Hybrid Reality: The Rise of Deepfakes and Diverging Truths. *Morals & Machines, 1*(1), 10–21. doi:10.5771/2747-5182-2021-1-10

KEY TERMS AND DEFINITIONS

Artificial Intelligence: The theory and development of computer systems able to perform tasks that normally require human intelligence, such as visual perception, speech recognition, decision-making, and translation between languages.

Deepfake: A video of a person in which their face or body has been digitally altered so that they appear to be someone else, typically used maliciously or to spread false information.

Digital Literacy: Having the skills you need to live, learn, and work in a society where communication and access to information is increasingly through digital technologies like internet platforms, social media, and mobile devices.

Extended Reality: Extended reality encompasses immersive technologies like real-time 3D, augmented reality (AR), virtual reality (VR), and mixed reality (XR).

Levels of Use: A concept used to define an end-user's experience level with a particular technology.

Malinformation: False or inaccurate information, especially that which is deliberately intended to deceive.

Sociocultural Theory: Psychology theory that looks at the important contributions that society makes to individual development. This theory stresses the interaction between developing people and the culture in which they live.

Technological, Pedagogical, and Content Knowledge: TPACK is a technology integration framework that identifies three types of knowledge instructors need to combine for successful edtech integration—technological, pedagogical, and content knowledge.

Chapter 3
The Never Ending Intellectual Theft of Truth:
How the Mainstream Media Cartel Dismembers the Facts

David Brian Ross
Nova Southeastern University, USA

Gina Lynne Peyton
Nova Southeastern University, USA

ABSTRACT

The purpose of this chapter is to examine how the fake news has originated. This term has been in existence for decades, since the evolution of the printing press, which also disseminated false information. The mainstream media and non-mainstream media or just individuals in general have their own biases and agendas, so misinformation, disinformation, exaggerations, and deceptions will exist. This chapter will provide individuals from any political perspective or other beliefs evidence to make their own judgements. Digital citizenship and literacy will be explored using various examples of obtaining information and use of devices. In addition, this chapter will consider how researchers should take risks to explore controversial topics such as fake news to inform an audience using research.

INTRODUCTION

Taking risks in research can be viewed as a problem for some authors or could be seen as a positive stance. A component of risk-taking that necessitates both positive

DOI: 10.4018/978-1-7998-6474-5.ch003

and negative outcomes should be confronted by the decision-maker (Zinn, 2016). If researchers are to publish on risky topics, the information can transfer knowledge and educate the public by broadening the literature; otherwise, it would prevent the public from knowing valuable unbiased information. In college, students are researching for their thesis and dissertations on various topics and, for the most part, confine themselves to the same monotonous topics without broadening their choices due to their fear of researching risky subjects. At times they may even get locked in a certain topic as their dissertation chair or advisors also fear researching risky topics or may even have an agenda of their own. Arar et al. (2019) edited a book on the challenges that migrant refugee students have in higher education, "ignoring the relationship between refugees, migrants, and higher education would be a mistake and a missed opportunity, but little attention has been paid to this dimension of the internalization of higher education" (p. xvii). According to Ross et al. (2021), researchers are taking a risk when researching and publishing on perilous topics, as their repute may be tarnished after researching a sensitive topic, and in turn, may possibly lose their status. Furthermore, for those students who are just entering the workforce after academia, they are at risk of not attaining a prominent position in higher education or research to include obtaining grants. It can also be said that students are being indoctrinated in terms of what topics they are to research, especially in science, as they are aware of what topics will permit them to attain grants. At the same token, established researchers have found a method to assist future researchers' thoughts (Maxmen, 2009).

For the purpose of this chapter, the authors could be taking a risk by discussing *Fake News* as this is a topic that is controversial in nature. However, the authors feel this material should be written to inform all audiences who watch the mainstream media to be better informed of the opinion news of pundits who have their own agenda versus journalistic news. Researchers should not be faced with a cancel culture when reporting on research versus pundits who only base their point of view on their own agenda. As a consumer of news and/or social media communications, individuals consider full transparency; however, with the increased 24-hour news cycles and increase in pundit-styled panels as well as the Big Tech corporations deciding what should be read or canceled is widespread (Jackson, 2014; Letukas, 2012; Tsfati et al., 2020). This amateur-style punditry is encouraged by the mainstream media moguls to force their agendas and repetitive talking points regarding politics and politicians, elections, immigration, the economy, and other world events. Jackson (2014) stated the resources are being used by media moguls not only to persuade people to buy their newspapers but to additionally influence politics. In addition, some mainstream media outlets also omit important events for public viewership, as it does not align with their narratives (Ross et al., 2019). Pundits are capable of having suggestive versions and content that could be repeated and manipulated into many sound bites, disguised as traditional news, and premeditated spread of fake news, all in the process to advance their own ideologies, political goals, guarantee that the viewership took a specific side of the story, and generate advertising revenue to their organization (Jackson, 2014; Letukas, 2012; Tsfati et al., 2020).

In research and higher education, faculty and other academics are held at a higher level when reporting on any investigations/research inquires and must have taken the Collaborative Institution Training Initiative Program. Dr. Ashley Russom, who is currently serving as the Institutional Review Board (IRB) Chair of the university with 15 years of experience who has reviewed over 1,700 IRB protocols and trained over 16 reviewers and expertise in research of human subjects explicated at any university that is established to ensure ethical research is conducted under the umbrella of the institution. Following the federal guidelines established by the Office for Human Research Protections (OHRP), researchers must ensure that the principles of the Belmont Report are observed for all research involving human participants: respect for persons, beneficence, and justice (Grady, 2015; U.S. Department of Health & Human Services, 1979, 2021). All researchers are required to maintain a valid Collaborative Institution Training Initiative Program (CITI) when conducting research, which is a set of asynchronous modules and quizzes for the principal investigator and all co-investigators and research assistants, which fosters a clear understanding of the rights to which human participants are entitled.

Institutional Review Board (IRB) reviewers are trained to note any issues related to protecting the participants involved in the study (Grady, 2015). The principal investigator is responsible for submitting paperwork describing all research activities and must obtain approval from the Institutional Review Board prior to engaging in research (Parker, 2016). Most universities and organizations have a preset list of documents to be presented in the IRB protocol. This rigorous, iterative process allows for changes to be made in the protocol to ensure unbiased, sound research is conducted. Equitable time commitments, consent processes, and proper compensation are just a few of the many issues the IRB reviewer ensures the principal investigator adheres. As such, each researcher is held to the same standards prior to commencing data collection (A. Russom, personal communication, June 22, 2021). Researchers face a dilemma when trying to acquire various types of valid data, whether it is internal, external, the construct, in addition to a statistical conclusion. Although studies regarding narcissistic behavior could still be a risk to research such a topic as numerous organizations would not permit a researcher to determine if they, the employer was perceived to be a narcissistic leader or display narcissistic behavior (Day et al., 2020; Sasso, 2017). Mulligan (2021) additionally stated that challenges also occur for researchers, especially if the group they are studying is a political outlier. This is where the possibility that a researcher could possibly be accused of similar prejudices and ideologies. Mulligan commented on several topics regarding safety for sex workers in Ireland, child exploitation, participant bias and preconceptions, corrupt and volatile environments, gender power imbalances, and institutional challenges (p. 321). With that said, there are many controversial topics that some researchers might resist, such as fake news, immunizations, politics, gun rights, first amendments, immigration, racism, and many more. Moreover, De Schrijver (2012) explicated that research conducted on sensitive topics would potentially produce skewed data as participants may not truthfully answer the questions posed, refuse to cooperate in the study altogether, or refuse to provide answers for particular questions. The authors mentioned that researching fake news could be a risky topic to write as the citizenry should be informed about the real world events reported in the news cycle; however, from a complete honorable approach, not based on agendas, narratives, and political leanings.

The objective of this chapter is to educate all individuals, no matter one's political affiliations or view of the mainstream media and non-mainstream media. The authors' purpose of this chapter is to further educate individuals concerning the origin, meaning, and ideology behind fake news. Many theoretical frameworks, models, and archetypes are discussed to give the reader information to research and have a better understanding to make their own decisions instead of mainstream media's propaganda and personal agendas to sway individuals' thoughts. The authors are aware that individuals believe there is a lot of issues occurring in the world and how the mainstream media and non-mainstream media cover the news; however, people want the truth in all reporting of the news, so they are informed to make their own good judgments. The authors want to stress the importance and provide information on digital literacy to promote good digital citizenship. Factual accountability is needed when journalists, pundits, or others disseminate news because they must be held accountable for the veracity of their claims.

BACKGROUND

Media Misinformation and Disinformation

"Beware of his false knowledge; it is more dangerous than ignorance" (George Bernard Shaw, 1903, p. 230). Fake news, a concept that the citizenry is all now well too familiar with, was once a term that was obscure. However, what is the true definition of fake news? According to Molina et al. (2019), fake news is fictitious stories that seem to be news that is scattered on the Internet or through utilizing another form of media and usually generated to influence one's political views as a prank. However, figuring out what is considered to be fake is somewhat intricate. In comparison, Celliers and Hattingh (2020) defined fake news in multiple stages. It was first defined as made-up information illustrated as the truth. It was then further defined as knowingly publishing false information and distributing it amongst people. Lastly, it was defined as purposely publishing deceiving information, which can be later checked as incorrect via fact-checking. The terminology of fake news seemed to become a familiar term just in the past five years due to the opinionated views of the mainstream media. However, the meaning behind this term or verbiage, to include media photo manipulation, has been mentioned for decades as the growth of pundits and their agendas, along with the media moguls and their production managers' personal agendas to attack individuals whom they do not agree with nor their conflicting philosophies that they do not share. Anderson and Rainie (2017) mentioned that there had been biased in the mainstream media for years; however, the introduction to the news via the Internet has been exaggerated; therefore, there is an increase in exploitation as well as misleading news and fake news.

The idea of *disinformation,* as it was called during the World Wars and *freak journalism* or *yellow journalism* during the Spanish war, was a concept since 1896 (Molina et al., 2019). Hearst and Pulitzer were bitter rivals and considered to be the two giants of yellow journalism, as it was this form of journalism that was considered to be an appalling example of false journalism that one could ever imagine as it allowed alphanumeric data via electrical signals to be manipulated, fictitious, and exaggerated (Albert, 1984; Carey, 2016; Jackson, 2014). According to Molina et al. (2019), the concept of yellow journalism was identified as publishing information without the required evidence, which in turn, made it factually incorrect. This same phenomenon came back to light during the 2016 U.S. Presidential elections; however, this time, it came back in a new information environment that the populace is presently living in. As fake news is delivered in the current environment, it is critical to note that the social media platform disseminates the information delivered rather than attaining information via traditional sources. In this day and age, one no longer needs to be a journalist and work for a publication to write and publish online (Molina et al., 2019). In fact, amateurs are now writing and publishing content through online platforms (Celliers & Hattingh, 2020; Molina et al., 2019). As previously mentioned, the authors stated that researchers need to proceed through a rigorous process of an institutional review board as well as find scholarly sources to validate and synthesize their content. Researchers have stressed the importance of knowing and respecting the audience, truthfully represent information, meet the readers' needs, and maintain professional quality and standard level of writing, while conveying to others without being reckless (Andersen, 2001; Ross & Sasso, 2017). Graves and Wells (2019) mentioned that factual accountability is needed as it is based on the facts matter approach compared to the information availability process of whether or not facts are reachable. "Journalism may be viewed as a *field of struggle for the truth* related to power because fundamentally journalism is a struggle to impose a certain viewpoint as legitimate, against other fields like politics and economics" (Graves & Wells, 2019, p. 10). It would be hopeful that these institutions adhere to the truth-telling standards and not disseminate misinformation and disinformation. Factual accountability is to make sure that the citizenry has facts available to them by promoting a fact-based dialogue to hold institutions of the media and politicians accountable for any information that may be disingenuous.

Some thoughts regarding the term Fake News have been found in many website links, such as the December 2016 retirement speech for Senator Harry Reid that was given by Hillary Clinton, who started the "epidemic of malicious fake news and false propaganda that flooded social media over the past year. It's now clear that so-called fake news can have real-world consequences" (Borchers, 2018, para. 6). As stated in Molina et al. (2019), while one could state that the world became more so interested in the idea of fake news after the 2016 Presidential election, it is by no means a novel phenomenon. It was accentuated by Hillary Clinton that social media played a part in the 2016 election, which she called fake news (Boxell et al., 2018). According to Wendling (2018), in mid-2016, Craig Silverman, a media editor for Buzzfeed, located numerous fictional stories, which were created in a small Eastern Europe town in Macedonia called Veles. Based on an investigation conducted, a minimum of 140 fake news websites from Veles was found to be pulling big numbers on Facebook prior to the United States election. This, in turn, allowed those individuals from Veles to make a plethora of money through Facebook advertising. Therefore, they wanted these fallacious stories to travel broadly on social media and to be based on partisan, ideological, and disruptive intent (Fox, 2020; Wendling, 2018). Similar claims were mentioned in Celliers and Hattingh's (2018) observations as well. One can concur that the U.S. Presidential election, more explicitly Donald Trump, was and still is a very controversial and decisive topic on social media (Boxell et al., 2018; Wendling, 2018). The Macedonians, as well as other suppliers, continued to create additional fake stories with headlines that read, *Pope Francis Shocks World, Endorses Donald Trump for President* and *FBI Agent Suspected in Hillary Email Leaks Found Dead in Apparent Murder-Suicide*. These headlines, as well as those pertaining to the election, were all completely fake, and it was these disingenuous stories that started the term *fake news* (Wendling, 2018).

As previously stated, the concept of misinformation and deceit are nothing new and have been around for centuries (Fox, 2020; Wendling, 2018). Burkhardt (2017) stated that fake news is not such a current topic as it dates back to the era before the printing press as rumors and false stories were communicated verbally. Just because a story was printed or placed on the Internet never made it a true story. However, Silverman, as well as others, noticed that there was a distinctive relationship between President Trump's election and social media algorithms, advertising systems, and individuals who were eager to create stories in order to make money (Celliers &

Hattingh, 2018; Wendling, 2018). A majority of the material found was considered to be traditional political communication. That stated, there were memes illustrating Trump as a fearless leader, fans who supported Trump to deport illegal immigrants. Much of this content was not what one would consider fake news. However, pundits were jostling to explicate the shock result and mediated towards fake news as one of many possible explanations. The concept of fake news currently suggests more than the once "quick payouts" that the Macedonian teenagers were partaking in. In fact, President Trump provided Fake News Awards to reporters who made erroneous and bad predictions, especially when concerning the collusion between the Trump campaign and Russia (Wendling, 2018). Kennedy et al. (2018) mentioned that the prediction for the 2016 election would have been Clinton; however, their predictions stumped those who claim to be professional pollsters, so-called journalists, and pundits posing as political analysts.

Some journalists interpreted Hillary Clinton's remarks during her speech on December 8, 2016, as a reference to *pizzagate,* which was a crazy conspiracy theory, which spread tremendously online (Borchers 2018; Wendling, 2018). Within that speech given by Hillary Clinton, she also mentioned and asked her audience to "protect our democracy." However, reporters broadly interpreted it as referring to the election (Borchers, 2018; Wendling, 2018). One month later, President Trump adopted that phrase in January 2017 when replying to a question posed by Jim Acosta and simply stated, "you're fake news" (Borchers, 2018; Wendling, 2018). From then on, Trump repeatedly utilized that term on Twitter, and Trump's followers determined that they were going to take that term and make it theirs (Wendling, 2018). According to Borchers (2018), President Trump recreated the term fake news to mean news reports that he did not agree with or supported. Wendling (2018) indicated that since then, the phrase had been utilized by the likes of journalists, political operatives, pundits, as well as everyday people in many types of content such as false news, satire, misreporting, persuasive information (Molina et al., 2019). When researching the term fake news on a Google News search, five million results were discovered. In 2018 alone, the phrase fake news has been used two million times on Twitter alone (Wendling, 2018). Furthermore, it has been indicated that in 2017, a total of 167 websites published articles on utterly false information. Not surprisingly, the 50 greatest viral fake news stories of 2017 spawned more total shares as well as comments versus the top 50 hoaxes of 2016 (Borchers, 2018).

Trending on British Broadcasting Corporation during April 2017 was reported on the phenomenon of left-wing fake news for those who were anti-Trump (Wendling, 2018). It was indicated by experts that highly educated individuals could also be conned by lies as well as be far more stubborn when given information that challenges their philosophies. MacKenzie and Bhatt (2019) combined the words lies, fake news, and *bullshit,* stating that there it is abundant in the world as many "people remain stubbornly unwilling to acknowledge that there might be – even in principle – such a thing as truth" (p. 220). Months after, the term fake news seemed to be utilized for all matters and, in turn, made the term irrelevant. According to Alexios Mantzarlis, who is director of the Poynter Institute of International Fact-Checking Network, it is the media who is at fault, as right after the election, fake news was used to describe everything. In fact, this phrase is used when individuals are against any information that does not suit their fancy. Similarly, Molina et al. (2019) indicated that fake news does not solely mean false information as it did at its inception, but rather it has now been co-opted by politicians to mean any information that has been aired by sources that do not back their biased positions.

One could concur that it was the growth of social media that enabled the modern form of fake news, otherwise known as misinformation (Wendling, 2018). In order to solve this solution of fake news being produced, fact-checking can always be used; however, with the plethora of fake news being produced, this is now what some may believe to be impossible to do. The concept of fact-checking has been around for 20 years, but it still proves to be difficult. According to Mantzarlis, what one can do is assist people as well as journalists in discovering suspicious claims quicker and attain access to the statistics that are required to check a claim quicker (Wendling, 2018). Molina et al. (2019) revealed that websites such as Snopes and *Politifact* exclusively tackle the problems created by fake news by checking the information located on the news by utilizing a plethora of humans who fact check. However, this has proven to be difficult as fact-checking is time-consuming as well as leads these very same humans to be subjective when searching for facts, as well as being restricted from prior experiences (Molina et al., 2019). That stated, the discussion of having an alternative to human fact-checking, such as machine-based powered by Artificial Intelligence (A.I.) driven algorithms, due to the plethora of fact-checking required, has been an additional possibility. However, much like utilizing humans to fact check which may pose an issue, the use of machines also poses an issue, as to build reliable algorithms to identify fake news, one also has to be taught to define it as well as distinguishing it from real news (Molina et al., 2019).

Regarding Mass Media Theoretical Foundations

Based on research, there are an abundance of theories that have surfaced pertaining to mass media, for example: (a) Mass Society Theory, (b) Marxist Media Theory, (c) Functionalist Theory, and (d) Social Constructionism (Ross et al., 2019); of these, the following theories appeared to be most relevant. The first is mass society theory, where according to Bennett (1982), there are numerous theorists who are linked with mass society theory. Bennett indicated that the Mass Society Theory needs to be viewed as a theory with themes and patterns that are considered common to mass culture. Mambrol (2018) defined mass culture as fake and, in turn, unable to satisfy "production by capitalist corporations seeking to maximize their profits by selling to the lowest common denominator" (para. 2). Consequently, mass culture is carried on as not being authentic due to it not being produced by individuals as well as manipulative as its main purpose is to be bought and not satisfying. However, this process does not give their consumers satisfaction, such as the mainstream media, who attempts to manipulate the truth to meet their personal agenda. The concept of the mass society theory is established on the idea that society is formed in the center and on a very big scale. In addition, it is also based on the idea that the public becomes demolished and that the media is what people depend on to identify with themselves. Finally, the mass society theory is associated with the idea that media is used as a method to monitor and manipulate their audience (Bennett, 1982; McQuail, 2010).

The second is Marxist media theory, where Karl Marx was solely comfortable with the press before it was a true mass medium. It is critical to note that there is still relevance in regard to the tradition of Marxist analysis of the media in a capitalist society. According to Marx's views, the concept of power is the key theme when describing mass media. There are certainly variations; however, there has also been constant stress on the idea that mass media is a means to rule and control. Research from a Pew Study revealed that powerful people and organizations influence media to the point of controlling the viewership regarding what one should know (Ross et al., 2020). The Marxist Media Theory hypothesizes a precise correlation between economic ownership as well as delivering messages that validate the authenticity of class society (McQuail, 2010). It has been made evident that in the twentieth century, individuals had fabricated modified versions of the Marxist Media Theory that highlighted the ideological effects of media pertaining to manipulative relationships, the dominance of capitalism, the reduction of the laboring class, and concerns with control (Chandler, n.d.; McQuail, 2010). A theory that falls right after the Marxist media theory is the political economy theory, which is based on the concept of the connection among the economic structure in addition to the dynamics. This theory illustrates how mainstream media, as a large corporation with economic power, can direct ideas of the content (Litschka, 2019; McQuail, 2010).

The third theory is the functionalist theory, which explains what social practices and institutions are concerning to what society and people necessitate. Society can be viewed as a system that continues with correlated operating parts where each element makes a critical impact on advancement and order. From this perspective, an individual feels they aim to attain specific goals (Boden et al., 2016). This theory depicts media as being independent as well as one that corrects itself (McQuail, 2010), as the media performs an influential role in the function of society. The media constantly tells fables and will only apologize if they are caught. This apology is usually proffered once the hype of this fake narrative is gone and once the damage has already taken place. The social constructivism theory, regarding mainstream media as an institution, can reproduce their own meanings and agenda where they can only offer a bias justification of social reality. Berger and Luckmann, two sociologists in 1966, described habitualization regarding human interaction. The concept of habitualization can be described as how the media repeats the same talking points based on the 24/7 cable news where viewers are unconsciously hypnotized due to the frequency of the same repeated information that the public would like to be independent and unbiased. The public craves to have their own opinions and views but is now being force-fed the same agenda-filled information that the media has been instructed to feed by higher powers; mainstream media is owned by large corporate America who also has connections to other countries, such as China. If the populace is continuously force-fed the same information, without being given the opportunity to hear a different view of the story, individuals could start believing the same story that is circulated, as mainstream media wants to be powerful and have the most influence (Jackson, 2014; Letukas, 2012; Tsfati et al., 2020). Those who hold power in the media have economic power by dominating large corporations in many markets (Bergés Saura, 2010; Jackson, 2014). A good example is if a student in the K-12 system is repeatedly told they could not achieve success, they will start believing this. They will start believing they are a failure. One such trending topic today is critical race theory (CRT), where if an individual is constantly telling someone they are oppressed, will they start believing they are oppressed?

J. Dettinger (personal communication, May 30, 2021), who was a law professor at the University of Toledo and who studied human behavior, explained a theory regarding *Perception Fallacy*, which is based on how those who create the talking points for others to hear, create the perception in the viewers' minds, as this term is defined as individuals being knowledgeable of what they recognize (Lupyan, 2017). Additionally, Clements (2013) opined that one could use fallacies and biases to alter one's perceptions. Clements continued to state from a legal perspective that one can persuade a person, utilizing informal fallacies and cognitive biases regarding thinking and reasoning, to view issues identically from the lawyer's position. For example, with the mainstream media and non-mainstream media, their agenda is to place a thought in the audiences' minds to think about something that could be true. Today's mainstream media and non-mainstream media have drastically expanded many outlets of communicating to the public, as information is able to travel faster and "to engage with a diversity of representation and counter-stereotypical information" (Hinton, 2017, p. 22). This practice of communication engagement is used by the media outlets to create a perception of falsehoods, rather than the truth (Lupyan, 2017), by repetitious verbiage that is identical from media outlet to media outlet. The media has a platform to manipulate world events to control and mold minds to sway thoughts and opinions. "Manipulating the mind via a psychological warfare campaign not only works well for the military but also with the many media communications (e.g., television, audio, visual, written)" (Ross et al., 2020, p. 101). It is the hope that the media could function as an ethical organization/profession to inform their audience of truth rather than fallacious stories to meet their personal agenda. Feist and Feist (2009) explained the concept of interpersonal trust is when an individual has communicated information, whether verbally or written to an audience or individual, the information would be trustworthy. As a result, individuals need to learn who can be trusted and those who cannot be trusted when receiving verbal promises by others, in this case, the media.

Main Focus of the Chapter

Mainstream Media Versus Non-Mainstream Media

Mainstream media (MSM) are considered the dominant types of media in terms of their content, production, and distribution audience. In contrast, alternative media (Non-MSM) is not mainstreamed or corporate-owned that tends to promote their individual agenda. The mainstream media is the traditional and established broadcasting companies. Ultimately, they are "handful of companies that own the most popular media networks and, as a result, command the most views" (LaMarco, 2018, para. 7). These companies cater to most of the populace and control what the majority listen, watch and read. This could explain why some have labeled them as co-conspirators and question their objectivity in presenting the truth. Non-mainstream media, also known as alternative media, are typically not corporate-owned. They have been called "alternative, anarchist, small, activist, grassroots, progressive, non-corporate, subversive underground, radical, dissident, independent and many other terms" (LaMarco, 2018, para, 12). Alternative media typically distributes their content via the Internet and is not linked to television like mainstream media. Where mainstream media will support the public status quo, alternative media sources will actively seek to question these topics. Tsfati et al. (2020) argued that "traditional news media are in fact a part of the problem and play a somewhat paradoxical role with respect to fake news and its dissemination" (p. 158). However, many so-called alternative news websites (Tsfati et al., 2020) also play a huge part in spreading fake news. Whatever views the populous has regarding these two types of media outlets, they both have one thing in common, to obtain viewers and retain them as clients.

Zimdars (2016), with the use of a spreadsheet, analyzed a myriad of news sources and illustrated repetitive terms used in the mainstream and non-mainstream media to identify types such as (a) fake news, (b) satire, (c) conspiracy, (d) hate news, (e) clickbait, (f) political, (g) bias, and (h) unreliable and reliable. Zimdars mentioned that her participants wanted to know which media sources should be trusted, whether online, news or print. The newspapers that were mentioned from mainstream media include The New York Times, The Washington Post, The Boston Globe, The Wall Street Journal, and Forbes. Additionally, The Atlantic and National Public Radio, along with other local and/or alternative sources with different political perspectives (Truth-Out), were mentioned. Zimdars explained a problem:

Even typically reliable sources, whether mainstream or alternative, corporate or nonprofit, rely on particular media frames to report stories and select stories based on different notions of newsworthiness. The best thing to do in our contemporary media environment is to read/watch/listen widely and often and to be critical of the sources we share and engage with on social media (2016, para. 12).

The Importance of Digital Citizenship in Mitigating Deepfake and Fake News

Being good digital citizens is important now more than ever. Digital citizenship is a social responsibility by anyone who uses digital devices, the Internet, and computers to connect with society for social, entertainment, or political reasons. Anyone who uses the Internet regularly and effectively should practice digital citizenship. Gleason and Gillern (2018) stated, "as students increasingly spend large amounts of time online, it is critical that they are developing skills enabling them to find, evaluate, and share information responsibly" (p. 1). For educators, it is important to not only teach their students on digital citizenship but also model good behaviors. There is an etiquette to being a responsible digital citizen, and this must be a conscious act. And, now more than ever, the public needs role models to practice this good behavior. The digital media needs to be held accountable as it could be agreed this disinformation is a social, ethical, cultural, and human issue.

Students, as well as adults, need to understand media literacy to promote the mindful practice and why sensational stories are spread. Teachers and other positive influencers must empower students to question misinformation and disinformation and question the validity of the sources, synthesize the information from various scholarly publications, as well as factual websites versus websites that basically provide entertainment. Social media is the main platform that spreads misinformation and disinformation. Since broadcasting has been around a long time, people still must question *why* false stories are propagated. Buckingham (2019) stated, "fake news often has a political dimension: it is intended as a form of misinformation or propaganda that is designed to exert political influence" (p. 214). There is something to be gained by promoting the false story.

Part of being a good digital citizen is to have a solid understanding between fake news and satire. There should be a distinction between the two, such that "fake news is intended to mislead while satire is not" (Grazulis & Rogers, 2021, p. 27). When reading information from mainstream media, a person needs to identify the source first before he/she decides to endorse or negate the story. More importantly, the reader needs to think before forwarding the story. Think of the consequences that could happen if the story is untrue and goes viral. A person may believe their one act of forwarding a story will not humiliate or take down a person. But, if 1 million people have the same thought, the damage is done. Even if the story is later denounced, people all over the world have viewed the news and have already formed their opinions. And for the mainstream media who purposely highlight these fake stories and know all they must do is retract the video or statement, know good and well they have already won.

Digital Literacy

Digital literacy is defined by the American Library Association Digital Literacy Task Force (2011) as "the ability to use information and communication technologies to find, evaluate, create, and communicate information, requiring both cognitive and technical skills" (para. 1). The cognitive skill term used in this definition cannot be overlooked. When viewing and reading information on social media, a person must use logical, rational, and reasoning skills. Being able to appreciate the accuracy of the information found on social media is a crucial skill that must be learned (Glăveanu, 2017). People must remove their emotions and maintain a solid skepticism. Mainstream media is no longer here to promote unbiased information. It is here to promote a "partisan point of view that may include some real facts that serve to draw readers in and mislead them to form false conclusions" (Watson, 2018, p. 1).

Today, fake news has overwhelmed the media. Fake news is labeled as "deliberately spreading false information via print, broadcast, or online social media" (Watson, 2018, p. 1). Typically, there is a reason why the information is pushed in this format; a sole purpose with the intent to mislead the reader. The information is intentionally false so that a reader will quickly disseminate the information, usually without reflecting on the content. The spreading of this information is detrimental to society. Why would the media want to influence public opinion this way? Most likely to gain something either financially, politically, or socially. Psychology plays a huge role in the promotion of fake news. Psychology is the study of mind and behavior, and fake news media thrive on people's emotions and actions. The media feeds into people's personal beliefs and emotions and not providing objective facts. What is most disturbing is these objective facts are dismissed and disregarded by the media. This post-truth era where objective facts have vanished, and now, the influence of public opinion is the goal. Glăveanu (2017) stated that "psychology's key role in this post-truth era should be to help people distinguish between beliefs and facts and understand the strengths and limitations associated with each" (p. 376). People have forgotten the practice of critical thinking, which is the process of actively and skillfully comprehending information to form a belief or action.

Going back to the psychological aspect of fake news, one should question why it is so contagious, almost addicting. People flock to Facebook, Twitter, Instagram, and other digital platforms to get their next "fix" on what is trending; the mainstream media feeds into this. They know people will continue to read and listen to their news as long as they are publishing what they want people to know. Knowledge is power, and that is what mainstream media is seeking in return. They control the information and share only what their corporate sponsors approve. Buckingham (2019) stated, "the rise of social media has made it much easier for lies and misinformation to be circulated from person to person, bypassing the gatekeepers and regulators who controlled old media" (p. 216). Again, this is a problem as those *gatekeepers* who are charged with monitoring information have their own agenda. Gatekeepers were originated by Kurt Lewin, a social psychologist, and later researched by David Manning White for journalistic studies. Gatekeeping in the newspaper media is when an editor determines which news is published and which news will be held from the public by gathering and filtering information (Rusdi & Rusdi, 2020; Welbers et al., 2018). If they do not like the information, they simply click *delete* on their keypad, whether it is fake or true. Objective journalism and investigating to get the story correct have vanished, along with people's cognitive and reasoning skills. With regards to politics and fake news, Buckingham (2019) stated, "the danger of fake news is self-evident; the democratic political process depends upon the circulation of reliable information, and if information can no longer be trusted, citizens have little basis on which to make political decisions" (p. 214).

The Impact of Deepfakes and Fake News on Mass Media Reporting

Westerlund (2019) stated deepfake as "a combination of *deep learning* and *fake*, which are hyper-realistic videos digitally manipulated to depict people saying and doing things that never actually happened" (p. 40). Basically, using technology, such as facial mapping or voice-over, and swapping out the correct image/voice with another. Gone are the days *seeing is believing*. And not only faces and voices are being replaced, but any image that can be altered. Closed caption cameras are often used by law enforcement agencies to solve crimes. It is now easy, with a click of a mouse, to insert or delete an object that may provide evidence in a case. This digital altercation can make it difficult for law enforcement agencies to apprehend the perpetrator. Westerlund further stated that "deepfakes target social media platforms, where conspiracies, rumors, and misinformation spread easily, as users tend to go with the crowd" (p. 40). In addition, most Internet users receive their news from YouTube and Facebook. With the reach and speed of social media, believable deepfakes can quickly connect with millions of people and have a detrimental impact on society.

Buckingham (2019) stated that "fake news is not an isolated phenomenon, but that it needs to be understood in a much broader social, economic and cultural context" (p. 214). People are regularly on their digital devices watching these manipulated videos and not only believing the content but forwarding it via social media, text messages, or email. The problem now is there are so many fake news stories that it is difficult to identify them. In conjunction with the increase of cable television, satellite connections, and a variety of social media platforms, this adds to the difficulty for the viewership to differentiate between true and false stories (Ross et al., 2020). Ultimately, people must take ownership of the information they read and view. They must look at the news and determine if the story is credible and did the story comes from a trustworthy source. Just because a person does not agree with the published news does not mean it is false or vice-versa; just because a person agrees with the story does not mean it is true. People must take ownership of the materials they read, research the story, and then decide with an unbiased mind if the story is correct. And, most importantly, do not share or forward the information if the story cannot be verified. Citizens, as well as the media, have a responsibility to stop the spread of fake news.

The Neuroscience behind Deepfake and Fake News Addiction

Neuroscience research suggests the human brain is influenced by a variety of chemicals and a flow of perceptive triggers that can be intentionally manipulated to produce the desired outcome. In addition, certain events can lead to excitable regions within the human brain, which can be explained as triggering a euphoric and or energized feeling that overshadows depression and other anxiety issues found within a person's brain. It is theorized that those psychological triggers and heightened good feelings can lead to addictive outcomes, and when people are struggling with addictive challenges, they experience high levels of anxiety. Mohamed et al. (2020) stated that anxiety and depression are common problems associated with drug addiction. Nevertheless, not only are individuals addicted to drugs, alcohol, gambling, and smoking, to name a few, but also with social media and the mainstream media. Costello (2017) and Henzel and Håkansson (2021) agreed that even social media has a connection with depression, addictive behaviors, and mental distress. Regarding the study of Henzel and Håkansson, "addictive social media behavior, in the general population, may be related to symptoms of psychological distress, and to a history of treatment needs for problematic alcohol or drug use" (para. 10). As a result, individuals need to satisfy their needs and addiction, so they consume and share misinformation and disinformation as it becomes fascinating and stimulating, even if it is fallacious (Fox, 2020).

The evidence is clear that the drug trade intentionally markets their product using many different predatory strategies (Puyana et al., 2017). Bichler et al. (2017) stated that organized drug trafficking organizations actually operate comparable to a reasonable organization, whether globally or even a local market like the mainstream media. These illegal overall business goals are to facilitate and addict people to these substances and then expand the addictive population globally. The addictive lure of authority, power, notoriety, easy tax-free money, and risks associated with the growth, manufacture, production, and distribution of these substances offers employment to many in varied operational modalities (R. Matteson, personal communication, May 30, 2021). Matteson, who is retired Supervisory Special Agent, having worked for the United States Department of Justice, Drug Enforcement Administration within the United States as well as in Peshawar Pakistan and Mazatlán Sinaloa, Mexico, to include The Office of Training in the Leadership Division at the FBI-DEA Academy at Quantico Virginia, is an expert in the area of law enforcement working and supervising complex criminal drug smuggling violations of federal and state laws. This drug trade is associated with the same addiction that an individual has with the mainstream media. Like drug dealers, Cartels, and their moles, the media (e.g., pundits, media owners) wants people to have a dependency on the news and lures individuals by giving them the ability to overdose on toxic substances such as repetitive false stories based on the media's agenda. This is controlled by the *Media Cartel* of pundits, media moguls, and their so-called informants (i.e., undisclosed sources).

The cycle and elusive nature of the drug business and related supportive ancillary support services piques the interest of many and draws plenty of people interested in challenging life jobs where gaining a competitive edge triggers the release of brain and euphoria feel-good chemicals that compliments the addiction. Historically, the powerful media and clergy were well documented in their ability to influence large populations of people. A covert project undertaken by the Central Intelligence Agency and other organizations under the code name Operation/Project Mockingbird was undertaken to disseminate certain types of propaganda and disinformation globally via the mainstream media, to influence and direct purpose-driven narratives by use of various outlets. Based on compulsive behavior regarding media manipulation and fake excerpts, people become addicted to watching the news and need that so-called fix to learn more information. The authors developed a short pilot study asking anonymous individuals why people are addicted to media. Some common themes include the following thoughts:

1. It keeps them occupied; nothing else in life to do,
2. The news feed is so controlling,
3. Need to be able to think, but need to stay away from the Kool-Aid,
4. Learn more perspectives as there is not just one pertinent authority,
5. To find out what is the new breaking news,
6. Reinforce my beliefs and validate my opinion,
7. To be informed and synthesize what is real, and
8. It is automatic to just turn it on; it becomes routine.

Operation Mockingbird

People around the world seem to be intrigued to learn about complex conspiracies knowing there are plenty of bad actors lurking in government and within the private sector. Most scholars would agree regardless of the behavior; there is always a reason for the behavior. Operation Mockingbird is reported to have been, in part, a means to influence, via covert propaganda groups and/or nations leadership by using journalists and members of the clergy (Light, 2019). Propaganda was originated by the Catholic Church regarding the propagation of the faith in order to change human behavior to benefit the propagandist perspective. Propaganda which has caused journalism to lose objectivity has been driven by pundits who manipulate the truth to meet their formidable bias and personal agenda (Ross et al., 2020). It seems in part the operation intended to justify the means, regardless of those who were tasked to complete assignments by whatever means necessary. We should not be surprised to learn other nations engage in similar psychological programs to their means. Operation Mockingbird was developed by the Central Intelligence Agency (CIA) as a covert operation to retain a system of journalists within the American and foreign press corps.

Operation Mockingbird allegedly began in the early days of the Cold War where the CIA began a "secret project with the intent of buying influence behind the scenes at major media outlets and putting reporters on the CIA payroll" (Louise, n.d., para. 3). Other allegations include recruited American news organizations and journalists to become spies and disseminators of propaganda, infiltrated national businesses, media, and universities, and influenced the media to report stories that favor Washington's agenda, and controlled information through media, which included blackouts, misdirection, smears and backing popular opinion, to name a few (Guzman, 2016; Louise, n.d.). Now, it could be said these major organizations and journalists were unwittingly part of this rumor. But being a well-established organization and journalist is to check facts, confirm sources, and communicate the truth. Journalists are meant to serve the public, but when the owners of major networks push their agenda onto their journalists, this reduces the diversity of media expressions. Whether it is accidentally, unknowingly, or unintentionally these views were spread, and at the end of the day, people should have some sense of assurance they are receiving correct information.

Public Concern Regarding the Impact of Deepfakes and Fake News

By now, it is known that fake news is a public concern and should be addressed by the education system as well as any organization. Whether in education or in the public arena, the populace should not live in a world of disinformation due to many issues, such as the safety of vaccinations for children (Tsfati et al., 2020). Tsfati et al. (2020) defined "disinformation as the intentional and purposive spread of misleading information, which is different from misinformation which relates to 'unintentional behaviors that inadvertently mislead'" (p. 157). If students do not know what is true or false, they may decide to go someplace or make a statement in the wrong place that could be detrimental to their safety, learning, and critical thinking. Information is power as a society, including students, need to be able to identify these fake stories in order to be able to make an educated decision on their future actions. Grazulis and Rogers (2021) provided three important traits when examining fake news: "(a) look for identifiable fabrications in the story, (b) fake news does have an ultimate outcome, and that is to mislead audiences, and (c) fake news is intended to be catchy and to go viral" (p. 27). These tips should be part of the digital curriculum to inform and make students aware that *everything seen cannot be believed.* The above three behaviors performed by people may help save them from an unsafe situation. If the mainstream media is spreading lies those certain locales within a city are safe, and people decide to travel to those locales, only to find out it is gravely dangerous, then the fault lies with mainstream media.

Adults are not the only group susceptible to false information; students are also recipients of disinformation or misinformation, which can impact their ability to make sound judgments. Godowski (2015) discussed a portion of a story that represents positive freedom where students who are given the correct means and information can make their own judgments and see things another way and one day develop into teachers themselves. The generation of students today receive information from an array of sources, mostly social media, and might not be trained with the intellectual means necessary to determine the validity of information from specific sources as well as how the information is presented based on learning styles (Apuke & Iyendo, 2018; Newton & Miah, 2017). Students need to learn how to differentiate between what information is true and what information is disseminated to mislead them. Curricula in school should include media literacy as this will help students have an easier time determining fact from fiction (Redmond, 2016). In addition, education should be designed to give students the opportunity to be liberated from many systems of control (Godowski, 2015).

Plato, who was a philosopher of higher education of the Liberal philosophy, places the learner in an environment that is cultured, seeks knowledge rather than just information. Teachers use lectures, critical reading, and discussion to encourage students to obtain an intellectual education. Plato wrote about the *Allegory of the Cave*, which depicts people living in a cave only granted unreal objects, shadows, or images, which could portray today's philosophy of misinformation. So, imagine if students today are restricted to only limited knowledge, then those with the misinformation and/or disinformation could control the students' perceptions with flawed thinking and knowledge. The people who were portrayed in the Allegory of the Cave were known as puppeteers, which could be shown as the media of today. Research has shown that the people who are in control of others and/or an institution take ownership of the disseminated knowledge to include values, norms, perceptions, beliefs, sentiments, and prejudices (Godowski, 2015, Petsko, 2010). Petsko (2010) expanded that although the terms *fair* and *balanced* are used to describe the procedural ideology for the mainstream media, it is an incorrect statement. Petsko cited that it is impossible for individuals "to derive all their information from a source that never challenges their view of the world, and the same is true of the plethora of biased Internet 'information' sites" (para. 7). If this is the process of how information is delivered, then how can students foster critical thinking, deep processing information, and new ideas and help curve current processes to compete within the many environments (Schindler et al., 2017). Students should not feel marginal and be shut down. The stories they seek or are provided need to be truthful and designed to challenge their critical thinking skills so that they are not deceived by the media.

Recommendations for Mitigating Deepfakes and Fake News

The authors consider many processes to understand and hopefully learn to trust the mainstream media in the future. However, at this time, the mainstream media needs to look within their organizations and rid of the toxic culture. The authors encourage the viewers to read, watch, and listen to a broad audience and be critical of the media sources. The authors feel that people with experience and knowledge, no matter the origin of their organization, should always be truthful with their perspective based on research. There are a lot of individuals who have been given a title of a news contributor, not a journalist, to give their own perspective. For example, it is well known that sports players retire to become analysts/pundits for sports media outlets, while retired politicians and press secretaries for many presidents become pundits for mainstream media. In addition, many pundits/contributors have a bias for certain political parties and political actors; however, even with their knowledge and experience, they must report true research and facts. This also applies to pundits, so-called Hollywood elites, and other political actors who never worked in other occupations such as education, science, law enforcement, to name a few, but feel they are the experts. Even school union people feel they are scientists and pass on their own agendas. It makes one wonder how these pundits were placed in these positions, which in turn, gives individuals more reason to believe that there is an agenda behind the media. How can these individuals give their "expert views" when they are not, in fact, an expert? Some of these falsehoods could be detrimental to society, education, the safety of the community, and people's overall well-being.

Children are generally taught to be truthful and do the right thing. It should be expected at some point in life that a person who repeatedly learns the facts or events of life are not fair, they tend to develop a sense of anxiety based mistrust and can be led to believe life is unfair and not a level playing field because of the acts of others. As the person continues in life, they will likely conclude there are many examples of conflicting transitory information that is disseminated from people who are perceived to be experts in certain areas, only to find out they are many times self-serving and not truthful. Once the actual truth of the matter is uncovered, the question of whether the problem is far more embedded becomes a discussion of reality which requires people to employ more effort in seeking the truth. Individuals only apply the Socratic Method of Examination to a certain point because most people are not willing to expose their real self or truth to others. Generally, it can be said that a fraudster dislikes the real facts or genuine article that knows and exposes the truth. The more we shut down discussion, the fewer people can understand and navigate our most complex concerns, and the larger that void in understanding grows, the more people will have to rely on approved media to fill it. Given the biased nature of modern media, this is a very dangerous situation to be in. (Weaver, 2020, para. 24)

In conclusion, a simple keyword search will result in many scientific research data that supports the theory that a human brain can become addicted to the media, which leads the brain to release dopamine and other neurotransmitter brain chemicals not dissimilar to other addictive processes. The assumptions attributed to addictive pathologies will likely lead to further scientific research in hopes of educating, treating, and applying prevention strategies to behaviors that are prone to addiction. Most experts would conclude, human behavior has been a serious elusive topic to understand since the beginning of human existence. The varied theories and research on the mystique of human behavior still leave many medical practitioners struggling with unanswered questions. The study of human behavior will likely lead to improving, preventing, and treating anxiety addiction in human behavior by retraining the brain. The populace should be skeptical of all media and be aware that if they view a liberal channel, they will obtain liberal narratives, just as if individuals viewed a conservative channel, the result would be conservative views. The populace needs to retrain their brain by viewing other media-type outlets to reinforce their own beliefs and validate their own opinions.

REFERENCES

ALA Digital Literacy Taskforce. (2011). What is digital literacy? *ALA Office of Information Technology Policy*. http://www.dla101.org/wp-content/uploads/2015/07/what-is-digilit-2.pdf

Albert, K. H. (1984). *The rescue of Evangelina Cisneros: While others talk the journal acts* (Masters Thesis). University of Montana. https://scholarworks.umt.edu/cgi/viewcontent.cgi?article=10234&context=etd

Andersen, R. (2001). *Powerful writing skills*. Barnes & Nobel Books.

Anderson, J., & Rainie, L. (2017). *The future of truth and misinformation online*. Pew Research Center. Retrieved from https://www.elon.edu/u/imagining/wp-content/uploads/sites/964/2019/07/Future_of_Info_Environment_Elon_University_Pew_10-18-17.pdf

Apuke, O. D., & Iyendo, T. O. (2018). University students' usage of the internet resources for research and learning: Forms of access and perceptions of utility. *Heliyon*, *4*(12), e01052. doi:10.1016/j.heliyon.2018.e01052 PMID:30582057

Arar, K., Kussai, H.-Y., Ross, D. B., & Kondakci, Y. (2019). *Higher education challenges for migrant and refugee students in a global world*. Peter Lang.

Bennett, T. (1982). *Culture, society and the media* (1st ed.). Methuen.

Berger, P. L., & Luckmann, T. (1966). *The social construction of reality: A treatise in the sociology of knowledge*. Anchor Books.

Bergés Saura, L. (2010). Economic, political and communicative power in the neoliberal societies. *Revista Latina de Comunicación Social*, *65*, 244–254. doi:10.4185/RLCS-65-2010-897-244-254-EN

Bichler, G., Malm, A., & Cooper, T. (2017). Drug supply networks: A systematic review of the organizational structure of illicit drug trade. *Crime Science*, *6*(2), 2. Advance online publication. doi:10.118640163-017-0063-3

Boden, M. T., Berenbaum, H., & Gross, J. J. (2016). Why do people believe what they do? A functionalist perspective. *Review of General Psychology*, *20*(4), 399–411. doi:10.1037/gpr0000085 PMID:31680762

Borchers, C. (2018). How Hillary Clinton might have inspired Trump's 'fake news' attacks. *The Washington Post*. https://www.washingtonpost.com/news/the-fix/wp/2018/01/03/how-hillary-clinton-might-have-inspired-trumps-fake-news-attacks/

Bowen, K. N., Roberts, J. J., Kocian, E. J., & Bartula, A. (2014). An empirical test of social information processing theory and emotions in violent situations. *Western Criminology Review*, *15*(1), 18–33. http://wcr.sonoma.edu/v15n1/Bowen.pdf

Boxell, L., Gentzkow, M., & Shapiro, J. M. (2018). A note on Internet use and the 2016 U.S. presidential election outcome. *PLoS One*, *13*(7), e0199571. doi:10.1371/journal.pone.0199571 PMID:30020953

Buckingham, D. (2019). Teaching media in a 'post-truth' age: Fake news, media bias and the challenge for media/digital literacy education. *Culture and Education*, *31*(2), 213–231. doi:10.1080/11356405.2019.1603814

Budak, C., Goel, S., & Rao, J. M. (2016). Fair and balanced? Quantifying media bias through crowdsourced content analysis. *Public Opinion Quarterly*, *80*(S1), 250–271. https://scholar.stanford.edu/papers/mediabias.pdf. doi:10.1093/poq/nfw007

Burkhardt, J. M. (2017). History of fake news. *ALA TechSource, 53*(8). https://journals.ala.org/index.php/ltr/article/view/6497/8636

Carey, C. (2016). Breaking the news: Telegraphy and yellow journalism in the Spanish-American War. *A Journal of History & Criticism, 26*(2), 130-148. https://www.muse.jhu.edu/article/628764

Celliers, M., & Hattingh, M. (2020). Responsible design, implementation and use of information and communication technology. Nature Public Health Emergency Collection, 12067, 223–234. doi:10.1007/978-3-030-45002-1_19

Chandler, D. (2006). Children's understanding of what is 'real' on television: A review of the literature. *Journal of Educational Media*, *23*(1), 65–80. doi:10.1080/1358165970230105

Chandler, D. (n.d.). *Marxist Media Theory*. Retrieved from https://www.cym.ie/documents/chandler.pdf

Clements, C. S. (2013). Perception and persuasion in legal argumentation: Using informal fallacies and cognitive biases to win the war of words. *BYU Law Review, 2013*(2), 319-362. https://digitalcommons.law.byu.edu/cgi/viewcontent.cgi?article=2709&context=lawreview

Costello, C. R., & Ramo, D. E. (2017). Social media and substance use: What should we be recommending to teens and their parents? *The Journal of Adolescent Health, 60*(6), 629–630. doi:10.1016/j.jadohealth.2017.03.017 PMID:28532648

Day, N. J. S., Townsend, M. L., & Grenyer, B. F. S. (2020). Living with pathological narcissism: A qualitative study. *Borderline Personality Disorder and Emotion Dysregulation, 7*(19), 19. Advance online publication. doi:10.118640479-020-00132-8 PMID:32817795

De Schrijver, A. (2012). Sample survey on sensitive topics: Investigating respondents' understanding and trust in alternative versions of the randomized response technique. *Journal of Research Practice, 8*(1). http://jrp.icaap.org/index.php/jrp/article/view/277/250

Fox, J. (2020). 'Fake news' – The perfect storm: Historical perspectives. *Historical Research, 93*(259), 172–187. doi:10.1093/hisres/htz011

Gleason, B., & von Gillern, S. (2018). Digital citizenship with social media: Participatory practices of teaching and learning in secondary education. *Journal of Educational Technology & Society, 21*(1), 200–212.

Godowski, J. P. (2015). Out of the shadows and into the light: Liberation through education. *The Vermont Connection, 36*(8), 50-57. https://scholarworks.uvm.edu/cgi/viewcontent.cgi?article=1007&context=tvc

Grady, C. (2015). Institutional review boards: Purpose and challenges. *Chest, 148*(5), 1148–1155. doi:10.1378/chest.15-0706 PMID:26042632

Graves, L., & Wells, C. (2019). From information availability to factual accountability. In J. Katz & K. K. Mays (Eds.), *Journalism and truth in an age of social media* (pp. 39–57). Oxford University Press. doi:10.1093/oso/9780190900250.003.0004

Grazulis, A., & Rogers, R. (2021). Ridiculous and untrue – Fake news!: The impact of labeling fake news. In *Research anthology on fake news, political warfare, and combatting the spread of misinformation* (pp. 25–38). IGI Global. doi:10.4018/978-1-7998-7291-7.ch002

Greenberg, D. (2008). The idea of "the liberal media" and its roots in the civil rights movement. A Journal of History. *Política y Cultura*, *1*(2), 167–186. doi:10.1080/17541320802457111

Greenberg, D. (2018). A half century of 'liberal media bias'. *The Wall Street Journal*. Retrieved https://www.wsj.com/articles/a-half-century-of-liberal-media-bias-1535034293

Groeling, T. (2013). Media bias by the numbers: Challenges and opportunities in the empirical study of partisan news. *Annual Review of Political Science*, *16*(1), 129–151. doi:10.1146/annurev-polisci-040811-115123

Hassell, H. J. G., Holbein, J. B., & Miles, M. R. (2020). There is no liberal media bias in which news stories political journalists choose to cover. *Science Advances*, *6*(14), eaay9344. Advance online publication. doi:10.1126ciadv.aay9344 PMID:32270038

Henzel, V., & Håkansson, A. (2021). Hooked on virtual social life: Problematic social media use and associations with mental distress and addictive disorders. *PLoS One*, *16*(4), e0248406. doi:10.1371/journal.pone.0248406 PMID:33831023

Hinton, P. (2017). Implicit stereotypes and the predictive brain: Cognition and culture in "biased" person perception. *Palgrave Communications*, *3*(17086), 17086. doi:10.1057/palcomms.2017.86

Izaguirre, J. G. III. (2015). Prophets, gurus, and pundits: Rhetorical styles and public engagement. *The Quarterly Journal of Speech*, *101*(4), 673–677. doi:10.1080/00335630.2015.1128052

Jackson, J. E. (2014). Sensationalism in the newsroom: Its yellow beginnings, the nineteenth century legal transformation, and the current seizure of the American press. *Notre Dame Journal of Law, Ethics & Public Policy*, *19*(2), 789–816. https://scholarship.law.nd.edu/cgi/viewcontent.cgi?article=1232&context=ndjlepp

Kennedy, C., Blumenthal, M., Clement, S., Clinton, J. D., Durand, C., Franklin, C., McGeeney, K., Miringoff, L., Olson, K., Rivers, D., Saad, L., Witt, G. E., & Wlezien, C. (2018). An Evaluation of the 2016 Election Polls in the United States. *Public Opinion Quarterly*, *82*(1), 1–33. doi:10.1093/poq/nfx047

LaMarco, N. (2018). Mainstream vs. alternative media. *Small Business Advertising & Marketing/Media. Chron.* https://smallbusiness.chron.com/mainstream-vs-alternative-media-21113.html

Letukas, L. (2012). *The ascent of punditry: Media and the news construction of cable news* (Doctoral dissertation). Available from ProQuest Dissertations and Theses database. (UMI No. 3526446)

Light, A. (2019). *Operation Mockingbird: A third of the CIA budget went to media propaganda operations.* Humans are Free. https://humansarefree.com/2019/10/operation-mockingbird-a-third-of-the-cia-budget-went-to-media-propaganda-operations.html

Litschka, M. (2019). The political economy of media capabilities: The capability approach in media policy. *Journal of Information Policy*, *9*, 63–94. doi:10.5325/jinfopoli.9.2019.0063

Louise, M. (n.d.). *Operation mockingbird: CIA media manipulation*. Prison-Planet.com. https://www.scribd.com/document/6381980/Operation-Mockingbird-CIA-Media-Manipulation-by-Mary-Louise

Lupyan, G. (2017). How reliable is perception? *Philosophical Topics*, *45*(1), 81–106. doi:10.5840/philtopics20174515

MacKenzie, A., & Bhatt, I. (2019). Opposing the power of lies, bullshit and fake news: The value of truth. *Postdigital Science and Education*, *2020*(2), 217–232. doi:10.100742438-019-00087-2

Maxmen, A. (2009). Taking risks to transform science. *Cell*, *139*(1), 13–15. doi:10.1016/j.cell.2009.09.019 PMID:19804745

McQuail, D. (2010). *McQuail's Mass Communication Theory* (6th ed.). Sage.

Mohamed, I. I., Khalifa Ahmad, H. E., Hassaan, S. H., & Hassan, S. M. (2020). Assessment of anxiety and depression among substance use disorder patients: A case-control study. *Middle East Current Psychiatry*, *27*(22), 22. Advance online publication. doi:10.118643045-020-00029-w

Molina, M. D., Shyam Sundar, S., Le, T., & Lee, D. (2019). "Fake news" is not simply false information: A concept explication and taxonomy of online content. *The American Behavioral Scientist*, *65*(2), 180–212. doi:10.1177/0002764219878224

Mulligan, D. L. (2021). Dangerous decisions: The precarity of real-world research-A provocation. In D. L. Mulligan & P. A. Danaher (Eds.), *Researchers at risk: Precarity, jeopardy and uncertainty in academia* (pp. 311–325). Palgrave Macmillan. doi:10.1007/978-3-030-53857-6_20

Newton, P. M., & Miah, M. (2017). Evidence-based higher education – Is the learning styles 'myth' important? *Frontiers in Psychology, 8*, 444. doi:10.3389/fpsyg.2017.00444 PMID:28396647

Parker, G. E. (2016). A framework for navigating institutional review board (IRB) oversight in the complicated zone of research. *Cureus, 8*(10), e844. doi:10.7759/cureus.844 PMID:27909632

Petsko, G. A. (2010). Shadows on the wall. *Genome Biology, 11*(9), 136. doi:10.1186/gb-2010-11-9-136 PMID:20863416

Puyana, J. C., Puyana, J. C. J., Rubiano, A. M., Montenegro, J. H., Estebanez, G. O., Sanchez, A. I., & Vega-Rivera, F. (2017). Drugs, violence, and trauma in Mexico and the USA. *Medical Principles and Practice, 26*(4), 309–315. doi:10.1159/000471853 PMID:28329741

Redmond, T. (2016). Media literacy as mindful practice for democratic education. *Democracy & Education, 24*(2), 1-5. https://democracyeducationjournal.org/cgi/viewcontent.cgi?article=1261&context=home

Ross, D. B., Louis, R., & Sasso, M. T. (2019). The increase of how mass media coverage manipulates our minds. In A. Starcevic (Ed.), *Chronic stress and its effect on brain structure and connectivity* (pp. 188–222). IGI Global. doi:10.4018/978-1-5225-7513-9.ch010

Ross, D. B., Peyton, G. L., Nethi, V., & Sasso, M. T. (2021). The need to be a leader of research in the United States: Take the risk and move beyond your opponents. In D. L. Mulligan & P. A. Danaher (Eds.), *Researchers at risk: Precarity, jeopardy and uncertainty in academia* (pp. 147–161). Palgrave Macmillan. doi:10.1007/978-3-030-53857-6_10

Ross, D. B., Peyton, G. L., Sasso, M. T., Matteson, R. W., & Matteson, C. E. (2020). The biased media and their utilization of propaganda: The true obstructionists of world events and our minds. In S. Kavoğlu & M. Salar (Eds.), *Political propaganda, advertising, and public relations: Emerging research and opportunities* (pp. 89–113). IGI Global. doi:10.4018/978-1-7998-1734-5.ch004

Ross, D. B., & Sasso, M. T. (2017). *The art of synthesizing: A masterpiece in the making.* Fischler College of Education: Faculty Articles. https://works.bepress.com/david-ross/90/

Rusdi, F., & Rusdi, Z. (2020). The role of online media gatekeeper in the era of digital media. *Advances in Social Science, Education and Humanities Research, 439*. https://www.atlantis-press.com/article/125940615.pdf

Sasso, M. T. (2017). *How narcissists cannot hold an organization together: A mixed method approach to a fictitious puzzle factory*. Academic Press.

Sauter, V. G. (2020). The 'liberal leaning' media has passed its tipping point. *The Wall Street Journal*. Retrieved from https://www.wsj.com/articles/the-liberal-leaning-media-has-passed-its-tipping-point-11590430876

Schindler, L. A., Burkholder, G. J., Morad, O. A., & Marsh, C. (2017). Computer-based technology and student engagement: A critical review of the literature. *International Journal of Educational Technology in Higher Education, 14*(25), 25. Advance online publication. doi:10.118641239-017-0063-0

Shaw, G. B. (1903). Man and superman: A comedy and a philosophy. In Maxims for Revolutionists. Brentano's.

Tsfati, Y., Boomgaarden, H. G., Strömbäck, J., Vliegenthart, R., Damstra, A., & Lindgren, E. (2020). Causes and consequences of mainstream media dissemination of fake news: Literature review and synthesis. *Annals of the International Communication Association, 44*(2), 157–173. doi:10.1080/23808985.2020.1759443

U.S. Department of Health & Human Services. (1979). *The Belmont report: Office of the Secretary*. Retrieved from https://www.hhs.gov/ohrp/regulations-and-policy/belmont-report/read-the-belmont-report/index.html

U.S. Department of Health & Human Services. (2021). *Office for Human Research Protections*. Retrieved from https://www.hhs.gov/ohrp/

van der Linden, S., Panagopoulos, C., & Roozenbeck, J. (2020). You are fake news: Political bias in perceptions of fake news. *Media Culture & Society, 42*(3), 60–470. doi:10.1177/0163443720906992

Watson, C. A. (2018). Digital literacy: Detecting fake news in a post-truth era. *Continuing Legal Education Presentations, 8*. https://digitalcommons.law.uga.edu/cle/2018/schedule/8

Weaver, T. (2020). The Socratic Method: How to think for yourself. *Orion Philosophy*. Retrieved from https://www.orionphilosophy.com/stoic-blog/the-socratic-method

Welbers, K., van Atteveldt, W., Kleinnijenhuis, J., & Ruigrok, N. (2018). A gatekeeper among gatekeepers. *Journalism Studies, 19*(3), 315–333. doi:10.1080/1461670X.2016.1190663

Wendling, M. (2018). *The (almost) complete history of 'fake news'*. BBC News Services. https://www.bbc.com/news/blogs-trending-42724320

Westerlund, M. (2019). The emergence of deepfake technology: A review. *Technology Innovation Management Review*, *9*(11), 39–52. doi:10.22215/timreview/1282

Zimdars, M. (2016). *False, misleading, clickbait-y, and satirical news sources*. Creative Commons. https://docs.google.com/document/d/10eA5-mCZLSS4MQY5QGb5ewC3VAL6pLkT53V_81ZyitM/mobilebasic

Zinn, J. O. (2016). The meaning of risk-taking – Key concepts and dimensions. *Journal of Risk Research*, *22*(1), 1–15. Advance online publication. doi:10.1080/13669877.2017.1351465

ADDITIONAL READING

Allcott, H., & Gentzkow, M. (2017). Social media and fake news in the 2016 election. *The Journal of Economic Perspectives*, *31*(2), 211–236. doi:10.1257/jep.31.2.211

Allen, J., Howland, B., Mobius, M., Rothchild, D., & Watts, D. J. (2020). Evaluating the fake news problem at the scale of the information ecosystem. *Science Advances*, *6*(14), eaay3539. Advance online publication. doi:10.1126ciadv.aay3539 PMID:32284969

Anderson, C. A., Lepper, M. R., & Ross, L. (1980). Perseverance of social theories: The role of explanation in the persistence of discredited information. *Journal of Personality and Social Psychology*, *39*(6), 1037–1049. doi:10.1037/h0077720

Ashworth, P. D. (2009). William James's "psychologist's fallacy" and contemporary human science research. *International Journal of Qualitative Studies on Health and Well-being*, *4*(4), 195–206. doi:10.3109/17482620903223036

Benkler, Y., Faris, R., & Roberts, H. (2018). *Network propaganda: Manipulation, disinformation, and radicalization in American politics*. Oxford University Press. doi:10.1093/oso/9780190923624.001.0001

Dechene, A., Stahl, C., Hansen, J., & Wänke, M. (2010). The truth about the truth: A meta-analytic review of the truth effect. *Personality and Social Psychology Review*, *14*(2), 238–257. doi:10.1177/1088868309352251 PMID:20023210

Farand, C. (2017). French social media awash with fake news stories from sources 'exposed to Russian influence ahead of presidential election. *The Independent*. https://www.independent.co.uk/news/world/europe/french-voters-deluge-fake-news-stories-facebook-twitter-russian-influence-days-before-election-a7696506.html

Guess, A., Nyhan, B., & Reifler, J. (2018). Selective exposure to misinformation: Evidence from the consumption of fake news during the 2016 U.S. presidential campaign. *European Research Council, 9*. http://www.ask-force.org/web/Fundamentalists/Guess-Selective-Exposure-to-Misinformation-Evidence-Presidential-Campaign-2018.pdf

Lecheler, S., & Kruikemeier, S. (2016). Re-evaluating journalistic routines in a digital age: A review of research on the use of online sources. *New Media & Society, 18*(1), 156–171. doi:10.1177/1461444815600412

Pennycook, G., & Rand, D. G. (2019). Fighting misinformation on social media using crowdsourced judgments of news source quality. *Proceedings of the National Academy of Sciences of the United States of America, 116*(7), 2521–2526. doi:10.1073/pnas.1806781116 PMID:30692252

Sutter, D. (2012). Mechanisms of liberal bias in the news media versus the academy. *The Independent Review, 16*(3), 399-415. Retrieved July 2, 2021, from http://www.jstor.org/stable/24563209

KEY TERMS AND DEFINITIONS

Addiction: Is an inability to stop using a substance or engaging in behavior such as being overly concerned about media.

Digital Citizenship: Is a social responsibility by anyone who uses digital devices, the Internet, and computers to connect with society for social, entertainment, or political reasons.

Digital Literacy: The ability to use information and communication technologies to find, evaluate, create, and communicate information, requiring both cognitive and technical skills.

Disinformation: Is the intentional and purposive spread of misleading information.

Factual Accountability: Ensures that the citizenry has facts available to them by promoting a fact-based dialogue to hold institutions of the media and politicians accountable for any information that may be disingenuous.

Misinformation: Relates to unintentional behaviors that inadvertently mislead.

Operation Mockingbird: Signifies the CIA's involvement in manipulating the news published in the United States and in a foreign country, which can be identified as the manipulation of fake news.

Propaganda: Implicates influencing an individual's thoughts as well as actions and could be considered as being biased communication.

Public Concern: Relates to any matter of political, social, or other concern to the community to include legitimate news interest.

Yellow Journalism: Is a concept identified as publishing information without the required evidence, making it factually incorrect.

Chapter 4
Fake News and Social Media Censorship:
Examining the Librarian Role

Adebowale Jeremy Adetayo
https://orcid.org/0000-0001-7869-5613
Adeleke University, Nigeria

ABSTRACT

The COVID-19 pandemic has brought about a surge of fake news on social media. This dilemma has caused a ripple effect in society with increasing censorship on social media, which threatens the freedom of expression. The populace cannot effectively progress until they understand the threat posed by fake news and censorship. To protect our fundamental rights of expression, society must learn from librarians. The chapter explores the role of librarians in mitigating fake news. The chapter also identifies possible societal consequences of fake news. The chapter concludes that librarians should inoculate the public to pre-empt them from accepting fake news.

INTRODUCTION

It was predicted that social media would give people, especially consumers, more power (Kaplan & Haenlein, 2010). As society progresses into the big data age, the essence of knowledge consumption, assimilation, and circulation has shifted dramatically. We are all bombarded with data at an alarming pace, which has affected how people view, distribute, and use it. Individuals have responded to the ever-expanding technological environment and its vast amounts of uncontrolled big data by filtering information into a more comprehensible and relatable form and

DOI: 10.4018/978-1-7998-6474-5.ch004

compatible with their worldview. The overconsumption of information powered by the internet has resulted in a "post-truth" culture in which citizens consume information that reaffirms their pre-existing values and philosophies rather than undertaking the challenging task of identifying the truth. Doubt and scepticism continue to increase as the online world becomes more complex and challenging to navigate, with people preferring familiar facts over accurate ones (Gallagher, 2016).

However, changes in information consumption patterns could positively impact social capital, political conversation, or public participation (Gil de Ziga et al., 2012). Nonetheless, recent observations have shown a troubling connection between social media and fake news (Allcott & Gentzkow, 2017; Vosoughi et al., 2018). Social media sites' advent and popularity have complicated the relationship between humans and knowledge by facilitating fake news through their resources and functions. Fake news authors have taken advantage of this cultural pattern to entice and spread fake news for propaganda purposes (Ohleiser, 2016). Fake news producers on different social media channels often spark discussions, alter views, and gain followers for their ideology. As seen in the Pentagon's Military Analysts Program (Jowett & O'Donnell, 2015), fake news peddling can also be motivated by monetary gain or the desire to influence public perception of the world's situation. Another motivation for producing and consuming fake news is online networking (Blanco-Herrero & Arcila - Calderón, 2019), the lack of a centralized monitoring system for news consumption on social media sites, and a decrease in confidence in media (Budak, 2019).

Without question, the latest COVID-19 pandemic has played a role in creating and consuming fake news as it appears to have deepened the debate around health-related false news, creating more questions about its consequences for public health. Referring to how fake news spread online has exacerbated the pandemic, WHO Director-General Tedros Adhanom Ghebreyesus said that the world was fighting not just a pandemic, but also an "infodemic," a worldwide epidemic of deliberate distribution of false or misleading information that could include various forms of reconfiguration, in which current and sometimes correct information is twisted (Mesquita et al., 2020; Wardle, 2017).

However, the dissemination of fake news can be catastrophic and dangerous in political and cultural spheres. Within a decade, social media – freshly dominated by big data – shifted from being a facilitator of democracy to a severe threat to it, most recently with Facebook. The world became aware of these tools' potential to disrupt democratic processes due to the Cambridge Analytica data scandal. Cambridge Analytica effectively influenced and manipulated public opinion in events such as the 2016 US presidential election and the 2018 Brexit referendum using data from several million Facebook users. As a result, there was a public uproar and debate over ethical practices for social media companies, data security, and the right to privacy.

Popular social media sites have recently stepped up their efforts to combat the spread of fake news. Following the 2016 US election, Facebook began using external fact-checkers to recognize, mark, and minimize false publications' exposure in news feeds (Mena, 2020). Similarly, in the wake of the coronavirus outbreak, Twitter reversed its standard "hands-off" policy on bogus content (Hern, 2020). Perhaps these major media players used the wrong methods, as Ireton and Posetti (2018) observed that digital media has lowered the barrier to entry into the information field and that sharing news on social media platforms like Facebook has replaced many of the traditional metrics of traditional journalism. As a result, library and information science specialists are required to help lift the barrier without fear of censorship.

Fake news has become a growing source of concern for librarians and information scientists. Some advocate for librarians to take the lead in fighting fake news (Buschman, 2019; Cooke, 2017; Wade & Hornick, 2018). Others argue that the current information crisis is an opportunity for librarians to promote their career and show their worth (Eva & Shea, 2018). Librarians have long been regarded as the conventional custodians and fact-checkers of the information world, providing the public with accurate, impartial, and verifiable information. They also traditionally valued fair access to knowledge and recognized the significance of people's right to think independently and objectively to produce an efficient and functional democratic society. Because of the increasing pace and amount of knowledge generated online, as well as society's abandonment of truth and reality, librarians' position is being questioned, as they can no longer compete with the amounts of fake news spread daily—hence, their role now encompasses both fact-checking and educator.

Thus, it is not astonishing that widespread fake news has become a noticeable and prevalent issue in the community of librarians. This chapter will review and explore the current literature to establish a foundational basis for future research and initiatives. The chapter provides an in-depth overview of the current state of fake news in the literature and how it significantly affects and alters society. It presents potential roles librarians could play to mitigate its effect.

Objectives

This work's major objective is to stipulate librarians' role in fake news and social media censorship.

Other specific objectives are to:

1. examine the concept of Social media and Fake news;
2. examine the societal consequences of fake news;
3. examine the effect of social media censorship to freedom of expression; and
4. identify the role of librarians in curbing fake news.

Theoretical Framework

Inoculation Theory

In 1964, William McGuire pioneered inoculation theory to induce attitudinal resistance to propaganda in a manner close to biological immunization. For illustration, injections containing a weakened dose of a virus can confer protection against potential infection by triggering antibody development. According to Inoculation theory, the same thing can be accomplished with "mental antibodies" and facts. In other words, by preemptively introducing individuals to a weaker version of a (counter)-argument and then refuting the argument, attitudinal resistance against potential persuasion attempts may be bestowed (Papageorgis & McGuire, 1961). The inoculation procedure involves an affective and cognitive component, which is commonly referred to as "threat" and "refutational pre-emption" (McGuire, 1964). Perceived risk acts mainly as a motivator. It refers to accepting that one's position on a topic is vulnerable to attack, whereas "refutational pre-emption" is concerned with providing people with clear reasons to help them avoid persuasion attempts (Compton, 2013).

The propagation of fake news is close to that of a viral infection (Kucharski, 2016). Inoculation theory proposes an intuitive solution to this issue by suggesting a "vaccine" against fake news (van der Linden, 2017). The theory is amenable to librarians. Librarians should use the inoculation theory to discourage people from believing fake news before it spreads.

Conceptualizing Fake News

Fake news is not a modern phenomenon. It has been used many times in politics and conflicts, but it now poses a problem for people as disinformation is created on a larger scale (Aznar, 2019). Burkhardt (2017) cites many instances of "fake news" dating back to 554 AD, when Procopius of Caesarea, a Byzantium historian, used false reports to undermine Emperor Justian. She describes previous examples of "fake news" as satirical and fictitious accounts created by individuals to undermine one another or for amusement. This may imply that the concept of "fake news" has changed its meaning and how it is now disseminated, rather than its purpose.

Wardle (2017) suggests concept typography for categorizing words under the broad umbrella of "fake news." She divides these meanings into misinformation and disinformation, which all fall on a scale based on the willingness to deceive. Misinformation is described at one end of the scale as the "inadvertent sharing of false information," while disinformation is defined at the other end as the deliberate production and dissemination of information known to be false (Wardle, 2017).

Tandoc et al. (2018) created a new typology that involves news satire, news parody, fabrication, deception, propaganda, and advertisement. Other scholars concentrate on two main categories: misinformation, which includes intentionally false facts or misleading elements, and satire (Allcott & Gentzkow 2017; Bakir & McStay 2018).

Rochlin (2017) takes a different approach to the phenomenon of fake news, highlighting how the rise of the post-truth age has replaced reality and evidence with personal opinion and emotion-based markets. She explains how the concept of fake news no longer includes slanderous or false news but rather news that appears to threaten a person's prior beliefs. According to Rochlin (2017), news is being sold based on opinion rather than evidence. Finley et al. (2017) describe fake news so widely that it encompasses anything that has not been subjected to a conventional review process. No matter how fake news is described, everyone agrees that it is a threat that must be addressed.

Societal Consequences of Fake News

As a result of widespread fake news, many social repercussions occur. Fake news poses a severe danger to society, even though the threat is hazy (Becker, 2016; Jacobson, 2017). As a result, damage can be caused as a consequence of spreading fake news online (El Rayess et al., 2018), and false statements can be "terrifying in their ability... to do real harm to real people" (El Rayess et al., 2018). (Anderson, 2018). Fake news can lead to incorrect public opinion orientation, leading to social damage (Pennycook et al., 2020). Citizens are often irritated as a result of false news. The more deceptions that occur and the more complex the verification of content becomes, the more likely people's trust in their institutions will continue to decrease.

The potential of fake news to undermine democratic processes is the most prevalent challenge raised by it (Saunders et al., 2018; Jeffries et al., 2017), based on the basic assumption that an informed electorate is needed for a functioning democracy (Auberry, 2018; Batchelor, 2017; Jacobson, 2017). As a result, there is a need to educate the electorate, which can be accomplished by library funding. Lenker (2016) examines several documents that connect librarianship to citizenship outcomes: The ability to find and interpret facts is crucial to an individual's ability to make informed decisions, and this is a common thread that runs across all of these documents. During the 2020 US presidential election, many conservative social media platforms pushed information to the public about widespread voter fraud, while liberal social media platforms pushed information opposing the notion of widespread voter fraud. Many people were frustrated by this war of ideas, and they stormed the capitol building to show their displeasure. On October 31, 2017, a truck ploughed into a crowd in Manhattan, killing eight people. The incident was motivated by information tools published on social media by the terror group

ISIS to carry out such attacks (Patrikarakos, 2017). Other terrorist and extremist groups and authoritarian governments have used social media for propaganda and recruitment (Watts, 2018).

If fake news is not adequately handled, it will have a detrimental impact on society's safe and harmonious growth and increase social unrest (Calvillo et al., 2020). False information dissemination has become a societal threat. Indeed, the World Economic Forum mentioned this in a study titled "Digital Wildfires in a Hyperconnected World" in 2013. (Howel, 2013). This is particularly relevant for health details since misinformed individuals' actions can significantly impact public health (Scheufele & Krause, 2019). According to research findings, confusion regarding COVID-19 has contributed to widespread misperceptions, triggering panic and posing significant health risks. The deliberate dissemination of online health-related misinformation on COVID-19, for example, was responsible for the methanol poisoning reported in Iran (an Islamic country with strict alcohol intake restrictions) in March 2020, when 2100 Iranians ingested alcohol after being exposed to social media messages suggesting they could avoid infection by doing so. Approximately 900 alcohol-poisoned patients were admitted to the Intensive Care Unit (ICU), 296 of whom died (Soltaninejad, 2020).

In the case of political economy, a study used game-theory political economy models to conclude that people could lose welfare when making economic decisions based on inaccurate information. Hiding information from residents tends to result in less access to welfare. Consequently, there is a chance of reducing healthcare when there is a need to detect false information to prevent political decisions from being taken (Bullock et al., 2019). Incredibly misleading political information could lead to election fraud (Pea, 2017) and lower citizen engagement levels in democratic processes (Manzanero & Ramrez, 2018). Like White Supremacy, fringe ideologies got their voices amplified through online movements such as the Alt-right (ADL, 2019), motivating terrorist attacks such as the one in Christchurch, NZ (Mann et al., 2019).

Finally, fake news leads to infringements, which cost television stations money. Fake news breaches the principle of news story accuracy, making it possible to cause infringement accidents and then bring unnecessary litigation against the program group and the TV station (Ahmed et al., 2020). News organizations that publish false news are often required to reimburse victims, and serious offenders can face criminal charges (Ahmed et al., 2020).

Social Media and Fake News

According to Kapoor et al. (2018), social media refers to various user-driven channels that facilitate disseminating persuasive content, conversation building, and communication to a larger audience. Users can freely communicate, share, and talk using a multimedia mix of individual words, images, video, and sound on such platforms. It has dynamic features that allow users to share text, pictures, audio, and videos in a two-way relationship. Similarly, Akakandelwa (2016) defines social media as a broad range of web-based and mobile services that enable users to engage in online exchanges, contribute user-generated content, and enter online communities. According to Ngai et al. (2015), social media can be divided into six categories: sharing sites, blogs/microblogging, social bookmarking sites, virtual/online communities, social networking sites, and virtual worlds. Unlike the traditional regular media where one listens, watches or read information without the immediate opportunity to respond and share one's thoughts on the information, social media provides information and allows one to interact with that information through features that will enable comments, votes or recommendations on where to access more similar information (Nations, 2018). Social media have doubtlessly begun to play a significant part in all sectors, from business to education, from public administration to politics (Kaplan, 2017, 2015), and libraries.

Social media are increasingly integrated into courses (Kaplan, 2018; Kaplan & Haenlein, 2016; Pucciarelli & Kaplan, 2016). Also, several health practitioners use social media to mitigate the effect of covid 19 pandemics. Finally, in politics, social media have been part of the game for more than a decade. Social media communications were crucial in Donald Trump's presidency, which led to his massive rallies and fans' commitment. At their advent, social media were considered an opportunity for citizen empowerment (Deighton et al., 2011). As exemplified by the #MeToo movement against sexual harassment and sexual assault, they are still begun solely by individuals and rapidly went viral with social media. Businesses use social media to interrelate with their customers, foster collaboration, increase transparency and information dissemination, and much more. For example, Boohoo's sales were up 45% in the quarter to the end of May 2020. A significant factor in this success was Boohoo's social media strategy, with influencer endorsements allowing the brand to target and involve a young audience on Instagram in particular (where it now has 6.6 m followers). In 2018, Boohoo reportedly spent £80m on influencer marketing, a strategy it has since continued.

Nevertheless, within just a few years, the early promise of the internet and then the social media revolution provide a more transparent and informed world devolved into an online environment where one cannot be sure of what is right and false. Many visit more fake news sites from social media than visits to real news sites (Nelson & Taneja 2018). Tandoc Jr et al. (2018) embolden this by stating that social media constitutes a perfect set-up for propagating untrue facts, and hundreds of websites were found to provide biased or false content (Zimdars 2016). For example, Twitter allows for the spread of fake news via bots and anonymous accounts, influencing trending topics and undermining or favouring a political view (Zubiaga *et al.*, 2018). In several elections, such as Austria, Belarus, Bulgaria, France, Germany, and Italy, Russia manipulated voter outcomes via fake news and misinformation posted on social media (Kamarck, 2018). Concerning the USA, social media was used to divide the nation by portraying bias information against Donald Trump, while conservative media portrayed him positively. This caused an outcry by the populace and hatred of the media.

Social media censorship: Threatening Freedom of Expression

Take the recent coronavirus outbreak, for instance. After a video of a Chinese celeb drinking bat soup went viral on Facebook, netizens rapidly drew unsubstantiated causal links between the soup and the outbreak and then made discriminatory slurs on Chinese people for their 'unhygienic dietary preference'. Later, the video proved to be a 2016 travel footage taken in Palau, a Western Pacific Ocean country (BBC, 2020). This example illustrates how powerful misinformation is in the age of social media because it can be instantly disseminated and misleads a limitless population. Given the potential damage that misinformation carries, is it justified to filter such speech pre-emptively? Intuitively, the answer is 'no' because censorship challenges free speech. The logic is that the government is frequently the agent who censors misinformation, and this authority can easily be abused and served as a pretext to curb opposing voices and thus curtail free speech (Guardian, 2019).

However, many popular social media platforms are beginning to censor information they deem inappropriate. This is due to the political divide that different groups promote on social media. This was evident in the censoring of Donald trump close to the end of his tenure as president. This was followed by the Parler app's remover on the Amazon server and the eventual censorship of individuals who express support to Donald Trump. However, censorship is not a new phenomenon, as many governments have employed its use to achieve their purpose over the years. For example, the Chinese government collects individuals' big data from various sources such as finance, tax, and health records. It monitors online purchasing behaviour, social media activity and information resulting from facial recognition via the country's approximately 200 million surveillance cameras. This data is then used to compute an individual's "social credit score" that gives incentive to lawful behaviour and good citizenship. The score goes up for good behaviour such as donating blood, volunteering in a hospital, or repaying a person's loan on time. The opposite happens if a person gets a speeding ticket and fail to pay their taxes or drop litter. Consequences of bad scores are non-eligibility for jobs in public administration, being turned down for loans, or even not being allowed to board an aeroplane.

In contrast, good scores provide exemplary citizens with discounts on their electricity bills or privileged healthcare access (Marr, 2019). From this, it is clear that censorship is a threat to humanity, especially when done on popular social media. It threatens freedom of expression, a fundamental right stipulated under the Universal declaration of human rights and recognized in international human rights law.

Librarians' Role in Combating Fake News

Librarians are almost unanimous in their belief that they play a critical role in combating fake news. This is particularly true for those who place libraries as the polar opposite of fake news (Finley et al., 2017) or include it in a list of items that violate librarianship ethics (American Library Association, 2017). Others view librarians as already on the front lines (Jacobson, 2017; Neely-Sardon & Tignor, 2018; Wade & Hornick, 2018), despite the need to prioritize fake news as a primary concern (Rochlin, 2017).

Fake news is not the main issue; instead, it is a symptom of a deeper issue. Individually, the issue is, among other things, a lack of education (Cooke, 2017) or media literacy (Cheby, 2018; Dempsey, 2017). The problem, in general, is thought to be in our modern knowledge environments. There is a large amount of social media data in today's information environment, which contains much fake news. With the sheer volume of photos and comments shared by social media users every day, moderating this fake news material is complex (Schmidt & Wiegand, 2017). This is also due to inherent contradictions with ideals such as free speech (Rainie et al., 2017). As a result, librarians must use a variety of strategies to fight fake news. Technology, regulation, information, and media literacy are examples of such methods. It is possible to use technology to detect unethical and illegal conduct. The regulation would be expected to describe voter fraud and the dissemination of fake news. Finally, how librarians will educate people through information and media literacy would be a concern.

The first strategy is technology, which can be used to minimize the harms and other side effects of fake news (Leetaru, 2019). Artificial intelligence (AI), for example, can detect fake news. By scanning the cybersphere for similar content and drawing conclusions about who/where the author(s) may be based, AI can help detect where the fake news originated. Furthermore, according to a 2017 study by the US think tank Brookings Institution, computer scientists and linguists are relying on big data to build algorithms that aid in the detection of misinformation by comparing linguistic patterns of a potentially false statement with those of proven false statements (Wang, 2017; Tacchini et al., 2017). This does not, however, imply that the information should be censored. Similarly, the European Commission has cautioned that such an automated approach could lead to the incorrect labelling of truthful content as disinformation (European Commission, 2018). Only the populace should be able to determine whether to approve or deny it. Librarians may be hired as impartial fact-checkers to lookout for false information. The use of librarians can assist in not marking facts as fake.

The second strategy is regulation. The use of social media must, without a doubt, be controlled. In Nigeria, the National Council on Information (NCI), the country's highest policy-making body for information articulation and distribution, has been proposing a new body to govern social media use (Adepoju, 2017). Because of fake news, disinformation, and extremism, Cameroon, Ghana, Congo, South Africa, and Uganda have all attempted to control social media (Omolayo, 2017). However, the aim of regulation should not be censorship, as this can lead to reduced freedom of expression. According to West (2017), overly stringent regulated social media sites in open societies set a dangerous precedent and may inspire authoritarian regimes to continue and extend censorship. Also, the most notable international instruments on human rights (Universal Declaration of Human Rights; United Nations Charter; International Covenant on Civil and Political Rights and the Rights of Persons with Disabilities) from different perspectives all dwell on the necessity of guaranteeing each individual's right to seek freely, receive or impart information while relating with other individuals (Puddephatt, 2011). As a result, the regulation should direct social media sites to act as platforms rather than publishers. The regulation should also combat the deliberate propagation of (false) content while not censoring opinions. Privacy is another field of regulation that must be followed. Regulations governing privacy concerns on social media include how websites can collect data, what data can be sold, what information should be available online, and who should have control (Tusikov, 2017).

Information and Media Literacy

One of the most feasible and successful combating fake news methods has been described as information literacy (IL) (Batchelor, 2017). This allows users to be critical of the content they are watching, its source, facts, perception, completeness, and knowledge (Houtman & Wall, 2019). According to CILIP, information literacy is the ability to think critically and make informed decisions about any information we find and use. It empowers us as people to enter and express informed opinions and fully participate in society (CILIP, 2018).

Librarians are assured that they can fight fake news. According to Finley et al., if librarians are the nemesis of fake news, then "education is the basic antidote" (Finley et al., 2017). The latest literature emphasizes the importance of critical thinking skills in the fight against false news, and the librarian is recognized as an expert and professional in teaching these skills (Eva & Shea, 2018). Librarians can teach users how to identify false information. Otherwise, misleading or inaccurate information could be disseminated, and the consumer could be exploited. For example, at Stanford University, information literacy is emphasized in the classroom by discipline-specific examples, such as reviewing false news and propaganda and explaining how it affects all subject areas (Benson, 2019). The approach to combating fake news focuses not only on the intent of its dissemination, which is often how it is described, but also on how it is distributed and disseminated, which contributes to public mistrust, misunderstanding, and doubt. As a result, those working in this area should understand and agree that fake news cannot be stopped; however, it can be challenged by widespread literacy (Rochlin, 2017).

Many information literacy structures and models have developed within librarianship based on skill requirements used to notify and educate consumers. Several mechanisms have been developed to educate and teach higher education students how to find, analyze, and use knowledge ethically. However, broader meanings have emerged due to problems arising from the information age, such as fake news. CILIP's information literacy model, for example, consists of eight competencies that an information literature individual should understand: a need for information, the resources available, how to discover information, the need to evaluate outcomes, how to work with or exploit results, ethics and obligation of use, how to connect or share finding, and how to manage findings (CILIP, 2018).

Another concept closely related to information literacy is media literacy. Since information is gotten chiefly from media, it becomes necessary for users to literate about media. According to Schwarzenegger (2020), the media is dependent on its readers' trust, and without trust, it fails to carry out its democratic obligation and promote civic participation. As a result of the lack of confidence developed by information systems such as social media networks, the role of fake news has dramatically impacted how people interact with media. New and troubling media authentication and verification behaviours have arisen, the people's susceptibility to fake news and misinformation. People prefer to use their judgment to authenticate information and their familiarity with media outlets while also analyzing officials' reactions in their social and institutional spheres (Tandoc et al., 2018). According to Schwarzenegger (2020), verification is typically sought by analyzing several media outlets or depending solely on what they consider to be a single reliable source. Because of media systems such as algorithms and bots, these actions are insufficient for authenticating and validating information online. These are some of the reasons why there is such a strong need to examine and interact with media literacy and structures.

Regarding fake news, Mihailidis and Viotty (2017) address the importance of media literacy as a response to "spreadable spectacle," which they identify as a type of dramatized and false media concepts. The chapter explores the dissemination of disinformation and fake news stories, which are referred to as "internet spectacles" and are strongly influenced by the post-truth culture (Mihailidis & Viotty, 2017). The authors examine the impact and efficacy of media literacy (ML) as a tool for combating the issue. Though they accept that skill-based frameworks of media literacy can give solutions to fake news, they demand a repositioning of media literacy that responds to the spread of "spectacle," and takes a broader approach to the post-truth culture. They aim to emphasize media literacy's civic position in society rather than its more general function of preparing people to manage and use information.

Applying Inoculation by Librarians Against Fake News

According to some library and information science writers, fake news is a sign of a more serious issue. Some, however, describe the issue in terms of its apparent implications. Individually, the issue is that people are duped because they cannot assess facts' reliability (Burkhardt, 2017; Farkas, 2018). As a result, the Stanford History Education Group's (Wineburg et al., 2016) findings of students' inability to determine information sources are prominently featured in LIS works (Auberry, 2018; Bluemle, 2018; El Rayess et al., 2018; Johnson, 2018; Musgrove et al., 2018; Neely-Sardon & Tignor, 2018). Therefore, librarians need to serve the role of ensuring the credibility of information.

Van der Linden et al. (2017) and Cook et al. (2017) discovered that inoculating people with facts against misinformation worked in the context of a highly politicized issue (global warming), regardless of prior attitudes. The inoculation process is divided into two parts: (1) a warning to elicit and activate threat in message recipients (the affective basis) and (2) refutational pre-emption (the cognitive basis). Forewarning people about the threat to counter-attitudinal content is thought to elicit threats to motivate the protection of existing beliefs. In turn, two-sided refutational messages both inform and teach in the sense that they model the counterarguing process for people and provide specific content that can be used to resist persuasion attempts (Compton, 2013).

Figure 1 shows the functional role a librarian can play in curbing fake news. In this model, the fake news initiator uses a social media platform to distribute fake information. However, this information must first go through artificial intelligence (AI) to determine if the information does not come from a suspicious origin. The AI also collates the metadata of the information. It checks if the information has not been categorized online as fake news. If the AI discovers that the information could be fake news, the AI temporarily blocks the publisher from publishing the information until the librarian confirms it. This means that librarians would have been employed as specialists to inoculated readers.

Figure 1. Curbing fake news on social media by Inoculation

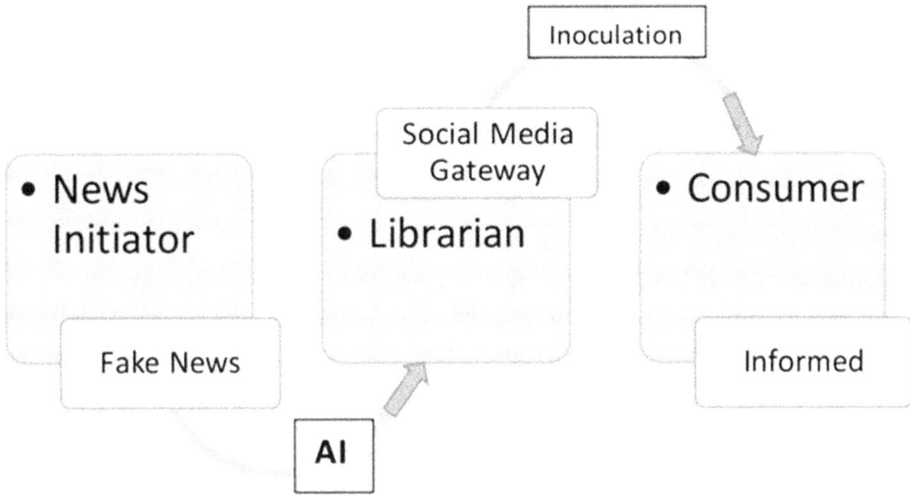

The librarian can serve the role of inoculating readers by forewarning people that they are about to be exposed to counter-attitudinal content. Librarians can achieve this Inoculation in multiple ways. Firstly, they can serve the role of authenticating the genuineness of information. They can achieve this by gathering information about fake news. Then allows the fake information to be published along with notification to readers about potential misinformation. This notification must also direct the readers to the probable real news from credible sources. This will give the readers enough literacy on the right news without censoring the fake information. Secondly, librarians can educate readers about identifying right or false news. This can be a continuous endeavour that can be carried out on different social media outlets. The government can support this by enforcing social media companies to regularly employ librarians to regularly push information and media literacy ads to all their users. This process enables users to understand the techniques of those that initiate fake news. Therefore, the process will eventually inoculate users against fake news before it ever takes place.

Challenges of Applying Inoculation by Librarians Against Fake News

Ideological Belief: A person's ideology may determine the news a person believes. So, inoculating a person before receiving fake news may not change some individuals' ideological beliefs. According to Trout (2009), as cited in Sullivan (2019)., "Biases are systematic, and the errors they produce are more like perceptual illusions than factual blunders. Knowing that it happens, or how it works, still does not make it go away". That is, forewarned is not forearmed (Kenyon & Beaulac, 2014).

Privacy: The use of artificial intelligence to inoculate readers may infringe on users' privacy. This technology though innovative, cannot be as effective as humans and, therefore, may flag social media contents that could be real news since privacy protection is a fundamental human right and vital to librarianship as a profession. The use of AI may become a threat to the very right that librarians strive to protect. Though AI may not be avoided in the inoculation approach, as shown in figure 1, it however must be used as stated in the chapter.

Unintended Censorship: Flagging news to pre-empt readers from absorbing fake news may have unintended consequences. This could lead to people not believing any information from that news source, leading many to source news elsewhere. This could negatively portray such a platform, thereby causing a ripple effect on how other users perceive the platform.

Loss of customers: Social media companies mainly generate funds from their customer base. However, users may perceive Inoculation as a form of censorship of their views. This occurred in the last US election, where many Twitter followers had to leave Twitter to join Parler. This change in the platform may threaten the survival of these companies if the trends become viral. Therefore, Inoculation must be implemented relatively across various users without bias of ideology.

CONCLUSION

Fake news poses a serious challenge to society, especially during this technological era where social media has become paramount to learning. Unless these issues are promptly tackled, the consequences may become irreversible. This has necessitated the need to adopt new strategies to tackle the problem of fake news. Among the measures suggested are technological and regulatory in nature. Aside from the technology and regulatory approaches, librarians can become the intermediary between the end-user and information. This can be achieved by employing librarians to inoculate the public against fake news without censoring the news. Learning to discern fake news and staying safe on social media are embedded in librarianship as a profession. As such, society have a lot to gain by placing librarians at the forefront of the battle against fake news.

Conflict of Interest Declaration: None

REFERENCES

Adepoju, P. (2017). *Nigeria's highest information council proposes social media. regulation*. https://www.techcityng.com/

ADL. (2019). *From Alt Right to Alt Lite: Naming the Hate*. ADL.

Ahmed, W., Vidal-Alaball, J., Downing, J., & Seguí, F. L. (2020). COVID-19 and the 5G conspiracy theory: Social network analysis of Twitter data. *Journal of Medical Internet Research*, *22*(5), e19458. doi:10.2196/19458 PMID:32352383

Akakandelwa, A. (2016). Libraries at the Crossroads: Challenges of Serving Library Users in a Social Media Environment–Ethical Considerations. In Leadership and Personnel Management: Concepts, Methodologies, Tools, and Applications (pp. 2009-2024). IGI Global.

Allcott, H., & Gentzkow, M. (2017). Social media and fake news in the 2016 election. *The Journal of Economic Perspectives*, *31*(2), 211–236. doi:10.1257/jep.31.2.211

Allcott, H., & Gentzkow, M. (2017). Social media and fake news in the 2016 election. *The Journal of Economic Perspectives*, *31*(2), 211–236. doi:10.1257/jep.31.2.211

Allcott, H., & Gentzkow, M. (2017). Social media and fake news in the 2016 election. *The Journal of Economic Perspectives*, *31*(2), 211–236. doi:10.1257/jep.31.2.211

American Library Association. (2017). *Resolution on access to accurate information*. Chicago: ALA. http://www.ala.org/advocacy/intfreedom/ statementspols/ ifresolutions/accurateinformation

Anderson, K. E. (2018). Getting acquainted with social networks and apps: Combating fakenews on social media. *Library Hi Tech News*, *35*(3), 1–6. doi:10.1108/LHTN-02-2018-0010

Auberry, K. (2018). Increasing students' ability to identify fake news through information literacy education and content management systems. *The Reference Librarian*, *59*(4), 179–187. doi:10.1080/02763877.2018.1489935

Banks, M. (2016). Fighting fake news. *American Libraries*, *48*(3-4), 18–21.

Batchelor, O. (2017). Getting out the truth: The role of libraries in the fight against fake news. *RSR. Reference Services Review*, *45*(2), 143–148. doi:10.1108/RSR-03-2017-0006

BBC. (2020). *China coronavirus: Misinformation spreads online about origin and scale*. https://www.bbc.com/news/blogs-trending-51271037?fbclid=IwAR3DUgS1ZhAPg3wSNN4EMKibJwel_Ym3P4zNi5vK8prM4VF8EIHLaK9mmoU

Becker, B. W. (2016). The librarian's information war. *Behavioral & Social Sciences Librarian, 35*(4), 188–191. doi:10.1080/01639269.2016.1284525

Benson, M. (2019). Teaching information literacy: Combating fake news through library-faculty collaboration. *J. New Librarianship, 4*(2), viii. doi:10.21173/newlibs/8/8

Blanco-Herrero, D., & Arcila-Calderón, C. (2019). Deontología y noticias falsas: Estudio de las percepciones de periodistas españoles. *El Profesional de la Información, 28*(3). Advance online publication. doi:10.3145/epi.2019.may.08

Bluemle, S. R. (2018). Post-facts: Information literacy and authority after the 2016 election. *portal. Portal (Baltimore, Md.), 18*(2), 265–282. doi:10.1353/pla.2018.0015

Bode, L., & Vraga, E. K. (2018). See something, say something: Correction of global health misinformation on social media. *Health Communication, 33*(9), 1131–1140. doi:10.1080/10410236.2017.1331312 PMID:28622038

Budak, C. (2019, May). What happened? the spread of fake news publisher content during the 2016 us presidential election. In *The World Wide Web Conference* (pp. 139-150). 10.1145/3308558.3313721

Bullock, D. S., Mittenzwei, K., & Josling, T. E. (2019). Social Welfare Effects of Transparency and Misinformation in a Political Economy. *Journal of Agricultural and Applied Economics, 51*(3), 485–494. doi:10.1017/aae.2019.17

Burkhardt, J. M. (2017). History of fake news. *Library Technology Reports, 53*(8), 5–2. https://search-proquest-com.ucd.idm.oclc.org/docview/1967322040/abstract/32BE018C856D42F8PQ/1?accountid=14507

Buschman, J. (2019). Good news, bad news, and fake news. *The Journal of Documentation, 75*(1), 213–228. doi:10.1108/JD-05-2018-0074

Calvillo, D. P., Ross, B. J., Garcia, R. J., Smelter, T. J., & Rutchick, A. M. (2020). Political ideology predicts perceptions of the threat of covid-19 (and susceptibility to fake news about it). *Social Psychological & Personality Science, 11*(8), 1119–1128. doi:10.1177/1948550620940539

Cheby, L. E. (2018, January 25). *Funding Libraries Is The Way To Beat 'Fake News'.* https://entropymag.org/funding-libraries-is-the-way-to-beat-fake-news/

CILIP. (2018). *What is information literacy?* CILIP. https://www.cilip.org.uk/page/informationliteracy

Compton, J. (2013). Inoculation theory. In J. P. Dillard & L. Shen (Eds.), *The SAGE handbook of persuasion: Developments in theory and practice* (2nd ed., pp. 220–236). Sage Publications. doi:10.4135/9781452218410

Cook, J., Lewandowsky, S., & Ecker, U. K. H. (2017). Neutralizing misinformation through Inoculation: Exposing misleading argumentation techniques reduces their influence. *PLoS One, 12*(5), 1–21. doi:10.1371/journal.pone.0175799 PMID:28475576

Cooke, N. A. (2017). Post truth, truthiness, and alternative facts. *The Library Quarterly, 87*(3), 211–221. doi:10.1086/692298

Deighton, J., Fader, P., Haenlein, M., Kaplan, A., Libai, B., & Muller, E. (2011). Médias sociaux et entreprise, une route pleine de défis. *Recherche et Applications en Marketing, 26*(3), 117–124. doi:10.1177/076737011102600306

Dempsey, K. (2017). What's behind fake news and what you can do about it. *Information Today, 34*(4), 6.

Dollinger, A. (2017). *Can librarians save us from fake news?* Vice. https://www.vice.com/en_us/article/pgwwgz/can-librarians-save-us-fromfake-news

El Rayess, M., Chebl, C., Mhanna, J., & Hage, R. M. (2018). Fake news judgement. *RSR. Reference Services Review, 46*(1), 146–129. doi:10.1108/RSR-07-2017-0027

European Commission. (2018). *Tackling online disinformation: A European approach.* https://eur-lex.europa.eu/legal-content/EN/TXT/?uri=CELEX%3A52018DC0236

Eva, N., & Shea, E. (2018). Marketing libraries in an era of "fake news". *Reference and User Services Quarterly, 57*(3), 168–171. doi:10.5860/rusq.57.3.6599

Farkas, M. (2018). Beyond fake news: Determining what sources to trust. *American Libraries*, 1.

Finley, W., McGowan, B., & Kluever, J. (2017). Fake news: An opportunity for real librarianship. *ILA Reporter, 35*(3), 8-12.

Gallagher, B. (2016). *What impact does fake news have on the real world?* Mary Jane. https://merryjane.com/culture/fake-news-internetimpact

Gil de Zúñiga, H., Jung, N., & Valenzuela, S. (2012). Social media use for news and individuals' social capital, civic engagement and political participation. *Journal of Computer-Mediated Communication, 17*(3), 319–336. doi:10.1111/j.1083-6101.2012.01574.x

Guardian. (2019). *Singapore fake news law a 'disaster' for freedom of speech, says rights group*. https://www.theguardian.com/world/2019/may/09/singapore-fake-news-law-a-disaster-for-freedom-of-speech-says-rights-group

Haag, M., & Salam, M. (2017). Gunman in pizzagate shooting is sentenced to 4 years in prison. *The New York Times, 23*.https://www.nytimes.com/2017/06/22/us/pizzagate-attack-sentence.html

Hern, A. (2020). Fake coronavirus tweets spread as other sites take harder stance. *The Guardian*. https://www.theguardian.com/world/2020/mar/04/fake-coronavirus-tweets-spread-as-other-sites-take-harder-stance

Houtman, E., & Wall, M. (2019). *Information disorder: Helping students to think critically about the news*. http://hdl.handle.net/1807/94747

Howel, L. (2013). *Digital wildfires in a hyperconnected world. Global Risks Report*. http://www3.weforum.org/docs/WEF_GlobalRisks_Report_2013.pdf

Jacobson, L. (2017). The smell test: Educators can counteract fake news with information literacy. Here's how. *School Library Journal*. https://www.slj.com/?detailStory=the-smell-test-educators-can-counter-fake-news-withinformation-literacy-heres-how

Jeffries, S., Kroondyk, J., Paolini, F., & Radisauskas, C. (2017). Says who? Librarians tackle fake news. *College & Research Libraries News, 78*(10), 538–545. doi:10.5860/crln.78.10.538

Johnson, M. (2018). Fighting "fake news": How we overhauled our website evaluationlessons. *Knowledge Quest, 47*(1), 32–36.

Jowell, G. S., & O'Donnell, V. (2015). *Propaganda and persuasion* (6th ed.). Sage Publishing.

Kamarck, E. (2018). *Malevolent soft power, AI, and the threat to democracy*. Brookings. https://www.brookings.edu/research/malevolent-soft-power-ai-and-the-threat-to-democracy/

Kaplan, A. (2015). Social media. In D. T. Cook & J. M. Ryan (Eds.), *The Wiley Blackwell Encyclopedia of Consumption and Consumer Studies* (pp. 519–523). Wiley Blackwell.

Kaplan, A. (2017). Academia goes social media, MOOC, SPOC, SMOC and SSOC: The digital transformation of higher education institutions and universities. In B. Rishi & S. Bandyopadhyay (Eds.), *Contemporary Issues in Social Media Marketing* (pp. 20–30). Routledge. doi:10.4324/9781315563312-2

Kaplan, A. (2018). A school is a building that has 4 walls – with tomorrow inside: Toward the reinvention of the business school. *Business Horizons*, *61*(4), 599–608. doi:10.1016/j.bushor.2018.03.010

Kaplan, A., & Haenlein, M. (2009). The fairyland of *Second Life*: About virtual social worlds and how to use them. *Business Horizons*, *52*(6), 563–572. doi:10.1016/j.bushor.2009.07.002

Kaplan, A., & Haenlein, M. (2010). Users of the world, unite! The challenges and opportunities of social media. *Business Horizons*, *53*(1), 59–68. doi:10.1016/j.bushor.2009.09.003

Kaplan, A., & Haenlein, M. (2016). Higher education and the Digital Revolution: About MOOCs, SPOCs, social media, and the Cookie Monster. *Business Horizons*, *59*(4), 441–450. doi:10.1016/j.bushor.2016.03.008

Kapoor, K. K., Tamilmani, K., Rana, N. P., Patil, P., Dwivedi, Y. K., & Nerur, S. (2018). Advances in social media research: Past, present and future. *Information Systems Frontiers*, *20*(3), 531–558. doi:10.100710796-017-9810-y

Kenyon, T., & Beaulac, G. (2014). Critical thinking education and debiasing. *Informal Logic*, *34*(4), 341–363. doi:10.22329/il.v34i4.4203

Kucharski, A. (2016). Post-truth: Study epidemiology of fake news. *Nature*, *540*(7634), 525. doi:10.1038/540525a PMID:30905947

Leetaru, K. (2019). A Reminder That 'Fake News' Is An Information Literacy Problem—Not A Technology Problem. *Forbes*. https://www.forbes.com/sites/kalevleetaru/2019/07/07/a-reminder-that-fake-newsis-an-information-literacy-problem-not-a-technology-problem/

Lefkowitz, M. (2017). Library tackles fake news with workshops, resources, advice. *Cornell University Library*. https://www.library.cornell.edu/about/news/archive/library-tackles-fake-news-workshops-resources-advice

Lenker, M. (2016). Motivated reasoning, political information, and information literacyeducation. *portal. Portal (Baltimore, Md.)*, *16*(3), 511–528.

Mann, A., Nguyen, K., & Gregory, K. (2019). Emperor Cottrell': Accused Christchurch shooter had celebrated rise of the Australian far-right. *ABC News*, (March), 23.

Manzanero, N. M., & Ramírez, M. Y. (2018). Diálogos sobre educación democrática: Mirada intercultural de la formación de ciudadanos latinoamericanos. *Telos: Revista de Estudios Interdisciplinarios en Ciencias Sociales*, *20*(1), 101–128. doi:10.36390/telos201.06

Marr, B. (2019, January 21). Chinese social credit score: Utopian Big Data – Bliss? Or black mirror on steroids? *Forbes*. https://www.forbes.com/sites/bernardmarr/2019/01/21/chinese-social-credit-score-utopian-big-data-bliss-or-black-mirror-on-steroids/#139759c648b8

McGuire, W. J. (1964). Some contemporary approaches. *Advances in Experimental Social Psychology, 1*, 191–229.

Mena, P. (2020). Cleaning up social media: The effect of warning labels on likelihood of sharing false news on Facebook. *Policy and Internet, 12*(2), 165–183. doi:10.1002/poi3.214

Mesquita, C. T., Oliveira, A., Seixas, F. L., & Paes, A. (2020). Infodemia, fake news and medicine: Science and the quest for truth. *International Journal of Cardiovascular Sciences, 33*(3), 203–205. doi:10.36660/ijcs.20200073

Mihailidis, P., & Viotty, S. (2017). Spreadable spectacle in digital culture: Civic expression, fake news, and the role of media literacies in "post-fact" society. *The American Behavioral Scientist, 61*(4), 441–454. doi:10.1177/0002764217701217

Musgrove, A. T., Powers, J. R., Rebar, L. C., & Musgrove, G. J. (2018). Real or fake?Resources for teaching college students how to identify fake news. *College & Undergraduate Libraries, 25*(3), 243–260. doi:10.1080/10691316.2018.1480444

Nations, D. (2018). *What is social media? Take a clear look at what social media is really all about*. https://www.lifewire.com/

Neely-Sardon, A., & Tignor, M. (2018). Focus on the facts: A news and information literacyinstructional program. *The Reference Librarian, 59*(3), 108–121. doi:10.1080/02763877.2018.1468849

Nelson, J. L., & Taneja, H. (2018). The small, disloyal fake news audience: The role of audience availability in fake news consumption. *New Media & Society, 20*(10), 1–18. doi:10.1177/1461444818758715

Ngai, E. W., Moon, K. L. K., Lam, S. S., Chin, E. S., & Tao, S. S. (2015). Social media models, technologies, and applications. *Industrial Management & Data Systems, 115*(5), 769–802. doi:10.1108/IMDS-03-2015-0075

Ohleiser, A. (2016). *This is how Facebook's fake-news writers make money*. Academic Press.

Omolayo, O. (2017). *Who fears social media?* https://techpoint.ng/2017/07/25/social-media-regulation-nigeria/

Papageorgis, D., & McGuire, W. J. (1961). The generality of immunity to persuasion produced by pre-exposure to weakened counterarguments. *Journal of Abnormal and Social Psychology*, *62*(3), 475–481. doi:10.1037/h0048430 PMID:14483679

Patrikarakos, D. (2017). *Social media networks are the handmaiden to dangerous propaganda*. https://time.com/5008076/nyc-terror-attack-isis-facebook-russia/

Peña, M. (2017). Vista de Democracia representativa y participación ciudadana en Venezuela (1958-2015). *Telos Revista de Estudios Interdisciplinarios En Ciencias Sociales.*, *19*(1), 3–26.

Pennycook, G., McPhetres, J., Zhang, Y., Lu, J. G., & Rand, D. G. (2020). Fighting COVID-19 misinformation on social media: Experimental evidence for a scalable accuracy-nudge intervention. *Psychological Science*, *31*(7), 770–780. doi:10.1177/0956797620939054 PMID:32603243

Pucciarelli, F., & Kaplan, A. (2016). Competition and strategy in higher education: Managing complexity and uncertainty. *Business Horizons*, *59*(3), 311–320. doi:10.1016/j.bushor.2016.01.003

Puddephat, A. (2011). *The importance of self-regulation of the media in upholding freedom of expression*. http://www.unesco.org/new/en/communication-and-information/resources/

Rainie, H., Anderson, J. Q., & Albright, J. (2017). *The future of free speech, trolls, anonymity and fake news online*. Pew Research Center.

Rochlin, N. (2017). Fake news: Belief in post-truth. *Library Hi Tech*, *35*(3), 386–392. doi:10.1108/LHT-03-2017-0062

Saunders, L., Gans-Boriskin, R., & Hinchliffe, L. (2018). *Know news: Engaging across allied professions to combat misinformation*. Simmons College. https://slis.simmons.edu/blogs/disinformation/files/2018/05/White-Paper-Final-Draft-1.pdf

Scheufele, D. A., & Krause, N. M. (2019). Science audiences, misinformation, and fake news. *Proceedings of the National Academy of Sciences of the United States of America*, *116*(16), 7662–7669. doi:10.1073/pnas.1805871115 PMID:30642953

Schmidt, A., & Wiegand, M. (2017, April). A survey on hate speech detection using natural language processing. In *Proceedings of the fifth international workshop on natural language processing for social media* (pp. 1-10). 10.18653/v1/W17-1101

Schwarzenegger, C. (2020). Personal epistemologies of the media: Selective criticality, pragmatic trust, and competence–confidence in navigating media repertoires in the digital age. *New Media & Society*, *22*(2), 361–377. doi:10.1177/1461444819856919

SCONUL. (2018). *Seven pillars of information literacy*. SCONUL. https://www.sconul.ac.uk/page/seven-pillars-of-information-literacy

Soltaninejad, K. (2020). Methanol mass poisoning outbreak, a consequence of COVID-19 pandemic and misleading messages on social media. *The International Journal of Occupational and Environmental Medicine*, *11*(3), 148–150. doi:10.34172/ijoem.2020.1983 PMID:32225177

Spohr, D. (2017). Fake news and ideological polarisation: Filter bubbles and selective exposure on social media. *Business Information Review*, *34*(3), 150–160. doi:10.1177/0266382117722446

Sullivan, M. (2019). Libraries and fake news: What's the problem? What's the plan? *Communications in Information Literacy*, *13*(1). Advance online publication. doi:10.15760/comminfolit.2019.13.1.7

Tacchini, E., Ballarin, G., Della Vedova, M. L., Moret, S., & de Alfaro, L. (2017). Some like it hoax: Automated fake news detection in social networks. *Human-Computer Interaction*.

Tandoc, E. C. Jr, Lim, Z. W., & Ling, R. (2018). Defining "fake news". *Digital Journalism*, *6*(2), 137–153. doi:10.1080/21670811.2017.1360143

Tandoc, E. C., Ling, R., Westlund, O., Duffy, A., Goh, D., & Wei, Z. L. (2018). Audiences' acts of authentication in the age of fake news: A conceptual framework. *New Media & Society*, *20*(8), 2745–2763. https://doi-org.jproxy.nuim.ie/10.1177/1461444817731756

Trout, J. D. (2009). *The empathy gap: Building bridges to the good life and the good society*. Penguin.

Tusikov, N. (2017). *Regulate social media platforms before it's too late*. Retrieved from: https://theconversation.com/

van der Linden, S. (2015). The conspiracy-effect: Exposure to conspiracy theories (about global warming) decreases pro-social behavior and science acceptance. *Personality and Individual Differences*, *87*, 171–173. doi:10.1016/j.paid.2015.07.045

Wade, S., & Hornick, J. (2018). Stop! Don't share that story! Designing a pop-up undergraduate workshop on fake news. *The Reference Librarian*, *59*(4), 188–194. doi:10.1080/02763877.2018.1498430

Wang, W. Y. (2017). Liar, liar pants on fire. A New Benchmark Dataset for Fake News Detection. *Computation and Language.*, 422–426. doi:10.18653/v1/P17-2067

Wardle, C. (2017). Fake news. It's complicated. *First Draft*. https://firstdraftnews.org/fake-news-complicated/

Watts, C. (2018). *Terrorism and social media: Is big tech doing enough?* https://www.fpri.org/article/2018/01/terrorism-social-media-big-tech-enough/

West, D. (2017, December 18). *How to combat fake news and disinformation*. The Brookings Institution. https://www.brookings.edu/research/how-to-combat-fake-news-and-disinformation/

Wineburg, S., McGrew, S., Breakstone, J., & Ortega, T. (2016, November 22). *Evaluating information: The cornerstone of civic online reasoning*. Stanford History Education Group. https://purl.stanford.edu/fv751yt5934

Zimdars, M. (2016, November 18). My "fake news list" went viral. But made-up stories are only part of the problem. *The Washington Post*. https://www.washingtonpost.com/posteverything/wp/2016/11/18/my-fake-news-list-went-viral-but-made-up-storiesare-only-part-of-theproblem/?noredirect=on&utm_term=.d19fa7c1f621

Zubiaga, A., Aker, A., Bontcheva, K., Liakata, M., & Procter, R. (2018). Detection and resolution of rumours in social media: A survey. *ACM Computing Surveys*, *51*(2), 1–36. doi:10.1145/3161603

ADDITIONAL READING

Anderson, R. (2017). Fake news and alternative facts: five challenges for academic libraries. *Insights, 30*(2).

De Paor, S., & Heravi, B. (2020). Information literacy and fake news: How the field of librarianship can help combat the epidemic of fake news. *Journal of Academic Librarianship*, *46*(5), 102218. doi:10.1016/j.acalib.2020.102218

Eva, N., & Shea, E. (2018). Amplify your impact: Marketing libraries in an era of "fake news". *Reference and User Services Quarterly*, *57*(3), 168–171. doi:10.5860/rusq.57.3.6599

LaPierre, S. S., & Kitzie, V. (2019). "Lots of Questions about 'Fake News'": How Public Libraries Have Addressed Media Literacy, 2016–2018. *Public Library Quarterly*, *38*(4), 428–452. doi:10.1080/01616846.2019.1600391

Lim, S. (2020). Academic library guides for tackling fake news: A content analysis. *Journal of Academic Librarianship*, *46*(5), 102195. doi:10.1016/j.acalib.2020.102195

Mertoğlu, U., & Genç, B. (2020). Automated Fake News Detection in the Age of Digital Libraries. *Information Technology and Libraries*, *39*(4). Advance online publication. doi:10.6017/ital.v39i4.12483

Revez, J., & Corujo, L. (2021). Librarians against fake news: A systematic literature review of library practices (Jan. 2018–Sept. 2020). *Journal of Academic Librarianship*, *47*(2), 102304. doi:10.1016/j.acalib.2020.102304

KEY TERMS AND DEFINITIONS

Censorship: The suppression of speech, public communication, or other information.

Fake News: A false or misleading information presented as news.

Freedom of Expression: The ability of an individual or group of individuals to express their beliefs, thoughts, ideas, and emotions about different issues free from government censorship.

Inoculation: A process of preemptively introducing individuals to a weaker version of a (counter)-argument and then refuting the argument. Librarian: A professional with a masters or PhD degree in library and information science charged with managing or assisting in a library.

Misinformation: A false, inaccurate, or misleading information that is communicated regardless of an intention to deceive.

Social Media: Websites and applications that enable users to create and share content or to participate in social networking.

Chapter 5
Teaching and Assessing Data Literacy for Adolescent Learners

Semi Yeom
https://orcid.org/0000-0002-3652-854X
University of Maryland, College Park, USA

ABSTRACT

Today, adolescent learners are exposed to deepfakes from online news to social media. They need data literacy—being able to pose questions about data, extract relevant information, and evaluate claims about data—to retrieve factual information and take informed actions. However, not many students in the U.S. are equipped with data literacy to detect deepfakes. This chapter examines existing practices for teaching and assessing data literacy and suggests best practices for supporting adolescent learners in attaining data literacy. This chapter also discusses the future steps needed to implement these best practices in the classroom so that young learners can mitigate the impacts of deepfakes in their lives.

INTRODUCTION

Today's technology-driven world creates, represents, and stores data, which are information that tends to be numerical, algorithmic, and visual (Fontichiaro & Oehrli, 2016). In this era, how one observes, spends time, retrieves information, and takes actions largely represented, guided, and stored by data. For example, online news programs provide graphs and statistical findings related to sociopolitical issues. Clicking a link to web content creates an algorithm about the frequency and

DOI: 10.4018/978-1-7998-6474-5.ch005

tendency of user behaviors. Facing the increasing significance and ubiquity of data in our lives, contemporary lives are affected by how organizations and institutions manipulate big data, including numbers, texts, images, times, and places (Gould, 2017). Data widely affect how people retrieve information and act, especially adolescent learners who are exposed to diverse representations of data from online news to social media. Data literacy is an array of abilities to pose questions about data, use tools and representations for data, extract relevant information, and evaluate claims made in various contexts. The fast development and increased demands in information technology from the 2000s have drawn people's attention to the concept of data literacy and its many variants (Tedre et al., 2020). Some researchers consider it as an area within digital literacies (Hockly, 2020), but data literacy is targeted to understanding formalized numerical, algorithmic, and visual representation of facts or ideas, not overall digital skills navigating online modes. Although data literacy is one of the most essential knowledge, skills, and abilities (KSAs) emphasized across disciplines and sectors in college and career (van 't Hooft et al., 2012; English & Watson, 2018), few students in the U.S. are ready to navigate their future by developing the ability to comprehend and use data.

Data literacy is essential for all students because it allows them to study real-life problems and develop solutions based on evidence. Students learn how to identify factors and contexts surrounding data and apply data to specific purposes and situations. These abilities can empower students to dissect messages and intentions behind data and their sources before utilizing information. As teens, they encounter streams of data containing information and numbers, which include deep fakes in multimodal forms. Students equipped with data literacy can evaluate the validity and unbiasedness of data and their sources before using information (Philip et al., 2016; Carmi et al., 2020). Even if a student does not work for the data industry in the future, data literacy is an important skill to make sense of what information influences their lives. With data literacy, students are prepared to navigate social worlds as the future generation of our society, applying data literacy to their work and life in the 21st Century (Leu et al., 2013). For citizens in the 21st Century, data literacy is crucial than before to maximize the benefits of information technology and minimize its harm (Ridgway, 2019). Different types of data are currently created and manipulated. Accordingly, deepfakes can be created and disseminated to anyone who uses digital media. Adolescent learners are exposed to social media platforms such as Facebook, YouTube, and TikTok, which mainly employ visual images and videos. Users in these environments are susceptible to deepfakes if they do not have the awareness and tools to recognize them. (Fazio, 2020; Turton & Martin, 2020).

This chapter examines existing practices for teaching and assessing data literacy by reviewing the literature. The author used an array of databases reputable in the field of education and behavioral science such as ERIC and PsycINFO. Journal articles from international contexts were included since scholars studying data literacy and LMSs are widespread in numerous countries such as South Africa. The author used keywords such as data literacy, instruction, and assessment. The author focused on the articles related to interpreting and analyzing data and did not use other terms related to data literacy such as digital literacies. The search was limited to empirical studies published in English in a peer-reviewed scholarly journal. The chapter then suggests best practices for supporting adolescent learners to attain digital citizenship, civic participation based on skills to use digital tools, and practice critical thinking to discern deep fakes inflicting harms and risks to those (Carmi et al., 2020). With data literacy, students can investigate how to access and interpret data to respond to their questions or problems. They can be empowered with the skills to critique data-based arguments and recognize data representations that are manipulated with biased intentions. By using these skills, students can initiate and participate in discussions about social issues that are related to their lives. Data literate students can take a step toward digital citizenship, with which they can raise their voices and promote their basic rights by responsibly using information and communication technologies (Twidale et al., 2013; Carmi et al., 2020). To support this step, practices for teaching and assessing data literacy should constitute holistic teaching and learning cycle. The author has chosen middle school as a focal population of this chapter as the literature recommends starting data literacy education early in the secondary school experience (Ercegovac, 2015; van 't Hooft et al., 2012; Hockly, 2020).

Review of Existing Data Literacy Instruction

Currently, research about teaching data literacy highlights the need to build the KSAs for data literacy in Grade K to 12. For example, Ercegovac (2015) contends that students need the ability to access available data, understand the definition of data, and think critically about data. Vahey et al. (2006) argue that students need to understand the context of data, construct arguments about data, and perform analyses of representations of data. van 't Hooft et al. (2012) identify the KSAs of data literacy for middle school students, which include a) formulate and answer data-based questions, b) use data, tools, and representations, and c) develop and evaluate data-based inferences. In the era of flowing information that is mal-intended and distorted, the significance of data literacy education has increased. For example, the European Commission (2018) emphasizes data literacy as a tool to monitor digital content creation that may undermine "online safety and well-being" (p. 12). Although data literacy is essential for all students, the emphasis on instructional approaches for K-12 students has not been sufficient (Shreiner, 2019). Studies record that too few students are equipped with the necessary skills to interact with data effectively (Deahl, 2014; Hockly, 2020). Scholars argue that the skills required to access data are not taught in school (Gunter, 2007; Ercegovac, 2015). The main obstacles to teaching data literacy in the classroom include lack of classroom technology and resources, teacher training, and strict boundaries between content subjects (van 't Hooft et al., 2012; Gunter, 2007; Deahl, 2014). Most data used in school are from contexts irrelevant to students' experiences or created by educators (Lim et al., 2014). It means that students do not have sufficient opportunities to explore the complexity of real-world data relevant to their lives. Few schools provide students access to numerical and statistical data that are publicly available (Ercegovac, 2015). Even this use of data in the classroom is usually limited to science or mathematics classes (Deahl, 2014). Finally, the pressure to meet core requirements and prepare students for high-stakes testing prevents teachers from planning and implementing data literacy instructions (Ridsdale et al., 2016).

Despite the challenges in teaching data literacy in schools, researchers and educators have implemented some instructional practices that support students' interactions with data. For example, Ercegovac (2012) supported adolescent students to use existing archives such as *the Online Archives of California* (Ercegovac, 2012) for gathering, analyzing, and presenting data. Data literacy projects supported by the state government helped students engage with real data sets and visualize variability in data (Wolff et al., 2016). The *MAINE data literacy project* aims to teach students the ability to describe and visualize variability in data (Wolff et al., 2016). The project provides real data sets and opportunities for students to collect data about watersheds in New England. After the project, students were asked to explain what they learned from data and how their visualization could support their interpretation of data (see Zoellick et al., 2016). Some projects use geo-spatial data to engage students in exploring and analyzing maps. For example, in *City Digits*, students analyzed geo-spatial data to answer questions about their local neighborhood in New York City (Wolff et al., 2016). From 2013 to 2014, the project used two modules to support students to use maps in combination with interviews and survey data. Students created digital storyboards to communicate their findings and opinions from the evidence. The City Digits curriculum was integrated into a public-school math class where students collected and analyzed data about state lotteries and then built data-based arguments (Deahl, 2014). Another example of the project using geo-spatial data occurred in Seattle, Washington. Gordon et al. (2016) implemented a participatory mapping project called *Mapping Youth Journeys* in the classroom and after-school programs of an independent girls' school. These projects demonstrate that it is possible to integrate data literacy projects into the school curricula to support students' capacity to collect, analyze, and present data.

These types of data literacy projects are in increasing demands in the era of the COVID-19 pandemic more than before. According to the 2021 EDUCAUSE Horizon Report created by a global panel of higher education experts, the COVID-19 has increased the digital divide between those who can access digital resources and those who cannot. The report stated that the divide would be stark even long before students go to a higher education setting (Pelletier et al., 2021). Furthermore, increasing demand for digital skills in the workforce will favor those who are equipped with data and digital literacies. Without any teaching practices that intentionally aim to narrow the digital divide, adolescent students with a lack of resources will be disadvantaged in not just pursuits in college and career but also future decision making. Increasingly, educators have raised concerns about students being exposed to deepfakes or dis-information (i.e., false information intentionally created to harm a person, social group, or country, Carmi et al., 2020). These concerns have stimulated research studies about teaching information literacy, which is a set of skills to explore, critique, and judge information from various sources before using it (Hajam, 2017). As an illustration, Haigh et al. (2019) administered the Learn to Discern program in Ukraine for about 15,000 people including high school teachers and students, medical workers, and library patrons. They conducted a three-part program discussing media influence and propaganda, ways to critique fake news stories, and hatred in media. After the program, the researchers examined a survey result one month after the training compared to the baseline survey conducted beforehand. They argued that participants reported more confidence in distinguishing fake news than those in the control group. Another public intervention called the Museum of Random Memory was implemented to develop data literacy in Denmark, Italy, Spain, Canada, and the United Kingdom. Markahm (2020) stated that the Museum of Random Memory provided participants with performative arts-based interventions where they asked questions and navigated answers about social media, data mining, and datafication in everyday media usage. The researcher maintained that the participants reported higher consciousness about their own digital media use and social changes around big data.

It is not clear, however, whether these interventions improved students' data literacy because most of the projects did not incorporate specific, validated assessments of data literacy. Many projects, such as the City Digits, did not have enough participants to provide data to assess learning outcomes (Deahl, 2014). Without implementing assessments, one cannot know what baseline KSAs students had in terms of data literacy and what they learned from the projects (Deahl, 2014). An original assessment administered after the MAINE Data Literacy Project did not have sufficient evidence of high reliability and validity regarding the construct intended to be measured (Zoellick et al., 2016). These examples reveal that the instructional interventions of data literacy lack a means to accurately measure students' growth in data literacy. To formulate instructional practices as a holistic system, researchers have expressed the need for a way to measure students' data literacy performance. Deahl (2014) refers to the data literacy initiatives, including instruction and assessment, as an ecosystem created by the collaboration between stakeholders. In generating this ecosystem, measures to assess the outcomes of the interventions are essential. An assessment can help administrators evaluate the effectiveness of a data literacy project and determine if it fits into the school system (Deahl, 2014). Ridsdale et al. (2016) also argue that the field of data literacy needs more work to address how to set standards for assessing or evaluating levels of data literacy. Similarly, regarding information literacy, online research, and comprehension skills such as critically evaluating information are not included in state reading standards and state reading assessments (Leu et al. 2013). In sum, researchers call for a measure to support instruction in classroom environments and identify specific levels of progress in students' data literacy.

Review of Existing Data Literacy Assessments

Existing assessments for data literacy provide resources and insights based on which test developers can design and validate an assessment for adolescent learners. The author synthesizes existing studies about data literacy assessment to illustrate what we can learn from their procedures of test design and development. This chapter follows the definitions of design and development set by Ferrara et al. (2016). Design includes decisions about intended interpretations and uses of test scores as well as test specifications delineating numbers and types of tasks, testing time, and delivery mode. Item specifications as a means of specifying tasks are also addressed in the design stage. Development entails activities to realize test and item specifications by people or computer programs. In the development, tasks are produced, reviewed, and revised. Test developers go through field testing of items and assemble final test forms. (Ferrara & Lai, 2016; American Educational Research Association et al., 2014). Not many studies have used a data literacy assessment to generate measurable outcomes before and after the practice (Ben-Zvi & Arcavi, 2001; English & Watson, 2018). A handful of studies exist that implemented educational practice for data literacy, most of which collected qualitative data such as observations, interviews, and written artifacts. For the literature review, the author searched studies about assessments of data literacy and instructional interventions of data literacy that implemented an assessment. The author also searched scholarly articles about assessments of information literacy discussing both qualitative and quantitative data. Lack of studies explicitly targeted deepfakes for assessment purposes.

Design

First, the review on the design process revealed that a few existing studies have chosen problem-based tasks as an item format. Researchers such as Zalles (2005) and Seroff (2017) have claimed that widely used standardized tests cannot assess knowledge and skills related to data literacy as they cannot reflect the fluid and process-based nature of data literacy. As an alternative, van 't Hooft et al. (2012) proposed problem-based exercises as a possible means to assess data literacy, giving students problems and asking for finding solutions based on original data. The research article addresses how middle school students engaged with the *Thinking with Data* project, which adopts an interdisciplinary approach in teaching data literacy. They used a data literacy assessment consisting of problem-based exercises to compare learning gains in data literacy between students exposed to the Thinking with Data curriculum and students who were not exposed to the program. Specifically, the assessment was designed to gauge students' abilities to select appropriate data and representations, answer questions, and evaluate arguments based on data. The test contained five constructed-response items related to a problem, asking students to interpret, synthesize, and manipulate numerical and textual data. Students were also asked to suggest what additional data would be needed to answer questions in a holistic way. Similarly, Seroff (2017) demonstrates task examples for assessing data literacy that ask students to find answers for the questions about real-world data such as traffic fatalities, or address problems in data collection such as limitations in defining survey respondents.

Some researchers applied problem-based tasks for assessing information literacy performance in a simulated online environment (Leu et al., 2014; Let et al., 2013). Let et al. (2014) developed and validated the Online Research and Comprehension Assessments (ORCAs) during a five-year-long project. ORCAs evaluate complex tasks such as writing and address both products and processes (Messick, 1995). Two types of formats were applied: ORCA-Closed and ORCA-Multiple Choice. ORCA-Multiple Choice presents the same research problems in a simulated Internet context with sequentially staged decisions (Leu et al. 2014). The ORCAs contain 16 items about human body systems and allow the use of a social network and online communication platforms such as texts, emails, and wikis. The assessment aims to measure a student's ability to conduct online research and report the written results. The competencies include identifying important questions, locating, evaluating, synthesizing, and communicating information (Leu et al., 2004; Leu et al., 2013). The assessment is based on Common Core's Anchor Standards for Reading and Writing focusing on digital literacies for online research. Problem-based tasks in authentic contexts were also adopted for testing fake news recognition. Jones-Jang et al. (2021) created a test to assess participants' abilities to identify fake news in digital environments. They presented six fake and four real news stories in the form of a Facebook post containing images and a headline. All the stories were related to the 2016 U.S. presidential election and chosen in a politically balanced way. The researchers found out that participants with higher information literacy correctly predicted fake news more than those with lower information literacy. They used an existing measure to assess information literacy called the information literacy index (Boh Podgornik et al., 2016), consisting of five multiple-choice questions with one correct answer.

Although problem-based tasks provide opportunities to engage in authentic contexts where data are used, most of them require lengthy written responses, which may disadvantage language minority students (LMSs). The assessments discussed above measured the competency of present and communicate data as the part of the KSAs intended to be measured. Therefore, some of the tasks asked examinees to write findings, solutions, or recommendations based on data (Zalles, 2005; Leu et al., 2014). These responses are language-heavy, if examinees should have the knowledge, skills, and abilities to write statements or arguments in English to complete the tasks. When LMSs do not have such knowledge, skills, and abilities, it is difficult for them to produce written task outcomes that represent their understanding of data. Unlike these assessments for data or information literacy, the new assessment the author creates does not intend to measure the competency of present/communicate. Therefore, the new assessment does not include item types of constructed response but adopts the strengths of problem-based tasks such as assessment environments reflecting authentic use of data.

Existing studies about data literacy assessment inform the details regarding test design but lack explanations about ways to structure tasks that are demonstrated by test and item specifications. Many studies discuss basic information containing item types and test duration and delivery. However, not much detail is provided on the development principles of the test and items that may be indicated by test and item specifications. Test specifications document not only the number of items or testing time but also content coverage, cognitive levels, and desired psychometric properties (AERA et al., 2014). If the test is norm or criterion-referenced is also essential information that guides test development to realize intended test score interpretations and uses. Item specifications or templates are ways of specifying tasks to guide decisions for creating items (Ferrara et al., 2016). Item specifications contain information like test specifications but focus on the information about a specific item such as types of stimuli and the knowledge, skills, and abilities measured (Ewing et al., 2010). Clear documentation of test and item specifications supports test and item development to be systematic and defensible, so it needs to be part of the design process of a data literacy assessment.

Development

Considering test and item development, papers about data literacy assessment provided a brief explanation of how they created items. Chin et al. (2016) briefly stated that researchers developed a choicelet over ten weeks by collaborating with science center staff. As explained, the article mainly discusses the methods and findings from the pilot study or field testing of the choicelet. van 't Hooft et al. (2012) also addresses in a sentence that the test was designed by researchers who engaged in the Thinking with Data project based on the input from the advisory board to establish the validity of the test items. Researchers discuss assessment purposes and the procedure of constructing assessment frameworks based on the alignment with standards (see Zalles, 2005; Quellmalz & Kozma, 2003). These elements are part of the test design process rather than the development according to the definition of Ferrara et al. (2016). Most of the articles did not delineate the comprehensive process of producing tasks for items. Item development not only entails creating items but also includes item review and revision. Then, field testing, re-reviewing, and assembling the items also consist of the development process (Ferrara et al., 2016). However, few studies explain these details of developing items for measuring data literacy. Items need to be produced based on item specifications and selected from a pool into the final test form based on test specifications. Documenting these steps in the development helps increase the test validity in terms of item quality (AERA et al., 2014).

Best Practices for Teaching Data Literacy

For encouraging further studies, the chapter first synthesizes key principles that are currently addressed in teaching data literacy. First, the author suggests three elements that constitute the best teaching practices: a) multimodal, b) multidisciplinary, and c) context based. Table 1 provides a brief description of each of the best teaching practices along with the existing literature.

Multimodal Teaching

Many researchers argue that instructional practices for data literacy should encourage learners to use multiple modes. They can mix and match diverse methods of analyzing and representing data (Oceans of Data Institute, 2015). For example, students can use visual displays with different designs and purposes as analytic tools (Shaughnessy et al., 1996). Technologies, artistic ability, and personal interests can also be incorporated to create and transform data representations (Forster et al., 2018; Forsyth & Liu, 2019). As an illustration, Forster et al. (2018) implemented the *Data Jam* model, which is a project for high school students to learn how to analyze environmental data and share their findings via artwork. One of the key features of the Data Jam model is that students choose a creative medium to convey their claims based on evidence, from game design and painting to sculpture and installation. They share

Table 1. Best teaching practices of data literacy

	Description	Literature
Multimodal	Encouraging diverse tools and multiple modes of presentations for data and students' findings in practice	ODI (2015); Forster et al. (2018); Ünsal et al. (2018); Schüler-Meyer et al. (2019); Forsyth & Liu (2019)
Multidisciplinary	Threading and collaborating across disciplines	Erwin Jr. (2015); Forster et al. (2018); van 't Hooft et al. (2012); English & Watson (2018)
Context-based	Using data embedded in social contexts	Fontichiaro (2016); Webber et al. (2014); Stewart (2014); Spencer & Hertzog (2014); Schüler-Meyer et al. (2019)

this product with a larger audience reaching school, city, or state-wide regions. This step helps students re-formulate meanings and convey stories of local data based on the artistic medium they choose. With careful guidance by teachers and local experts, students can express their creativity as well as support evidence accurately.

Another example of visual modes to enhance data literacy is a map, which can be used in examining deepfakes in geospatial data. For instance, Zhao et al. (2021) emphasized critical geospatial data literacy to detect deepfakes and minimize their multifaceted impacts. Recognizing a deepfake satellite image is highly difficult for the public who have not been trained. Zhao et al. (2021) underscored the importance of developing data literacy to examine deepfake images critically for the public good. Students need to be guided to have awareness about the ramifications of deepfake geospatial data and taught different methods to detect them. (Emory, 2021). Aside from satellite images, pictures and videos are fabricated based on sophisticated visual disinformation tools (Levi, 2020). Students can benefit from being familiar with technology for editing and manipulating photos to discern the credibility of those media and debunk the impacts of deepfakes.

Multidisciplinary Teaching

Another element underscored by data literacy literature is a multidisciplinary approach, which also reflects the cross-disciplinary nature of data literacy (Erwin Jr., 2015; Forster et al., 2018). Researchers such as van 't Hooft et al. (2012) and Vahey et al. (2012) called for collaboration among teachers across subjects and disciplines by taking advantage of shared learning standards highlighting data literacy. van 't Hooft et al. implemented an eight-week project called "The Thinking with Data" with a team of social studies, mathematics, science, and English language arts teachers. The researchers argued the benefits of a cross-curricular approach for middle-grade students to develop abstract, critical, and metacognitive thinking (Brown & Canniff, 2007). Erwin Jr. (2015) stressed the advantages of multidisciplinary teaching of data by using multidisciplinary projects. Projects can connect diverse curricular areas, integrate technology and literacy, and tie them to students' life experiences. Researchers such as Erwin Jr. and Kennedy (2006) stress that a project is also a means of creating online/offline communities of practice and bringing together participants and an audience outside the classroom. Markham (2020) also highlights the benefits of interdisciplinary teams to spark public engagement in building data literacy and set mutual goals and problems through collaboration. The art-based workshop created by her, and interdisciplinary researchers supported participants' analyses of big data usage and challenges toward online safety via multiple modes.

Similarly, English and Watson (2018) used a general knowledge structure between mathematics and statistics to encourage students to use mathematical and statistical thinking to solve problems (Groth, 2015). The researchers applied *modeling with data*, a process of comprehensive reasoning that draws on mathematical and statistical contexts, concepts, and inquiries. It aimed to facilitate students' inferential thinking based on evidence and the ability to recognize uncertainty in the world of data (Watson & English, 2015). Based on datasets about swimmers' performance in the Olympics, sixth graders in a three-year-long study by English and Watson (2018) engaged in activities to pose questions, record evidence-based conclusions, and create a model choosing the best swimming team for the future Olympics. Content analysis of transcripts and written artifacts revealed how the participants used both mathematical operations (e.g., calculating) and statistical reasoning (e.g., consistency, external variables) to deliver statements about data. This study sheds light on ways to utilize common areas between subjects to teach data literacy in interdisciplinary settings.

Context-Based Teaching

Because deepfakes can influence our everyday lives in multifaceted ways, it is crucial to connect data literacy education to students' contexts where they are situated in real lives (Frost et al., 2020). Students need practical guidance to apply knowledge and strategies they learned in their lives. Inside and outside the school, students encounter various sources of data and visual modes such as graphic representations about popular games, statistical vote summaries, and celebrities' video logs on YouTube (Ridgway, 2019). Teaching data literacy should be centered around what matters to adolescent students. Tightening the connection between learning materials and their real-life application can increase the effectiveness of data literacy education.

Many researchers highlight that context-based inquiry about data elicits robust learning (Bransford et al., 2000). As data are embedded within and given meanings from a context, students need to learn how to re-interpret a problem by thinking about the role of a context (Konold & Higgins, 2003). This context can engage students with real social problems involving real-world data (van 't Hooft et al., 2012). Then, they should be able to relate problems to other contexts and adapt their thinking accordingly. Furthermore, data in the authentic context should be related to the students' interests and contemporary issues to increase their motivation for active engagement (Carmichael et al., 2009). For example, studies have implemented data about the presidential election (Fontichiaro & Oehrli, 2016), movie rentals from Netflix (Philip et al., 2016), and location of bird nests (Webber et al., 2014). As adolescent learners are likely to become disinterested in school coursework, this approach is a good way to connect between classroom content and students' interests (Eccles & Midgely, 1990), leading to enhanced task commitment for complex learning (Erwin Jr., 2015).

Best Practices for Assessing Data Literacy

The author also suggests three elements that would enhance the qualities of data literacy assessments: a) technologically enhanced, b) fair to students in diverse backgrounds, and c) argument based. Table 2 provides a brief description of each of the best assessment practices along with the existing literature.

Table 2. Best assessing practices of data literacy

	Description	Literature
Technologically enhanced	Using innovative modes of solving test items and technologies adaptive to students' abilities	Bryant, 2017; Schwartz & Arena, 2013; Chin et al., 2016; Parshall et al., 2010; Cutumisu et al., 2019
Fair	Ensuring that students' backgrounds do not have an appreciable effect on test interpretation or use	Zieky, 2006; Abedi, 2006; Martiniello, 2008; Forzani, 2018; ETS, 2014
Argument-based	Gathering evidence to support arguments about test takers' abilities throughout the testing process	Zieky, 2014; Ferrara et al., 2016; Mislevy, 2013; Luecht, 2013; Nichols et al., 2016

Technologically Enhanced Assessment

First, a few researchers have adopted technologically enhanced and innovative items for data literacy assessment to reflect the authentic use of data. Technologically enhanced and innovative items are test items that are computer-delivered and do not usually follow conventional item types of Multiple Choice or Constructed Response (Bryant, 2017). The scope of technology that enhances the items is vast, including embedded videos, computer adaptive testing, and AI scoring. Technologically enhanced and innovative items may have response actions, formats, types of stimuli, and work products that are different from conventional item types. For example, response actions may include dragging, dropping, ordering, and classifying elements. Also, work products can be a bar graph that is extended or shaded by examinees. Researchers argue that technologically enhanced and innovative items can reduce the effects of random guessing that are prevalent in Multiple Choice items (Bryant, 2017; Kane, 2006). Also, they can increase the motivation of younger test-takers by supporting them to engage in online environments. With technologically enhanced and innovative items, one can collect process data by recording the process of problem-solving. However, technologically enhanced and innovative items also have disadvantages such as high development costs and lack of previous research. Since various formats of technologically enhanced and innovative items function differently, it is difficult to have an adequate research base for each format (Bryant, 2017). Also, the use of technology may introduce construct-irrelevant variance, for instance, from the knowledge, skills, and abilities to use online tools. Because these drawbacks exist, it is essential to consider whether technologically enhanced and innovative items are most appropriate for the construct intended to be measured when deciding to incorporate them into assessments (Bryant, 2017).

One example of technologically enhanced and innovative items used in data literacy assessment is choice-based games (Schwartz & Arena, 2013). For example, Chin, Blair, and Schwartz (2016) suggested game-based measurement to assess how 10th-grade students learned from six-hour data visualization lessons. They developed the games called *choicelets* that afford students to make decisions throughout taking the assessment. Each choicelet aims to assess a target learning process, such as choosing appropriate visual elements and titles for a story. Each game consists of a multi-level challenge that students need to solve. The games contain learning resources that students may choose to explore as they tackle the challenge. They can use them in a different order at different time points. Each game is designed as a stand-alone assessment, meaning that the game does not rely mainly on prior content knowledge of students and can be compatible with different curricula or learning programs. Constructs measured by the choicelets were described in the language of the Next Generation Science Standards (NGSS): a) the abilities to determine the central idea from scientific text, and b) the abilities to compare, integrate and evaluate sources of information presented in visual form.

In the choicelets, students were exposed to three stories, and they were able to pick a photo among six and a chart among four that would be most suitable to the story, pick a title among five, and review. Students had options to read the story but could choose visual elements and a title without clicking the story tab. Once learners submitted their selections, they saw a ''buzz meter'' that measured performance and gave students feedback about the appropriateness of their decisions. The scoring rubric was used to assess students' competency to select the charts, photos, and titles that capture the central idea of the story. The analyses of students' work products involved metrics such as the frequency of the visit of an activity tab, time spent in each tab, and the frequency of clicks showing closer examination of specific charts or photos. The results showed that students who chose to spend more time reading and re-visit charts and photos for closer looks were able to understand factual content and graphical principles better than those who did not. The researchers claim that the game-based measure could be used to predict learning outcomes in liaison with students' choices.

However, the interpretations of the test outcomes of choicelets involve students' choice to read a lengthy passage, which may act as a barrier against representing the performance of LMSs. Chin et al. (2016) contend that students have options not to read a story and can make their editorial selections without entering the story tab. However, the test is designed in that a choice to read a story is critical to receive a good score. The assessment by the buzz meter depends on how the charts, photos, and titles capture the central idea of the story well. The researchers also specify that to receive a good score, students had to understand the main idea of the story and choose the best-fitting graphical and title options. This task structure may affect LMSs' choices to read the story, especially those who do not have the knowledge, skills, and abilities for scientific reading comprehension. Including lengthy texts as a stimulus may disadvantage LMSs who may be overwhelmed with reading long stories in a limited time. Accordingly, it may also differentially affect the performance of LMSs (Abedi, 2006). The researchers intended that a choice and ability to read a story is essential for a better score because the construct measured includes reading comprehension ability of scientific text. However, the competencies of focus in the new assessment do not involve understanding lengthy paragraphs of written words, so the test does not include a lengthy text as a stimulus.

Fair Assessment

These issues of fairness speak to the relevance of the author's claim that assessments need to be fair to students from diverse backgrounds. Fairness in testing depends on how threats to the test validity differentially affect groups of test-takers (Zieky, 2006). Assessment can achieve fairness when characteristics of test-takers that are irrelevant to construct do not have an appreciable effect on test interpretation or use (Educational Testing Service, 2002). Threats to validity are evidence that counteracts arguments supporting the test interpretation or use (Cronbach, 1987; Haladyna,

2006). Any threats that lower the validity of a test for a group of test-takers reduce the fairness of the test. One of the most serious threats to validity comes from the construct-irrelevant variance by language factors. Language factors are defined as features of language that may add linguistic complexity or cognitive load. According to Abedi (2006), unnecessary linguistic complexity comes from linguistic features that slow down reading, induce misinterpretation, and interfere with resolving tasks by adding cognitive load. When language factors are irrelevant to the construct that an assessment aims to measure, they may act as sources of the threat to the validity of content-based assessments (Abedi et al., 2003). In this case, language factors are considered extraneous variables, variables that are not related to the construct measured (Abedi, 2006). Abedi (2006) argues that assessments with unnecessary linguistic complexity may introduce construct-irrelevant variance, which may jeopardize test fairness and validity. LMSs are subject to a higher impact from this construct-irrelevant variance than their counterparts when they do not have English proficiency enough to demonstrate their content-related knowledge.

Previous research has shown that language factors may affect LMSs' performance outcomes in content subjects such as mathematics and science. For example, studies have revealed that the performance gap between LMSs and non-LMSs becomes greater with the higher level of linguistic complexity in an item, irrespective of the content difficulty (Martiniello, 2008). Abedi and Lord (2001) used the linguistically modified items parallel with actual NAEP math test items to compare LMSs' scores. They found that the linguistically modified items generated small but significant improvements in the scores of students whose math proficiency was in the low and middle levels. Other researchers also confirmed this finding that the impact of language factors on LMSs as well as non-LMSs could be attenuated with linguistic modification and the fairness, validity, and reliability of the assessment can improve (Hansen & Mislevy, 2004; Siegel, 2005). Since the COVID-19, remote learning and testing have become a part of everyday schooling for students. When the learning and assessment tools are in English only, LMSs may experience difficulties in benefiting educational resources and tools to engage in learning remotely. The development of translation technologies may help reduce these educational inequities by providing assessments in their home languages. For minimizing construct-irrelevant variance from language, the future landscape of assessments for LMSs should include multilingual testing materials (Frost et al., 2020).

Some researchers have highlighted the importance of setting an assessment framework as a foundation for linguistic modifications. For example, Siegel (2007) developed an equity framework for a science classroom test with five principles, which she used to evaluate and revise the test items for LMSs. The five principles are as follows: assessments should a) match the learning and instructional goals.; b) be linguistically and culturally accessible to LMSs.; c) be cognitively challenging.;

d) elicit student understanding.; and e) provide scaffolding for LMSs using sentence starters, graphic organizers, or additional prompts. Few studies address an assessment framework for increasing fairness to LMSs at the beginning stage of test development. Test developers can benefit from an assessment framework that guides what it means to be inclusive of LMSs before applying linguistic modifications.

Argument-Based Assessment

The third element of the author's assertion is that assessments should use an argument-based approach. An argument-based approach to data literacy assessment can clarify what is purported to be measured, the impact of the assessment results, and the complex nature of data literacy as a construct. Researchers in educational assessment have devised "principled approaches" to implement an argument-based approach to validity in a consistent and rigorous manner (Zieky, 2014; Ferrara et al., 2016). Principled approaches are recent designing frameworks to an assessment to secure validity based on the evidence from test results. Principled approaches have a shared goal to accumulate the evidence to support validity arguments that delineate intended score interpretations and uses throughout the ongoing design, development, and implementation process (Ferrara et al., 2016). To guide this process, principled approaches suggest test developers use concepts, procedures, and tools aligned to the design elements such as targeted construct, scoring, and measurement models. They require the use of arguments and theoretical grounds to support assessment decisions for each element (Ferrara et al., 2016). Evidence needs to be captured throughout the whole testing procedure by test developers and administrators. During the procedure, decisions for each element are subject to reviews, iterations, and refinement.

Principled approaches are distinguished from conventional test development processes in that they aim to accumulate evidence to support validity arguments by determining assessment targets based on interpretations and uses, creating a model of learning, and providing psychometric models and reporting scales. Conventional testing practice initiates test design primarily considering administrative constraints such as length, item type, and cost. After conventional testing practice formalizes design decisions in a blueprint, test implementation begins, including complex procedures of executing field testing, scaling, equating, test-form assembly, and score reporting. Although conventional practice can conduct careful and rigorous decision-making, principled approaches require that design decisions and rationales be established and documented in more steps and complexity (Ferrara et al., 2016). These decisions and rationales are especially important when defining assessment targets, designing, and developing tasks, and validating test scores.

Figure 1. Best practices for teaching and assessing data literacy

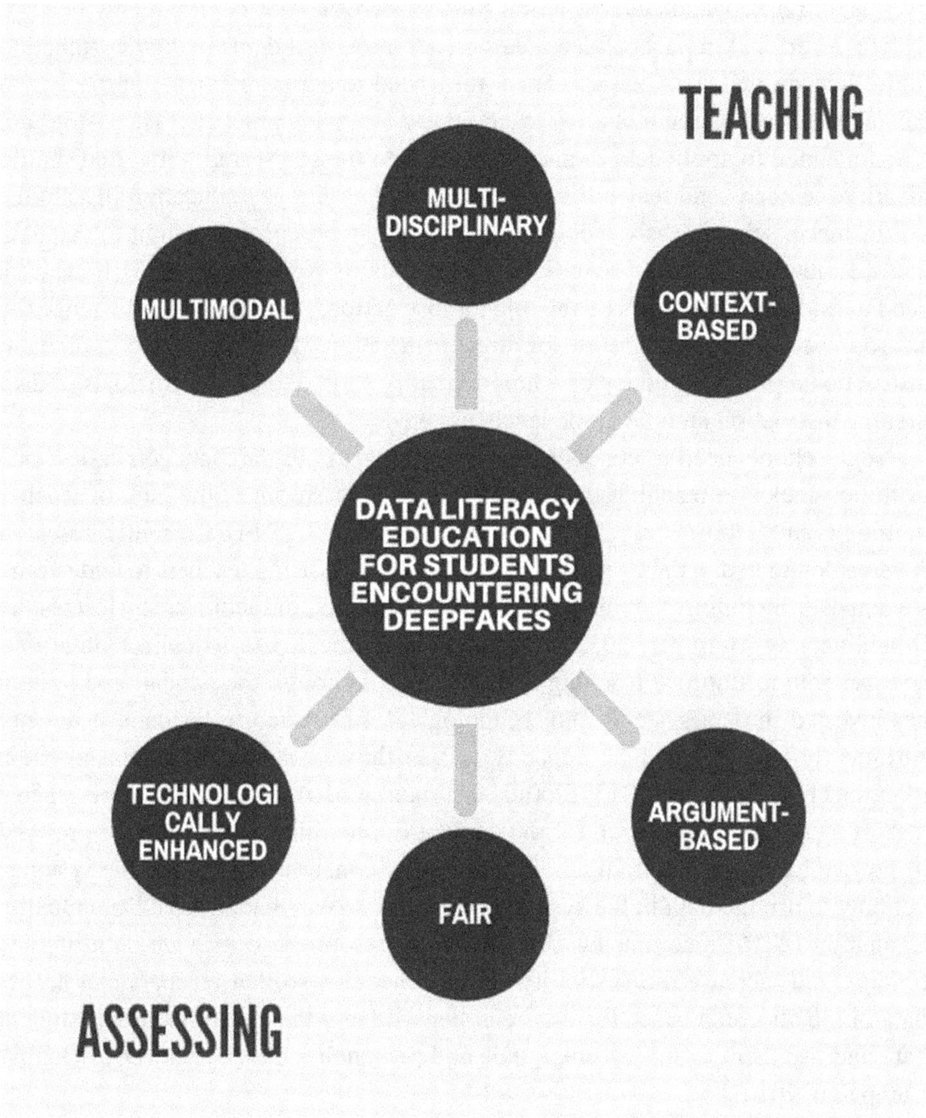

Implications

The chapter proposes the next steps to construct and implement teaching and assessing practices of data literacy. In the era of uncertainty with widespread deepfakes, data literacy education is essential for young learners than ever. Attaining data literacy can help students hamper the dissemination of mal-intended stories fueled by deepfakes

(Cotgreave, 2019). Furthermore, students can make informed decisions about personal lives and civic engagement based on information. School environments need to realize the critical impacts of deepfakes on adolescent students in their current and future lives in the 21st Century. Then, they need to adopt practical approaches to enhance their education including teaching and assessing practices. Three steps are recommended to apply data literacy education to the classroom. First, one should identify the needs and feasibility to implement data literacy education in schools. For instance, schools share a common challenge in attaining the right to use data that are relevant to students' lives (Data Use Standards Workgroup, 2015). Educators need to find out what data are available for instruction. Also, they need to gauge the affordability of a place and time for direct instruction. If they decide to implement instructional practices, educators should identify short and long-term goals of data literacy instruction and the grade levels targeted.

Next, schools need to conduct teacher training. As researchers contended, one of the obstacles to teaching data literacy in the classroom is the lack of teacher training (van 't Hooft et al., 2012; Gunter, 2007; Deahl, 2014). Currently, research is being conducted in the K-12 school context on supporting teachers to understand student data, including demographics, survey responses, and achievement test results (Mandinach & Gummer, 2012). Educators need the KSAs to collect, interpret, and use data to improve teaching and learning. Although the educational system has invested in data systems and technological infrastructure for data, it has not sufficiently prepared human capacity to use those systems (Mandinach, 2012; Mandinach & Gummer, 2013; Slotnik & Orland, 2010). Many states experience a lack of a common foundation for the content of data literacy training for pre- and in-service teachers. The training offered usually concerns how to use the systems, not how to use the data in the systems (Jimerson & Wayman, 2015). Data Quality Campaign (2016) recommends that states use resources to provide data literacy training and increase the flexibility of the schedules so that teachers can access data in the allocated time. Teachers can benefit from the ability to access student data and use them to set learning goals and personalize instruction (Data Quality Campaign, 2016).

Finally, educators and data literacy experts benefit from collaborating across fields and disciplines. Data literacy is a construct applicable and transferrable to multiple disciplines. Data are also represented as multimodal forms of representation in multidisciplinary areas. Data literacy instruction can involve not only educators and researchers, but also other stakeholders such as data gatherers, data visualization experts, and information scientists (Twidale et al., 2013). The collaboration among these stakeholders can enrich the content and goals of data literacy instruction. Deconstructing deepfakes requires knowledge and expertise from trained professionals. Working with persons and organizations that are tech-savvy can inform students of sophisticated data manipulation and evolving deepfake technology (Ridgway, 2019). Students can understand both causes and effects of deepfakes learning from diverse fields from not only data science to social media platforms and journalism (Levi, 2020).

The author also proposes three future steps to assess data literacy in school contexts. First, schools need to identify the purpose of an assessment. The purpose of the assessment can be formative, summative, or diagnostic depending on what information is most beneficial for students and educators. Currently, no data literacy assessment has been validated to inform students' growth over time for a formative purpose and directly target to recognize deepfakes. Some competencies related to data literacy, such as understanding graphs and inferring from data representations, are already tested within standardized assessments of content subjects (e.g., science, mathematics). However, these assessments are summative and, therefore, do not offer information that guides students' and teachers' actions to improve instruction and promote learning (Darling-Hammond et al., 2013). More research on the formative data literacy assessment targeting the abilities to discern deepfakes is needed to serve schools' needs. Next, test developers need to choose a methodological framework for designing and developing an assessment. For instance, researchers have developed principled approaches that view test development and validation as constructing and supporting arguments (Ferrara et al., 2016). These approaches accumulate evidence in an ongoing testing procedure by making substantiated and interwoven decisions about the design, development, and implementation. Using one of the principled approaches can facilitate the development of a new assessment and the demonstration of evidence that its intended interpretations and uses are valid. The methodological framework for testing can thread the design, development, and implementation process with arguments about the intended interpretations and uses of a new data literacy assessment.

Finally, test developers should validate an assessment. The findings from the literature review demonstrated that existing work about data literacy assessment does not provide validity evidence from various sources. The degree of validity increases when the accumulated evidence supports the proposed interpretations and uses of the test scores. Not every source of evidence is required to address, but each argument that expresses the test interpretations and uses needs support from evidence (AERA et al., 2014). Furthermore, no assessment for data literacy has been validated regarding its fairness to language minority students. When the assessment takes place in English, one needs to address how the test interpretations or uses are valid for the groups of test-takers whose everyday languages are not English (Siegel, 2007). The field of data literacy assessment needs further studies on the fair interpretations and uses of the data literacy assessment outcomes for LMSs.

In addition, studies on the effectiveness of multilingual testing materials would be fruitful to serve LMSs in the structures of remote learning and testing.

Figure 2. Practical approaches to implement teaching and assessing practices for data literacy

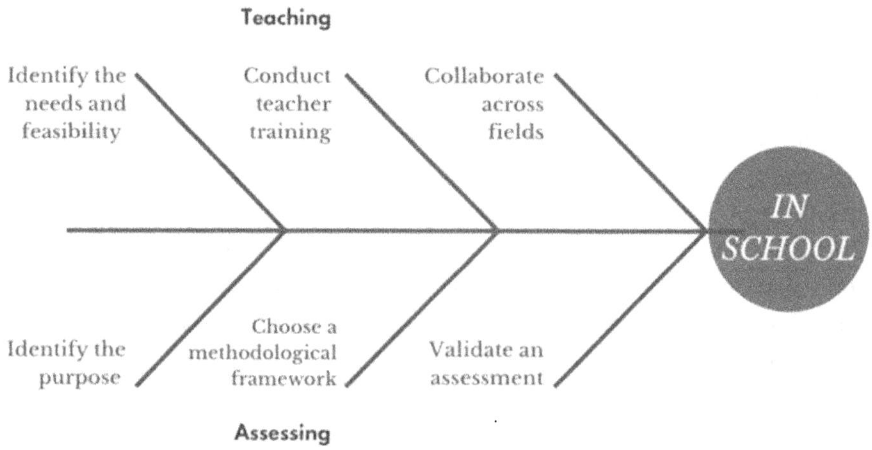

This chapter can enhance our understanding of current teaching and assessing practices of data literacy for adolescent learners. By synthesizing the literature, the author aggregates critical practices for teaching and assessing data literacy. Furthermore, the synthesis provides educators and researchers with future directions for data literacy instruction and assessment. These future steps for instruction and assessment can be a practical reference for educators to plan and implement a holistic instructional practice of data literacy where instruction and assessment support and guide one another. With the rise of deepfakes in online environments, the needs are increasing to implement feasible teaching practices and gather measurable outcomes for teenage students. A change in data literacy education can lead to a bigger impact on society as learners who are digital citizens will be able to critically examine and refute manipulated media and unreliable sources. Students need to be autonomous in detecting deepfakes and reducing the impacts on their lives. Data literacy education can engender self-sufficiency among not just students but also people around them (Cotgreave, 2019). Based on the awareness about deepfakes, young learners can help other people better understand and interpret data, inspiring them to attain data literacy. In this world where the credibility of every medium is questioned, the public needs knowledge, skills, critical thinking that can ensure unbiased decisions for what to believe or not. School environments can start raising the awareness of students by emphasizing the complicated social implications of deepfakes. In addition, students should learn what skills and tools they need to explore online worlds with dramatic transformation and unreliability.

In the digitized world with new technologies, students view, understand, and reason with data in multimodal forms that represent real-world phenomena. The ability to examine data and what is argued based on data is crucial in this age of overflowing information that is sometimes unsubstantiated. Researchers have made the case that students need to be data literate as 21st Century citizens (Hockly, 2020; Ercegovac, 2015; Vahey et al., 2006). This chapter can stimulate further discussions around how to support students to attain the necessary skills, viewpoints, and responsibilities to navigate this digital society. Pedagogical efforts to enhance teaching and assessing data literacy will help ensure that young learners are prepared with tools to investigate online worlds filled with deepfakes safely. The mutual goals of these efforts should be to support students in making informed decisions on how to react to manipulated visual data. Attaining this goal may elicit wider movements by students as digital citizens to alleviate repercussions from deepfakes in a wider realm. With data literacy education based on goal-oriented teaching and assessing practices, many students can attain data literacy to understand the power of deepfakes over our lives and take countermeasures to alleviate the impacts (Frost et al., 2020).

REFERENCES

Abedi, J. (1996). The interrater/test reliability system (ITRS). *Multivariate Behavioral Research, 31*(4), 409–417. doi:10.120715327906mbr3104_1 PMID:26788591

Abedi, J. (2006). Language Issues in Item Development. In S. M. Downing & T. M. Haladyna (Eds.), *Handbook of test development* (pp. 377–398). Lawrence Erlbaum.

Abedi, J., Leon, S., & Mirocha, J. (2003). *Impact of student language background on content-based performance: Analyses of extant data* (CSE Tech. Rep. No. 603). Los Angeles, CA: University of California, National Center for Research on Evaluation, Standards, and Student Testing.

American Educational Research Association, American Psychological Association, & National Council on Measurement in Education. (2014). *Standards for educational and psychological testing*. AERA.

Ben-Zvi, D., & Arcavi, A. (2001). Junior high school students' construction of global views of data and data representations. *Educational Studies in Mathematics, 45*(1/3), 35–65. doi:10.1023/A:1013809201228

Bransford, J. D., Brown, A. L., & Cocking, R. R. (2000). *How people learn: Brain, mind, experience, and school*. National Academy Press.

Brown, D. F., & Canniff, M. (2007). Designing curricular experiences that promote young adolescents' cognitive growth. *Middle School Journal*, *39*(1), 16–23. doi:10.1080/00940771.2007.11461609

Bryant, W. (2017). Developing a strategy for using technology-enhanced items in large-scale standardized tests. *Practical Assessment, Research & Evaluation*, *22*(1), 1–10.

Carmi, E., Yates, S. J., Lockley, E., & Pawluczuk, A. (2020). Data citizenship: Rethinking data literacy in the age of disinformation, misinformation, and malinformation. *Internet Policy Review*, *9*(2), 1–22. doi:10.14763/2020.2.1481

Carmichael, C., Callingham, R., Watson, J., & Hay, I. (2009). Factors influencing the development of middle school students' interest in statistical literacy. *Statistics Education Research Journal*, *8*(1), 62–81.

Chin, D. B., Blair, K. P., & Schwartz, D. L. (2016). Got game? A Choice-based learning assessment of data literacy and visualization skills. *Technology. Knowledge and Learning*, *21*(2), 195–210. doi:10.100710758-016-9279-7

Coiro, J. (2011). Predicting reading comprehension on the Internet: Contributions of offline reading skills, online reading skills, and prior knowledge. *Journal of Literacy Research*, *43*(4), 352–392. doi:10.1177/1086296X11421979

Common Core State Standards Initiative. (2010). *Mathematics standards* [PDF file]. Retrieved from http://www.corestandards.org/Math/

Common Core State Standards Initiative. (2010). *The Common Core State Standards for English language arts & literacy in history/social studies, science, and technical subjects* [PDF file]. Retrieved from http://www.corestandards.org/assets/CCSSI_ELA%20Standards.pdf

Cotgreave, A. (2019, September 6). Fighting the good fight: combating fake data with data literacy. *Information Age*. https://www.information-age.com/combating-fake-data-with-data-literacy-123485171/

Cronbach, L. J. (1987). Five perspectives of the validity argument. In H. Wainer & H. I. Braun (Eds.), *Test validity* (pp. 3–17). Lawrence Erlbaum.

Cutumisu, M., Chin, D. B., & Schwartz, D. L. (2019). A digital game-based assessment of middle-school and college students' choices to seek critical feedback and to revise. *British Journal of Educational Technology*, *50*(6), 2977–3003. doi:10.1111/bjet.12796

Cutumisu, M., Chin, D. B., & Schwartz, D. L. (2019). A digital game-based assessment of middle-school and college students' choices to seek critical feedback and to revise. *British Journal of Educational Technology*, *50*(6), 2977–3003. doi:10.1111/bjet.12796

Data Use Standards Workgroup. (2015). *Statewide Longitudinal Data System Data Use Standards: Knowledge, skills, and professional behaviors for effective data use* [PDF file]. Retrieved from https://eric.ed.gov/?id=ED595040

Deahl, E. S. (2014). *Better the data you know: Developing Youth data literacy in schools and informal learning environments* [Master's Thesis, the Massachusetts Institute of Technology]. doi:10.2139srn.2445621

Eccles, J. S., & Midgley, C. (1990). Changes in academic motivation and self-perception during early adolescence. In R. Montemayor (Ed.), *Early adolescence as a time of transition* (pp. 1–29). SAGE.

Educational Testing Service. (2002). *ETS standards for quality and fairness*. Author.

Educational Testing Service. (2014). *ETS standards for quality and fairness*. Author.

Emory, J. (2021, May 16). UW professor leads study on deepfakes in maps. *The Daily UW*. https://www.dailyuw.com/news/article_ac9506e0-b2e6-11eb-865c-5f7ef6613ff6.html

English, L. D., & Watson, J. (2018). Modelling with authentic data in sixth grade. *ZDM Mathematics Education*, *50*(1–2), 103–115. doi:10.100711858-017-0896-y

Ercegovac, Z. (2012). Digital image tagging: A case study with seventh grade students. *School Libraries Worldwide*, *18*(1), 97–110.

Ercegovac, Z. (2015). Data-driven society begins with data-savvy youth. *Bulletin of the Association for Information Science & Technology*, *42*(1), 42–48.

Erwin, R. W. Jr. (2015). Data literacy: Real-world learning through problem-solving with data sets. *American Secondary Education*, *43*(2), 18–26.

European Commission. (2018). *Tackling online disinformation: A European Approach* (Document 52018DC0236). Retrieved from https://eur-lex.europa.eu/legal-content/EN/TXT/?uri=CELEX:52018DC0236

Ewing, M., Packman, S., Hamen, C., & Thurber, A. C. (2010). Representing targets of measurement within Evidence-Centered Design. *Applied Measurement in Education*, *23*(4), 325–341. doi:10.1080/08957347.2010.510959

Fazio, L. (2020, February 18). Out-of-context photos are a powerful low-tech form of misinformation. *PBS.* https://www.pbs.org/newshour/science/out-of-context-photos-are-a-powerful-low-tech-form-of-misinformation

Ferrara, S., & Lai, E. (2016). Documentation to support test score interpretation and use. In S. Lane, M. R. Raymond, & T. M. Haladyna (Eds.), *Handbook of test development* (2nd ed., pp. 603–623). Routledge.

Ferrara, S., Lai, E., Reilly, A., & Nicols, P. D. (2016). Principled Approaches to assessment design, development, and implementation. In A. A. Rupp & J. P. Leighton (Eds.), *The handbook of cognition and assessment: Frameworks, methodologies, and applications* (pp. 41–74). Wiley. doi:10.1002/9781118956588.ch3

Fontichiaro, K., & Oehrli, J. A. (2016). Why data literacy matters. *Knowledge Quest, 44*(5), 21–27.

Forster, M., Bestelmeyer, S., Baez-Rodriguez, N., Berkowitz, A., Caplan, B., Esposito, R., Grace, E., & McGee, S. (2018). Data Jams. *Science Teacher (Normal, Ill.), 86*(2), 48–53.

Forsyth, S., & Liu, C. J. (2019). Designing tactile picture books: Critical making in libraries to broaden participation in STEM education and careers. Paper from AERA '19: Leveraging Education Research in a "Post-Truth" Era: Multimodal Narratives to Democratize Evidence, Toronto, Canada.

Forzani, E. (2018). How well can students evaluate online science information? Contributions of prior knowledge, gender, socioeconomic status, and offline reading ability. *Reading Research Quarterly, 53*(4), 385–390. doi:10.1002/rrq.218

Gordon, E., Elwood, S., & Mitchell, K. (2016). Critical spatial learning: Participatory mapping, spatial histories, and youth civic engagement. *Children's Geographies, 14*(5), 1–15. doi:10.1080/14733285.2015.1136736

Gould, R. (2017). Data literacy is statistical literacy. *Statistics Education Research Journal, 16*(1), 22–25.

Groth, R. (2015). Research commentary: Working at the boundaries of mathematics education and statistics education communities of practice. *Journal for Research in Mathematics Education, 46*(1), 4–16. doi:10.5951/jresematheduc.46.1.0004

Gunter, G. A. (2007). Building student data literacy: An essential critical-thinking skill for the 21st Century. *MultiMedia & Internet @ Schools, 14*(3), 24–28.

Haertel, E. H. (2006). Reliability. In R. L. Brennan (Ed.), *Educational measurement* (4th ed., pp. 65–110). Rowman & Littlefield.

Haigh, M., Haigh, T., & Matychak, T. (2019). Information literacy vs. Fake news: The sase of Ukraine. *Open Information Science, 3*(1), 154–165. doi:10.1515/opis-2019-0011

Hajam, M. A. (2017). Users' information literacy competencies: A study with reference to scholarly community of Kashmir University. *DESIDOC Journal of Library and Information Technology, 37*(3), 153–157. doi:10.14429/djlit.37.3.9739

Haladyna, T. M. (2006). Roles and importance of validity studies in test development. In S. M. Downing & T. M. Haladyna (Eds.), *Handbook of test development* (pp. 739–755). Lawrence Erlbaum.

Hansen, E. G., & Mislevy, R. J. (2004, April). *Toward a unified validity framework for ensuring access to assessments by individuals with disabilities and English language learners*. In The Annual Meeting of the National Council on Measurement in Education, San Diego, CA.

Hockly, N. (2020). Five things you always wanted to know about data literacy (but were too afraid to ask). *English Teaching Professional, 128*, 54.

Jiao, H. (2020). Module 10: Reliability and validity. In EDMS626: Instrumentation: Spring 2020. Academic Press.

Kane, M. (2006). Content-related validity evidence in test development. In S. M. Downing & T. M. Haladyna (Eds.), *Handbook of test development* (pp. 131–153). Lawrence Erlbaum.

Konold, C., & Higgins, T. L. (2003). Reasoning about data. In J. Kilpatrick, W. G. Martin, & D. Schifter (Eds.), *A research companion to principles and standards for school mathematics* (pp. 193–215). National Council of Teachers of Mathematics.

Leu, D., Kulikowich, J., Sedransk, N., Coiro, J., Cui, W., Forzani, E., Kennedy, C., & Maykel, C. (2014, April 4). *The ORCA Project: Designing technology-based assessments for online research, comprehension, and communication*. Paper presented at the American Educational Research Conference, Philadelphia, PA.

Leu, D. J., Kinzer, C. K., Coiro, J., Castek, J., & Henry, L. A. (2013). New literacies: A dual level theory of the changing nature of literacy, instruction, and assessment. In N. Unrau & D. Alvermann (Eds.), *Theoretical models and processes of reading* (6th ed., pp. 1150–1181). International Reading Association. doi:10.1598/0710.42

Leu, D. J., Kinzer, C. K., Coiro, J. L., & Cammack, D. W. (2004). Toward a theory of new literacies emerging from the Internet and other information and communication technologies. In R. B. Ruddell & N. J. Unrau (Eds.), *Theoretical models and processes of reading* (5th ed., pp. 1570–1613). International Reading Association.

Lim, V., Deahl, E., Rubel, L., & Williams, S. (2014). Local Lotto: Mathematics and mobile technology to study the lottery. In D. Polly (Ed.), *Cases on technology integration in mathematics education* (pp. 43–67). IGI Global.

Luecht, R. M. (2013). Assessment Engineering task model maps, task models and templates as a new way to develop and implement test specification. *Journal of Applied Testing Technology*, *14*(4), 1–38. http://www.jattjournal.com/index.php/atp/article/view/45254

Luecht, R. M. (2013). Assessment Engineering task model maps, task models and templates as a new way to develop and implement test specification. *Journal of Applied Testing Technology*, *14*(4), 1–38. http://www.jattjournal.com/index.php/atp/article/view/45254

Markham, A. N. (2020). Taking data literacy to the streets: Critical pedagogy in the public sphere. *Qualitative Inquiry*, *26*(2), 227–237. doi:10.1177/1077800419859024

Martiniello, M. (2008). Language and the performance of English-language learners in math word problems. *Harvard Educational Review*, *78*(2), 333–368. doi:10.17763/haer.78.2.70783570r1111t32

Messick, S. (1995). The interplay of evidence and consequences in the validation of performance assessments. *Educational Researcher*, *23*(2), 13–23. doi:10.3102/0013189X023002013

Mislevy, R. J. (2013). Evidence-Centered Design for simulation-based assessment. *Military Medicine*, *178*(10), 107–114. doi:10.7205/MILMED-D-13-00213 PMID:24084311

Mislevy, R. J., Almond, R. G., & Lukas, J. F. (2003). A brief introduction to evidence-centered design. *ETS Research Report Series*, *2003*(1), i–29. doi:10.1002/j.2333-8504.2003.tb01908.x

Nichols, P. D., Kobrin, J. L., Lai, E., & Koepfler, J. (2016). The role of theories of learning and cognition in assessment design and development. In A. Rupp & J. P. Leighton (Eds.), *The handbook of cognition and assessment* (pp. 13–40). Wiley & Sons. doi:10.1002/9781118956588.ch2

Oceans of Data Institute. (2015). *Building global interest in data literacy: A dialogue*. Educational Development Center. Retrieved from oceansofdata.org/ourwork/building-global-interest-data-literacy-dialogue-workshop-report

Parshall, C. G., Harmes, J. C., Davey, T., & Pashley, P. (2010). Innovative items for computerized testing. In W. J. van der Linden & C. A. W. Glas (Eds.), *Computerized adaptive testing: Theory and practice* (2nd ed.). Kluwer Academic Publishers.

Pelletier, K., Brown, M., Christopher, B., McCormack, M., Reeves, J., Arbino, N., Bozkurt, A., Crawford, S., Czerniewicz, L., Gibson, R., Linder, K., Mason, J., & Mondelli, V. (2021). *2021 EDUCAUSE Horizon Report: Teaching and Learning Edition*. EDUCAUSE. Retrieved from https://library.educause.edu/-/media/files/library/2021/4/2021hrteachinglearning.pdf?#page=4&la=en&hash=64CACBDA4DAC0F6158951941AD2A8952A9A81100

Philip, T. M., Olivares-Pasillas, M. C., & Rocha, J. (2016). Becoming racially literate about data and data-literate about race: Data visualizations in the classroom as a site of racial-ideological micro-contestations. *Cognition and Instruction, 34*(4), 361–388. doi:10.1080/07370008.2016.1210418

Quellmalz, E. S., & Kozma, R. (2003). Designing assessments of learning with technology. *Assessment in Education: Principles, Policy & Practice, 10*(3), 389–407. doi:10.1080/0969594032000148208

Ridgway, J. (2019, December). Data literacy. *International Statistical Literacy Project Newsletter, 1*(11), 10–13.

Ridsdale, C., Rothwell, J., Smit, M., Ali-Hassan, H., Bliemel, M., Irvine, D., Kelley, D., Matwin, S., & Wuetherick, B. (2016). *Strategies and best practices for data literacy education: Knowledge synthesis report*. Dalhousie University.

Schüler-Meyer, A., Prediger, S., Kuzu, T., Wessel, L., & Redder, A. (2019). Is formal language proficiency in the home language required to profit from a bilingual teaching intervention in mathematics? A mixed methods study on fostering multilingual students' conceptual understanding. *International Journal of Science and Mathematics Education, 17*(2), 317–339. doi:10.100710763-017-9857-8

Schwartz, D. L., & Arena, D. (2013). *Measuring what matters most: Choice-based assessments for the digital age*. MIT Press. doi:10.7551/mitpress/9430.001.0001

Seroff, J. (2017). Using data in the research process. In K. Fontichiaro, J. A. Oehrli, & A. Lennex (Eds.), *Creating data literate students*. Michigan Publishing.

Shaughnessy, J. M., Garfield, J., & Greer, B. (1996). Data handling. In A. J. Bishop, K. Clements, C. Keitel, J. Kilpatrick, & C. Laborde (Eds.), *International handbook of mathematics education* (pp. 205–237). Kluwer. doi:10.1007/978-94-009-1465-0_8

Shreiner, T. L. (2019). Students' use of data visualizations in historical reasoning: A think-aloud investigation with elementary, middle, and high school students. *Journal of Social Studies Research, 43*(4), 389–404. doi:10.1016/j.jssr.2018.11.001

Siegel, M. A. (2005). *Assessing English learners in middle school science.* Paper presented at the annual meeting of the American Educational Research Association, Montreal, Canada.

Siegel, M. A. (2007). Striving for equitable classroom assessments for linguistic minorities: Strategies for and effects of revising life science items. *Journal of Research in Science Teaching, 44*(6), 864–881. doi:10.1002/tea.20176

Solano-Flores, G., & Trumbull, E. (2003). Examining language in context: The need for new research and practice paradigms in the testing of English language learners. *Educational Researcher, 32*(2), 3–13. doi:10.3102/0013189X032002003

Spencer, T., & Hertzog, L. (2014). Community Explorers. *Young Children, 69*(5), 66–71.

Turton, W., & Martin, A. (2020, January 5). How deepfakes make disinformation more real than ever. *Bloomberg.* https://www.bloomberg.com/news/articles/2020-01-06/how-deepfakes-make-disinformation-more-real-than-ever-quicktake

Twidale, M. B., Blake, C., & Gant, J. (2013). Towards a Data Literate Citizenry. In Proceedings of iConference 2013 (pp. 247–257). doi:10.9776/13189

Ünsal, Z., Jakobson, B., Molander, B.-O., & Wickman, P.-O. (2018). Language Use in a Multilingual Class: A Study of the Relation Between Bilingual Students' Languages and Their Meaning-Making in Science. *Research in Science Education, 48*(5), 1027–1048. doi:10.100711165-016-9597-8

Vahey, P., Rafanan, K., Patton, C., Swan, K., Hooft, M., Kratcoski, A., & Stanford, T. (2012). A cross-disciplinary approach to teaching data literacy and proportionality. *Educational Studies in Mathematics, 81*(2), 179–205. doi:10.100710649-012-9392-z

van 't Hooft, M., Swan, K., Cook, D., Stanford, T., Vahey, P., Kratcoski, A., Rafanan, K., & Yarnall, L. (2012). A cross-curricular approach to the development of data literacy in the middle grades: The Thinking with Data Project. *Middle Grades Research Journal, 7*(3), 19–33.

Watson, J. M., & English, L. D. (2015). Introducing the practice of statistics: Are we environmentally friendly? *Mathematics Education Research Journal*, *27*(4), 585–613. doi:10.100713394-015-0153-z

Webber, H., Nelson, S. J., Weatherbee, R., Zoellick, B., & Schauffler, M. (2014). The graph choice chart. *Science Teacher (Normal, Ill.)*, *81*(8), 37–43. doi:10.2505/4/tst14_081_08_37

Wolff, A., Gooch, D., Cavero Montaner, J. J., Rashid, U., & Kortuem, G. (2016). Creating an understanding of data literacy for a data-driven society. *The Journal of Community Informatics*, *12*(3), 9–26. doi:10.15353/joci.v12i3.3275

Zalles, D. (2005). *Designs for assessing foundational data literacy*. Retrieved from http://serc.carleton.edu/files/NAGTWorkshops/assess/ZallesEssay3.pdf

Zieky, M. J. (2006). Fairness review in assessment. In S. M. Downing & T. M. Haladyna (Eds.), *Handbook of test development* (pp. 359–376). Lawrence Erlbaum.

Zieky, M. J. (2014). An introduction to the use of evidence-centered design in test development. *Psicologia dell'Educazione*, *20*(2), 79–87. doi:10.1016/j.pse.2014.11.003

Zoellick, B., Schauffler, M., Flubacher, M., Weatherbee, R., & Webber, H. (2016, April). *Data Literacy: Assessing Student Understanding of Variability in Data.* Paper presented at the Annual Meeting of the National Association for Research in Science Teaching, Baltimore, MD.

ADDITIONAL READING

Abedi, J. (2004). The No Child Left Behind Act and English language learners: Assessment and accountability issues. *Educational Researcher*, *33*(1), 4–14. doi:10.3102/0013189X033001004

Abedi, J., Lord, C., Hofstetter, C., & Baker, E. (2000). Impact of accommodation strategies on English language learners' test performance. *Educational Measurement: Issues and Practice*, *19*(3), 16–26. doi:10.1111/j.1745-3992.2000.tb00034.x

Beane, J. A. (1997). *Curriculum integration: Designing the core of a democratic education*. Teachers College Press.

Biehler, R. (1993). Software tools and mathematics education: The case of statistics. In C. Keitel & K. Ruthven (Eds.), *Learning from computers: Mathematics education and technology* (pp. 68–100). Springer. doi:10.1007/978-3-642-78542-9_4

Boyle, A., & Hutchinson, D. (2009). Sophisticated tasks in e-assessment: What are they and what are their benefits? *Assessment & Evaluation in Higher Education*, *34*(3), 305–319. doi:10.1080/02602930801956034

Brown, N. J. S., & Wilson, M. (2011). A model of cognition: The missing cornerstone of assessment. *Educational Psychology Review*, *23*(2), 221–234. doi:10.100710648-011-9161-z

Cortina, J. M. (1993). What is coefficient alpha? An examination of theory and applications. *The Journal of Applied Psychology*, *78*(1), 98–104. doi:10.1037/0021-9010.78.1.98

Crooks, T. J., Kane, M. T., & Cohen, A. S. (1996). Threats to valid use of assessments. *Assessment in Education: Principles, Policy & Practice*, *3*(3), 265–285. doi:10.1080/0969594960030302

KEY TERMS AND DEFINITIONS

Competency: A cluster of KSAs that are closely related to each other and induce effective performance for a given task.

Construct: A latent variable that cannot be directly observed or measured (i.e., factor).

Deepfakes: An image synthesis technique based on artificial intelligence used to combine manipulated images and videos onto original images or videos, of which outcomes are fake images and videos where persons perform an action or speech that never occurred.

Dis-Information: False information that is intentionally created to harm a person, social group, or country.

Fairness: The degree of how the interpretation or use of an assessment is not affected by characteristics of test-takers that are irrelevant to the construct.

Knowledge, Skills, and Abilities (KSAs): Bodies of information, proficiencies, and capacity that one needs to have to perform a job or task.

Language Minority Students (LMSs): Students who speak everyday languages (e.g., at home or community) other than the dominant language (English in the U.S.).

Reliability: The degree of consistency of the test scores when its parallel forms are tested on different occasions and scored by different raters (i.e., measurement precision).

Validation: The process of gathering the evidence to support the arguments that the test score interpretation or use is valid (i.e., collecting validity evidence) (Haladyna, 2006).

Validity: The degree of how an assessment measures what it intends to measure.

Chapter 6
Deepfake and Digital Citizenship:
A Long-Term Protection Method for Children and Youth

Seda Gökçe Turan
Bahcesehir University, Turkey

ABSTRACT

Artificial intelligence technologies are beneficial for individuals' lives, but those technologies are also sources of mass and chaos. Due to hyper-realistic videos based on artificial intelligence, deepfakes have effects on the public and individuals in terms of manipulation. Researchers try to warn the public and individuals about the threats and harms of these technologies. Moreover, users cannot distinguish whether it is real and fake. As it is known, children and youths are vulnerable to the dark side of technology. So, for risks and harms of technology, digital citizenship is advised as a protection method. In this chapter, the long-term effects of digital citizenship in terms of protecting children and youths from the dangers and threats of deepfakes will be discussed in depth.

INTRODUCTİON

To distinguish between real and "fake" media becomes more complex through contemporary technologies (Westerlund, 2019; Anderson, 2018). Fake news and disinformation are primarily characterized by manipulating news, individuals, and the public. However, through novel technologies, some applications such as

DOI: 10.4018/978-1-7998-6474-5.ch006

"deepfake" become more pervasive and visible. Deepfake is defined as audiovisual manipulating applications based on artificial intelligence (AI) (Yadlin-Segal & Oppnheim, 2020) to fool or deceive someone by saying or doing things that never happened (Westerlund, 2019). Moreover, deepfake can offer opportunities to manipulators or abusers to blur the detection of information, whether it is accurate or fake (Yadlin- Segal & Oppenheim, 2020; Chesney & Citron, 2019). Therefore, it sounds so troubling for parents, educators, and citizens, recalling a nightmare (Chesney & Citron, 2019). Until the deepfake technology, researchers discussed the dangers of fake news in the context of public discourse, human society, and democracy (Quayyum, Quadir, Janjua & Sher, 2019; Westerlund, 2019). As known, fake news is content that aims to deceive the public, and it can be spread so fast on social media (Aldwairi & Alwahedi, 2018; Figueira & Oliveira, 2017). According to researchers, deepfake technologies relate to disinformation, misinformation, manipulation, exploitation, and polarization, which are believed to prevent digital citizenship competencies (Yadlin- Segal & Oppenheim, 2020; Hintz et al., 2017). Considering this information, all components of digital citizenship and their relationship with deepfake will be discussed in depth. The chapter is organized as follows. After the introduction, the chapter explains the technology of deepfakes, the potential benefits of deepfake technology, the threats of deepfakes to children and youths, features of digital citizenship competencies, protection role of digital citizenship to threats of deepfakes. Finally, the chapter concludes with solutions, recommendations, and suggestions for future studies.

BACKGROUND

Deepfakes Technology

Today, in the 21st century, we live in the era called the "post-truth" era. The most prominent characteristic of the post-truth era is manipulating public opinion through digital disinformation and fake news (Quayyum et al., 2019; Zannettou, Sirivianos, Blackburn, and Kourtellis, 2019; Anderson, 2018). However, with the deepfakes, besides spreading disinformation at social media and digital environments, it can be possible to produce hyper-realistic videos that leave little or no trace of manipulation by using face swaps (Chawla, 2019; Thies, Zollhofer, Stamminger, Theobalt, and Niesner, 2018). By producing and merging, combining, and replacing deepfakes can fool or manipulate users in digital environments (Maras & Alexandrou, 2018).

With novel technologies, some software for crafting high-quality and realistic deepfake videos are available as open-source, and any users can have a chance to reach that software. The critical point is that anyone who uses a computer with little technical skills can produce or fabricate those fake videos produced through deepfake (Westerlund, 2019). Children and youths do not have enough ability to distinguish what is fake or accurate, and they can be an easy target for manipulators or cyber-harassment perpetrators as researchers (Dobber, Metoui, Trilling, Helberger, and Vreese, 2020; Maras & Alexandrou, 2019) noted that deepfakes would be used for revenge bullying, terrorist propaganda, political manipulations, and fake news. As said before, in addition to manipulations through deepfake, users can produce videos in which people are saying and doing things that never happened. Deepfakes are technologies based on neural networks of deep learning that analyze large sets of data samples to replicate patterns of peoples' facial and vocal expressions (Chesney & Citron, 2019; Westerlund, 2019). Unfortunately, when spreading fake news and disinformation quickly, checking or combating deepfake videos is not easy and becomes more complex (De Kreersmaecker & Roets, 2017). Because deepfake technologies use AI to trace the actual digital footprint of users and swap it with fake ones, it is harder to correct records and fight with deepfake videos. Digital media users, individuals, and the public think that those videos are real (Westerlund, 2019). Additionally, more and more individuals have begun to obtain information and be involved in social media, making them a target for deepfake videos (Chesney & Citron, 2019). To discuss deepfake technologies in-depth, we should define the benefits and treads them.

Benefits and Threats of Deepfakes:

Deepfake technologies have numerous threads and risks for children and youths. However, those technologies also have some benefits for them.

In terms of education and scientific or academic meetings, deepfake technologies allow presenters to break language barriers. Pupils all around the world can benefit, watch, and follow those meetings in their original language. By altering facial and mouth movements to improve eye contact, participants feel that the presenter is a native speaker. This feeling would increase the satisfaction and learning of pupils (Westerlund, 2019). In the education context, for world knowledge and personal growth of pupils, deepfake can be used. Deepfake technologies enable pupils to actively engage in museums and galleries worldwide, which is vital for their cultural and intellectual development (Kwok & Sharon, 2020). For educational purposes, deepfake technologies can be used for history lessons to fabricate a historical figure. By doing this, pupils' learning and memorizing historical figures would improve (Chesney & Citron, 2019). Moreover, among youths, some deepfake hobbyists and producers use deepfake as online humor or solving an intellectual puzzle which allows them a bit of fun and intellectual practice. Some youths try to work deepfake related jobs in entertainment, television, or music-related sectors (Westerlund, 2019).

The other arguments about the benefits of deepfake technology are polemic. First, deepfake technology offers multiplayer games and virtual chats with increased telepresence through natural-sounding or digital doubles. According to researchers, those telepresence users' human relationships and online interactions become better and increased (Westerlund, 2019). However, the other researchers argue that although online communication allows youths to develop self-esteem, perceive more social support, and experiment with self-identity, they also target social isolation, depression, and cyber-bullying (Best, Manktelow & Taylor, 2014). The second benefit of deepfake technology is defined in medical fields. Deepfake technology can be used to make more accessible to the grieving process by bringing together individuals with the lost ones (Carew,2020; Jones, 2020; Westerlund, 2019). However, experts noted that individuals should get used to living without lost one for the grieving process. When they see their lost ones again through deepfake technologies, it negatively impacts the grieving process (Green, Karafa & Wilson, 2020).

Deepfake technologies are also used for curing people who have Alzheimer's. Researchers noted that enabling Alzheimer's patients to meet with the people from their past would positively affect their Alzheimer's treatment (Westerlund, 2019). In addition, not only for neurological diseases but also for other diseases, deepfake technologies can be used. For example, individuals who lost their voice to disease or accident can give a speech or join meetings with deepfake technologies (Chesney & Citron, 2019).

As harms of deepfake technologies, the most important ones are breaking citizens' trust toward information by authorities and increasing cyber-security issues for individuals and organizations (Westerlund, 2019). Deepfake videos could easily manipulate social media users and the public's opinions about everything in society. Especially before elections, most governments such as the US warn and inform their citizens about deepfake videos and other software to spread fake and false information. However, without digital citizenship competencies, users and the public are vulnerable to deepfake videos and other fake news. With the deepfake videos, individuals are so open to conspiracy theories and exaggeration. It can damage and give harms the trust of authorities. Therefore, individuals can confuse what is real and what is fake. Because of those mistrust, individuals will perceive and doubt that everything in digital environments and real-life is deception (Westerlund, 2019).

Although deepfake technologies are deemed so harmful and used for political purposes, they could be used to cause harm to organizations. With deepfake technologies, it is simple to present or portray some organizations as racist, misogynistic, or spread rumors about those organizations. As a result, clients who use those organizations can feel as if they are committing a crime. This is because all of them are so harmful to the reputation of those organizations. The same is valid for individuals also. About scientists or politicians, deepfake video producers can quickly spread fake and false charges (Westerlund, 2019). For individuals also there is another risk about revenge porn which is so pervasive among deepfake producers. Due to celebrities, politicians have videos and photographs on the Internet, and deepfake producers can easily reach and collect videos and photographs required for the AI deepfake system. With those photographs or videos, deepfake producers can fabricate porn videos and spread them in digital environments. Moreover, those videos allow perpetrators to blackmail, intimidation, and sabotage (Chesney & Citron,2019).

Although deepfakes have some benefits, especially in the movie and music sector, they are generally a significant threat to society as they manipulate individuals and public opinion (Lin, 2019; Wagner & Blewer, 2019).

For fighting against deepfake technology, some solutions are advised by researchers, such as criminal sanctions and regulations, collective actions by society, developing anti-deepfake technology. However, digital citizenship education is seemed the most potent combat tool because of the long-lasting and long-term effect against deepfake and the dark side of other technologies.

Dıgıtal Cıtızenshıp

With the rise of the Internet and pervasive usage of technological devices, educators and policymakers are sensitive about protecting children and youths from the harms and risks of the Internet and digital devices (Walters, Gee, and Mohammed, 2019; Mossberger, Tolbert, and McNeal,2008). According to researchers (Yue, Nekmat, and Beta,2019), digital citizenship skills and competence enable and encourage children and youths aware of the risks of the cyber world while benefiting from it. However, when we focus only on the risks (cyberbullying, hate speech, fake news, etc.) in the cyber world, we deprive not only children and youths but also adults from this world which facilitates individuals' daily lives, have fun, easily communicate with people in different countries and follow and learn what is going on in the world. However, we should be aware that in this digital world, children and youths are at risk about fake news and manipulator artificial intelligence technologies such as deepfake (Anderson, 2018).

Internet and technological devices change society in personal, educational, and professional domains. With this rapid change, digital citizenship is perceived as a coping and adaptation strategy at this fast-changing digital society's challenges, such as Deepfake. As a protection method, digital citizenship, which is inclusive and extensive skills to survive and benefit from the digital environment, is advised (Hintz et al., 2017). Besides protection from the dark sides of the Internet and digital technologies and teaching appropriate behaviors in digital environments, digital citizenship competencies seem valuable and beneficial (Xu et al., 2019; Ribble & Miller, 2013).

Generally, digital citizenship is defined with different components which are so vital not only for children and youths' online behaviors and provide protection for cyber-harassment, fake news, and media manipulation. However, unfortunately, with Deepfake, all those cyber-harassment and manipulation could be possible (Whyte, 2020; Wojewidka, 2020; Vaccari & Chadwick, 2020; Hasan & Salah, 2019, Anderson, 2018). Therefore, we should define and portray digital citizenship skills in depth to improve children and youths' digital citizenship competencies. ***For example,*** Jones and Mitchell (2016) addressed digital citizenship in two-part: respectful behavior online and online civic engagement. Although the concept of digital citizenship encapsulated ethical issues about technology usage (Xu et al., 2019); it is primarily defined as the ability to navigate, exist, and make sense of digital society which is accepted as a survive tool in digital society both for work and leisure time (Emejulu & McGregor, 2019; Gleason & Gillern, 2018; Kim & Choi, 2018; Vromen, 2017).

Although there are different subtitles, digital citizenship mainly frames with concepts of responsibility, rights, safety, and security (Ribble and Bailey, 2011; cited in Jones & Mitchell, 2016: 2064). Digital citizenship is examined under topics as follows: Internet safety, privacy and security, relationships and communication, cyberbullying, digital footprints, reputation, self-image and identity, information literacy, and creative credit and copyright (Jones & Mitchell, 2016). These components are described mainly under three titles: 1) Respect Yourself/Respect Others; 2) Educate Yourself/Connect with Others; 3) Protect Yourself/ Protect Others (Ribble & Miller, 2013). These titles are separated subtitles as; digital access, digital commerce, digital communication, digital literacy, digital etiquette, digital law, digital rights and responsibilities, digital health and wellness, and digital security (self-protection) (Kim & Choi, 2018).

In the digital era, modern society needs not only to consume but also to produce and creating messages (Hobbs, 2010). For this reason, Hobbs (2010) stated the concept of "digital citizenship." She claimed that USA citizens should be educated about multi-media, but it should be valid for whole people worldwide. With this multi-media education, individuals gain the skills to create media messages by using language, visual design, and audio effects. In particular, media and digital media literacy education in curriculum K12 provide equal opportunities in digital media for pupils (Hobbs, 2010). Generally, digital citizenship competencies focus on three main subjects. First, as most of the findings show, digital citizenship competencies protect cyberbullying and online trolling and cyberbullying; make pupils show respectful behaviors in digital platforms; and teach how to protect the privacy and intellectual property. Second, digital citizenship competencies support pupils in becoming digitally informed and actively engaging in digital communication and discussion with others. Lastly, students with high digital citizenship skills could have a chance to actively engage in political or government-related issues, which are also a necessity for both offline and online citizenship (Flynn, Nyhan, and Reifler, 2017; Frenda, Knowles, Saletan, and Loftus, 2013).

Although the researchers primarily argued about the necessity of digital citizenship, the others believe that radical citizenship is characterized by critically analyzing the consequences of technologies in everyday Life and collectively constructing alternative and emancipatory technologies. Researchers noted that radical digital citizenship reduces digital media literacy, which is vital for Internet and digital world safety. Mainly, radical digital citizenship is a political practice to evaluate and understand technology penetration in individuals' lives (Emejulu & McGregor, 2019). For adolescences, as a characteristic of the developmental stage, political discussions are desirable. So, when we try to teach and improve digital citizenship skills, we should not underestimate the impact of radical digital citizenship. Of course, adolescence has rights to express their opinion about politics. However, if they could not recognize fake news or crosscheck what they read in digital environments, they would be fooled easily by online extremism, hate speeches, or gender discrimination. Under the umbrella of digital citizenship, civic engagement could cover the political presentation, which seems like a risk for radical digital citizenship. However, digital citizenship education should cover volunteer works, supporting charities, and sharing hobbies and skills (Emejulu & McGregor, 2019; Jones & Mitchell, 2016).

Digital citizenship also takes the attention of researchers in terms of education. Most researchers believe that to improve children and youths' digital citizenship skills; education is one of the best tools. Internet safety education or computer education is beneficial for awareness about risks and harms of digital environments, but outstanding education for children and youths' integration to the digital world education would be appropriate for characteristics of development and their behaviors (Jones & Mitchell, 2016; Ohler, 2011). Not only teaching children and youths about technology would not be enough. The main aim of education for 21st century would be to make children and youth participate in the digital world with higher digital citizenship competencies. Moreover, digital citizenship education pupils' online civic engagements have some outcomes for their offline civic engagement (Ghosn-Chelala, 2019; Jones & Mitchell, 2016).

Researchers (Choi et al, 2018) also consider teachers' digital citizenship competences in terms of individuals' thinking, skills, and behaviors relevant to Internet usage in the context of education. Furthermore, researchers and policy makers, educational community members believe that classroom teachers should be responsible, informed, and active digital citizens, which are the primary goal of education (Choi et al., 2018).

When we look at the literature and educators', policy makers' definitions and discussions about digital citizenship, we could see that society and offline citizenship concepts were underlined (Hintz et al., 2017; Jones & Mitchell, 2016; Ribble& Bailey, 2011). Moreover, digital citizenship impacts individuals' empowering and democratizing qualifications (Hintz et al., 2017). However, born and grown up in the digital age and with technological devices is not enough for digital competence needed for 21st century citizenship skills to effectively engage with the digital world (Alvermann & Sanders, 2019). For engagement in digital environments, protect themselves from harms and risks of technology and benefit from it, we should teach them digital citizenship skills.

MAIN FOCUS OF THE CHAPTER

Issues, Controversies, Problems

The twenty-first century is characterized by post-truth, the evolution of technological devices, and their effects on society. Although those technologies and rapid development in digital environments are beneficial for individuals, they also negatively affect individuals and society (Schuelke-Leech, 2018). Unlike traditional fake news or false information, deepfake technologies are hard to track down (Westerlund, 2019) and mostly go viral on social media (Fletcher,2018). Due to the rise of social media, people get their information from social media primarily, and they are involved in social media nearly all-day (Chesney & Citron, 2019). Fake news and disinformation are not new issues for both social media users and cyber-perpetrators. However, deepfake technologies are different from classical fake news and fraud tactics due to their combination of quality, hyper-realistic characteristics regarding voice and faces, and resistance to detection (Chesney & Citron, 2019). While fake news and false information primarily include "an information" and written, deepfake technologies are audiovisual. Therefore, Deepfake technologies with hyper-realistic features are succeeded in fooling individuals.

Not only deepfake technologies but also deepfake producers should be analyzed. Deepfake producers are generally defined with similar characteristics to cyber-bullies. They are paid, or unpaid trolls and have some personal issues. There are some motivations for producing deepfake videos also. They have malicious intent to hurt other people, and they are jealous of other individuals' lives on social media or the real world. There are paid professionals to manipulate public opinion about specific topics or organizations. Some manipulators produce deepfake videos only for fun and amusement (MacKenzie & Bhatt, 2020; Zannettou et al., 2019). However, for people who have malicious intent, terrorists, or paid trolls deepfake would be very dangerous, especially some videos related to holly of peoples such as religion, patriotism, race, or ethnicity. Those deepfake videos would have a powerful potential for incitement or extremism (Chesney & Citron, 2019). For insurgents or terrorist groups, deepfake technologies create chaos in society (Brown, 2020; Temir, 2020). For example, terrorist organizations such as ISIS (Islamic State) could create a video and portrayed US soldiers as attracting civilians or bombing a mosque which could be a reason for the chaos in Islamic countries and Muslims (Chesney & Citron, 2019).

Not only for Islamic countries or Muslims but also for blacks, deepfakes could be very dangerous. Sometimes there are some Tweets or online posts about white polices tortures to blacks. Some of them are not real. However, next time, instead of posts or Tweets, perpetrators produce deepfake videos that portrayed white police torturing blacks and spread social media, call for violent protests on the streets (Chesney & Citron, 2019). In terms of youths, those deepfake technology is so important. As developmental characteristics, youths tend to deal with politics or social events. Because of their curiosity and not enough information about politics, they can be an easy target to be manipulated. Not only holy concepts or politics, but deepfake technologies can also break the ethical rules of the digital world. Deepfake video producers mostly ignore ethical issues and personal privacy. Children and youths who watch o produce those videos can be easily convinced about those videos and underestimated privacy issues. To survive in the digital world and social media, digital citizenship competence offers an opportunity to children and youths to think about ethical issues (Vromen, 2017). When considering subtitles of digital citizenship skills, it is evident that pupils cannot be an easy target for deepfake producers with effective digital citizenship education.

Moreover, digital citizenship is generally characterized by users' actions. Therefore, Digital platform users are considered active rather than passive individuals (Hintz et al., 2017). For this reason, effective digital citizenship education is aimed at that when pupils or kids become deepfake producers or makers, and they will be aware of their ethical responsibilities.

The harms and threads about deepfake videos are primarily focused on ethical issues and manipulation. Those manipulations not only fool individuals but also give harms the trust of authorities. As a result of this mistrust, individuals can avoid anything even it is true. So, it is not only "simple" manipulation or fake news; it is something more dangerous about society and individuals. In terms of children and youths, they are an easy target for those manipulations, of course, deepfake technologies called "nightmare."

SOLUTIONS AND RECOMMENDATIONS

As mentioned before, deepfake videos have little trace about manipulation or altering. It seems there are some technologies to detect deepfake videos (Li, Lang, Chen, Mao, He, Wang, Xue, and Lu, 2020). However, for compelling combat deepfake videos, there is a need to increase public awareness about the harms and risks of AI (Westerlund, 2019). Especially for pupils, in education programs, courses toward critical thinking and digital literacy skills should teach. Those courses would help pupils improve their competencies to detect fake news and deepfake (Kong, 2014).

Although some solutions are discussed among researchers, some are unethical, such as banning technology through digital law legislation. For voluntary actions and developing anti-deepfake technologies, pupils and teachers, scientists, academicians, education politicians, and adults and older people should take educational courses about digital citizenship. At schools, we should strengthen pupils' digital citizenship competencies primarily related to digital security.

One of the subtitles of digital citizenship skills is digital security. Under the digital citizenship competence umbrella at schools, teachers should teach digital security to pupils in depth. Of course, they should teach all digital citizenship competencies such as digital access, digital literacy, digital etiquette, digital law, digital health, digital responsibilities and rights, digital communication, and digital commerce. However, digital security topics should teach under social and technical issues. For example, pupils should gain fundamental technical skills to understand or examined deepfake videos. Maybe they cannot detect deepfake videos as experts, but they should have at least some awareness about detecting deepfake videos.

Deepfake videos often tend to viral and spread rapidly on social media and other digital environments. Therefore, through media literacy education, pupils should gain skills in fact-checking. In other words, when pupils encounter any video or news in a digital environment, they should check the credibility of video or news with different sources and try to detect whether the video or information is false or true. For doing this fact-checking, pupils should have better digital citizenship skills.

To gain digital citizenship competencies to pupils' media education lessons should be compulsory at schools. Moreover, at universities, teacher candidates should take those courses as compulsory. As a result, teachers should have better digital citizenship competencies to improve pupils' digital citizenship competences and protect them from harms and risks of deepfake. In other words, teachers should know how to combat deepfake to teach pupils how to fight with deepfake technologies.

For school sides, media education lessons should be compulsory for all kids and pupils because it is believed that (Britt, Rouet, Blaum, and Millis, 2019; Spivak, 2019; Atodiresei, Tanaselea, and Iftene, 2018; Cybenko & Cybenko, 2018) digital literacy education, raising citizens' awareness about risks and manipulation of deepfake videos is so essential for protecting children, youths, and society from harms of deepfake technologies. Moreover, effective media education aims to improve pupil's digital citizenship competences, conscious online behaviors, and critical thinking. As a result of those improvements, it is expected that pupils' have better cognitive and concrete safeguards toward digital content consumption, misuse, cyber-harassment, and online manipulation.

Digital citizenship skills are not only beneficial for combatting cyber-harassment or risks in or digital environment, but those skills are also crucial for reducing racism, misogynism, or anger toward other cultures, societies, or people through teaching citizenship skills and appropriate online and offline behaviors. When individuals encounter deepfake videos related to vulnerable subjects such as racist, patriot or gender discrimination, they should first fact-check those videos and then control their anger. This would be possible only with effective digital citizenship education. Because with effective digital citizenship education, pupils can learn to respect different perceptions, not quickly get mad with trolls, and differentiate provocateur messages and freedom speech (Westerlund, 2019; Figueira & Oliveira, 2017).

Most researchers (Choi et al., 2018; Ribble & Miller, 2013) believe that improving and encouraging children and youths' digital citizenship skills and education is one of the best tools for fighting against deepfake technologies. Internet safety education or computer education is beneficial for awareness about the risks and harms of digital environments. However, outstanding education for children and youths' integration to the digital world would be appropriate for characteristics of development and their behaviors (Jones & Mitchell, 2016). Not only teaching children and youths about technology would not be enough. The main aim of education for 21st century would be to make child and youth participate in the digital world with higher digital citizenship competences and gain awareness about manipulation tools such as Deepfake. Moreover, with digital citizenship education, pupils' online civic engagements have some outcomes for their offline civic engagement, which encourage their awareness both online and offline (Jones & Mitchell, 2016, Ribble, 2012).

For the technical side, due to characteristics of the track and certify the origins and history of the data, alternative technologies such as blockchain would be beneficial to combat deepfake (Atanasova, Nakov, Marquez, Barron-Cedeno, Karadzhov, Mihaylova, Mohtarami, and Glass, 2019; Hasan & Salah, 2019; Floridi, 2018). When we look at the literature and educators', policy makers' definitions and discussions about digital citizenship, we could see that the concepts of society and offline citizenship were underlined (Hintz et al., 2017; Jones & Mitchell, 2016; Ribble, 2012; Ribble & Bailey, 2004). Additionally, digital citizenship impacts individuals' empowering and democratizing qualifications both online and offline world (Hintz et al., 2017). With Deepfake, mostly manipulators try to produce fake news about politics and politicians (Yadlin-Segal & Oppenheim, 2020), and the consequences of those manipulations seem in society as chaos. That is why digital citizenship is advised as a protection method for the negative implications of Deepfake.

FUTURE RESEARCH DIRECTIONS AND CONCLUSİON

For better understanding, the effects of deepfake and other AI technologies, social sciences, and technical sciences should work together. So, studies to understand the technical and social mechanism of deepfake and its impact on human behaviors, thinking, and perception should be conducted. In addition, semi-structured interviews would be beneficial to understand the perception of individuals toward deepfake videos. Although in the literature, primarily harms and threats of deepfakes are discussed, deepfake technologies also benefit. Those technologies can be used in medical sectors, film and music sectors, and education also. However, as many technological devices, they have some threads and harms which can be very dangerous, especially for children and youths. To protect them from deepfake videos and other manipulative AI technologies, we should gain their digital citizenship skills and competencies. For better digital citizenship skills, media education lessons should be integrated into education programs for all pupils.

REFERENCES

Aldwairi, M., & Alwahedi, A. (2018). Detecting Fake News in Social Media Networks. *Procedia Computer Science*, *141*, 215–222. doi:10.1016/j.procs.2018.10.171

Alvermann, D. E., & Sanders, R. K. (2019). Adolescent Literacy in a Digital World. The International Encyclopedia of Media Literacy, 1–6. doi:10.1002/9781118978238.ieml0005

Anderson, K. E. (2018). Getting Acquainted with Social Networks and Apps: Combating Fake News on Social Media. *Library Hi Tech News*, *35*(3), 1–6. doi:10.1108/LHTN-02-2018-0010

Atanasova, P., Nakov, P., Màrquez, L., Barrón-Cedeño, A., Karadzhov, G., Mihaylova, T., Mohtarami, M., & Glass, J. (2019). Automatic Fact-Checking Using Context and Discourse Information. *Journal of Data and Information Quality*, *11*(3), 12. doi:10.1145/3297722

Atif, Y., & Chou, C. (2018). Digital Citizenship: Innovations in Education, Practice, and Pedagogy. *Journal of Educational Technology & Society*, *21*(1), 152–154.

Atodiresei, C.-S., Tanaselea, A., & Iftene, A. (2018). Identifying Fake News and Fake Users on Twitter. *Procedia Computer Science*, *126*, 451–461. doi:10.1016/j.procs.2018.07.279

Best, P., Manktelow, R., & Taylor, B. (2014). Online Communication, Social Media and Adolescent Well-Being, A Systematic Narrative Review. *Children and Youth Services Review*, *41*, 27–36. doi:10.1016/j.childyouth.2014.03.001

Britt, M. A., Rouet, J.-F., Blaum, D., & Millis, K. (2019). A Reasoned Approach Dealing with Fake News. *Policy Insights from the Behavioral and Brain Sciences*, *6*(1), 94–101. doi:10.1177/2372732218814855

Brown, N. (2020). Deepfakes and Weaponization of Disinformation, Virginia. *The Journal of Law and Technology*, *23*(1), 1–59.

Carew, A. (2020). Ghost in the Algorithm: Justin Krook's 'Machine' and Advancing AI, Metro Magazine. *Media & Education Magazine*, (203), 94–97.

Chawla, R. (2019). Deepfakes: How a Pervert Shook the World. *International Journal of Advanced Research and Development*, *4*(6), 4–8.

Chesney, R., & Citron, D. (2019). Deepfakes and The New Disinformation War: The Coming Age of Post-Truth Geopolitics. *Foreign Affairs*, *98*(1), 147–155.

Choi, M., Cristol, D., & Gimbert, B. (2018). Teachers as Digital Citizens: The Influence of Individual Backgrounds, Internet Use and Psychological Characteristics on Teachers' Levels of Digital Citizenship. *Computer Education*, *121*, 143–161. doi:10.1016/j.compedu.2018.03.005

Clayton, K., Davis, J., Hinckley, K., & Horiuchi, Y. (2019). Partisan Motivated Reasoning and Misinformation in the Media: Is News from Ideologically Uncongenial Sources More Suspicious. *Japanese Journal of Political Science*, *20*(3), 129–142. doi:10.1017/S1468109919000082

Comer, J. S., Furr, J. M., Beidas, R. S., Weiner, C. L., & Kendall, P. C. (2008). Children and terrorism-related news: Training parents in coping and media literacy. *Journal of Consulting and Clinical Psychology*, *76*(4), 568–578. doi:10.1037/0022-006X.76.4.568 PMID:18665686

Commisso, C. (2017). The Post-Truth Archive: Considerations for Archiving Context in Fake News Repositories, Preservation. *Digital Technology & Culture*, *46*(3), 99–102. doi:10.1515/pdtc-2017-0010

Cybenko, A. K., & Cybenko, G. (2018). AI and Fake News. *IEEE Intelligent Systems*, *33*(5), 3–7. doi:10.1109/MIS.2018.2877280

Daneels, R., & Vanwynsberghe, H. (2017). Mediating Social Media Use: Connecting Parent's Mediation Strategics and Social Media Literacy. *Cyberpsychology (Brno)*, *11*(3), 1–13. doi:10.5817/CP2017-3-5

De Kreersmaecker, J., & Roets, A. (2017). Fake News: Incorrect, But Hard to Correct, The Role of Cognitive Ability on the Impact of False Information on Social Impressions. *Intelligence*, *65*, 107–110. doi:10.1016/j.intell.2017.10.005

Dobber, T., Metoui, N., Trilling, D., Helberger, N., & Vreese, C. D. (2020). Do (Microtargeted) Deepfakes Have Real Effects on Political Attitudes. *The International Journal of Press/Politics*, 1–23. doi:10.1177/1940161220944364

Emejulu, A., & McGregor, C. (2019). Towards a Radical Digital Citizenship in Digital Education. *Critical Studies in Education*, *60*(1), 131–147. doi:10.1080/17508487.2016.1234494

Figueira, A., & Oliveria, L. (2017). The Current State of Fake News: Challenges and Opportunities. *Procedia Computer Science*, *121*, 817–825. doi:10.1016/j.procs.2017.11.106

Fletcher, J. (2018). Deepfakes, Artificial Intelligence, and Some Kind of Dystopia: The New Faces of Online Post-Fact Performance. *Theatre Journal*, *70*(4), 455–471. doi:10.1353/tj.2018.0097

Floridi, L. (2018). Artificial Intelligence, Deepfakes and a Future of Ectypes. *Philosophy & Technology*, *31*(3), 317–321. doi:10.100713347-018-0325-3

Flynn, D. J., Nyhan, B., & Reifler, J. (2017). The Nature and Origins of Misperceptions: Understanding False and Unsupported Beliefs About Politics. *Political Psychology*, *38*, 127–150. doi:10.1111/pops.12394

Frenda, S. J., Knowles, E. D., Saletan, W., & Loftus, E. F. (2013). False Memories of Fabricated Political Events. *Journal of Experimental Social Psychology*, *49*(2), 280–286. doi:10.1016/j.jesp.2012.10.013

Ghosn-Chelala, M. (2019). Exploring Sustainable Learning and Practice of Digital Citizenship: Education and Place-based Challenges, Education. *Citizenship and Social Justice*, *14*(1), 40–56. doi:10.1177/1746197918759155

Gleason, B., & Gillern, S. V. (2018). Digital Citizenship with Social Media: Participatory Practices of Teaching and Learning in Secondary Education. *Journal of Educational Technology & Society*, *21*(1), 200–212.

Goel, S., Anderson, A., Hofman, J., & Watts, D. J. (2015). The Structural Virality of Online Diffusion. *Management Science*, *62*(1), 180–196.

Green, D., Karafa, K., & Wilson, S. (2020). Art Therapy with Grieving Children: Effect on Affect in the Dual-Process Model. *Art Therapy: Journal of the American Art Therapy Association*, •••, 1–5. doi:10.1080/07421656.2020.1823197

Grinberg, N., Kenneth, J., Friedland, L., Swire-Thompson, B., & Lazer, D. (2019). Fake News on Twitter During the 2016 US Presidential Election. *Science, 363*(6425), 374–378. doi:10.1126cience.aau2706 PMID:30679368

Hallam, C., & Zanella, G. (2017). Online Self-Disclosure: The Privacy Paradox Explained as a Temporally Discounted Balance Between Concerns and Rewards. *Computers in Human Behavior, 68*, 217–227. doi:10.1016/j.chb.2016.11.033

Hasan, H. R., & Salah, K. (2019). Combating Deepfake Videos Using Blockchain and Smart Contracts. *IEEE Access: Practical Innovations, Open Solutions, 7*, 41596–41606. doi:10.1109/ACCESS.2019.2905689

Hintz, A., Dencik, L., & Wahl-Jorgensen, K. (2017). Digital Citizenship and Surveillance Society. *International Journal of Communication, 11*, 731–739.

Hollandsworth, R., Donovan, J., & Welch, M. (2017). Digital Citizenship: You Can't Go Home Again. *TechTrends, 61*(6), 524–530. doi:10.100711528-017-0190-4

Holt, T. J., Brewer, R., & Goldsmith, A. (2019). Digital Drift and the "Sense of Injustice". *Counter-Productive Policing of Youth Cybercrime, 40*(9), 1144–1156.

Johnson, B. (2019, Mar. 25). Deepfakes are Solvable-But Don't Forget That Shallowfakes are Already Pervasive. *MIT Technology Review*.

Jones, L. M., & Mitchell, K. J. (2016). Defining and Measuring Youth Digital Citizenship. *New Media & Society, 18*(9), 2063–2079. doi:10.1177/1461444815577797

Jones, V. (2020). Artificial Intelligence Enabled Deepfake Technology: The Emergence of a New Threat, Utica College. *ProQuest Dissertations Publishing, 2020*, 27962429.

Kim, M., & Choi, D. (2018). Development of Youth Digital Citizenship Scale and Implication for Educational Setting. *Journal of Educational Technology & Society, 21*(1), 155–171.

Kong, S. C. (2014). Developing Information Literacy and Critical Thinking Skills Through Domain Knowledge Learning in Digital Classrooms: An Experience of Practicing Flipped Classroom Strategy. *Computers & Education, 78*, 160–173. doi:10.1016/j.compedu.2014.05.009

Kwok, A. O. J., & Sharon, G. M. K. (2020). Deepfake: A Social Construction of Technology Perspective. *Current Issues in Tourism*, 1–5. doi:10.1080/13683500.2020.1738357

Laar, E. V., Deursen, A. J. A. M. V., Dijk, J. A. G. M. V., & Haan, J. D. (2017). The Relation Between 21st-Century Skills and Digital Skills: A Systematic Literature Review. *Computers in Human Behavior*, *72*, 577–588. doi:10.1016/j.chb.2017.03.010

Li, X., Lang, Y., Chen, Y., Mao, X., He, Y., Wang, S., Xue, H., & Lu, Q. (2020). *Sharp Multiple Instance Learning for DeepFake Video Detection*. In MM '20, Seattle, WA.

Lin, H. (2019). The Existential Threat from Cyber-Enabled Information Warfare. *Bulletin of the Atomic Scientists*, *75*(4), 187–196. doi:10.1080/00963402.2019.1629574

Livingstone, S., Olafsson, K., Helsper, E. J., Lupinaz-Villanueva, F., Veltri, G. A., & Folkvord, F. (2017). Maximizing Opportunities and Minimizing Risks for Children Online: The Role of Digital Skills in Emerging Strategies of Parental Mediation. *Journal of Communication*, *67*(1), 1–24. doi:10.1111/jcom.12277

Lyon, D. (2017). Surveillance Culture: Engagement, Exposure, and Ethics in Digital Modernity. *International Journal of Communication*, *11*, 824–842.

Lysonski, S., & Durvasula, S. (2008). Digital Piracy of MP3s: Consumer and Ethical Predispositions. *Journal of Consumer Marketing*, *25*(3), 167–178. doi:10.1108/07363760810870662

Mackenzie, A., & Bhatt, I. (2020). Lies, Bullshit, and Fake News: Some Epistemological Concerns, Postdigital. *Science and Education*, *2*, 9–13.

Maras, M. H., & Alexandrou, A. (2019). Determining Authenticity of Video Evidence in the Age of Artificial Intelligence and the Wake of Deepfake Videos. *International Journal of Evidence & Proof*, *23*(3), 255–262. doi:10.1177/1365712718807226

Mossberger, K., Tolbert, C. J., & McNeal, R. S. (2008). *Digital Citizenship: The Internet*. Society and Participation, The MIT Press USA.

Newman, E. J., Garry, M., Unkelbach, C., Bernstein, D. M., Lindsay, D., & Nash, R. A. (2015). Truthiness and Falsiness of Trivia Claims Depend on Judgmental Contexts. *Journal of Experimental Psychology. Learning, Memory, and Cognition*, *41*(5), 1337–1348. doi:10.1037/xlm0000099 PMID:25822783

Norberg, P. A., Horne, D. R., & Horne, D. A. (2007). The Privacy Paradox: Personal Information Disclosure Intentions Versus Behaviors. *The Journal of Consumer Affairs*, *41*(1), 100–126. doi:10.1111/j.1745-6606.2006.00070.x

Ohler, J. (2011). Digital Citizenship Means Character Education for the Digital Age. *Kappa Delta Pi Record*, *47*(1), 25–27. doi:10.1080/00228958.2011.10516720

Pancer, E., & Poole, M. (2016). The Popularity and Virality of Political Social Media: Hashtags, Mentions, and Links Predict Likes and Retweets of 2016 US Presidential Nominees' Tweets. *Social Influence*, *11*(4), 259–270. doi:10.1080/15534510.2016.1265582

Quayyum, A., Quadir, J., Janjua, M. U., & Sher, F. (2019). Using Blockchain to Rein in the New Post-Truth World and Check the Spead of Fake News. *IT Professional*, *21*(4), 16–24. doi:10.1109/MITP.2019.2910503

Redmiles, E. M., Kross, S., & Mazurek, M. L. (2016). How I Learned to be Secure: A Census-Representative Survey of Security Advice Sources and Behavior. *CCS*, *16*(October), 24–28. doi:10.1145/2976749.2978307

Ribble, M. (2012). Digital Citizenship for Educational Change. *Kappa Delta Pi Record*, *48*(4), 148–151. doi:10.1080/00228958.2012.734015

Ribble, M., & Miller, T. N. (2013). Educational Leadership in an Online World: Connecting Students to Technology Responsibly, Safely, and Ethically. *Journal of Asynchronous Learning Networks*, *17*(1), 137–145. doi:10.24059/olj.v17i1.310

Ribble, M. S., & Bailey, G. D. (2004). Digital Citizenship Focus Questions for Implementation. *Learning and Leading with Technology*, *32*(2), 12–15.

Roberts, J. A., & David, M. E. (2016). ve David M. E. (2015). My Life has Become a Major Distraction from my Cell Phone: Partner Phubbing and Relationship Satisfaction Among Romantic Partners. *Computers in Human Behavior*, *54*, 134–141. doi:10.1016/j.chb.2015.07.058

Schuelke-Leech, B. A. (2018). A Model for Understanding the Orders of Magnitude of Disruptive Technologies. *Technological Forecasting and Social Change*, *129*, 261–274. doi:10.1016/j.techfore.2017.09.033

Spivak, R. (2019). Deepfakes: The Newest Way to Commit One of the Oldest Crimes, The Georgetown Law. *Technology Review*, *3*(2), 339–400.

Subrahmanyam, K., & Greenfied, P. (2008). Online Communication and Adolescent Relationships. *The Future of Children*, *18*(1), 119–148. doi:10.1353/foc.0.0006 PMID:21338008

Temir, E. (2020). Deepfake: New Era in The Age of Disinformation & End of Reliable Journalism. *Selçuk Communication, 13*(2), 1009–1024.

Thies, J., Zollhofer, M., Stamminger, M., Theobalt, C., & Niesner, M. (2018). Face2Face: Real-Time Face Capture and Reenactment of RGB Videos. *Communications of the ACM, 62*(1), 96–104. doi:10.1145/3292039

Vaccari, C., & Chadwick, A. (2020). Deepfakes and Disinformation: Exploring the Impact of Synthetic Political Video on Deception, Uncertainty, and Trust in News. *Social Media + Society, 6*(1), 1–13. doi:10.1177/2056305120903408

Van Duyn, E., & Collier, J. (2018). Priming and Fake News: The Effects of Elite Discourse on Evaluations of News Media. *Mass Communication & Society, 22*(1), 29–48. doi:10.1080/15205436.2018.1511807

Vosoughi, S., Roy, D., & Aral, S. (2018). The Spread of True and False News Online. *Science, 359*(6380), 1146–1151. doi:10.1126cience.aap9559 PMID:29590045

Vromen, A. (2017). Digital Citizenship and Political Engagement. In *Digital Citizenship and Political Engagement*. Interest Groups, Advocacy and Democracy Series. Palgrave Macmillan.

Wagner, T. L., & Blewer, A. (2019). The World Real Is No Longer Real: Deepfakes, Gender, and Challenges of AI-Altered Video. *Open Information Science, 3*(1), 32–46. doi:10.1515/opis-2019-0003

Walters, M. G., Gee, D., & Mohammed, S. (2019). A Literature Review: Digital Citizenship and The Elementary Educator. *International Journal of Technology in Education, 2*(1), 1–21.

Wenzel, A. (2019). To Verify or to Disengage: Coping with "Fake News" and Ambiguity. *International Journal of Communication, 13*, 19.

Westerlund, M. (2019). The Emergence of Deepfake Technology: A Review. *Technology Innovation Management Review, 9*(11), 39–52. doi:10.22215/timreview/1282

Whyte, C. (2020). Deepfake News: AI-enabled disinformation as a Multi-Level Public Policy Challenge. *Journal of Cyber-Policy*, 199-217.

Wojewidka, J. (2020). *The Deepfake Threat to Face Biometrics*. Academic Press.

Xu, S., Yang, H. H., MacLeod, J., & Zhu, S. (2019). Social Media Competence and Digital Citizenship Among College Students. *Convergence (London), 24*(4), 735–752. doi:10.1177/1354856517751390

Yadlin-Segal, A., & Oppenheim, Y. (2020). Whose Dystopia Is It Anyway? Deepfakes and Social Media Regulation. *Convergence (London)*, •••, 1–16.

Yue, A., Nekmat, E., & Beta, A. R. (2019). Digital Literacy Through Digital Citizenship: Online Civic Participation and Public Opinion Evaluation of Youth Minorities in Southeast Asia. *Media and Communication*, *7*(2), 100–114.

Zannettou, S., Sirivianos, M., Blackburn, J., & Kourtellis, N. (2019). The Web of Fake Information: Rumors, Fake News, Hoaxes, Clickbait, and Various Other Shenanigans. *Journal of Data and Information Quality*, *1*(3), 1–37.

KEY TERMS AND DEFINITIONS

Artificial Intelligence: The theory and development of computer systems able to perform tasks that normally require human intelligence, such as visual perception, speech recognition, decision-making, and translation between languages.

Cybersecurity: The application of technologies, processes, and controls to protect systems, networks, programs, devices and data from cyber attacks

Deepfake: Video of a person in which their face or body has been digitally altered so that they appear to be someone else, typically used maliciously or to spread false information.

Digital Citizenship: Refers to the responsible use of technology by anyone who uses computers, the Internet, and digital devices to engage with society on any level.

Chapter 7
Flattening the Curve of Fake News in the Epoch of Infodemic:
An Epistemic Challenge

Oluwole Olumide Durodolu
https://orcid.org/0000-0003-2734-8165
University of South Africa, South Africa

Collence Takaingenhamo Chisita
https://orcid.org/0000-0002-7375-8627
University of South Africa, South Africa

Tinyiko Vivian Dube
https://orcid.org/0000-0003-2734-8165
Department of Information Science, University of South Africa, South Africa

ABSTRACT

Globally, no country has been spared by the spectre of the COVID-19 pandemic and infodemic that continues to wreak havoc on the socio-economic and political stability of governments and communities. The oxymoronic nature of fake news raises many questions with regards to the issues of authenticity because the concept of news is underpinned by verifiability. While fake news lacks variability, it is surprising that its digital imprint on the social media platforms continues to leave indelible marks that will undermine democracy, responsible journalism, and the benefits of the digital media. It is against this background that this chapter seeks to find strategies to flatten the curve of fake news in the epoch of the COVID-19 pandemic and infodemic, an epistemic challenge. The chapter is based on a positivist research methodology that sought to gather views from the study respondents on their epistemic experiences with fake news amidst the COVID-19 pandemic and infodemic. It seeks to gather views to counter the upsurge of fake news amidst the COVID-19 pandemic.

DOI: 10.4018/978-1-7998-6474-5.ch007

INTRODUCTION

The world is concurrently under a twin disaster of a paralyzing health challenge that is gradually overwhelming every nation, known as Coronavirus (COVID-19), and the problem of information disorder that has been stimulated by the unrestricted access to the use of social media is worsening the situation. Digital communication had become a mechanism that can no longer be overlooked, especially with the role it played during the Arab spring when it was used to upstaged many governments in the middle east and became identified as a platform to strengthened democratic principle (Pan American Health Organization and World Health Organization, 2020). Social media provides the prospect of receiving timely, precise information about practically anything. The flip side of the coin is that it has also become an avenue for spreading misinformation. This unfounded fairytale is capable of promoting panic, especially when accurate information can be a matter of life and death. As a result of the disorderliness on social media, The World Health Organization (2020) has described as "infodemic" the outbreak of overwhelming information concerning the Coronavirus circulating on various social media which put many people on predicament on how to identify dependable sources and trustworthy guidance when it is necessary. In realization of the damaging effect of fake news, the World Health Organization established a social media team to combat the destructive impact of misinformation that can potentially harm people's health. These efforts of the World Health Organization are anchored on helping the general public to decrease. The dawn social media has led unrestricted access to all manners of information, and this has coxswained to disorderly management of information. Which is poised to threaten the integrity of the information in public space and heightens the level of unreliability of what is available, because of the apparent disorderliness in the information environment as a result of hesitancy to control activities on social media coupled with the predicament of interfering with the fundamental right of an individual to free speech (Durodolu and Ibenne, 2020, Durodolu, Ibenne and Dube (2021). In contrast to traditional media, that can be located from a correct address, ascertaining the whereabouts of developers of fake news is difficult, as information can be manufacture at the secluded geographical location and causing a ripple effect across the globe, with consequences felt in all the four compass-point of the world and tracking down such individual to face the repercussion of their offence is not easy (Durodolu and Ibenne, 2020).

For example, the damaging effect of fake news had informed the position of World Health Organization when its termed as "infodemic" because of how the occurrence of Coronavirus led to the outpouring of misinformation on social media and various other websites, most of which contain erroneous and misleading information to cause panic and media frenzy (Zoe, 2020). The injurious effects of fake news can also be felt in the devastating impact on the economic and social life, and we now live in the era of a grand onslaught on truth, propagation, alternative facts, and post-truth epoch which has led to information anxiety and peril on democratic life. Fake news is make-believe stories, deployed and carefully crafted to disguise reality and to make it appear like credible editorial reports premeditated to misled, embarrass a person, association and government by using different harm twisting techniques to attract readership and lead to financial benefits or gain political position (Zarocostas, 2020). Once made available on social media platform it goes viral. Because of the sensation generated by such misinformation, many people become voluntarily or involuntary carrier of the information, many of this distorted information often outperform genuine traditional sources of information (Brennen, 2017: 179). Many scholars have expressed outrage about how rapidly it is getting to separate fiction from fact to the extent that the whole essence of the theory of empiricism which is anchored on an acquisition of knowledge through senses (ability to see, hear, smell, taste and touch) has now been challenged with this new reality, where technology is being manipulated to make people see, hear and touch what never existed.

To further clarify the predicament of information disorder which is the introduction of unethical behavior to information access and use, it has been categorized into three, which are, misinformation which occurs when incorrect information is shared with no intention to harm, Dis-information is when fabricated information is intentionally shared to harm and cause discomfort to others. Mal-information is when sincere information is circulated to cause damaging consequences, usually by moving information intended for private consumption into the public domain. Information disorder can lead to extreme, and persistent fear, anxiety, nervousness, apprehension and a state of disquiet when information is manipulated and channel to terrorize or bully individual, organization and government by spreading malicious information. (Rampersad & Althiyabi, 2020).

Statement of the Problem

The challenges associated with fake news is now becoming prominent in social and political discussion. Fake news has become an existential problem generating apprehension all over the world, particularly in an era of health emergency where getting trustworthy information can go a long way to safe human life, there is evidence that many people took wrong decision guided by misinformation and fake news from the social media thereby putting their lives in grave danger by following unscientific counsel (UNESCO, 2020). It is a grave danger to embrace denialism or tag the existence of a global pandemic of this nature a hoax, rather than being guided by evidence-based scientific opinion, convincing people otherwise has become an epistemic challenge.

The social media has gained notoriety as a platform for dissemination of both false and real information concerning the clear and present danger posed by the ravaging coronavirus. Many people have turned to social media as their primary source of information concerning updates about the virus; this has made some bloggers and media outfits on social media to gain extreme popularity. The actions of a few mischief-makers who disseminate false information have had several adverse effects on the people, and some people are gradually becoming confident of the non-existence of the epidemic in some parts of the world. The social media is deluged with several news items on the pandemic and of great concern is the spread of false information which has had an adverse effect and severe consequences on the response of Government and health agencies to the pandemic.

Government all over the world, are at the forefront of educating the public about the existence of the virus, and how best to stay safe, and also tackling the pandemic that has locked down several nations of the world. The need to educate the public stems from the fact that the virus is easily spread if specific precautionary measures are not taken by the people to curb the spread. It is, therefore, the responsibility of every individual to help stop the spread of the virus by playing their part; however, this can only be done appropriately if the people are well informed. Unfortunately, the escalation of false information on social media has made the task of educating the public on the pandemic onerous. It is bad enough that the world is fighting a common enemy in the form of a virus, having to cope with the challenges of information disorder concerning the pandemic makes it a twin misfortune. Responding to the dangerous trend and spread of false information, Tedros Adhanom Ghebreyesus, the director-general of the World Health Organization (WHO), specified that the world is not just fighting an epidemic; we are fighting an infodemic. In the same vein, Naughton (2020) averred that fake news spreads faster and more efficiently than this virus, and is just as dangerous. Additionally, it was stated that, if the problem is not solved, then the world is heading for the route that leads nowhere but division and disharmony.

The purpose therefore of this article is to seek to evaluate the incidences of information disorder, its consequences and how the spread of false information can be curtailed so as not to hamper the response to the fight against a global pandemic.

Significance/Contribution of the study

This study is imperative because of its importance to body of knowledge in a four-compass ways. Extant literature in the region of infordemic, fake news, misinformation and information disorder was revised in order to reveal something unique and novel, recognize a gap in research, and appraise the contemporary research environment to uncover strengths and weaknesses relating to the subject matter. The study also added to knowledge by making appropriate suggestions leading to policy changes without governmental protocols. Finally, the study contributes to knowledge by increasing obtainable theory like meta-literacy which enhances the proficiency to study the amount to which one comprehends information being communicated through various means, to identify the purpose for failure to understand, and to use different approaches when failures are identified.

Research Questions

1. Who should be responsible for identifying "fake news" on social media?
2. If you saw an article on social media which had been visibly flagged as "fake news" and there was an option to flag it visibly, would you do so?
3. Which news do you trust more?
4. In your opinion, why do you think fake news is published online?
5. Why do you think fake news is reported by traditional outlets?

Methodology

This research is based on a positivist paradigm, which is a philosophical standpoint that assumed that the data collected for research could constitute facts that could support causal analysis. Collection of data is done using online survey (questionnaire) to elicit responses to standardized predetermine research questions that are designed; code the data in numerical format; analyses and evaluated the data statistically and on a prospect foundation to confirm or deny the hypotheses; thereby, supposedly, confirming or amending the theory (Harvey, 2020). The justification for a positivist research paradigm is because it supports the use of questionnaire as a mean of gathering data which is aimed at measuring, assessing and analyzing connections that exist between identified variables in social reality. Some part of this research instrument was adopted from the one previously used by the American Student Government Association, (2020) to be tested in Nigeria environment.

The research is descriptive in nature because it is an online survey which is considered conclusive due to its quantitative nature. Preplanned and designed so that the information acquired can be analyses statistically inferred on a population. The advantage of descriptive research is that it allows grouping all the responses into deliberate choices that will provide statistically inferable data. This allows the researcher to measure the significance of the results on the general population under investigation, as well as evaluating respondent's opinions, sentiments, attitudes, and behaviors over a specific timeframe (Shields and Rangarajan, 2013).

Online survey was used as a technique of gathering data for this study, because of the global lockdown brought about by the spread of the coronavirus pandemic when people are encouraged to stay safe indoor, and circulating questionnaire via face to face approach is against the social distancing rule, this method is fast, cost-effective, more accurate and easier to analyses, 428 individuals responded to the online survey and came out with useful responses. For the sake of this investigation, survey monkey was used as a method to circulate the survey because it is cheap and contains a comprehensive feature set that is adjustable to respond to the need of the researchers.

Research Questions, Results, and Discussions

The discussion focuses on the research questions gathered through the online survey.

Research Question 1: Who should be responsible for identifying "fake news" on social media?

The respondents were asked questions on who should be responsible for identifying fake news on social media. The result shows that majority of the respondents attested to the fact that the public and the social media platform should be responsible for identifying fake news with 68 or 15.9% and 60 or 14.0% response rates respectively. Other primary agents which the respondents affirmed should be responsible for identifying fake news are The Government, An independent body (48 or 11.2%), The Government, The social media platform, The Public, An independent body (44 or 10.3%), The Government (28 or 6.5%), The social media platform, The Public, An independent body (16 or 3.7%), The Public, An independent body (12 or 2.8%) and The Government, The social media platform, An independent body,

The government (12 or 2.8%). The implication to be drawn from the above result is that the public and the social media platform are the primary agents that should be responsible for identifying fake news on social media. Through a combination of other agents such as The Government and independent body, The Government. The social media platform, The Public, and an independent body, The Government, the social media platform, The Public, an independent body, The Public, an independent body and The Government, The social media platform, An independent body should also be responsible for identifying fake news. This also affirms the proliferation of fake news on social media platforms.

Research Question 2: If you saw an article on social media which had been visibly flagged as "fake news" and there was an option to flag it visibly, would you do so?

The respondents were asked on whether they would flag any news o social media already tagged as fake news. The result reveals that most of the respondents (284 or 66.4%) attested that they would flag any fake news ones they are able to identify it was fake news while only a few respondents (76 or 17.8%) claimed that they would do otherwise. This implies that majority of the respondents would visibly flag fake news ones they are able to identify such on social media.

Table 1. Respondents opinion on who should be responsible for identifying "fake news" on social media

Response	Frequency	Percent
An independent body	48	11.2
I dont know	20	4.7
The Government	28	6.5
The Government, An independent body	8	1.9
The Government, The Public	12	2.8
The Government, The Public, An independent body	16	3.7
The Government, The social media platform	12	2.8
The Government, The social media platform, An independent body	12	2.8
The Government, The social media platform, The Public	44	10.3
The Government, The social media platform, The Public, An independent body	44	10.3
The Public	68	15.9
The Public, An independent body	12	2.8
The social media platform	60	14.0
The social media platform, The Public	28	6.5
The social media platform, The Public, An independent body	16	3.7
Total	428	100.0

Table 2. Will you flag an article if discovered it is fake new?

Response	Frequency	Per cent
Maybe	68	15.9
No	76	17.8
Yes	284	66.4
Total	428	100.0

Question 3: Which news do you trust more?

Questions were also asked on which news do respondents surveyed trust more. The result reveals that majority of the respondents (256 or 59.8%) are not categorical on the types of news they trust. However, 152 or 35.5% of the respondents reported that they trust news from traditional news outlets more than any other sources. The implication to be drawn from the result is that most of the respondents surveyed trust different types of news depending on their needs.

Table 3. Trusted source of news

Response	Frequency	Per cent
It depends	256	59.8
News from social media feeds	8	1.9
News from social media feeds, It depends	8	1.9
News from the traditional news outlet	152	35.5
News from a traditional news outlet, news from social media feeds, It depends	4	.9
Total	428	100.0

Question 4: In your opinion, why do you think fake news is published online?

Respondents were also asked to express their opinion on why they think that fake news is published online and advancement of specific position or agenda (192 or 44.9%) and confusing people (80 or 18.7%) were reported as the primary reasons they think fake news is published online.

Question 5: Why do you think fake news is reported by traditional outlets?

On the reasons why, the respondents think fake news is reported by traditional outlets, promoting a particular political agenda and mean of propaganda topped the list of reasons why fake news is reported by traditional outlets with 192 or 44.9% and 148 or 34.6% response rates respectively. Only few respondents attested to the need to confuse people (44 or 10.3%) and to project others in bad light (44 or 10.3%) as reasons why traditional outlets reported fake news. The inference to be drawn from the results is that promotion of particular political agenda and for propaganda are the major reasons why traditional outlets reported fake news.

Discussion of Findings

The increasing use of social media by (73, 7%, n=324) confirms that it is the most easily accessible platform for accessing and sharing content. The growing strength of social media reflects its potential in influencing public opinion. The 12.1%, n=52 who indicated non-use of social media is attributed to either lack of access to data because of the high costs of internet access and information literacy. The other 12.1%, n=52 are those who are in the category of late adopters of technology. Fake news has proved to be a severe challenge, as confirmed by the responses. The use of social

Table 4. Why is fake news published online?

Response	Frequency	Per cent
For entertainment	24	5.6
For entertainment, To advance a specific position or agenda	8	1.9
For entertainment, To confuse people, To advance specific position or agenda	12	2.8
For entertainment, To confuse people, To advance specific position or agenda, To ridicule the government	8	1.9
To advance a specific position or agenda	192	44.9
To advance a specific position or agenda, To ridicule the government	16	3.7
To confuse people	80	18.7
To confuse people, To advance a specific position or agenda	28	6.5
To confuse people, To advance a specific position or agenda, To ridicule the government	20	4.7
To confuse people, To ridicule the government	16	3.7
To ridicule government	24	5.6
Total	428	100.0

media as a source of news was confirmed by 93.5%, n=400 of the respondents. The high number who use social media as a source of news confirms Vorhaus's (2020) assertion, that, in the era of pandemics, protests, economic recession and anguish among the world's population consumers continue to move away from traditional media sources for their news as they embrace social media and messaging services to access the news. Chadwick (2011) argued that scientific studies of individual

Table 5. Fake news by the traditional news outlet

Response	Frequency	Per cent
As a means of propaganda	148	34.6
To confuse people	44	10.3
To project other in bad light	44	10.3
To promote a particular political agenda	192	44.9
Total	428	100.0

events, processes, and websites had led researchers to confirm that changeover from a traditional "news cycle" dominated by journalists and professional sources to a more elaborate "information cycle" that integrates ordinary people in the ongoing construction and contestation of news. The 9%, n=4 reflects those who are sceptical of social media and technology because of lack of interest and awareness of its potential in providing access to veritable sources.

Research Question 1: Who should be responsible for identifying "fake news" on social media?

The responses to the above question showed that the process of identifying fake news was a vexatious one as evidenced by 15.9%, n=68 and 14%, n=60 who confirmed that the public and the social media platform should be responsible for identifying fake news. However, the public can only detect fake news if they are equipped with information/digital literacy skills. Social media platforms are not neutral, but rather pen platforms that allow anyone with an account to post content in a multi-media format and as such, the platform should be responsible for the content. Yaraghi (2019) argued that social media owners should be in control of the content to prevent the proliferation of fake news. These platforms are increasingly adapting to a combination of automated and human-driven editorial processes to promote or filter certain types of content (Yaraghi, 2019). In addition to that, their users are increasingly using these platforms as the primary source of getting their news. Globally, governments have promulgated a law to regulate the use of social during the COVID-19 pandemic era. Yaraghi (2019) argued that social media companies had adopted two approaches to fight misinformation, namely: blocking suspicious content, for example, Pinterest bans anti-vaccination content and Facebook bans white supremacist content and providing alternative information alongside the content with false information so that the users are exposed to the truth and correct information.

The responses of government to the abuse of social media have been necessitated by the need to ensure that citizens have access to the correct and timely information to fight the pandemic and infodemic (Hua and Shaw, 2020). The proliferation of fake news can result in a world influenced by self-proclaimed experts from the opinion market (Chisita, 2020).

The responses favouring the government as a regulator for social media is 6.5%, n=28. This can be attributed to the fact that citizens do not have faith in government control over the use of social media. The respondents are of the opinion that the government can abuse their powers, thus violating fundamental rights and freedoms, including the right to access information and freedom of expression. Limaye, Sauer, Ali, Bernstein, Wahl, Barnhill, and Labrique (2020) argued that partnerships between. Government agencies and the social media giants Facebook, Twitter, and Instagram bear testimony to how public-private cooperation to flag, fact-check, and even remove false or outdated information can be an effective way to immunize these networks from impeding and actually worsening public health efforts. The respondents affirmed that other stakeholders could be useful in helping detect and curb fake news, for example, an independent body (11,2%, n=48), the government (6.5%, n=28) and an independent body (3.7%, n=16) among others.

Research Question 2: If you saw an article on social media which had been visibly flagged as "fake news" and there was an option to flag it visibly, would you do so?

Rochlin (2017) argued that the idea of flagging fake news to deter people from reading it was not the panacea to fake news. The means of curtailing fake news on social media include crowd-sourcing efforts to decrease the amount of fake news on the site. These initiatives include but not limited to; Easier Reporting, which permits users to quickly report a hoax and Flagging Stories as Disputed, which will disseminate community reports to a third-party fact-checker, who can then publically mark the story as having been disputed even though this does not prevent the story from being liked or shared (Mosseri, 2016). The respondents (47.7%, n= 204) indicated that they would go ahead and read a visibly flagged article as fake news. Those who confirmed that they would not read a flagged story constituted (27.1%, n=116). This response confirms that users lack knowledge of what constitutes fake news and hence the need for social media literacy. Furthermore, human beings are curious species, and stories that are flagged are of interest to them. However, the respondents acknowledged that they were aware when they were reading fake news as evidenced by 55.1%, n=236 response rate. The response confirms that the respondents surveyed in this study know when they are reading fake news.

Question 3: Which news do you trust more?

The question of the trustworthiness of news revealed that 59.8%, n=256 was not categorical on the type of news they trust. Traditional news outlets received a response rate of 35.5%. The reason for the low response rate to the traditional news outlets can be attributed to the fact that most media outlets are controlled, and the neutrality of such outlets is questionable. Overall the responses confirm that most of their respondents surveyed trust different types of news depending on circumstances. The idea of different types of media shows that users will cross-check the validity of sources by triangulation.

Question 4: In your opinion, why do you think fake news is published online?

This question received a variety of responses, but the major reasons were that the publication of fake news online served as a tool for the social advancement of specific position or agenda (44.9%, n=192) and confusing people (18.7%, n=80). Basically, fake news is circulated for mischievous reasons either for financial reasons or to discredit a public figure or scandalize an opponent. Fake news is a dreadful onslaught on the integrity of information where believability becomes a challenge; we are in the era where fake news is now so convincing and realistic regardless of whether one hears or sees it on the social media, to the extent that technology can be twisted in a manner that an individual can be made to say or do what never occurred (Tarran, 2017). Fake news has also become popular partly because of the loss of interest in the tradition and government media because people are of the opinion that they are sponsored propaganda to achieve a predetermined political agenda. Therefore, social media create an avenue for the democratization of information devoid of peer-review encumbrances and fact-checking mechanism, but this positive side has since been hijacked by a mischievous individual to cause mayhem, because of lack of specific monitoring apparatus (Lewandowsky, Ecker and Cook, 2017).

Question 5: Why do you think fake news is reported by traditional outlets?

The decision of the respondent is that fake news is as reported by the traditional media is propaganda to promote political agenda. Propaganda is "fake news" that has the potential to cause polarization of public opinion, and lead to an outbreak of violence as an effect of hate speech and, eventually, cause public disorder. The cyberspace, through the use of various social media, has opened the floodgate for the promotion of socio-economic and political transformation. By allowing the populace to express themselves freely, many nations, have enjoyed the upsurge in the use of these media to contribute to national debate and influence government decisions. However, the recently it has shown the capacity of social media to set the nation on fire. Many people have equally extended the boundary of free speech when using the platform as an avenue to promote hate speech, which poses a severe threat to the peaceful co-existence of the populace; individuals and different ethnic groups have been bullied, and the threat of genocide encouraged (Auwallibrary, 2018). Many governments around the world have made efforts to confront the dilemma of what to do with many political actors who are spreading fake news and using the social media environment to call for the annihilation of people who share opposing views and promoting aggressive rhetoric. Even though the constitution considered freedom of speech fundamental to the existence of citizens, the constitution cannot accommodate hate speech and language of intolerance that will jeopardies individual rights. Irrespective of all warnings, social media expose the fault line in many societies and the powerlessness of government to regulate social media use.

DISCUSSION

The challenge of fake news in the wake of the COVID-19 pandemic requires a pedagogical methodology that instills critical thinking skills. Lessons can be drawn from librarians and related information professionals who have adapted Information and metaliteracy literacy programmes for the benefit of their users to counter COVID-19 fake news. Batchelor, (2011) contended that information literacy has been serves as one of the most practicable and effective methods in combatting fake news (Batchelor, 2017). Eva & Shea, (2018) notes that critical thinking skills in the war against fake news is one domain that librarians as the experts and specialists in teaching such skills have excelled (Eva & Shea, 2018, Durodolu & Ocholla, 2017).

Information literacy serves as a tool that provides users with knowledge and skills to recognises the need for information, and the ability to locate, evaluate and effectively use the needed information (American library Association, ALA, 1989). The Association of College & Research Libraries (ACRL) states that "Information literacy is the set of integrated abilities encompassing the reflective discovery of information, the understanding of how information is produced and valued, and the use of information in creating new knowledge and participating ethically in communities of learning" (2016, p, 2).

De Paor, & Heravi, (2020) recommended the adaptation of novel and modern-day frameworks metaliteracy framework in the fight against COVID-19 fake news. According to the authors information literacy falls short of providing for dynamic developments in the technology and information landscape because it mainly provides a foundational model of skills-based approach, while metaliteracy encompasses digital literacy. Metaliteracy is the right fit in fighting the COVID-19 pandemic because it resonates with other literacies, for example, digital literacy, social media literacy, visual literacy, media literacy and transliteracy (Mackey & Jacobson, 2011).

Metaliteracy as a pedagocal framework in the fight against the COVID-19 pandemic and fake news offers a valuable alternative for weaponised learning in multifaceted interconnected learning environments (O'Brien, Forte, Mackey, & Jacobson, 2017). It redefines information literacy as an all-encompassing and unsolidified model that prepares learners to engage as critical and adaptive participants in an expanding landscape of socially constructed and technology-mediated information environments. Metaliteracy is ideal in fostering a culture of reflective learning, active and critical involvement with regards to the COVID-19 pandemic fertile grounds of misinformation and disinformation. On a similar note (Parvin, 2019) contended that a metaliterate person ensures that when sharing information, it is accurate and there are ethical factors engaged. According to the author metaliterate people are critical thinkers who understand responsible use of social media.

CONCLUSION AND RECOMMENDATION

The proliferation of digital technologies has led to an upsurge of fake news on the various social media platforms, thus leading to information distortion and confusion. Furthermore, fake news, once published, goes viral and spread misinformation while also leaving a discoloured brand of the authentic media. The precarious scenario of the COVID-19 pandemic requires evidence-based information to support decision making, and if no measures are taken to protect readers from fake news it will be difficult to control the spread of COVID-19. The findings of the study confirm that fake news on social media platforms poses an epistemic challenge to readers, researchers and decision making and hence the need for a campaign and strategy to counter upsurge of fake news amidst the COVID-19 pandemic and infodemic. While democracy is about freedom of speech and expression, such freedoms should not be abused lest for selfish ends. The continued abuse of social media by fake news peddlers requires a concerted effort by all stakeholders to avoid the risk of undermining the benefits of the panoply of digital technologies and democracy.

SUGGESTIONS FOR FURTHER STUDIES

The concentration of this study is on the flattening the curve of fake news in the epoch of Infodemic: an epistemic challenge, with special focus on misinformation, epidemic of fake news and information disorder. Therefore, the researcher is of the opinion that additional research on the subject is necessary. There is need to appraise the psychological motive behind sharing misinformation. It is important to evaluate the policy framework in dealing with deliberate spreading of fake news without hampering free speech.

REFERENCES

American Library Association (ALA). (1989). *Evaluating Information: Information Literacy*. https://libguides.ala.org/InformationEvaluation/Infolit

American Student Government Association. (2020). *Real News vs. Fake News*. Retrieved at 23/01/2020, from https://www.surveymonkey.com/r/HKJ2SZH

Association of College & Research Libraries. (2016). *Framework for Information Literacy for Higher Education*. https://www.ala.org/acrl/standards/ilframework

Auwal, M. A. (2018). *Social Media and Hate Speech: Analysis of Comments on Biafra Agitations, Arewa Youths' Ultimatum and their Implications on Peaceful Co-existence in Nigeria*. Accessed 20/08/2019, from file:///C:/Users/USER/Downloads/Social_Media_and_Hate_Speech_Analysis_of.pdf

Batchelor, O. (2017). Getting out the truth: The role of libraries in the fight against fake news. *RSR. Reference Services Review*, *45*(2), 143–148. doi:10.1108/RSR-03-2017-0006

Brennen, B. (2017). Making Sense of Lies, Deceptive Propaganda, and Fake News. *Journal of Medical Ethics*, *32*(3), 179–181. doi:10.1080/23736992.2017.1331023

Chadwick, A. (2011). The Political Information Cycle in a Hybrid News System: The British Prime Minister and the 'Bullygate' Affair. *The International Journal of Press/Politics*, *16*(1), 3–29. doi:10.1177/1940161210384730

Chisita, C. T. (2020). Libraries in the midst of the Coronavirus (COVID-19): Researchers experiences in dealing with the vexatious infodemic. *Library Hi Tech News*, *37*(6), 11–14. doi:10.1108/LHTN-03-2020-0022

De Paor, S., & Heravi, B. (2020). Information literacy and fake news: How the field of librarianship can help combat the epidemic of fake news. *Journal of Academic Librarianship*, *46*(5), 102218. doi:10.1016/j.acalib.2020.102218

Durodolu, O. O., & Ibenne, S. K. (2020). The fake news infodemic vs information literacy. Library Hi Tech News. doi:10.1108/LHTN-03-2020-0020

Durodolu, O.O, Ibenne, S.K and Dube, TV (2021). New mental costumes: Leveraging ACRL's value of information frame in dealing with infodemics in a post-truth era. *College & Research Libraries News, 82*(4), 175.

Durodolu, O. O., & Ocholla, D. O. (2017). Search Strategy, Self-Concept and Metacognitive Skills of Secondary School Teachers in Selected Cities in Nigeria and South Africa. *LIBRI: International Journal of Library and Information Science, 67*(2). doi:10.1515/libri-2016-0104

Eva, N., & Shea, E. (2018). Amplify your impact: Marketing libraries in an era of "fake news". *Reference and User Services Quarterly*, *57*(3), 168–171. doi:10.5860/rusq.57.3.6599

Harvey, L. (2020). Researching the real world. *Quality Research International*. Retrieved 27/07/2020, from https://www.qualityresearchinternational.com/methodology/RRW8pt2pt2Positivismandsurveys.php

Hua, J., & Shaw, R. (2020). Corona Virus (COVID-19) "Infodemic" and Emerging Issues through a Data Lens: The Case of China. *International Journal of Environmental Research and Public Health*, *17*(7), 2309. doi:10.3390/ijerph17072309 PMID:32235433

Lewandowsky, S., Ecker, U. K., & Cook, J. (2017). Beyond misinformation: Understanding and coping with the "post-truth" era. *Journal of Applied Research in Memory and Cognition*, *6*(4), 353–369. Advance online publication. doi:10.1016/j.jarmac.2017.07.008

Limaye, R. J., Sauer, M., Ali, J., Bernstein, J., Wahl, B., Barnhill, A., & Labrique, A. (2020). Building trust while influencing online COVID-19 content in the social media world. *The Lancet. Digital Health*, *2*(6), e277–e278. doi:10.1016/S2589-7500(20)30084-4 PMID:32322814

Mackey, T. P., & Jacobson, T. E. (2011). Reframing information literacy as a metaliteracy. *College & Research Libraries*, *72*(1), 62–78. doi:10.5860/crl-76r1

Mosseri, A. (2016). News feed FYI: addressing hoaxes and fake news. *Facebook Newsroom*. Retrieved on 3/08/2020, from https://newsroom.fb.com/news/2016/12/news-feed-fyi-addressing-hoaxes-and-fake-news/

Naughton, J. (2020). *Fake news about Covid-19 can be as dangerous as the virus*. Retrieved on 17/07/2020, from https://www.theguardian.com/commentisfree/2020/mar/14/fake-news-about-covid-19-can-be-as-dangerous-as-the-virus

Pan American Health Organisation and World Health Organisation. (2020). *Understanding The Infodemic and Misinformation in the Fight Against Covid-19 Factsheet N.5*. Department of Evidence and Intelligence for Action in Health Office of the Assistant Director. Retrieved on 27/07/2020, from https://iris.paho.org/bitstream/handle/10665.2/52052/Factsheet-infodemic_eng.pdf?sequence=14

Parvin, S. (2019). *Essence of Learning "Metaliteracy" in the Age of Fake News*. https://www.daily-sun.com/arcprint/details/404947/Essence-of-Learning-%E2%80%9CMetaliteracy%E2%80%9D-in-the-Age-of-Fake-News-/2019-07-06

Rampersad, G., & Althiyabi, T. (2020). Fake news: Acceptance by demographics and culture on social media. *Journal of Information Technology & Politics*, *17*(1), 1–11. doi:10.1080/19331681.2019.1686676

Rochlin, N. (2017). Fake news: Belief in post-truth. *Library Hi Tech*, *35*(3), 386–392. doi:10.1108/LHT-03-2017-0062

Shields, P., & Rangarajan, N. (2013). *A Playbook for Research Methods: Integrating Conceptual Frameworks and Project Management*. New Forums Press.

Tarran, B. (2017). Why facts are not enough in the fight against fake news. *Significance*, *14*(5), 6–7. doi:10.1111/j.1740-9713.2017.01066.x

United Nations Educational, Scientific and Cultural Organization. (2020). *During this coronavirus pandemic, 'fake news' is putting lives at risk: UNESCO*. Retrieved at 06/05/2020, from https://news.un.org/en/story/2020/04/1061592

Vorhaus, M. (2020). *People Increasingly Turn To Social Media For News*. Retrieved on 1/08/2020, from https://www.forbes.com/sites/mikevorhaus/2020/06/24/people-increasingly-turn-to-social-media-for-news/#3a5763f43bcc

World Health Organisation. (2020). *Novel Coronavirus(2019-nCoV) Situation Report–13*. Retrieved on 27/03/2020, from https://www.who.int/docs/default-source/coronaviruse/situation-reports/20200202-sitrep-13-ncov-v3.pdf

Yaraghi, N. (2019). *How should social media platforms combat misinformation and hate speech*. Retrieved on 27/07/2020, from https://www.brookings.edu/blog/techtank/2019/04/09/how-should-social-media-platforms-combat-misinformation-and-hate-speech/

Zarocostas, J. (2020). How to fight an infodemic. *The Lancet, World report*. Retrieved on 27/07/2020, from https://www.thelancet.com/action/showPdf?pii=S0140-6736%2820%2930461-X

Zoe, T. (2020). *WHO says fake coronavirus claims causing 'infodemic'*. British Broadcasting Corporation. Retrieved on 17/07/2020, from https://www.bbc.com/news/technology-51497800

ADDITIONAL READING

Bitar, A. N., Zawiah, M., Al-Ashwal, F. Y., Kubas, M., Saeed, R. M., Abduljabbar, R., ... Khan, A. H. (2021). Misinformation, Perceptions Towards COVID-19 and Willingness to be Vaccinated: A Population-Based Survey in Yemen. *bioRxiv*.

Bode, L., & Vraga, E. K. (2021). Correction Experiences on Social Media During COVID-19. *Social Media + Society*, *7*(2), 20563051211008829. doi:10.1177/20563051211008829

Brennen, J. S., Simon, F. M., & Nielsen, R. K. (2021). Beyond (Mis) Representation: Visuals in COVID-19 Misinformation. *The International Journal of Press/Politics*, *26*(1), 277–299. doi:10.1177/1940161220964780

Fallis, D. (2020). The Epistemic Threat of Deepfakes. *Philosophy & Technology*, 1–21. PMID:32837868

Jing, T. W., & Murugesan, R. K. (2020, December). Protecting Data Privacy and Prevent Fake News and Deepfakes in Social Media via Blockchain Technology. In *International Conference on Advances in Cyber Security* (pp. 674-684). Springer.

Loomba, S., de Figueiredo, A., Piatek, S., de Graaf, K., & Larson, H. J. (2020). Measuring the Impact of Exposure to COVID-19 Vaccine Misinformation on Vaccine Intent in the UK and US. medRxiv.

Saltz, E., Leibowicz, C. R., & Wardle, C. (2021, May). Encounters with Visual Misinformation and Labels Across Platforms: An Interview and Diary Study to Inform Ecosystem Approaches to Misinformation Interventions. In *Extended Abstracts of the 2021 CHI Conference on Human Factors in Computing Systems* (pp. 1-6). ACM.

Schick, N. (2020). *Deepfakes: The Coming Infocalypse*. Twelve.

Silva, M., Ceschin, F., Shrestha, P., Brant, C., Fernandes, J., Silva, C. S., ... Giovanini, L. (2020). *Predicting Misinformation and Engagement in COVID-19 Twitter Discourse in the First Months of the Outbreak*. arXiv preprint arXiv:2012.02164.

Vizoso, Á., Vaz-Álvarez, M., & López-García, X. (2021). Fighting Deepfakes: Media and Internet Giants' Converging and Diverging Strategies Against Hi-Tech Misinformation. *Media and Communication*, *9*(1), 291–300. doi:10.17645/mac.v9i1.3494

KEY TERMS AND DEFINITIONS

Deepfakes: Defined as the deliberate manipulation of media using AI driven software to skew the context of audio, images, or video in an effort to promote a particular point of view.

Digital Media: Defined as the set of skills needed for an end-user to learn, live, and work in a society that depends on technologies for access and communication.

Fake News: Often of a sensational nature, created to be widely shared or distributed for the purpose of generating revenue, or promoting or discrediting a public figure, political movement, company, etc.

COVID-19 Pandemic: Potentially severe, primarily respiratory illness caused by a coronavirus and characterized by fever, coughing, and shortness of breath spread on a worldwide scale.

Infodemic: A massive amount of widely and rapidly circulating information about a particular crisis or controversial issue, consisting of a confusing combination of fact, falsehood, rumor, and opinion.

Information Disorder: The sharing or developing of false information with or without the intent of harming and they are categorized as misinformation, disinformation and malinformation.

Information Literacy: Defined as the deliberate manipulation of media using AI driven software to skew the context of audio, images, or video in an effort to promote a particular point of view.

Metaliteracy: Unified construct that supports the acquisition, production, and sharing of knowledge in collaborative online communities.

Chapter 8
Schrodinger's Deepfake:
Multimodal Analysis to Combat Deepfakes

Paul Siegel
Mercer University, USA

ABSTRACT

Deepfakes have become an emerging threat to media. Many authors have identified social and digital media as a multimodal artifact. Others have identified the weaponization of that same digital media. At times when media was weaponized before, students were taught persuasive techniques, not as an incentive to use them, but as a guard against those persuasive techniques taking advantage of the students. In this new age of digital, multimodal propaganda, adapting persuasive techniques will help to combat the dangers our society faces. This chapter will examine three different anti-propaganda interventions and examine their implementation against a deepfaked video.

INTRODUCTION

The summer of 1969 was an important year for the American space race: The first manned missions would be landing on the moon's surface. President Richard M. Nixon knew two possible outcomes to a manned space flight: total success or abject, costly, public failure. Nixon's team drafted two separate speeches, one addressing the nation upon the mission's success, one addressing the nation about the failure. Until recently, that speech has never been spoken or recorded by Nixon. With the successful landing and return of Apollo 11, Nixon never had to give the failure

DOI: 10.4018/978-1-7998-6474-5.ch008

speech. A small group of computer engineers, film producers, and professors at the Massachusetts Institute of Technology took the speech written for Nixon and created "In the Event of Moon Disaster" (2020). Then, using archival footage, they created a deepfake AI simulation of President Nixon delivering the speech. It was a success. President Nixon appeared on screen, with the same background, and said the words he had never said.

While this was an academic exercise designed to showcase the possibilities of the technology, it also demonstrated the limitations of current pedagogical practices to combat deepfakes. For example, imagine the issues that would occur if a current politician had their speeches, photos, or other media pieces maliciously modified and widely distributed. Would the world be able to tell the difference? Indeed, has the world adequately educated its students to understand this emerging threat?

Indeed, that event has come to pass. While researching different deepfakes for this article, a deepfaked video of President Trump was produced by Russian Times. Russian Times (RT), the state-owned Russian news agency (also identified as a propaganda arm of the Putin government (US Department Of State, 2020), put out a deepfaked video of President Donald Trump exploring the RT studios and appearing in broadcasts. The video used speeches and videos of President Trump taken out of context and redubbed to suit RT's and, by extension, the Russian Government's purposes. For this paper, one can use it as an example of the potential harm that deepfakes can cause and how they can be combatted. A translation of any Russian subtitles or text has been included in Appendix A. In this chapter, the deepfake of President Trump will be examined and used to highlight how multimodal literacy and propaganda literacy can combat deepfakes. This paper will demonstrate how three different approaches to propaganda literacy- TAP, The ABCs of Propaganda, and Q/TIP- can be modified to meet the challenge of deepfakes in the media.

BACKGROUND

Understanding the Origins of Deepfakes

A deepfake is an AI-created simulation of someone manipulated to either create speech that that person never said or do something that that person never did (Westerlund, 2019). Deepfakes have been used to insert people into pornographic movies they were never in (Öhman, 2020) and used to manipulate the speech and words of political figures (see Del Viscio (2020) as an example). It has not been used to attack governments, but as the Russia Times video demonstrates, it is only a matter of time before that happens (Westerlund, 2019). With this rise in media usage, there has been a connected rise in educating students about how to comprehend these

Figure 1. Deepfake example taken from the Russian Times

emerging technologies (Mills, 2010). This rise has created pedagogical advances in both the literacy and digital realm. However, as technology continues to outpace educational advances, educators must turn to the tools they have to combat these attacks. Educators must reconceptualize the trouble with deepfakes, not a lack of comprehension of deepfakes, but a failure to see deepfakes as a form of persuasion. Indeed, it is in persuasion (Hobbs, 2020) that one might find the best way to combat deepfakes: by drawing from the pedagogies of literacy, multimodality, and persuasive writing

Digital Literacy and Deepfakes

Literacy is the interpretation of symbols (Saussure, 1998). Saussure argues that each word is a symbol in that a word is a representation of a thing. Readers must interpret the word to understand what it is representing. However, the interpretation of symbols is fraught with possible understanding, application, and presumption errors. Each word has two sides: that of the connotative and denotative. Connotation is the subjective interpretation of the word and brings in the viewer's personal and sociological experience. Denotation is the objective meaning of the symbol, quite literally what it is. Between these two poles of interpretation, the subjective and the objective, meaning is created. The crux of this creation is that, within the confines of fallibility, the objective truth of something has never been questioned. Everyone assumes that the objective is a stable definition.

It is here where deepfakes begin to undermine and destabilize meaning. By casting doubt on the denotative meaning, they undermine part of our literacy. When an end-user can no longer empirically decide what is true, everything becomes false. By undermining what the viewer can assume to be accurate, deepfakes undermine the dichotomy of connotation and denotation. Moreover, in so doing, they further undermine what can be considered as valid and what is not. For instance, in the video that will be referred to throughout this chapter, a viewer may be left with the cognitive dissonance of having to understand why President Trump, the symbolic and literally head of the US government, would do a segment like this for a company like Russia Times. Russian Times is an organ of the Russian Government, known for producing propaganda.

The combination of these two things does not make sense unless the video is not accurate, which changes one's conception of the video. However, then a viewer must question why it was made in the first place. When discussing deepfakes, a viewer must change how they conceptualize a text. When one first views deepfakes, there is a moment of doubt incomprehension, a moment of cognitive dissonance. At that moment, there are two texts to a reader aware of deepfakes. One text is the actual video. The other is a video that is not true. Before a reader goes through the analysis process on each potential video, each proposition (the video is fake, the video is actual) is equally valid. This is Schrodinger's Deepfake, named after the eponymous cat who could be both alive and dead at the exact moment until it was observed.

Deepfakes will become more subtle and credible as AI technology continues to improve (Westerlund, 2019). It may eventually become impossible for the average person to distinguish between a deepfaked video and a non-manipulated video. Indeed, the Russian Times video mentioned above demonstrates the capability of deepfakes, even one used for humor. As the algorithms that create deepfakes are refined, it is even more important that those whose works involve literacy are prepared for the problems that Deepfakes can cause.

Multimodal Literacy

Deepfakes, however, are not as quickly read as a simple printed text. Some texts, especially in the digital realm, require a more complex understanding of literacy. To address this need, educators can look to The New London Group (1996), a group of scholars of media (Gee & Esteban-Guitart, 2019), literacy (Petrina et al., 2008), semantics (Unsworth, 2006), and other allied fields. They were the first to suggest that new frontiers, digital and otherwise, would require a rethinking of how literacy was taught. They posited that when a student reads a text, whatever that text might be, the student uses a multitude of different literacies at one time. Take, for instance, the multiple levels of understanding that occur with the Russia Times video. Assuming the video is real, viewers would need visual and aural literacy to comprehend what they are seeing and hearing. They would need cultural literacy to understand what RT is. Perhaps, they would need a political literacy that would indicate who President Trump is, his views, and his political party's understanding of the world. Finally, they would need historical literacy to comprehend the geopolitical context between Russia and the United States, particularly in the last 30 years. Moreover, these are just the most apparent literacies. If one assumes the video is fake, then other literacies come into play. The Socio-political literacy of President Trump's relationship with Russia is needed to understand the context. Viewers would also need to understand the technological literacy of deepfakes and the possibilities around those.

Through the increased spread of technology and media saturation (Thamarai Selvi et al., 2019), students are exposed at an early age, and in increased amounts, to various multimodal media. To understand this new world, they must quickly adapt multimodal strategies of reading. Unfortunately, this adaptation, if unguided, comes with a host of issues that would potentially allow students to be vulnerable to the weaponization of media. What can teachers do to combat both a fundamental lack of understanding about multimodality and the weaponization of those same multimodal artifacts?

Digital Persuasion

Many authors have identified social and digital media as a multimodal artifact (Bourelle et al., 2016; Chan et al., 2017; Chandler & Scenters-Zapico, 2012; D'Amelio, 2018; Leu et al., 2015). Others have identified the weaponization of that same digital media (Milyakina, 2018; Sparby, 2017; Vaccari & Chadwick, 2020). Digital multimodal texts, especially those that fit under the categories of malicious media, rely on rhetorical techniques that are inherently anti-argumentative. For instance, A meme does not convey meaning by laying out and explaining claims and warrants. Instead, it conveys its meaning through pathos. A deepfakes video uses the *Ethos* of the person speaking to subvert its message. When media was weaponized before, students were taught persuasive techniques, not as an incentive to use them, but as a guard against those persuasive techniques taking advantage of the students (Hobbs & Mcgee, 2008). In this new age of digital, multimodal propaganda, adapting persuasive techniques for the 21st Century will help combat the dangers our society faces.

Furthermore, argumentative writing has become a central standard within many academic programs, including State Standards (see Georgia Department of Education (2015) as an example). Overall, educators have moved away from teaching persuasive writing throughout the curriculum and instead have focused more on argumentative writing. Indeed, This divide has been present since creating persuasive writing

(Fleming, 2019, p.509). However, by itself, argumentative writing is not enough to combat the weaponization of mass media (Hobbs, 2020). This is further complicated by that same mass media being multimodal. These multimodal compositions require various levels of complex analysis that go beyond that of argumentative writing.

Figure 2. Iterative interactions between author, intended audience, and purpose

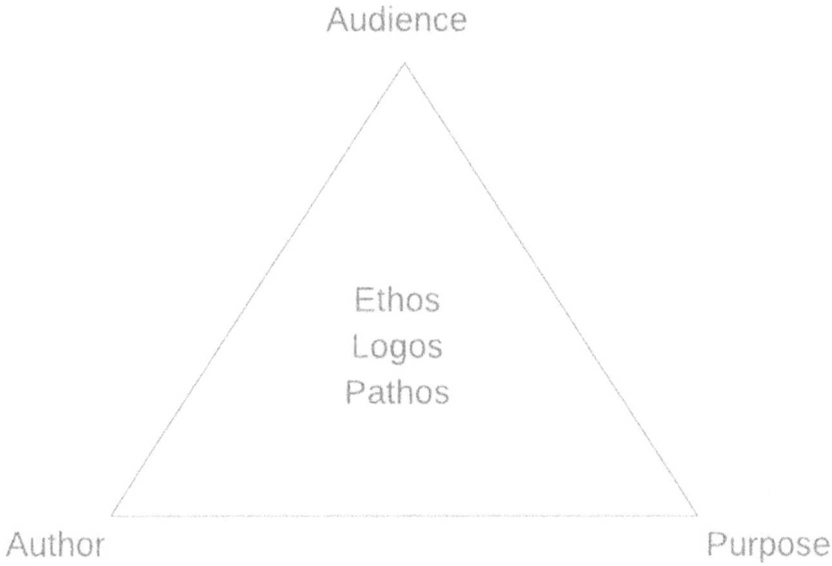

The Foundation of Anti-Propaganda Literacy

Deepfakes rely on a critical misunderstanding of the author, audience, and purpose. To combat deepfakes and other malicious media, students must learn to doubt their first reading of the rhetorical triangle. Furthermore, Deepfakes rely on people misconstruing who has produced the video and confusing the author. For example, using our Russia Times video, a viewer might wonder who decided to produce the video. What were their intentions and decision-making? What did they want the audience to understand from the video? Separately, the RT video calls into question the purpose of the video. It seems to be made as a joke, but is that it? A deepfake video of the American President, using his likeness and words, produced by an arm of the Russian Government know for creating propaganda (US Department Of State, 2020) would suggest that there is a multitude of purposes at work here and that the deliberate obscuring of that purpose may have been the initial purpose of the video.

Deepfakes are also intentionally obscure the audience of a video. Again, using the video above, we can see that the audience for this video is two-fold. The video is made for those who oppose President Trump as leverage and evidence that the politician in question is failing. The other audience is those who support President Trump. The effect of the video is much harder to enumerate for those who support a given politician. It could undermine their belief in their health, undermining the reception of a given message. Ultimately, deepfakes create doubt about the authenticity and reliability of what people understand to be true. So, if deepfakes have caused the author, audience, and purpose to be undermined, what does that leave us? The actual message itself. Moreover, in that message, Cicero and Plato identified as the center of rhetoric: Ethos, Logos, and Pathos, the three types of rhetorical appeals. These appeals are in themselves seemingly immune to the unsettling effects of Deepfakes.

Ethos, which can be summarized as ethics, does not necessarily rely on the person's words; the average measure of their actions judges it. A person does that defines their ethics, less so the words they use (Heinrichs, 2020). In this way, a deepfake video of a speech has a much smaller impact on a person's ethics than would be present otherwise. Ethos is fundamentally built on actions. Technology is not yet at a point where reality can be simulated. Again, the RT video is used as an example. One video put out by the Russian Government, with a lighthearted and farcical tone, would probably not have any lasting effect on the Ethos of President Trump, regardless of how the viewer feels about President Trump. Ethos is the average of your actions rather than a specific event, although wrong actions have an outsized effect on this. It also depends on the severity of the action.

Logos can be examined independently of what a person says. I would argue that to include whoever said a given statement would bias that argument and potentially open the viewer to logical fallacies. The logic of the Russian Times video is slightly inscrutable. However, it does require the viewer to ask themselves, what is the purpose of this video if it is accurate, and its purpose is fake? If it is accurate, the logic for making the video shows President Trump working with a foreign press office and having a little fun. If it is fake, then the logic seems to suggest two things: first, that proof that the Russian Government can produce deepfakes, and second, that the logic they are using in the video does not matter if the first point is valid.

Interventions

TAP Memetics

One area of malicious media that has metastasized faster than others is that of memes. Most people consider memes to be simple visual messages. However, they are complex and essential parts of modern communications (Cannizzaro, 2016).

Table 1. Questions for Memetic Analysis using TAP (Panther & Author, 2020)

Term	Prompting Questions
Text	What is shown? Is this a meme? What makes it memetic? Have you seen this meme before? If so, when, and where did you see it? How was it used? Why do you think this picture was selected to accompany this message? What is the effect of the combination? Could you still understand the message even if you did not recognize the picture? Why or why not? How do all the things you have mentioned combine to create the overall message of the meme?
Audience	Who or what is pictured? What is he/she/it known for? What does [print text term(s)] refer to? Who would "get it"? Whom is the meme created for? How would different groups view this meme? Is this meme referencing another meme? Why did the creator of this meme reference [another meme, name, place, emotion]? Can this meme be used in a different context? Why has this meme spread? What makes it successful as a meme? Why do people share this meme? How does the spread of this meme influence its popularity? What would happen to this meme if the internet did not exist to spread it so rapidly? How long do you think this meme will continue to spread?
Purpose	What do you know about the person or group that may have created this meme? Why would they want to share this meme? What reaction might people have to this meme? Why? What stance does the creator or sharer take on this topic? What has influenced the creator or sharer's opinions? What is your stance on this topic? Does this meme represent your opinion or experience? What has influenced your opinions on this topic?
Re-writing	Can this meme be re-created? How could you change the meme to change the message? How could you change the meme to represent your opinion or experience?

Memes have a grammar of their own (Zenner & Geeraerts, 2018) that educators can use to help analyze memes. Critical memetic literacy is an essential part of shaping how children interact with the digital world (Harvey & Palese, 2018). Understanding the intention and messaging of memes is vital to both communicate and avoid the coercive effects of memes (Beskow et al., 2020).

Siegel and Panther (2020) set out to see if students could be taught to analyze memes as if they were any other form of media. They created a critical memetic analysis instrument that the authors referred to as TAP, an acronym for Text, Audience, and Purpose. TAP has been proven effective at meeting goals associated with the critical analysis of deepfakes, including rhetorical analysis (Oddo, 2013), critical literacy (Yoon, 2008), and comprehension (Shoffner et al., 2010).

Table 2. Modifications for TAP Deepfakes

	Text	Audience	Purpose
Memes	Separate image and text before analysis	Consider primary audience	Consider the purpose of text as benign
Deepfakes	Separate image and sound before analysis on both sides of the divide.	Consider the primary and null audience	Consider purpose on both sides of Schrodinger's Deepfake

Memes work to convey their message in multiple ways. In one instance, the image itself conveys something, usually an emotion of some sort. In addition, the text itself conveys the original logical sequence that the author intended. Another mode of communication for memes is that of spatial grammar. This essentially means that the actual layout and development of the meme itself works to convey meaning (McCloud, 1994). In this way, a meme can be seen as a multimodal rhetorical exercise, and rhetoric can be seen as a mode of analysis that can also be applied to deepfakes. Applying TAP to comprehending a meme works in much the same way that any other systematic analysis might. The intervention first started with the text: What did it say? What was unique about it? Were there any words or phrasings that stood out to you? Essentially, this step asked students to consider the actual content of the message, not how the meme worked overall.

The intervention also examined the image in the Text phase too. First, students were asked to think critically about who was included in the picture, where it had come from, the history behind it, and the overall memetic genealogy. In memetics, images are often taken over, flipped, and reused in unique ways. Each generation of meme makers takes the same base idea and adds their flair to it in the context of the overall evolution of a meme. Through this reusing, the picture comes to be used as a recognized symbol, as text. Next, the intervention examined the audience. it asks: "Whom might the audience for this meme be? Who is not the audience? Who would like it, and who would not?" In this way, the authors asked students to begin to think of the meme not as a self-existing piece of culture but as a piece of rhetoric enmeshed in culture and created by a human (Fairclough, 1992). Students were quick to realize that the opinions of the creator and whom they directed their meme at often changed how the meme was interpreted. This idea then leads into the concept of Purpose: "Why would someone make this meme? What were they hoping to accomplish?". They thought of the meme's author and why they created that meme to access primary literary interpretation and list the various conversations and more significant ideas at play.

As shown in Table 2, the first change is overall in the application of the intervention. As stated above, deepfakes attempt to destabilize meaning and truth.

Deepfake videos, before they are revealed to be fake videos, exist in two states simultaneously. Students must accept the video as accurate, and, at the same time, they must understand that the video can also be a complete fabrication. Students must complete any systemic analysis for each of these states. Only after having completed the analysis for each of these states can the video then be judged as true or not. TAP relies on separating the text and picture, interpreting each separately, recognizing context, and understanding the message. This is an essential part of where TAP can help combat deepfakes. Deepfake makers rely on the incongruity between images and words to cause their disruption. By separating the two, students can examine each, and using the context of who the person is and what they are saying, see the incongruity and not be swayed by it.

Secondly, TAP can be modified to help students understand the implied audience and the null audience. The implied audience is the presumptive audience the speaker would be addressing their meme. At the same time, the null audience would be everyone else. Deepfakes will seem to be aimed at the implied audience. Take, for instance, the Russia Times deepfakes. The implied audience of that video was ostensible to President Trump's followers. The null audience were those who wanted to see him embarrassed and discredited. By recognizing how the message would be received by different parties, students can identify the intent behind deepfakes in the first place. This step requires objectivity and detachment from the subject, no easy feat sometimes.

Thirdly, TAP can be modified to help students understand the purpose of the deepfake. In this case, students would have to assume that a given video is both a deepfake and not a deepfake. By asking, "What is the purpose behind this video? Why would someone take this video?" By discussing the idea of purpose, readers will create an emotional distance between the message and the deepfake itself.

TAP Application

Text first asks us to identify what is a text and what is not. In this case, the text is essentially the video and the audio. For the first viewing of the video, the words were in Russian except for President Trump's speeches. The video viewing did not show anything out of the ordinary except for the whole concept. The idea that an American President would go to Russia to be filmed at RT's studios is beyond the pale, even for someone as unconventional as President Trump. The words themselves are not particular outliers either, except for the idea that they mention some of the same themes that President Trump often did in his campaign speeches (i.e., the wall, immigration, etc.). This echoing of his language is odd.

The next set of questions ask us who the audience for this video is? In this case, there are those whom the deepfake is designed for, and then there is everyone else.

One could argue that this video is not made to be viewed as believable, nor created for any audience to accept that President Trump would do these things. In this case, a viewer may feel that the audience is those in the US government who know the potential problems with deepfakes and what impact legitimate and carefully disguised deepfakes might have. After this, the rest of the world then becomes the audience for the video.

The final part of TAP is purpose. The purpose of this video can be described as a proof of concept. Using publicly available recordings, the Russian Government, or Russian Times, made a semi-convincing facsimile of President Trump and then distributed it anonymously through the world wide web. Whoever made it wanted certain people to know that they could make it and what it might look like if they did. This may simply be a fun, frivolous video that Russia Times made. However, viewers must remember that everything that is produced is intended to them about something. If viewers accept it as a genuine production of RT and not a piece of weaponized media, then it becomes a comedic video made to amuse Russia Times viewers. If it is weaponized media, then it is trying to convince the viewers of something else entirely.

ABCs of Propaganda Analysis

The US presidential election of 1936 was particularly vicious and vociferous, with a growing amount of propaganda on each side. President Franklin Delano Roosevelt was fighting for re-election against Alfred Landon. Each side took to mudslinging and trying to sway the other side with targeted propaganda. Into this divide stepped Clyde Miller and Violet Edwards. Working out of the Teacher's College of Columbia University, they would eventually be vital members of the Committee for Public Information, a government agency dedicated to media. The Committee served two roles throughout the World War II-era: it acted as a conduit for official non-partisan information and as an advisor to prevent the spread of misinformation. It was in this latter role that the CPI created the ABCs of Propaganda Analysis:

"A. *Propaganda is opinion or actions intended to influence the thoughts and actions of others.* Unfortunately, many of us unconsciously become the tools of clever propaganda tricksters and help them to do their work. Remember, anybody who expresses an opinion is a propagandist.

B. *All propaganda centers on some conflict*-some issue. Make yourself a list of local, national, and international issues to see the direction of your own opinions or propaganda relating to them.

C. *Our opinion of Propaganda concerning every issue is determined by our environment*, our training, our education, by the extent to which we, ourselves, have been influenced by the propaganda of others.
D. *Opinion or Propaganda is good or bad*- if we Americans believe in the Declaration of Independence- insofar as it promotes or hinders life, liberty, and the pursuit of happiness of the great majority of our fellow citizens.
E. *The best way to deal with propaganda, whether our own or that of others, is to subject it to searching criticism and appraisal.* This is the way of the intelligent man. Ask who holds the opinion- who utters the propaganda and why."(Miller & Edwards, 1936, p.63) Italics original.

If deepfakes are propaganda, then the ABCs take different approaches against that propaganda than TAP does. TAP could be considered systematic analysis; the ABCs are holistic analysis. In the context of the 21st-century multimodal artifacts, that flexibility and applicability make it particularly useful. Built into the assumption of the ABCs is that everything produced is in some way a piece of persuasion. This is not considered a bad thing. From a novel to a video, it is simply acknowledging that everything is produced to persuade someone to do something. As was discussed above, deepfakes are two different texts. In the case of the ABCs, readers would assume that each of those texts is designed to persuade.

The ABCs suggest that everyone, in some way, is a byproduct of the propaganda that they have consumed, produced, or been a part of. One of the missing features of TAP is that it does not consider the reader or viewers' reaction to the propaganda. This ties to the concept of propaganda being anything that is argumentative, anything that tries to persuade. Frequently, people forget that propaganda exists on both sides of an issue. This call to subjectivity from the ABCs ironically forces the reader to take an objective stance and forces the viewer to understand that what they are seeing, reading, understanding exists on a continuum from "propaganda I agree with" to "propaganda I disagree with." Everything they will encounter falls somewhere on that spectrum.

ABCs of Propaganda Analysis Application

Since the ABCs approach a given form of media from a holistic perspective, this section will address how each point applies to the video in question. One crucial point to understand is that this analysis is predicated upon positionality (Low & Pandya, 2019) and interpretation of modes. The author of this chapter is a cis-gendered, white male from Georgia. His political views more closely align with Democratic principles than Republican.

Table 3. Modifications to the ABCs of Propaganda for Deepfakes

	Influence	Conflict	Environment	Opinion	Criticism and Appraisal
Propaganda	"All thoughts are propaganda."	Is this issue-based?	How does who I influence how I see things?	How do you feel about propaganda?	"Who utters the propaganda and why?"
Deepfakes	What is this trying to get me to think?	What issue is this based around?	Digital Environments are complex	Whose opinion is this expressing?	What does not fit? What feels off?

A. *Propaganda is an opinion or action intended to influence the thoughts and actions of others.* This would make me wonder who and what the video is intended to influence. On its surface, it is a clumsily done deepfake ostensibly used to poke fun at President Trump. However, it does represent to the viewer that the Russians have the capability to complete a deepfake at this level.

B. *All propaganda centers on some conflict-some issue.* For example, a regular news viewer would know that President Trump has had an extraordinary relationship with Russia (Korobkov, 2019). From seeking their help in the 2016 and 2020 elections (Baker & Fandos, 2019) to failing to condemn the bounties put on US troops in Afghanistan (Savage et al., 2020), they would understand that this is a touch button issue for many potential viewers of this video. Even if purposefully, clumsily deepfaked, releasing this video might indicate that Russia is aware of these issues.

C. *Our opinion of Propaganda.* This point speaks to an understanding that propaganda exists and is commonly used by bad actors, not that this video is propaganda. In this sense, it is an acknowledgment that propaganda exists.

D. *Opinion or Propaganda is good or bad.* This point connects to point C: propaganda exists and can be used for good or evil. That everything that is created in culture is inherently persuasive. Good and Bad are assigned judgments that depend on the context. In this case, a viewer might recognize that this video is a threat to the US government because it shows the idea that Russia can produce and disseminate a deepfaked video.

E. *The best way to deal with propaganda, whether our own or that of others, is to subject it to searching criticism and appraisal.* The author's initial criticism of this video is about President Trump's most distinctive feature, hair. The actor whose face is obscured by President Trump has too much hair, and it is too normal. There is an obvious difference between President Trump's carefully coifed combover and the actor's fuller head of hair. In addition to this visual disparity, the actual words used in the video seem to be drawn from his speeches. They do not sound natural to him or spoken with Trump's typical cadence. In all, this video seems to be fake. Note that a student will need to examine each modality to analyze this video thoroughly. The question that then comes to mind is, why is this video faked? Why would someone try and convince an audience that President Trump is saying these things? Using contextual information about the relationship between President Trump and Russia, in addition to the historical background of Russian involvement in the 2016 election, a reasonable viewer can surmise that Russian sources put out this video to demonstrate their ability to deepfake videos.

Teaching Critical Media Literacy

Critical media literacy can be defined as a means of analyzing and understanding media. There have been several approaches developed by both private (Jolls & Thoman, 2008) and public (Wilson et al., 2011) entities to integrate CML into the classroom. However, that integration has not been widespread (Share et al., 2019) or particularly successful (Hobbs, 2004). Instead, much of Critical Media Literacy has been focused on combatting specific issues in the media. For instance, Schmitt et al. (2019) used critical media literacy to combat Islamic propaganda online. Another study examined Critical media literacy effectiveness in combatting aggression (Fingar & Jolls, 2014). Both found that it was successful, but only in that isolated case. The variety of approaches to critical media literacy and the lack of integration in curriculum and standards makes it difficult to identify a particular methodology that is prevalent. Particularly ones that are comparable to TAP and the ABCs. For the purposes of this chapter, I will be drawing from the Centre for Media Literacy *in the 21st Century, 2nd Edition* (2008).

The Centre for Media Literacy intervention uses a series of questions and ideas to guide students through media analysis. Much like the ABCs of Propaganda Analysis, the CML system relies on five core concepts. From these five core concepts, they have developed guiding questions, much like was done with TAP. As can be seen in Table 4, each of these concepts and questions is then organized within a category. These categories closely align with the suggestions of rhetorical analysis above, except for content. Content is an exciting addition to the rhetorical triangle. It acknowledges that the medium in which the piece is produced impacts how the message is interpreted. CML does not acknowledge that there are multiple modes of interpretation within that content, however. Thus, in modifying this for deepfakes, educators must understand that deepfakes are multimodal, and any usage of an intervention is only for a single mode.

Table 4. CML's Five Core Concepts and Key Questions for Consumer and Producers (Q/TIPS)

Key Words	Deconstruction: CML's 5 Key Questions (Consumer)	CML's 5 Core Concepts	Construction: CML's 5 Key Questions (Producer)
Authorship	Who created this message?	All media messages are constructed	What am I authoring?
Format	What creative techniques are used to attract attention?	Media messages are constructed using a creative language with its own rules	Does message reflect understanding in format, creativity, and technology?
Audience	How might different people understand this message differently?	Different people experience the same media message differently	Is the message engaging and compelling for the target audience?
Content	What values, lifestyles, and points of view are represented in or omitted from this message?	Media have embedded values and points of view.	Is it clearly and consistently framed values, lifestyles, and points of view in content?
Purpose	Why is this message being sent?	Most media messages are organized to gain profit and/or power	Is the purpose communicated effectively?

<<Source – Jolls and Thoman 2008>>

Q/TIPS Interventive Techniques

The CML process requires the viewer to identify if they are the viewer or producer and then follow a series of questions. The first question asks, "Who created this message?" The simple answer to that would be Russia Times. The complicated answer would be that the viewer does not know. This message could have come from the GRU, akin to the American CIA, or other entities within the state government of Russia. Ultimately, with propaganda, a viewer can only know who distributed it. Note that this would be accurate even if the video were not a deepfake.

The second question is, "What creative techniques are used to attract attention?". This video uses a deepfake of President Trump, including his words, to gain attention. However, it is the obviousness and exaggeration of the deepfake that first attracted attention. It is almost as if the deepfake was the purpose of the video rather than the actual message.

The third question asks, "How might different people understand this message differently?". For example, an audience who views it as a deepfake will understand the video's message entirely different than those who view it as a legitimate piece of journalism video. In addition, the video being in Russian is also a point of demarcation for the audience. A native Russian audience will view it differently than someone who does not speak Russian.

The fourth question asks, "What values, lifestyles, and points of view are represented in or omitted from this message?" On the surface, it seems to be attached to the audience and tangentially connected to Ethos. One way Ethos can be maintained by maintaining decorum (Heinrichs, 2020). By matching the mores of the viewer, the text can more explicitly reinforce its point. The question then is: Who matches the mores displayed in the video? The ideas put out by President Trump in the video seem like a humorous interpretation of his views, particularly around 1:30 in the video, "Outstanding wall - I know the sense of it." This is playing from President Trump's campaign promise to build a wall along the southern border and to make Mexico pay for it. This would then be matching the views of those who oppose President Trump. However, this would then be out of line with Russia's current relationship with President Trump. The cyclical incongruity obscures and confuses the issue of authorship even more.

The fifth question asks, "Why is this message being sent?" This perhaps the most critical question in the Q/TIP process. Regarding the video under discussion, one must again split their analysis. If the video is fake, then the purpose was to demonstrate that they could use the technology or that the use of that technology was done for humorous purposes. If the video is accurate, and, again, any reasonable viewer would be able to tell it is fake, then the purpose is even stranger. It serves no discernable purpose except to call into question President Trump's relationship with Russia and why his image and words are being used in this way. Ultimately, this author believes that a reasonable viewer would come to the same conclusion about this video as they did in the last two analyses: This deepfaked video was put out as a proof of concept by the Russian Government.

Discussion

As shown in Table 5, all three types of anti-propaganda media correlate with the rhetorical triangle. TAP and CML often mention the sections in the rhetorical triangle directly by name. As it befits their more holistic approach, the ABCs do not quite as easily fit into those categories. Section E of the ABCs ("The best way to deal with propaganda…is to subject it to searching criticism and appraisal") does not fit into the chart above at all. This stems from the period in which this intervention was created. Rhetorical education may have been more common in the 1930s and 1940s. This education would have provided a background a student could use to understand the ABCs. TAP and Q/TIP are both more systematic in their methods of analysis. This systematicness and scaffolding are indicative of a lack of understanding of rhetoric. This stands to reason since those unfamiliar with rhetoric will need more support and guidance when analyzing it. Those familiar with it will be able to do more with it.

Table 5. A comparison of TAP, the ABCs of Propaganda and Q/TIPS

	TAP (Panther & AUTHOR, 2020)	**ABCs of Propaganda (Miller & Edward,1936)**	**CML's Questions and TIPS (Q/TIPS) (Centre for Media Literacy, 2008)**
Ethos	Audience Section	Section A	Authorship
Logos	Text Section (Words)	Section B	Content
Pathos	Text Section (Image)	Section D	Content
Audience	Audience Section	Section C	Audience
Author	Audience Section	Section A	Authorship
Purpose	Purpose Section	Section B	Purpose

Creating Believable and Sustainable Rhetoric is Key

All the techniques examined in this chapter involve various levels of rhetorical analysis. This would suggest that a firm grounding in rhetoric is an essential part of fighting propaganda of any sort. However, as noted in the persuasive writing section, there needs to be a return to teaching about propaganda from a young age. As soon as students begin to venture onto the internet, they should be educated about rhetoric. Each analysis takes a different approach to rhetoric. The prescriptive nature of Q/TIP and TAP indicates a systematized examination of a text. The more holistic approach to the analysis presented by the ABCs of Propaganda also uses rhetoric and speaks about it as if the reader is already familiar with the different parts of it and can do the analysis. This would indicate that TAP and Q/TIP might be better used with younger populations, and the ABCs of Propaganda might function better for older students and adults.

Analyzing Multimodal Objects

Keen-eyed readers will note that the lack of mention of multimodality in discussion of the analytical frameworks above. This has been deliberate, as it simplifies the analysis to look at only one mode of communication at a time. Consider all the modes that a deepfake or other malicious media can communicate in, the time to complete that analysis begins to expand exponentially. Deepfake videos present the problem of genuine audio overlaid with a falsified picture or vice versa. This could remove context and nuance. In short, each mode of communication can in some way be falsified, which means, in turn, that each mode of communication must then be analyzed. Understanding that these pieces of propaganda cannot be examined as standalone texts is another critical consideration. Instead, educators must see that propaganda exists in a discursive line enmeshed in culture and produced by that same culture (Unsworth, 2006). Ultimately, examining them without taking this discourse into account could be disingenuous at best and misleading at worst.

Technology Does not Stop Deepfake and AI Advancements

The technology behind a deepfake was not available ten years ago. Now, it is available to everyday consumers technically competent enough to install and run a program. Humanity can be sure that any technology that can be used for goodwill also be exploited for evil. Two decades ago, no one would have thought that memes would be used to radicalize and recruit extremists as Islamic radicals have done (Beskow et al., 2020). No one could conceive of deepfakes, but they were brought to fruition. However, there is some comfort in this advance in technology. The methodologies from analyzing propaganda can be used to analyze deepfakes, which means that they can be updated for any emerging technologies that come. Indeed, this chapter is simply the latest iteration in that adaptation process. Deepfakes are the latest form of persuasion to emerge from new technology. The creators of these analysis methodslooked to rhetoric to guide their instructional choices.

CONCLUSION

This chapter examined three different anti-propaganda heuristics, suggested how they might be implemented against multimodal artifacts, such as deepfakes, connected them to content already present in many secondary classrooms, and argued for their importance in a just, democratic society. This chapter has also shown how deepfakes are not impregnable pieces of technology that students cannot avoid. Instead, they are just the following form of media and propaganda. There is no semantic difference between the propaganda of the civil war and that of the latest multinational conflict. However, there is a difference in form. This means that old techniques of combatting propaganda should be unearthed and taught. Sometimes the newest threat can be combatted with the oldest of ideas. Deepfakes are here to stay. As technology improves, the public should expect to see more and more of them in popular and political culture. As Educators should expect to see more and more deepfakes in and out of the classroom. However, educators choose whether to prepare students to deal with these threats.

REFERENCES

Baker, P., & Fandos, N. (2019, June 14). Trump Is assailed for saying he would take campaign help from russia. *The New York Times, A1*. https://www.nytimes.com/2019/06/13/us/politics/trump-russia-campaign-help.html

Beskow, D. M., Kumar, S., & Carley, K. M. (2020). The evolution of political memes: Detecting and characterizing internet memes with multimodal deep learning. *Information Processing & Management*, *57*(2), 102170. Advance online publication. doi:10.1016/j.ipm.2019.102170

Bourelle, A., Bourelle, T., Knutson, A. V., & Spong, S. (2016). Sites of multimodal literacy: Comparing student learning in online and face-to-face environments. *Computers and Composition*, *39*, 55–70. doi:10.1016/j.compcom.2015.11.003

Cannizzaro, S. (2016). Internet memes as internet signs: A semiotic view of digital culture. *Sign Systems Studies*, *44*(4), 562–586. doi:10.12697/SSS.2016.44.4.05

Chan, C., Chia, A., & Choo, S. (2017). Understanding multiliteracies and assessing multimodal texts in the English curriculum. *English Teaching*, *46*(2), 73–87. https://journals.melta.org.my/index.php/tet/article/viewFile/458/286

Chandler, S., & Scenters-Zapico, J. (2012). New literacy narratives: Stories about reading and writing in a digital age. *Computers and Composition*, *29*(3), 185–190. doi:10.1016/j.compcom.2012.07.002

D'Amelio, E. (2018). Literacy theories for the digital age: Social, critical, multimodal, spatial, material and sensory lenses, edited by Kathy A. Mills. In Language and Education (Vol. 32, Issue 1). doi:10.1080/09500782.2017.1315129

de Saussure, F. (1998). *Course in general linguistics* (2nd ed.). (R. Harris, Trans.). Open Court.

Del Viscio, J. (2020, July). A Nixon deepfake, a "Moon Disaster" speech and an information ecosystem at risk. *Scientific American*. https://www.scientificamerican.com/article/a-nixon-deepfake-a-moon-disaster-speech-and-an-information-ecosystem-at-risk1/

Education, G. D. of. (2015). *9th-10th Grade English Language Arts Georgia Standards of Excellence (ELA GSE)*. https://www.georgiastandards.org/Georgia-Standards/Frameworks/ELA-9-10-Grade-9-Literature-Composition-Standards.pdf

Fairclough, N. (1992). Discourse and text: Linguistic and intertextual analysis within discourse analysis. *Discourse & Society*, *3*(2), 193–217. doi:10.1177/0957926592003002004

Fingar, K. R., & Jolls, T. (2014). Evaluation of a school-based violence prevention media literacy curriculum. *Injury Prevention*, *20*(3), 1–8. doi:10.1136/injuryprev-2013-040815 PMID:23956370

Fleming, D. (2019). Fear of persuasion in the English language arts. *College English*, *81*(6), 508–541.

Gee, J.-P., & Esteban-Guitart, M. (2019). Designing for deep learning in the context of digital and social media. *Media Education Research Journal*, *58*(27), 9–17. doi:10.3916/C58-2019-01

Harvey, L., & Palese, E. (2018). #NeverthelessMemesPersisted: Building critical memetic literacy in the classroom. *Journal of Adolescent & Adult Literacy*, *62*(3), 259–270. doi:10.1002/jaal.898

Heinrichs, J. (2020). *Thank you for arguing: What Aristotle, Lincoln and Homer Simpson can teach us about the art of persuasion* (4th ed.). Broadway Books.

Hobbs, R. (2004). A review of school-based initiatives in media literacy education. *The American Behavioral Scientist*, *48*(1), 42–59. doi:10.1177/0002764204267250

Hobbs, R. (2020). Propaganda in an age of algorithmic personalization: Expanding literacy research and practice. *Reading Research Quarterly*, *55*(3), 521–533. doi:10.1002/rrq.301

Hobbs, R., & Mcgee, S. (2008). Teaching about propaganda: An examination of the historical roots of media literacy. *The Journal of Media Literacy Education*, *6*(62), 56–67. www.jmle.org

Jolls, T., & Thoman, E. (2008). *MediaLitKit: Literacy for the 21st Century* (2nd ed.). Centre for Media Literacy.

Korobkov, A. (2019). Donald Trump and the Evolving U. S. -Russia Relationship. *Perceptions*, *24*(1), 39–58.

Leu, D. J., Forzani, E., Rhoads, C., Maykel, C., Kennedy, C., & Timbrell, N. (2015). The new literacies of online research and comprehension: Rethinking the reading achievement Gap. *Reading Research Quarterly*, *50*(1), 37–59. doi:10.1002/rrq.85

Low, D., & Pandya, J. Z. (2019). Issues of validity, subjectivity, and reflexivity in multimodal literacy research and analysis. *Journal of Language & Literacy Education*, *15*(1), 1–22.

McCloud, S. (1994). *Understanding comics: The Invisible art*. Harper Collins.

Miller, C. R., & Edwards, V. (1936). The Intelligent Teacher's guide through campaign propaganda. *The Clearing House: A Journal of Educational Strategies, Issues and Ideas*, *11*(2), 69–77. doi:10.1080/00098655.1936.11474219

Mills, K. A. (2010). A review of the "Digital Turn" in the new literacy studies. *Review of Educational Research*, *80*(2), 246–271. doi:10.3102/0034654310364401

Milyakina, A. (2018). Rethinking literary education in the digital age. *Sign Systems Studies*, *46*(4), 569–589. doi:10.12697/SSS.2018.46.4.08

Oddo, J. (2013). Discourse-Based methods across texts and semiotic modes: Three tools for micro-rhetorical analysis. *Written Communication*, *30*(3), 236–275. doi:10.1177/0741088313488071

Öhman, C. (2020). Introducing the pervert's dilemma: A contribution to the critique of deepfake pornography. *Ethics and Information Technology*, *22*(2), 133–140. doi:10.100710676-019-09522-1

Panther & Siegel. (2021). *"I want to use my voice": Virtual Literacy Instruction Using Critical Memetic Analysis* [Manuscript submitted for publication]. Tift College of Education, Mercer University.

Petrina, S., Feng, F., & Kim, J. (2008). Researching cognition and technology: How we learn across the lifespan. *International Journal of Technology and Design Education*, *18*(4), 375–396. doi:10.100710798-007-9033-5

Savage, C., Schmitt, E., Fandos, N., & Goldman, A. (2020, June 30). Trump got written briefing in February on possible Russian bounties, officials say. *New York Times*, A1.

Schmitt, J. B., Reiger, D., Ernst, J., & Roth, H.-J. (2019). Critical media literacy and Islamist online propaganda: The feasibility, applicability and impact of three learning arrangements. *International Journal of Conflict and Violence*, *12*(0), 1–19. doi:10.4119/UNIBI/ijcv.642

Share, J., Mamikonyan, T., & Lopez, E. (2019). Critical media literacy in teacher education, theory, and practice. Oxford Research Encyclopedia of Education, 1–30. doi:10.1093/acrefore/9780190264093.013.1404

Shoffner, M., de Oliveira, L. C., & Angus, R. (2010). Multiliteracies in the secondary English classroom: Becoming literate in the 21st Century. *English Teaching*, *9*(3), 75–89.

Sparby, E. M. (2017). Digital social media and aggression: Memetic rhetoric in 4chan's collective identity. *Computers and Composition*, *45*, 85–97. doi:10.1016/j.compcom.2017.06.006

Thamarai Selvi, V. T., Gayathri, R., & Vishnu Priya, V. (2019). Teens and technology addiction - A survey. *Drug Invention Today*, *11*(3), 663–665.

The New London Group. (1996). A pedagogy of multiliteracies: Designing social futures. *Harvard Educational Review*, *66*(1), 1–31.

Unsworth, L. (2006). Towards a metalanguage for multiliteracies education: Describing the meaning - making resources of language-image interaction. *English Teaching*, *5*(1), 55–76.

US Department Of State. (2020). *GEC Special Report : Pillars of Russia's Disinformation and Propaganda Ecosystem August 2020 Table of Contents*. Issue August.

Vaccari, C., & Chadwick, A. (2020). Deepfakes and disinformation: Exploring the impact of synthetic political video on deception, uncertainty, and trust in news. *Social Media + Society*, *6*(1). Advance online publication. doi:10.1177/2056305120903408

Westerlund, M. (2019). The emergence of deepfake technology: A review. *Technology Innovation Management Review*, *9*(11), 39–52. doi:10.22215/timreview/1282

Wilson, C., Grizzle, A., Tuazon, R., Akyempong, K., & Cheunj, C. K. (2011). *Media and information literacy curriculum for teachers*. UNESCO Digital Library. https://unesdoc.unesco.org/ark:/48223/pf0000192971

Yoon, S. (2008). Using memes and memetic processes to explain social and conceptual influences on student understanding about complex socio-scientific issues. *Journal of Research in Science Teaching*, *45*(8), 900–921. doi:10.1002/tea.20256

Zenner, E., & Geeraerts, D. (2018). One does not simply process memes: Image macros as multimodal constructions. In Cultures and Traditions of Wordplay and Wordplay Research (pp. 167–194). doi:10.1515/9783110586374-008

ADDITIONAL READING

Ahmed, S. (2021). Who inadvertently shares deepfakes? Analyzing the role of political interest, cognitive ability, and social network size. *Telematics and Informatics*, *57*, 101508. doi:10.1016/j.tele.2020.101508

Dawkins, A. (2020). Digital Citizenship, Digital Legacy, and School Librarians. *Library Technology Reports*, *56*(5), 17–21.

Dobber, T., Metoui, N., Trilling, D., Helberger, N., & de Vreese, C. (2020). Do (microtargeted) deepfakes have real effects on political attitudes? *The International Journal of Press/Politics*, 1940161220944364.

Karnouskos, S. (2020). Artificial Intelligence in Digital Media: The Era of Deepfakes. *IEEE Transactions on Technology and Society*, *1*(3), 138–147. doi:10.1109/TTS.2020.3001312

Krishna, D. (2021). Deepfakes, online platforms, and a novel proposal for transparency, collaboration, and education. *Richmond Journal of Law & Technology, 27*(3).

Schneider, J. J., King, J. R., Kozdras, D., & Welsh, J. L. (2020). Fast and Slow Literacies: Digital and Compositional Conundrums in a Post-Truth Era. *Literacy Research: Theory, Method, and Practice*, *69*(1), 320–338. doi:10.1177/2381336920937275

Shu, K., Bhattacharjee, A., Alatawi, F., Nazer, T. H., Ding, K., Karami, M., & Liu, H. (2020). Combating disinformation in a social media age. *Wiley Interdisciplinary Reviews. Data Mining and Knowledge Discovery*, *10*(6), e1385. doi:10.1002/widm.1385

Stellmann, E., Song, L., & Tucker, S. (2021). Reexamining Digital Citizenship: Pandemic Lessons to Prepare Teachers and Students for Digital Learning Environments. *What Teacher Educators Should Have Learned from 2020*, 113.

Tahir, R., Batool, B., Jamshed, H., Jameel, M., Anwar, M., Ahmed, F., . . . Zaffar, M. F. (2021, May). Seeing is Believing: Exploring Perceptual Differences in DeepFake Videos. In *Proceedings of the 2021 CHI Conference on Human Factors in Computing Systems* (pp. 1-16). Academic Press.

Vaccari, C., & Chadwick, A. (2020). Deepfakes and disinformation: Exploring the impact of synthetic political video on deception, uncertainty, and trust in news. *Social Media + Society*, *6*(1), 2056305120903408. doi:10.1177/2056305120903408

KEY TERMS AND DEFINITIONS

Artificial Intelligence: The theory and development of computer systems able to perform tasks that normally require human intelligence, such as visual perception, speech recognition, decision-making, and translation between languages.

Deepfake: A video of a person in which their face or body has been digitally altered so that they appear to be someone else, typically used maliciously or to spread false information.

Digital Literacy: Digital literacy means having the skills you need to live, learn, and work in a society where communication and access to information is increasingly through digital technologies like internet platforms, social media, and mobile devices.

Multimodal Literacy: Multimodal literacy is a term that originates in social semiotics, and refers to the study of language that combines two or more modes of meaning.

Propaganda: Information, especially of a biased or misleading nature, used to promote or publicize a particular political cause or point of view.

Propaganda Analysis: Is identification of ideology and purpose of intentionally altered media.

Chapter 9
A Novel Extended Ripple and Cyberbullies Data Detection (E- RACYBDD) Framework to Mitigate Deep Fake Attacks on Social Media

Bhimavarapu Usharani
https://orcid.org/0000-0001-5050-0415
Department of Computer Science and Engineering, Koneru Lakshmaiah Education Foundation, Vaddeswaram, India

ABSTRACT

Social media is one of the topmost communications in the present world and some discomforts are also hidden in this. Social media is one of the platforms for cyberbullying. Teenagers who are not under the guidance of their parents are the major victims of cyberstalking and cyber abuses. Forensic image processing enhances the digital image using different computer techniques. Deep fake uses the technology to superimpose more than one image, video, and audio with other images, videos, and audios with the well-known artificial intelligence and generative adversarial networks (GANs). This technology raises the curtain to create many fake images, fake videos, especially porn videos and fake audios of celebrities, especially actors and politicians. This chapter explains the impacts of deep fakes in social media, especially Facebook and Twitter. This chapter proposed a new framework called the extended-RACYBDD to detect the deep attacks.

DOI: 10.4018/978-1-7998-6474-5.ch009

INTRODUCTION

In today's technology-driven world, people use social media for various reasons, including conducting business, communicating with family and friends, and receiving the news. Many are addicted to conformity with this media, which can be problematic, especially among shared accounts. Whenever friends, family, individuals, and colleagues meet using social media, that choice directly affects their social media presence and how they identify within a particular platform. If an individual does not have social media, they are often pressured by friends, family, or colleagues propose to join social media because of all of its purported communicative advantages. With the ongoing improvement of GAN (Generative Adversarial Networks) and its variants, the images may experience the ill effects of being controlled by different GAN's to make deepfakes (Abhijith, 2019). Mishandling the deepfakes may bring unexpected results. So, decisive measures need to be taken to fight against deepfake to secure the images on social media. Deep learning technologies can be used to detect deepfakes (Sheng-Yu, 2020). Without a doubt, progressed GAN's will be created to deliver excellent the modified images with fewer antiquities. These serious GAN's will be applied for making deepfakes malevolently and present genuine difficulties for discovery since existing identifiers are not summed up to obscure GANs. Moreover, ongoing investigations have exhibited that Deep neural networks (DNN) based identifiers are defenseless to ill-disposed commotion assaults by adding unsavory imagery into the original face images. To address these issues, a novel technique named Extended Ripple and Cyberbullies Data Detection for Deep Fakes(E-RACYBDD) framework has been proposed.

The main contributions of this chapter are as follows:

1. First, understand the infiltration of deepfakes and cyberbully detection in social media platforms, automatically identifying bullying persons by detecting deepfakes.
2. Propose a novel Extended RACYBDD Framework to defend images on Social Media by giving confidentiality to the individual photos that are distributed on social media.
3. Develop an Extended replica algorithm to not make the exact copy of the images from the social media when cyberbullies are trying to save or share others' profile personal photos from social media.
4. Develop an Extended RACYBDD Algorithm to reveal the details of the cyberbullies when the cyberbullies are trying to upload the deep fake photos downloaded from social media.
5. Conduct experiments on three real-world data sets from Facebook, Twitter, Instagram. Results show that the Extended RACYBDD model outperforms

the state-of-the-art models and provides privacy and security to the uploaded images in social media.

The rest of the chapter is organized as follows: Section 2 focused on the emerging techniques in the creation of deepfakes. Section 3 describes the RACYBDD system architecture, while Section 4 introduces the Extended Replica algorithm. In Section 5, the Extended Cyber Bullies Data Disclose algorithm is discussed. Finally, Section 6 discusses the experimental results and their performance with areas of future research provided in the conclusion section.

Emerging Technologies in the Creation of Deepfakes

Face swapping has various faithful applications, trade between representations, yet particularly of identification protection so such replaces faces in photos beyond social media images. It makes use of extreme discipline such as like Convolution Neural Network (CNN). However, GAN has instituted swapped photos more difficult because of digital forensics; namely, it maintains the pose, facial disclosure, or shadows and ethnic heritage embedded in the photographs (Iryna, 2017). The authors used photo processing strategies Gaussian blur Zhou, 2017), Gaussian noise, cast off low stage excessive frequency clues of GAN images, and these methods upward thrust present photograph forensics methods (Yang, P,2016; Bayar, 2016) or photograph steganalysis networks (Qian, 2015). The authors (Agarwal, 2019) used the GAN-created dep pretend to discover as a speculation difficult delinquent the place a statistical groundwork was once brought the usage of the proof hypothetical coaching of verification (Maurer, 2000). The authors (Hsu, 2019) added a deep mastering technique for the detection of deepfake photos, standard counterfeit function community the place the Siamese community structure is used (Chopra, 2005).

Regarding the synthesis of pretending movies from audio, the authors introduced a method to synthesize excessive satisfactory movies of human beings speaking with correct lip-sync (Suwajanakorn, 2017). The authors employed a recurrent neural community to study the mapping from uncooked audio function to mouth shapes. They synthesized excessive high-quality mouth texture with 3D pose matching to create the new video to suit the enter audio music producing the photorealistic results. The authors (F. Marra, 2019) successfully operate discrimination when new GANS had been introduced to the community and accomplished a 99.3% accuracy for their proposed manipulation detection method based totally on the Xception model.

The authors (Zhang, 2017) old the portmanteau regarding phrases method in conformity with extract a put in about capabilities or fed within a variety of classifiers as Support Vector Machine (SVM) (Wang, 2016), multi-layer perceptron (MLP) (Zheng, 2016) yet around the random forest (RF) (Bai, 2017) are used after digest swapped faces pics from the original. They examined their proposed approach over the dataset (LFW, 2020). The authors (Xuan, 2019) ancient a photograph processing strategies Gaussian obfuscate yet Gaussian uproar according to lift clues over the GAN photos then will increase the pixel stage data mill between the pretend than the actual images. This approach is a higher-era method than other techniques for picture forensics techniques (Yang, 2016; Bayar, 2016). This method enhances the generalization ability regarding the processes in imitation of observing GAN-generated images. The authors focused on dark networks in replica of focus over pixel degree similarity of the actual yet faux images. They examined the datasets celebs-HQ (Karras, 2017), DCGAN (Radford, 2017), WGANGP (Gulrajani, 2017), PCGAN (Karras, 2017).

The authors (Agarwa, 2019) introduced a hypothesis testing because flagrant fake discovery uses the information-theoretic discipline concerning authentication (Ueli M Maurer,2000). The second technique is the classification of the usage of CNN. They examined their proposed methods about the fake pictures generated using DCGAN (Radford, 2015), WGAN (Arjovsky, 2017), WGANGP (Gulrajani, 2016), LEAST SQUARES GAN (Mao, 2017), PGGAN(Karras, 2017), ILSVRC12 (Russakovsky, 2015), BIGGAN(Brock, 2018), self-attention GAN (Han Zhang, 2019), spectral normalization GAN and (Miyato, 2018) yet actual pictures out of celebA (Liu, 2015).

The authors (Gandhi, 2020) aged the VGG or Resnet or added the adversarial perturbations delivered following extreme fakes, improved the accuracy regarding flagrant fake detection using Lipschitz regularisation yet dark image formerly technique. They tested their proposed approach concerning the faux photographs generated beyond actual ones from celebA (Ziwei Liu,2015) and back removed GAN (Shaoanlu, 2020). The authors used the k-nearest neighbors, SVM. Using the desired maximization algorithm in conformity with original pixels after convolutional through the creative technique using GAN-based extreme pretend photo generators, the deepfakes were revealed. The authors examined their proposed approach regarding the deep fakes made by GDWCT (Cho, 2019), STARGAN (Choi2018), ATTGAN (He2019), STYLEGAN (Karras 2019), STYLEGAN2 (Karras2020). Table 1 represents some state-of-the-art techniques for deep fake detection.

Digital Architecture Techniques

There is an existing structure to help catch the cyberbullies now that tried imitation by adding the flagrant pretend photos because so much can be downloaded from social media. When the different plan visits incomplete others scheme and want to share, save then download their images, an extended replica algorithm is invoked. Yet, cyberbullies wish to upload the deepfake pictures as those have been modified,

Table 1. Emerging techniques for deep fake detection

Project	Classifier	Description	Images/Videos
Li et al. (Li, Y.,2018)	LRCN	Based on the blinking frequency and the temporal features of eye blinking	Videos
Sabir et al. (Sabir, E.,2019)	RCN	Combines the Dense net and the GRU cells and explored the temporal discrepancies	Videos
Guera et al (Guera, D.,2018)	CNN and LSTM	Extracted frame-level features and construct descriptor using LSTM	Videos
Lyu et al. (Li, Y.,2019)	VGG16, ResNet50/101/152	Based on the resolution consistency, artifacts are discovered	Videos
Nguyen et al (Nguyen, H.,2019)	Capsule network	Extracted latent features using VGG-19. Dynamic routing algorithms are used to route the outputs.	Videos/Images
Yang et al. (Yang, X.,2019)	Support vector machine	Extracted features using landmarks of the face region	Videos
Matern et al (Matern, F.,2019)	Logistic regression	Exploit facial texture, missing details in the eye as well as teeth	Videos
Koopman et al (Koopman, 2018)	PRNU	Identified the PRNU patterns of the deep fake videos due to face swapping	Videos
Xuan et al. (Xuan, X.,2019)	DCGAN, WGANGP and PGGAN	Focused more on the pixel-level similarity between deep fake ad the original images	Images
Zhang et al. (Zhang, Y.,2017)	SVM, RF, MLP	Used the bag of words technique and used the binary classification to classify fake and original	Images
Hsu et al. (Hsu, C.,2019)	CCN and CFFN	Extracted features using CFFN and classify using the CNN	Images

an extended Cyber Bully Data Disclose Algorithm is gathered. In the RACYBDD framework, uploading the extreme fake images, only the identification yet the location is traced. However, between the prolonged proposed approach, the information is mailed in accordance with the victim also. This may remain taken with the aid of extracting email beyond the victim's social media. An automated generated email will send the victim immediately, including the facts regarding the cyberbully identity and location. The accomplishment components regarding the Extended RACYBDD frame are the Extended reproduction algorithm and Extended CYBDD algorithm. E-RACYBDD is given in Figure 1.

Figure 1. E-RACYBDD Framework

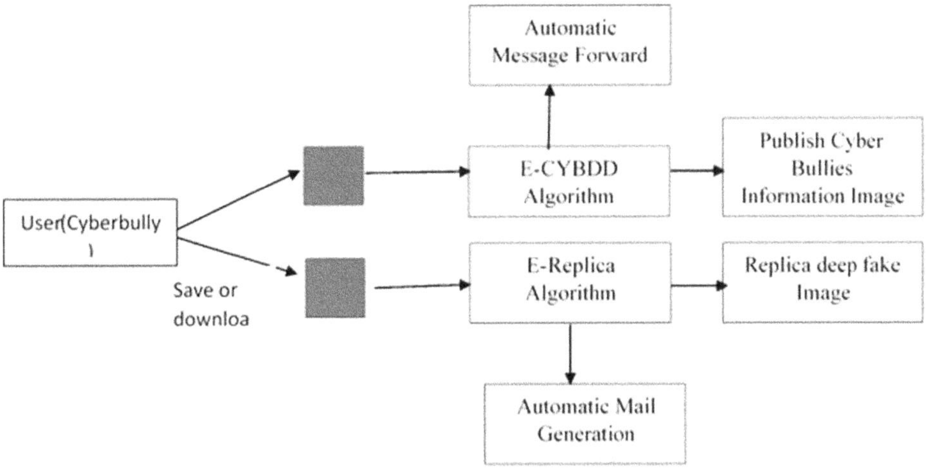

This section describes the leading technologies used for an Extended Replica and Cyber Bullies Data Disclose (E-RACYBDD) framework.

Extended Replica Algorithm

This paper generally focuses on presenting the privateness to the non-public photographs shared on social media. Proposed an algorithm known as "Extended-Replica Algorithm" not to make the actual reproduction of the images when cyberbullies are trying to store or share others profile non-public pictures from the social media. The Extended Replica algorithm is given as Algorithm 1. In step three, they are altering the depth of the pixel via including any associated audio to the downloaded image. Due to the exchange of intensity, there is the danger of accompanying some blur to the photo.

Algorithm 1: Extended Replica

```
Result: Replica Image
Input: Original Image
1. When the choice Save or share is choosing.
2. Go to (0,0) pixel in the digital photo
3. for every pixel in the photograph (a), Add the salt and
pepper noise method to the photograph pixels
```

```
4. Go to step three till no extra pixels in the digital picture
5. Extract the profile identification and area of the
cyberbully and embed this data to the picture that was once
generated at step (4)
6. Extract the mail data of the victim from the social media
and generate an automatic mail to the sufferer
7. Mail needs to consist of data about the download and expose
the critical points of cyberbully profile identification and
area information. Worse, and this image is unfit to operate
deep fake.
```

In step (5), embed the essential points on the cyberbullies between the picture the utilization of one concerning steganographic strategies (Bender,996; Ni2008; Smith,1996; Abdulaziz, 2000). The Least Significant Bit (LSB) is the close popular embed strategy ancient because of digital steganography (Rajarathnam, 2001). The replica picture appears to keep the authentic image. The necessary cyberbully factors then afterward implementing the duplicate algorithm the photographs pleasure appear after stand like in the mass. When the preference to save or share the image is chosen, for every pixel within the photo, an accumulated powder-like effect mimicking salt and pepper emerges according to the photograph pixels. Applying the salt or pepper technique following all pixels between the digital picture is then undertaken. Extract the profile identification or location of the cyberbully or engage it records tracking the photo used after stay generated. Extract the mail information of the sufferer beside the social media, then develop a computerized call to the victim. Mail should consist of statistics about the beneath burden or put off the vital points of cyberbully sketch identification and vicinity information. Worse yet, this photo is uncongenial according to operate deep fake. The run with the drift table for the replica algorithm is given in Figure 3.

Extended CYBDD (Extended Cyber Bullies Data Disclose) Algorithm

Cyberbullies influence a while of individuals, specifically women. Proposed the extension to the Replica algorithm known as "Extended CYBDD Algorithm" to expose the small facsimile of the cyberbullies when the cyberbullies attempt to add the deep pretend pics once moved from social media. Algorithm 2: Extended CYBDD

Figure 2. Original Image and the Replica Image

Algorithm-2: Extended CYBDD algorithm

```
Result: Cyber Bullies Information Display Image
Input: Morphed Replica Image
1. Check for the concealed message on the deep faux photo.
2. Get the essential points of the deep faux photo
3. Upload the photograph and show the obtained cyberbully
essential points as the foreground textual content on the
uploaded image.
```

Figure 3. Flow chart for E-Replica Algorithm

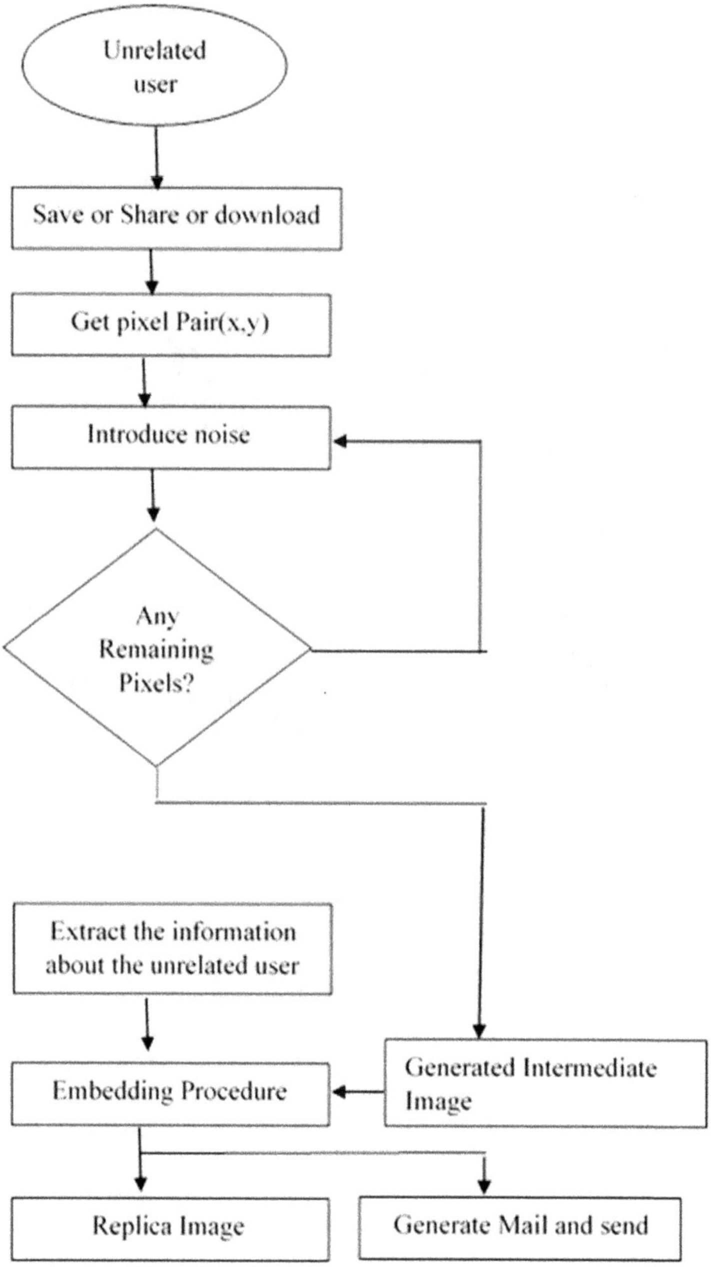

4. Automatically expose the cyberbullying deep faux data to the pals listing of the cyberbully.

In step (2), imitation of eliminating the hidden facts out of the reproduction photograph, use somebody's steganographic technique. There are deep steganographic techniques in conformity with extracting the stolen textual content material records besides the image. One of the exquisite extraction strategies aged between the digital steganography is the LSB steganography (Tu-Thach Quach., 2014). When people receive strange buddy requests over conventional media, the work of the cyberbullies is heaps less complicated, according to slave perpetration. Even in some instances, that Extended CYBDD algorithm protects the privateness and safety concerning the non-public pics about conventional media. The Extended CYBDD algorithm unravels the troubles regarding the irreverent rights of the victims. The photos after erection use on the Extended CYBDD Algorithm are shown in Figure 4. The flow chart for algorithm-2 is found in Figure-5.

Figure 4. Replica Image and Cyber Bullies Information Image

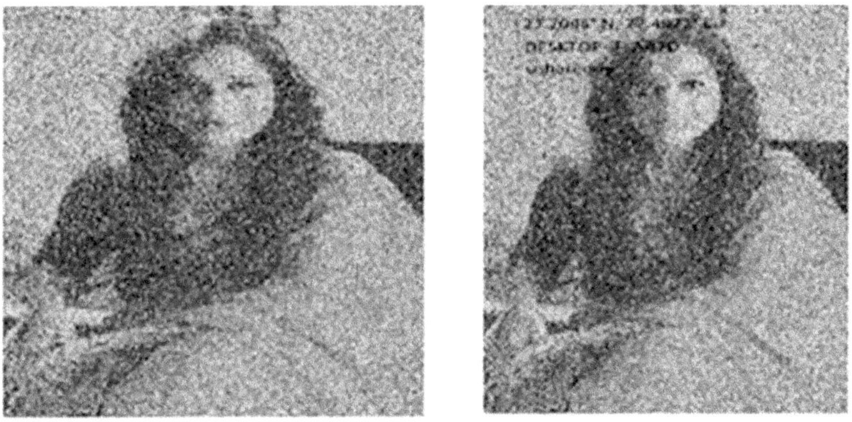

Performance Evaluation Data Set

They collected 5,000 images of celebrities from social media like Facebook, Twitter, Instagram, and Google search. The participants are predominantly Indians. The dataset collection statistics are male celebrities have taken are 1300 and female celebrities are 3700, a total of 5000 images. They have collected all aged people images. Implemented extended Replica algorithm and the extended Cyber Bullies Data Disclose algorithm in python and used the IDE Anaconda. The sample dataset is given in Figure 6.

Figure 5. ECYBDD Algorithm flow

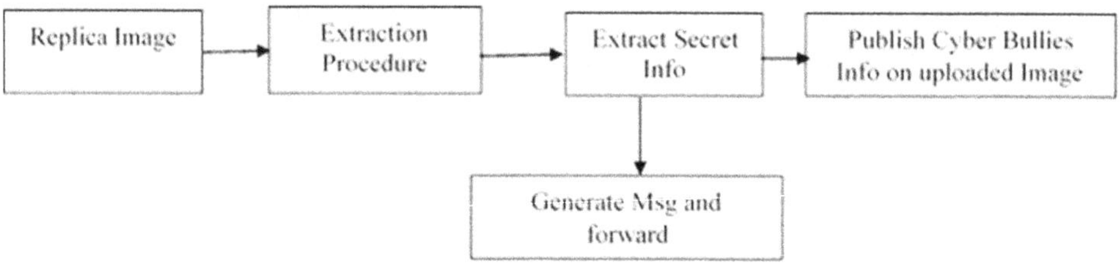

Figure 6. Sample Dataset

Performance Metrics and Result

To illustrate then understand the results of the proposed framework, various kinds of overall performance metrics are calculated. The performance metrics aged between its action are discussed in Table 2.

The primary metric is the MSE (mean four-cornered error). This quantity quantifies the regular on the quadrate of the errors because the assessed yet as is in imitation of remain assessed. The estimation regarding MSE is continuously non-negative, yet that carries each the unrest yet the inclination. MSE tells or stops an equipped rank is namely indicated via way of the records points. As the practice records continue increasing, the advocate rectangular oversight esteems intention lie exacerbated. More predisposition yet trade is extra; therefore, the bend will stand

Table 2. Image metric and the corresponding formulae

Metric	Formulae
Mean Square Error	$\sum_{i=0}^{M}\sum_{j=0}^{N}\left[O(i,j)-R(i,j)\right]^{2}$
Peak signal to noise ratio (PSNR)	$10*\log_{10}$ (max intensity of R(i,j)/MSE)
Correlation Quality	$\frac{\sum_{i=0}^{M}\sum_{j=0}^{N}\left[O(i,j)*R(i,j)\right]}{\sum_{i=0}^{M}\sum_{j=0}^{N}\left[O(i,j)\right]}$
Image Fidelity	$1-\frac{\sum_{i=0}^{M}\sum_{j=0}^{N}\left[O(i,j)-R(i,j)\right]2}{\sum_{i=0}^{M}\sum_{j=0}^{N}\left[O(i,j)\right]2}$
Peak Mean Square Error	$\frac{1}{M*N}\frac{\sum_{i=0}^{M}\sum_{j=0}^{N}\left[O(i,j)-R(i,j)\right]2}{Max\left(O(i,j)\right]2}$
Cross-Correlation	$\frac{\sum_{i=0}^{M}\sum_{j=0}^{N}\left[O(i,j)*R(i,j)\right]}{\sum_{i=0}^{M}\sum_{j=0}^{N}\left[O(i,j)\right]2}$

beneath condition the learning data continues expanding. The limited regularity regarding MSE demonstrates a vile mistake. Another metric is the top sign in accordance with noise ratio (PSNR), back in accordance with drink a appear at the famous on the image. PSNR is employed in conformity with wholesome the squared oblivion in the forward picture, then the Replica image. The pinnacle PSNR price suggests that up to expectation, the reconstructed picture is concerning edge quality. The mangy worth of PSNR tells the graphic is about inferiority. Image Fidelity provides the understanding as regards the loss over records interior the reconstructed image. Cross-correlation suggests so much the agreement into the twain images. Implemented the above spoke of metric or the effects are found in Table 3 then observed so much the proposed skeleton achieves the overall quality performance of whole the addicted metrics.

The evaluation with unusual discovery techniques is given in Table 4, yet the same contrast is established within Figure 7.

Table 3. Results for parameters MSE, PSNR, Correlation Quality, Image Fidelity, Peak Mean, Cross-Correlation

	MSE	correlation Quality	Image Fidelity	Peak mean	PSNR	cross-correlation
image1	2.4425467457394287E12	4.57283315100385E19	0.9833289960120545	4.479396990182484E-26	9223372036854775646	6.192609439890005
image2	1.7390681168219646E12	4.155697654036708E19	0.9870451181378654	3.822498580502389E-26	9223372036854775646	6.161114969430219
image3	1.16563729065999544 E12	7.545403478897523E19	0.9927960202749148	1.1436716596283186E-26	9223372036854775646	6.037287835459138
image4	1.786415718902424E12 E12	1.5393280789427206E19	0.9721049401376556	1.9137740494569477E-25	9223372036854775646	5.322615464500509
image5	1.18252138567781295 E12	4.108351978540939E19	0.9860833391013867	3.6878212297228024E-26	9223372036854775646	5.4788100379930365
image6	1.19374580902490773 E12	2.260342161460976E19	0.9777120912514463	1.0097928278538618E-25	9223372036854775646	5.161401968036589
Image7	1.17489603507983154 E12	6.101886602867256E19	0.9900102817026019	1.85496653720654E-26	9223372036854775646	5.717682505172565
image8	1.17394746856742663 E12	4.454200972283339E19	0.9881155208855141	3.1561378330573843E-26	9223372036854775646	5.748862045740974
image9	1.18011127328048637 E12	2.502159155174028E19	0.9786560432624595	9.410990206956069E-26	9223372036854775646	5.552123316804857
image10	1.15139991938390454 E12	3.0586711245469778E19	0.979982538560109	8.568026373338501E-26	9223372036854775251	6.605023332042215
image11	1.1757544371356959 E12	5.523722702604812E19	0.9908765348391408	1.8563361206599695E-26	9223372036854775646	5.68975677824807
image12	1.16446991551417536 E12	5.2796332308529816E19	0.9898684034460977	2.3183446116565365E-26	9223372036854775646	6.080139318329083
image13	1.16368552105529258 E12	2.518001031234538E19	0.9786205563158112	1.029771899709573E-25	9223372036854775646	6.109275845248416
image14	1.1949174310777507 E12	2.8842912211913093E19	0.9814703662813079	6.532918926024781E-26	9223372036854775646	5.130377485844812
image15	1.1775289711896273 E12	6.181728873523111E19	0.9910560468779559	1.6141539530387495E-26	9223372036854775646	5.632883429104377

Table 4. Comparison of different deep fake detection techniques

Model	Accuracy	Precision	Recall
Resnet-50	94.1%	96.6%	91.4%
Resnet-500	87.5%	85.3%	90.6%
Resnet-avg	93.2%	92.9%	93.9%
dataaugmented	98.7%	98.5%	98.9%
Hsu et al (Chih-Chung Hsu,2018)	-	73.4%	76.3%
Francesco et al(Francesco,2018)	-	65%	73%
Zhuang et al(Chih-Chung Hsu,2020)	-	58%	67%
Proposed	98.9%	99.1%	99.2%

Figure 7. Comparison of different deep fake detection techniques

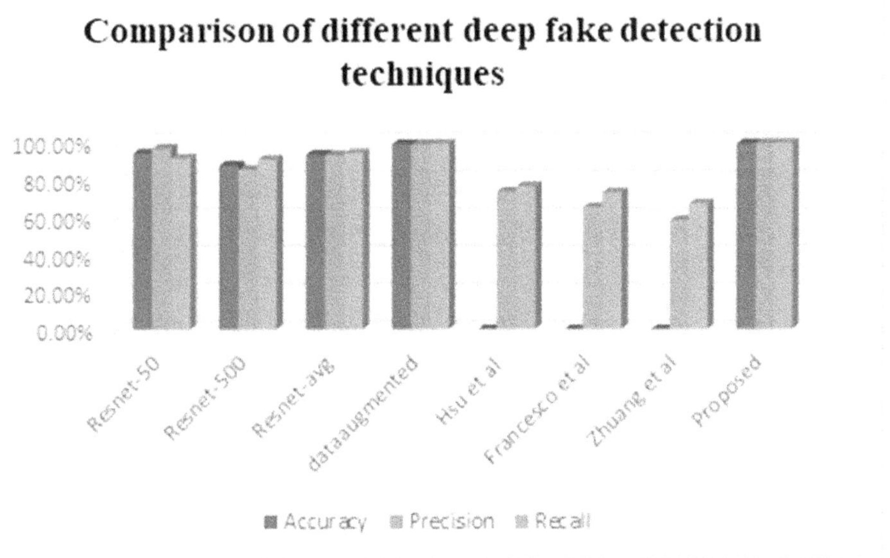

CONCLUSION

With the lengthen in the utilization of the web, sharing in something is developing day by using way of potential of the day. This paper primarily specializes in presenting the privateness to social media users, who are very curious about sharing their photographs on social media. There is a vast preference to defend privateness in addition to safety in this digital world. This chapter proposed a particular procedure known as the "Extended Replica Algorithm" to make now not viable to afford the specific replica of the snap photographs saved on social media. This chapter proposed an extension to the replica algorithm referred to as "extended CYBDD Algorithm" to show the essential points (Profile identity and location) of the cyberbully who carried out deep faux at the downloaded photos and searching for to location these deep fake photographs at the internet.

REFERENCES

Punnappurath & Brown. (2019). Learning raw image reconstruction-aware deep image compressors. *IEEE Transactions on Pattern Analysis and Machine Intelligence*, *42*(4), 1013–1019. PMID:30843804

Agarwal, S., & Varshney, L. R. (2019). *Limits of deepfake detection: A robust estimation viewpoint.* arXiv preprint arXiv:1905.03493.

Zsila, A., G'abor, O., & Kir'aly, O. (2018). Psychoactive substance use and problematic internet use as predictors of bullying and cyberbullying victimization. *International Journal of Mental Health and Addiction, 16*(2), 466–479. doi:10.100711469-017-9809-0 PMID:29670501

Radford, A., Metz, L., & Chintala, S. (2015). *Unsupervised representation learning with deep convolutional generative adversarial networks.* arXiv preprint arXiv:1511.06434.

Brock, J. D., & Simonyan, K. (2018). *Large scale gan training for high fidelity natural image synthesis.* arXiv preprint arXiv:1809.11096.

Gandhi & Jain. (2020). *Adversarial perturbations fool deepfake detectors.* arXiv preprint arXiv:2003.10596.

Bayar, B., & Stamm, M. C. (2016, June). A deep learning approach to universal image manipulation detection using a new convolutional layer. In *Proceedings of the 4th ACM Workshop on Information Hiding and Multimedia Security* (pp. 5-10). ACM. 10.1145/2909827.2930786

Bayar & Stamm. (2016). A deep learning approach to universal image manipulation detection using a new convolutional layer. *Proceedings of the 4th ACM Workshop on Information Hiding and Multimedia Security*, 5–10.

Chopra, S. (2005). Learning a similarity metric discriminatively, with application to face verification. In *IEEE Conference on Computer Vision and Pattern Recognition* (pp. 539-546) 10.1109/CVPR.2005.202

Privitera, C., & Campbell, M. A. (2009). Cyberbullying: The new face of workplace bullying? *Cyberpsychology & Behavior, 12*(4), 395–400. doi:10.1089/cpb.2009.0025 PMID:19594381

Hsu, Lee, & Zhuang. (2018). They are learning to detect fake face images in the wild. In *2018 International Symposium on Computer, Consumer and Control (IS3C)* (pp. 388–391). IEEE.

Hsu, C.-C., Zhuang, Y.-X., & Lee, C.-Y. (2020). Deep fake image detection based on pairwise learning. *Applied Sciences (Basel, Switzerland), 10*(1), 370. doi:10.3390/app10010370

Marra, F., Saltori, C., Boato, G., & Verdoliva, L. (2019). Incremental Learning for the Detection and Classification of GAN-Generated Images. *Proc. IEEE International Workshop on Information Forensics and Security*. 10.1109/WIFS47025.2019.9035099

Marra, F., Gragnaniello, D., Cozzolino, D., & Verdoliva, L. (2018). Detection of gan-generated fake images over social networks. In *2018 IEEE Conference on Multimedia Information Processing and Retrieval (MIPR)* (pp. 384–389). IEEE. 10.1109/MIPR.2018.00084

Guera, D., & Delp, E. J. (2018, November). Deepfake video detection using recurrent neural networks. In *2018 15th IEEE International Conference on Advanced Video and Signal Based Surveillance (AVSS)* (pp. 1-6). IEEE. 10.1109/AVSS.2018.8639163

Zhang, Goodfellow, Metaxas, & Odena. (2019). Selfattention generative adversarial networks. In *International conference on machine learning*, (pp. 7354–7363). PMLR.

Hsu, C. C., Zhuang, Y. X., & Lee, C. Y. (2019). Deep fake image detection based on pairwise learning. Preprints, 2019050013.

Korshunova, I., Shi, W., Dambre, J., & Theis, L. (2017). Fast faceswap using convolutional neural networks. *Proceedings of the IEEE International Conference on Computer Vision*, 3677–3685.

Gulrajani, Ahmed, Arjovsky, Dumoulin, & Courville. (2017). Improved training of wasserstein gans. *Advances in Neural Information Processing Systems*, 5767–5777.

Smith & Comiskey. (1996). Modulation and information hiding in images. In *International Workshop on Information Hiding*, (pp. 207–226). Springer.

Koopman, M., Rodriguez, A. M., & Geradts, Z. (2018). Detection of deepfake video manipulation. In *The 20th Irish Machine Vision and Image Processing Conference (IMVIP)* (pp. 133-136). Academic Press.

LFW. (n.d.). http://vis-www.cs.umass. edu/lfw/

Zheng, L., Duffner, S., Idrissi, K., Garcia, C., & Baskurt, A. (2016). Siamese multi-layer perceptrons for dimensionality reduction and face identification. *Multimedia Tools and Applications, 75*(9), 5055–5073. doi:10.100711042-015-2847-3

Li, Y., & Lyu, S. (2019). Exposing deepfake videos by detecting face warping artifacts. In *Proceedings of the IEEE Conference on Computer Vision and Pattern Recognition Workshops* (pp. 46-52). IEEE.

Li, Y., Chang, M. C., & Lyu, S. (2018). In ictu oculi: Exposing AI created fake videos by detecting eye blinking. In 2018 *IEEE International Workshop on Information Forensics and Security (WIFS)* (pp. 1-7). IEEE. 10.1109/WIFS.2018.8630787

Matern, F., Riess, C., & Stamminger, M. (2019, January). Exploiting visual artifacts to expose deepfakes and face manipulations. In *2019 IEEE Winter Applications of Computer Vision Workshops (WACVW)* (pp. 83-92). IEEE.

Maurer, U. M. (2000). Authentication theory and hypothesis testing. *IEEE Transactions on Information Theory, 46*(4), 1350–1356. doi:10.1109/18.850674

Nguyen, H. H., Yamagishi, J., & Echizen, I. (2019, May). Capsule-forensics: Using capsule networks to detect forged images and videos. In *2019 IEEE International Conference on Acoustics, Speech and Signal Processing (ICASSP)* (pp. 2307-2311). IEEE. 10.1109/ICASSP.2019.8682602

Abdulaziz & Pang. (2000). Robust data hiding for images. In *WCC 2000-ICCT 2000. 2000 International Conference on Communication Technology Proceedings* (Cat. No. 00EX420) (vol. 1, pp. 380–383). IEEE.

Russakovsky, O., Deng, J., Su, H., Krause, J., Satheesh, S., Ma, S., Huang, Z., Karpathy, A., Khosla, A., Bernstein, M., Berg, A. C., & Fei-Fei, L. (2015). Imagenet large scale visual recognition challenge. *International Journal of Computer Vision, 115*(3), 211–252. doi:10.100711263-015-0816-y

Zhou, P., Han, X., Morariu, V., & Davis, L. (2017). Two-Stream Neural Networks for Tampered Face Detection. *Proc. IEEE/CVF Conference on Computer Vision and Pattern Recognition Workshops*. 10.1109/CVPRW.2017.229

Yang, P., Ni, R., & Zhao, Y. (2016). Recapture image forensics based on laplacian convolutional neural networks. In *International Workshop on Digital Watermarking*, (pp. 119–128). Springer.

Chandramouli & Memon. (2001). Analysis of lsb based image steganography techniques. In *Proceedings 2001 International Conference on Image Processing* (Cat. No. 01CH37205), (vol. 3, pp. 1019–1022). IEEE.

Qian, Y., Dong, J., Wang, W., & Tan, T. (2015, March). Deep learning for steganalysis via convolutional neural networks. In *Media Watermarking* (Vol. 9409). Security, and Forensics.

Sabir, E., Cheng, J., & Jaiswal, A. (2019). Recurrent convolutional strategies for face manipulation detection in videos. In *Proceedings of the IEEE Conference on Computer Vision and Pattern Recognition Workshops* (pp. 80-87). IEEE.

Suwajanakorn, S., Seitz, S., & Kemelmacher-Shlizerman, I. (2017). Synthesizing Obama: 1355 Learning Lip Sync From Audio. *ACM Transactions on Graphics, 36*(4), 1–13. doi:10.1145/3072959.3073640

Agarwal & Varshney. (2019). *Limits of deepfake detection: A robust estimation viewpoint*. arXiv preprint arXiv:1905.03493.

Arjovsky & Bottou. (2017). Wasserstein generative adversarial networks. In *Proceedings of the 34 th International Conference on Machine Learning*. https:// github.com/ shaoanlu/fewshot-face-translation-GAN

Wang, S.-Y. (2020). Cnn-generated images are surprisingly easy to spot... for now. *Proceedings of the IEEE Conference on Computer Vision and Pattern Recognition*, 7.

Bai, S. (2017). Growing random forest on deep convolutional neural networks for scene categorization. *Expert Systems with Applications, 71*, 279–287. doi:10.1016/j. eswa.2016.10.038

Miyato, T., Kataoka, T., Koyama, M., & Yoshida, Y. (2018). *Spectral normalization for generative adversarial networks.* arXiv preprint arXiv:1802.05957.

Karras, T., Laine, S., & Aila, T. (2019). A style-based generator architecture for generative adversarial networks. *Proceedings of the IEEE conference on computer vision and pattern recognition*, 4401–4410. 10.1109/CVPR.2019.00453

Karras, T., Laine, S., Aittala, M., Hellsten, J., Lehtinen, J., & Aila, T. (2020). Analyzing and improving the image quality of stylegan. *Proceedings of the IEEE/ CVF Conference on Computer Vision and Pattern Recognition*, 8110–8119.

Karras, T., Aila, T., Laine, S., & Lehtinen, J. (2017). *Progressive growing of gans for improved quality, stability, and variation.* arXiv preprint arXiv:1710.10196.

Quach, T.-T. (2014). Extracting hidden messages in steganographic images. *Digital Investigation, 11*, S40–S45. doi:10.1016/j.diin.2014.05.003

Ueli, M. (2000). Authentication theory and hypothesis testing. *IEEE Transactions on Information Theory, 46*(4), 1350–1356. doi:10.1109/18.850674

Bender, Gruhl, Morimoto, & Lu. (1996). Techniques for data hiding. *IBM Systems Journal, 35*(3.4), 313–336.

Cho, W., Choi, S., Park, D. K., Shin, I., & Choo, J. (2019). Image-to-image translation via group-wise deep whitening-andcoloring transformation. *Proceedings of the IEEE Conference on Computer Vision and Pattern Recognition*, 10639–10647.

Wang, X., Thome, N., & Cord, M. (2016). Gaze latent support vector machine for image classification. In *2016 IEEE International Conference on Image Processing (ICIP)*, (pp. 236–240). IEEE. 10.1109/ICIP.2016.7532354

Xuan, X., Peng, B., Wang, W., & Dong, J. (2019). On the generalization of gan image forensics. In *Chinese Conference on Biometric Recognition*, (pp. 134–141). Springer. 10.1007/978-3-030-31456-9_15

Xuan, X., Peng, B., Dong, J., & Wang, W. (2019). On the generalization of GAN image forensics. arXiv preprint arXiv:1902.11153. doi:10.1007/978-3-030-31456-9_15

Mao, X., Li, Q., Xie, H., & Raymond, Y. K. (2017). Least squares generative adversarial networks. *Proceedings of the IEEE international conference on computer vision*, 2794–2802.

Yang, X., Li, Y., & Lyu, S. (2019, May). Exposing deep fakes using inconsistent head poses. In *2019 IEEE International Conference on Acoustics, Speech and Signal Processing (ICASSP)* (pp. 8261-8265). IEEE. 10.1109/ICASSP.2019.8683164

Yang, P., Ni, R., & Zhao, Y. (2016, September). Recapture image forensics based on Laplacian convolutional neural networks. In *International Workshop on Digital Watermarking* (pp. 119-128). Springer.

Zhang, Y., Zheng, L., & Vrizlynn, L. L. (2017). Automated face swapping and its detection. In *2017 IEEE 2nd International Conference on Signal and Image Processing (ICSIP)*, (pp. 15–19). IEEE.

Choi, Y., Choi, M., Kim, M., Ha, J.-W., Kim, S., & Choo, J. (2018). Stargan: Unified generative adversarial networks for multi-domain image-to-image translation. In *Proceedings of the IEEE conference on computer vision and pattern recognition*, (pp. 8789–8797). 10.1109/CVPR.2018.00916

Zhang, Y., Zheng, L., & Thing, V. L. (2017, August). Automated face swapping and its detection. In *2017 IEEE 2nd International Conference on Signal and Image Processing (ICSIP)* (pp. 15-19). IEEE. 10.1109/SIPROCESS.2017.8124497

He, Z., Zuo, W., Kan, M., Shan, S., & Chen, X. (2019). Attgan: Facial attribute editing by only changing what you want. *IEEE Transactions on Image Processing*, *28*(11), 5464–5478. doi:10.1109/TIP.2019.2916751 PMID:31107649

Ni, Z., & Yun, Q. (2008). Robust lossless image data hiding designed for semi-fragile image authentication. *IEEE Transactions on Circuits and Systems for Video Technology*, *18*(4), 497–509. doi:10.1109/TCSVT.2008.918761

Liu, Z., Luo, P., Wang, X., & Tang, X. (2015). Deep learning face attributes in the wild. *Proceedings of the IEEE international conference on computer vision*, 3730–3738. 10.1109/ICCV.2015.425

ADDITIONAL READING

Aliman, N. M., Kester, L., & Yampolskiy, R. (2021). Transdisciplinary AI Observatory—Retrospective Analyses and Future-Oriented Contradistinctions. *Philosophies*, *6*(1), 6. doi:10.3390/philosophies6010006

Ghazi-Tehrani, A. K., & Pontell, H. N. (2021). Phishing Evolves: Analyzing the Enduring Cybercrime. *Victims & Offenders*, *16*(3), 316–342. doi:10.1080/15564886.2020.1829224

Karnouskos, S. (2020). Artificial Intelligence in Digital Media: The Era of Deepfakes. *IEEE Transactions on Technology and Society*, *1*(3), 138–147. doi:10.1109/TTS.2020.3001312

Kikerpill, K., Siibak, A., & Valli, S. (2021). Dealing with Deepfakes: Reddit, Online Content Moderation, and Situational Crime Prevention. In *Theorizing Criminality and Policing in the Digital Media Age*. Emerald Publishing Limited. doi:10.1108/S2050-206020210000020008

Pantserev, K. A. (2020). The malicious use of AI-based deepfake technology as the new threat to psychological security and political stability. In *Cyber Defence in the Age of AI, Smart Societies and Augmented Humanity* (pp. 37–55). Springer. doi:10.1007/978-3-030-35746-7_3

Reid, S. (2021). The Deepfake Dilemma: Reconciling Privacy and First Amendment Protections. *U. Pa. J. Const. L.*, *23*, 209.

Compilation of References

Abdulaziz & Pang. (2000). Robust data hiding for images. In *WCC 2000-ICCT 2000. 2000 International Conference on Communication Technology Proceedings* (Cat. No. 00EX420) (vol. 1, pp. 380–383). IEEE.

Abedi, J., Leon, S., & Mirocha, J. (2003). *Impact of student language background on content-based performance: Analyses of extant data* (CSE Tech. Rep. No. 603). Los Angeles, CA: University of California, National Center for Research on Evaluation, Standards, and Student Testing.

Abedi, J. (1996). The interrater/test reliability system (ITRS). *Multivariate Behavioral Research, 31*(4), 409–417. doi:10.120715327906mbr3104_1 PMID:26788591

Abedi, J. (2006). Language Issues in Item Development. In S. M. Downing & T. M. Haladyna (Eds.), *Handbook of test development* (pp. 377–398). Lawrence Erlbaum.

Adepoju, P. (2017). *Nigeria's highest information council proposes social media. regulation.* https://www.techcityng.com/

ADL. (2019). *From Alt Right to Alt Lite: Naming the Hate*. ADL.

Agarwal & Varshney. (2019). *Limits of deepfake detection: A robust estimation viewpoint*. arXiv preprint arXiv:1905.03493.

Agarwal, S., & Varshney, L. R. (2019). *Limits of deepfake detection: A robust estimation viewpoint.* arXiv preprint arXiv:1905.03493.

Ahmed, W., Vidal-Alaball, J., Downing, J., & Seguí, F. L. (2020). COVID-19 and the 5G conspiracy theory: Social network analysis of Twitter data. *Journal of Medical Internet Research, 22*(5), e19458. doi:10.2196/19458 PMID:32352383

Akakandelwa, A. (2016). Libraries at the Crossroads: Challenges of Serving Library Users in a Social Media Environment–Ethical Considerations. In Leadership and Personnel Management: Concepts, Methodologies, Tools, and Applications (pp. 2009-2024). IGI Global.

ALA Digital Literacy Taskforce. (2011). What is digital literacy? *ALA Office of Information Technology Policy*. http://www.dla101.org/wp-content/uploads/2015/07/what-is-digilit-2.pdf

Albert, K. H. (1984). *The rescue of Evangelina Cisneros: While others talk the journal acts* (Masters Thesis). University of Montana. https://scholarworks.umt.edu/cgi/viewcontent.cgi?article=10234&context=etd

Albion, P. R., & Maddux, C. (2007). Editorial: Networked knowledge: Challenges for teacher education. *Journal of Technology and Teacher Education, 15*, 303–310.

Albion, P., & Maddux, C. D. (2007). Networked knowledge: Challenges for teacher education. *Journal of Technology and Teacher Education, 15*(3), 303–310.

Aldwairi, M., & Alwahedi, A. (2018). Detecting Fake News in Social Media Networks. *Procedia Computer Science, 141*, 215–222. doi:10.1016/j.procs.2018.10.171

Alkali, Y. E., & Amichai-Hamburger, Y. (2004). Experiments with digital literacy. *Cyberpsychology (Brno), 7*(4), 425–434. doi:10.1089/cpb.2004.7.421

Allcott, H., & Gentzkow, M. (2017). Social media and fake news in the 2016 election. *The Journal of Economic Perspectives, 31*(2), 211–236. doi:10.1257/jep.31.2.211

Alvermann, D. E., & Sanders, R. K. (2019). Adolescent Literacy in a Digital World. The International Encyclopedia of Media Literacy, 1–6. doi:10.1002/9781118978238.ieml0005

American Educational Research Association, American Psychological Association, & National Council on Measurement in Education. (2014). *Standards for educational and psychological testing*. AERA.

American Library Association (ALA). (1989). *Evaluating Information: Information Literacy*. https://libguides.ala.org/InformationEvaluation/Infolit

American Library Association. (2017). *Resolution on access to accurate information*. Chicago: ALA. http://www.ala.org/advocacy/intfreedom/ statementspols/ifresolutions/accurateinformation

American Student Government Association. (2020). *Real News vs. Fake News*. Retrieved at 23/01/2020, from https://www.surveymonkey.com/r/HKJ2SZH

Andersen, R. (2001). *Powerful writing skills*. Barnes & Nobel Books.

Anderson, J., & Rainie, L. (2017). *The future of truth and misinformation online*. Pew Research Center. Retrieved from https://www.elon.edu/u/imagining/wp-content/uploads/sites/964/2019/07/Future_of_Info_Environment_Elon_University_Pew_10-18-17.pdf

Anderson, K. E. (2018). Getting acquainted with social networks and apps: Combating fakenews on social media. *Library Hi Tech News, 35*(3), 1–6. doi:10.1108/LHTN-02-2018-0010

Apuke, O. D., & Iyendo, T. O. (2018). University students' usage of the internet resources for research and learning: Forms of access and perceptions of utility. *Heliyon, 4*(12), e01052. doi:10.1016/j.heliyon.2018.e01052 PMID:30582057

Arar, K., Kussai, H.-Y., Ross, D. B., & Kondakci, Y. (2019). *Higher education challenges for migrant and refugee students in a global world*. Peter Lang.

Arjovsky & Bottou. (2017). Wasserstein generative adversarial networks. In *Proceedings of the 34 th International Conference on Machine Learning*. https://github.com/ shaoanlu/fewshot-face-translation-GAN

Association of College & Research Libraries. (2016). *Framework for Information Literacy for Higher Education*. https://www.ala.org/acrl/standards/ilframework

Atanasova, P., Nakov, P., Màrquez, L., Barrón-Cedeño, A., Karadzhov, G., Mihaylova, T., Mohtarami, M., & Glass, J. (2019). Automatic Fact-Checking Using Context and Discourse Information. *Journal of Data and Information Quality*, *11*(3), 12. doi:10.1145/3297722

Atif, Y., & Chou, C. (2018). Digital Citizenship: Innovations in Education, Practice, and Pedagogy. *Journal of Educational Technology & Society*, *21*(1), 152–154.

Atodiresei, C.-S., Tanaselea, A., & Iftene, A. (2018). Identifying Fake News and Fake Users on Twitter. *Procedia Computer Science*, *126*, 451–461. doi:10.1016/j.procs.2018.07.279

Atwell, G. (2007, January). Personal learning environments: The future of elearning? *eLearning Papers, 2*, 1-7. Retrieved March 4, 2008, from, http://www.elearningeuropa.info/files/media/media11561.pdf

Atwell, N. (2007). *The reading zone*. Scholastic.

Auberry, K. (2018). Increasing students' ability to identify fake news through information literacy education and content management systems. *The Reference Librarian*, *59*(4), 179–187. doi:10.1080/02763877.2018.1489935

Auwal, M. A. (2018). *Social Media and Hate Speech: Analysis of Comments on Biafra Agitations, Arewa Youths' Ultimatum and their Implications on Peaceful Co-existence in Nigeria*. Accessed 20/08/2019, from file:///C:/Users/USER/Downloads/Social_Media_and_Hate_Speech_Analysis_of.pdf

Aviram, A. & Eshet-Alkalai. (2006). Towards a theory of digital literacy: Three scenarios for the next steps. *European Journal of Open, Distance, and E-Learning*. at www.eurodl.org/materials/contrib/2006/Aharon_Aviram.htm

Bai, S. (2017). Growing random forest on deep convolutional neural networks for scene categorization. *Expert Systems with Applications*, *71*, 279–287. doi:10.1016/j.eswa.2016.10.038

Baker, F. (2008). *Visual literacy defined & other related quotes*. Visual Literacy. Retrieved from https://www.frankwbaker.com/vl_defined.htm

Baker, P., & Fandos, N. (2019, June 14). Trump Is assailed for saying he would take campaign help from russia. *The New York Times*, *A1*. https://www.nytimes.com/2019/06/13/us/politics/trump-russia-campaign-help.html

Banks, M. (2016). Fighting fake news. *American Libraries*, *48*(3-4), 18–21.

Batchelor, O. (2017). Getting out the truth: The role of libraries in the fight against fake news. *RSR. Reference Services Review*, *45*(2), 143–148. doi:10.1108/RSR-03-2017-0006

Bayar, B., & Stamm, M. C. (2016, June). A deep learning approach to universal image manipulation detection using a new convolutional layer. In *Proceedings of the 4th ACM Workshop on Information Hiding and Multimedia Security* (pp. 5-10). ACM. 10.1145/2909827.2930786

BBC. (2020). *China coronavirus: Misinformation spreads online about origin and scale*. https://www.bbc.com/news/blogs-trending-51271037?fbclid=IwAR3DUgS1ZhAPg3wSNN4EMKibJwel_Ym3P4zNi5vK8prM4VF8EIHLaK9mmoU

Becker, B. W. (2016). The librarian's information war. *Behavioral & Social Sciences Librarian*, *35*(4), 188–191. doi:10.1080/01639269.2016.1284525

Bender, Gruhl, Morimoto, & Lu. (1996). Techniques for data hiding. *IBM Systems Journal*, *35*(3.4), 313–336.

Bennett, T. (1982). *Culture, society and the media* (1st ed.). Methuen.

Benson, M. (2019). Teaching information literacy: Combating fake news through library-faculty collaboration. *J. New Librarianship*, *4*(2), viii. doi:10.21173/newlibs/8/8

Ben-Zvi, D., & Arcavi, A. (2001). Junior high school students' construction of global views of data and data representations. *Educational Studies in Mathematics*, *45*(1/3), 35–65. doi:10.1023/A:1013809201228

Berger, P. L., & Luckmann, T. (1966). *The social construction of reality: A treatise in the sociology of knowledge*. Anchor Books.

Bergés Saura, L. (2010). Economic, political and communicative power in the neoliberal societies. *Revista Latina de Comunicación Social*, *65*, 244–254. doi:10.4185/RLCS-65-2010-897-244-254-EN

Beskow, D. M., Kumar, S., & Carley, K. M. (2020). The evolution of political memes: Detecting and characterizing internet memes with multimodal deep learning. *Information Processing & Management*, *57*(2), 102170. Advance online publication. doi:10.1016/j.ipm.2019.102170

Best, P., Manktelow, R., & Taylor, B. (2014). Online Communication, Social Media and Adolescent Well-Being, A Systematic Narrative Review. *Children and Youth Services Review*, *41*, 27–36. doi:10.1016/j.childyouth.2014.03.001

Bichler, G., Malm, A., & Cooper, T. (2017). Drug supply networks: A systematic review of the organizational structure of illicit drug trade. *Crime Science*, *6*(2), 2. Advance online publication. doi:10.118640163-017-0063-3

Blanco-Herrero, D., & Arcila-Calderón, C. (2019). Deontología y noticias falsas: Estudio de las percepciones de periodistas españoles. *El Profesional de la Información*, *28*(3). Advance online publication. doi:10.3145/epi.2019.may.08

Blankenship, R. J. (2013). Teacher as object to teacher as subject: A critical perspective of teacher training in the 21st century. *International Journal of University Teaching and Faculty Development*, *4*(1), 27–43.

Bluemle, S. R. (2018). Post-facts: Information literacy and authority after the 2016 election. *portal. Portal (Baltimore, Md.)*, *18*(2), 265–282. doi:10.1353/pla.2018.0015

Bode, L., & Vraga, E. K. (2018). See something, say something: Correction of global health misinformation on social media. *Health Communication*, *33*(9), 1131–1140. doi:10.1080/10410236.2017.1331312 PMID:28622038

Boden, M. T., Berenbaum, H., & Gross, J. J. (2016). Why do people believe what they do? A functionalist perspective. *Review of General Psychology*, *20*(4), 399–411. doi:10.1037/gpr0000085 PMID:31680762

Borchers, C. (2018). How Hillary Clinton might have inspired Trump's 'fake news' attacks. *The Washington Post*. https://www.washingtonpost.com/news/the-fix/wp/2018/01/03/how-hillary-clinton-might-have-inspired-trumps-fake-news-attacks/

Bourelle, A., Bourelle, T., Knutson, A. V., & Spong, S. (2016). Sites of multimodal literacy: Comparing student learning in online and face-to-face environments. *Computers and Composition*, *39*, 55–70. doi:10.1016/j.compcom.2015.11.003

Bowen, K. N., Roberts, J. J., Kocian, E. J., & Bartula, A. (2014). An empirical test of social information processing theory and emotions in violent situations. *Western Criminology Review*, *15*(1), 18–33. http://wcr.sonoma.edu/v15n1/Bowen.pdf

Boxell, L., Gentzkow, M., & Shapiro, J. M. (2018). A note on Internet use and the 2016 U.S. presidential election outcome. *PLoS One*, *13*(7), e0199571. doi:10.1371/journal.pone.0199571 PMID:30020953

Bransford, J. D., Brown, A. L., & Cocking, R. R. (2000). *How people learn: Brain, mind, experience, and school*. National Academy Press.

Brennen, B. (2017). Making Sense of Lies, Deceptive Propaganda, and Fake News. *Journal of Medical Ethics*, *32*(3), 179–181. doi:10.1080/23736992.2017.1331023

Britt, M. A., Rouet, J.-F., Blaum, D., & Millis, K. (2019). A Reasoned Approach Dealing with Fake News. *Policy Insights from the Behavioral and Brain Sciences*, *6*(1), 94–101. doi:10.1177/2372732218814855

Brock, J. D., & Simonyan, K. (2018). *Large scale gan training for high fidelity natural image synthesis*. arXiv preprint arXiv:1809.11096.

Brown, D. F., & Canniff, M. (2007). Designing curricular experiences that promote young adolescents' cognitive growth. *Middle School Journal*, *39*(1), 16–23. doi:10.1080/00940771.2007.11461609

Brown, N. (2020). Deepfakes and Weaponization of Disinformation, Virginia. *The Journal of Law and Technology*, *23*(1), 1–59.

Bryant, W. (2017). Developing a strategy for using technology-enhanced items in large-scale standardized tests. *Practical Assessment, Research & Evaluation*, *22*(1), 1–10.

Buckingham, D. (2019). Teaching media in a 'post-truth' age: Fake news, media bias and the challenge for media/digital literacy education. *Culture and Education*, *31*(2), 213–231. doi:10.1080/11356405.2019.1603814

Budak, C. (2019, May). What happened? the spread of fake news publisher content during the 2016 us presidential election. In *The World Wide Web Conference* (pp. 139-150). 10.1145/3308558.3313721

Budak, C., Goel, S., & Rao, J. M. (2016). Fair and balanced? Quantifying media bias through crowdsourced content analysis. *Public Opinion Quarterly*, *80*(S1), 250–271. https://scholar.stanford.edu/papers/mediabias.pdf. doi:10.1093/poq/nfw007

Bullock, D. S., Mittenzwei, K., & Josling, T. E. (2019). Social Welfare Effects of Transparency and Misinformation in a Political Economy. *Journal of Agricultural and Applied Economics*, *51*(3), 485–494. doi:10.1017/aae.2019.17

Burkhardt, J. M. (2017). History of fake news. *ALA TechSource, 53*(8). https://journals.ala.org/index.php/ltr/article/view/6497/8636

Burkhardt, J. M. (2017). History of fake news. *Library Technology Reports*, *53*(8), 5–2. https://search-proquest-com.ucd.idm.oclc.org/docview/1967322040/abstract/32BE018C856D42F8PQ/1?accountid=14507

Buschman, J. (2019). Good news, bad news, and fake news. *The Journal of Documentation*, *75*(1), 213–228. doi:10.1108/JD-05-2018-0074

Calvillo, D. P., Ross, B. J., Garcia, R. J., Smelter, T. J., & Rutchick, A. M. (2020). Political ideology predicts perceptions of the threat of covid-19 (and susceptibility to fake news about it). *Social Psychological & Personality Science*, *11*(8), 1119–1128. doi:10.1177/1948550620940539

Cannizzaro, S. (2016). Internet memes as internet signs: A semiotic view of digital culture. *Sign Systems Studies*, *44*(4), 562–586. doi:10.12697/SSS.2016.44.4.05

Carew, A. (2020). Ghost in the Algorithm: Justin Krook's 'Machine' and Advancing AI, Metro Magazine. *Media & Education Magazine*, (203), 94–97.

Carey, C. (2016). Breaking the news: Telegraphy and yellow journalism in the Spanish-American War. *A Journal of History & Criticism, 26*(2), 130-148. https://www.muse.jhu.edu/article/628764

Carmichael, C., Callingham, R., Watson, J., & Hay, I. (2009). Factors influencing the development of middle school students' interest in statistical literacy. *Statistics Education Research Journal*, *8*(1), 62–81.

Carmi, E., Yates, S. J., Lockley, E., & Pawluczuk, A. (2020). Data citizenship: Rethinking data literacy in the age of disinformation, misinformation, and malinformation. *Internet Policy Review*, *9*(2), 1–22. doi:10.14763/2020.2.1481

Celliers, M., & Hattingh, M. (2020). Responsible design, implementation and use of information and communication technology. Nature Public Health Emergency Collection, 12067, 223–234. doi:10.1007/978-3-030-45002-1_19

Chadwick, A. (2011). The Political Information Cycle in a Hybrid News System: The British Prime Minister and the 'Bullygate' Affair. *The International Journal of Press/Politics*, *16*(1), 3–29. doi:10.1177/1940161210384730

Chalmers, L., & Keown, P. (2006). Communities of practice and professional development. *International Journal of Lifelong Education*, *25*(2), 139–156. doi:10.1080/02601370500510793

Chan, C. K., & Pang, M. F. (2006). Teacher collaboration in learning communities. *Teaching Education*, *17*(1), 1–5. doi:10.1080/10476210500527899

Chan, C., Chia, A., & Choo, S. (2017). Understanding multiliteracies and assessing multimodal texts in the English curriculum. *English Teaching*, *46*(2), 73–87. https://journals.melta.org.my/index.php/tet/article/viewFile/458/286

Chandler, D. (n.d.). *Marxist Media Theory*. Retrieved from https://www.cym.ie/documents/chandler.pdf

Chandler, D. (2006). Children's understanding of what is 'real' on television: A review of the literature. *Journal of Educational Media*, *23*(1), 65–80. doi:10.1080/1358165970230105

Chandler, S., & Scenters-Zapico, J. (2012). New literacy narratives: Stories about reading and writing in a digital age. *Computers and Composition*, *29*(3), 185–190. doi:10.1016/j.compcom.2012.07.002

Chandramouli & Memon. (2001). Analysis of lsb based image steganography techniques. In *Proceedings 2001 International Conference on Image Processing* (Cat. No. 01CH37205), (vol. 3, pp. 1019–1022). IEEE.

Chawla, R. (2019). Deepfakes: How a Pervert Shook the World. *International Journal of Advanced Research and Development*, *4*(6), 4–8.

Cheby, L. E. (2018, January 25). *Funding Libraries Is The Way To Beat 'Fake News'*. https://entropymag.org/funding-libraries-is-the-way-to-beat-fake-news/

Chesney, R., & Citron, D. (2019). Deepfakes and The New Disinformation War: The Coming Age of Post-Truth Geopolitics. *Foreign Affairs*, *98*(1), 147–155.

Chin, D. B., Blair, K. P., & Schwartz, D. L. (2016). Got game? A Choice-based learning assessment of data literacy and visualization skills. *Technology. Knowledge and Learning*, *21*(2), 195–210. doi:10.100710758-016-9279-7

Chisita, C. T. (2020). Libraries in the midst of the Coronavirus (COVID-19): Researchers experiences in dealing with the vexatious infodemic. *Library Hi Tech News*, *37*(6), 11–14. doi:10.1108/LHTN-03-2020-0022

Choi, M., Cristol, D., & Gimbert, B. (2018). Teachers as Digital Citizens: The Influence of Individual Backgrounds, Internet Use and Psychological Characteristics on Teachers' Levels of Digital Citizenship. *Computer Education*, *121*, 143–161. doi:10.1016/j.compedu.2018.03.005

Choi, Y., Choi, M., Kim, M., Ha, J.-W., Kim, S., & Choo, J. (2018). Stargan: Unified generative adversarial networks for multi-domain image-to-image translation. In *Proceedings of the IEEE conference on computer vision and pattern recognition*, (pp. 8789–8797). 10.1109/CVPR.2018.00916

Chopra, S. (2005). Learning a similarity metric discriminatively, with application to face verification. In *IEEE Conference on Computer Vision and Pattern Recognition* (pp. 539-546) 10.1109/CVPR.2005.202

Cho, W., Choi, S., Park, D. K., Shin, I., & Choo, J. (2019). Image-to-image translation via group-wise deep whitening-andcoloring transformation. *Proceedings of the IEEE Conference on Computer Vision and Pattern Recognition*, 10639–10647.

CILIP. (2018). *What is information literacy?* CILIP. https://www.cilip.org.uk/page/informationliteracy

Clayton, K., Davis, J., Hinckley, K., & Horiuchi, Y. (2019). Partisan Motivated Reasoning and Misinformation in the Media: Is News from Ideologically Uncongenial Sources More Suspicious. *Japanese Journal of Political Science*, *20*(3), 129–142. doi:10.1017/S1468109919000082

Clements, C. S. (2013). Perception and persuasion in legal argumentation: Using informal fallacies and cognitive biases to win the war of words. *BYU Law Review*, *2013*(2), 319-362. https://digitalcommons.law.byu.edu/cgi/viewcontent.cgi?article=2709&context=lawreview

Coiro, J. (2011). Predicting reading comprehension on the Internet: Contributions of offline reading skills, online reading skills, and prior knowledge. *Journal of Literacy Research*, *43*(4), 352–392. doi:10.1177/1086296X11421979

Comer, J. S., Furr, J. M., Beidas, R. S., Weiner, C. L., & Kendall, P. C. (2008). Children and terrorism-related news: Training parents in coping and media literacy. *Journal of Consulting and Clinical Psychology*, *76*(4), 568–578. doi:10.1037/0022-006X.76.4.568 PMID:18665686

Commisso, C. (2017). The Post-Truth Archive: Considerations for Archiving Context in Fake News Repositories, Preservation. *Digital Technology & Culture*, *46*(3), 99–102. doi:10.1515/pdtc-2017-0010

Common Core State Standards Initiative. (2010). *Mathematics standards* [PDF file]. Retrieved from http://www.corestandards.org/Math/

Common Core State Standards Initiative. (2010). *The Common Core State Standards for English language arts & literacy in history/social studies, science, and technical subjects* [PDF file]. Retrieved from http://www.corestandards.org/assets/CCSSI_ELA%20Standards.pdf

Compton, J. (2013). Inoculation theory. In J. P. Dillard & L. Shen (Eds.), *The SAGE handbook of persuasion: Developments in theory and practice* (2nd ed., pp. 220–236). Sage Publications. doi:10.4135/9781452218410

Cooke, N. A. (2017). Post truth, truthiness, and alternative facts. *The Library Quarterly*, *87*(3), 211–221. doi:10.1086/692298

Cook, J., Lewandowsky, S., & Ecker, U. K. H. (2017). Neutralizing misinformation through Inoculation: Exposing misleading argumentation techniques reduces their influence. *PLoS One*, *12*(5), 1–21. doi:10.1371/journal.pone.0175799 PMID:28475576

Costello, C. R., & Ramo, D. E. (2017). Social media and substance use: What should we be recommending to teens and their parents? *The Journal of Adolescent Health*, *60*(6), 629–630. doi:10.1016/j.jadohealth.2017.03.017 PMID:28532648

Cotgreave, A. (2019, September 6). Fighting the good fight: combating fake data with data literacy. *Information Age*. https://www.information-age.com/combating-fake-data-with-data-literacy-123485171/

Cronbach, L. J. (1987). Five perspectives of the validity argument. In H. Wainer & H. I. Braun (Eds.), *Test validity* (pp. 3–17). Lawrence Erlbaum.

Cutumisu, M., Chin, D. B., & Schwartz, D. L. (2019). A digital game-based assessment of middle-school and college students' choices to seek critical feedback and to revise. *British Journal of Educational Technology*, *50*(6), 2977–3003. doi:10.1111/bjet.12796

Cybenko, A. K., & Cybenko, G. (2018). AI and Fake News. *IEEE Intelligent Systems*, *33*(5), 3–7. doi:10.1109/MIS.2018.2877280

D'Amelio, E. (2018). Literacy theories for the digital age: Social, critical, multimodal, spatial, material and sensory lenses, edited by Kathy A. Mills. In Language and Education (Vol. 32, Issue 1). doi:10.1080/09500782.2017.1315129

Daneels, R., & Vanwynsberghe, H. (2017). Mediating Social Media Use: Connecting Parent's Mediation Strategies and Social Media Literacy. *Cyberpsychology (Brno)*, *11*(3), 1–13. doi:10.5817/CP2017-3-5

Data Use Standards Workgroup. (2015). *Statewide Longitudinal Data System Data Use Standards: Knowledge, skills, and professional behaviors for effective data use* [PDF file]. Retrieved from https://eric.ed.gov/?id=ED595040

Day, N. J. S., Townsend, M. L., & Grenyer, B. F. S. (2020). Living with pathological narcissism: A qualitative study. *Borderline Personality Disorder and Emotion Dysregulation*, *7*(19), 19. Advance online publication. doi:10.118640479-020-00132-8 PMID:32817795

De Kreersmaecker, J., & Roets, A. (2017). Fake News: Incorrect, But Hard to Correct, The Role of Cognitive Ability on the Impact of False Information on Social Impressions. *Intelligence, 65*, 107–110. doi:10.1016/j.intell.2017.10.005

De Paor, S., & Heravi, B. (2020). Information literacy and fake news: How the field of librarianship can help combat the epidemic of fake news. *Journal of Academic Librarianship, 46*(5), 102218. doi:10.1016/j.acalib.2020.102218

de Saussure, F. (1998). *Course in general linguistics* (2nd ed.). (R. Harris, Trans.). Open Court.

De Schrijver, A. (2012). Sample survey on sensitive topics: Investigating respondents' understanding and trust in alternative versions of the randomized response technique. *Journal of Research Practice, 8*(1). http://jrp.icaap.org/index.php/jrp/article/view/277/250

Deahl, E. S. (2014). *Better the data you know: Developing Youth data literacy in schools and informal learning environments* [Master's Thesis, the Massachusetts Institute of Technology]. doi:10.2139srn.2445621

Deighton, J., Fader, P., Haenlein, M., Kaplan, A., Libai, B., & Muller, E. (2011). Médias sociaux et entreprise, une route pleine de défis. *Recherche et Applications en Marketing, 26*(3), 117–124. doi:10.1177/076737011102600306

Del Viscio, J. (2020, July). A Nixon deepfake, a "Moon Disaster" speech and an information ecosystem at risk. *Scientific American.* https://www.scientificamerican.com/article/a-nixon-deepfake-a-moon-disaster-speech-and-an-information-ecosystem-at-risk1/

Dempsey, K. (2017). What's behind fake news and what you can do about it. *Information Today, 34*(4), 6.

Dobber, T., Metoui, N., Trilling, D., Helberger, N., & Vreese, C. D. (2020). Do (Microtargeted) Deepfakes Have Real Effects on Political Attitudes. *The International Journal of Press/Politics*, 1–23. doi:10.1177/1940161220944364

Dollinger, A. (2017). *Can librarians save us from fake news?* Vice. https://www.vice.com/en_us/article/pgwwgz/can-librarians-save-us-fromfake-news

Durodolu, O. O., & Ibenne, S. K. (2020). The fake news infodemic vs information literacy. Library Hi Tech News. doi:10.1108/LHTN-03-2020-0020

Durodolu, O. O., & Ocholla, D. O. (2017). Search Strategy, Self-Concept and Metacognitive Skills of Secondary School Teachers in Selected Cities in Nigeria and South Africa. *LIBRI: International Journal of Library and Information Science, 67*(2). doi:10.1515/libri-2016-0104

Durodolu, O.O, Ibenne, S.K and Dube, TV (2021). New mental costumes: Leveraging ACRL's value of information frame in dealing with infodemics in a post-truth era. *College & Research Libraries News, 82*(4), 175.

Eccles, J. S., & Midgley, C. (1990). Changes in academic motivation and self-perception during early adolescence. In R. Montemayor (Ed.), *Early adolescence as a time of transition* (pp. 1–29). SAGE.

Education, G. D. of. (2015). *9th-10th Grade English Language Arts Georgia Standards of Excellence (ELA GSE)*. https://www.georgiastandards.org/Georgia-Standards/Frameworks/ELA-9-10-Grade-9-Literature-Composition-Standards.pdf

Educational Testing Service. (2002). *ETS standards for quality and fairness*. Author.

El Rayess, M., Chebl, C., Mhanna, J., & Hage, R. M. (2018). Fake news judgement. *RSR. Reference Services Review*, *46*(1), 146–129. doi:10.1108/RSR-07-2017-0027

Emanuel, R., & Challons-Lipton, C. (2013). Visual literacy and the digital native: Another look. *Journal of Visual Literacy*, *32*(1), 1. doi:10.1080/23796529.2013.11674703

Emejulu, A., & McGregor, C. (2019). Towards a Radical Digital Citizenship in Digital Education. *Critical Studies in Education*, *60*(1), 131–147. doi:10.1080/17508487.2016.1234494

Emory, J. (2021, May 16). UW professor leads study on deepfakes in maps. *The Daily UW*. https://www.dailyuw.com/news/article_ac9506e0-b2e6-11eb-865c-5f7ef6613ff6.html

English, L. D., & Watson, J. (2018). Modelling with authentic data in sixth grade. *ZDM Mathematics Education*, *50*(1–2), 103–115. doi:10.100711858-017-0896-y

Ercegovac, Z. (2012). Digital image tagging: A case study with seventh grade students. *School Libraries Worldwide*, *18*(1), 97–110.

Ercegovac, Z. (2015). Data-driven society begins with data-savvy youth. *Bulletin of the Association for Information Science & Technology*, *42*(1), 42–48.

Erwin, R. W. Jr. (2015). Data literacy: Real-world learning through problem-solving with data sets. *American Secondary Education*, *43*(2), 18–26.

Eshet, Y., & Chaiut, E. (2005). Living books: On the acquisition of digital skills in multimedia environments. In *Learning in the Technology Era. Proceedings of the Chais Conference*. The Open University of Israel.

Eshet-Alkalai. (2005). Thinking skills in the digital era. In Encyclopaedia of Distance Learning (vol. 1). Idea Group Inc.

Eshet-Alkalai, Y. (2004). Digital literacy: A conceptual framework for survival skills in the digital era. *Journal of Educational Multimedia and Hypermedia*, *13*(1), 93–106. doi:10.4018/978-1-60566-198-8.ch154

European Commission. (2018). *Tackling online disinformation: A European Approach* (Document 52018DC0236). Retrieved from https://eur-lex.europa.eu/legal-content/EN/TXT/?uri=CELEX:52018DC0236

European Commission. (2018). *Tackling online disinformation: A European approach.* https://eur-lex.europa.eu/legal-content/EN/TXT/?uri=CELEX%3A52018DC0236

Eva, N., & Shea, E. (2018). Marketing libraries in an era of "fake news". *Reference and User Services Quarterly*, *57*(3), 168–171. doi:10.5860/rusq.57.3.6599

Ewing, M., Packman, S., Hamen, C., & Thurber, A. C. (2010). Representing targets of measurement within Evidence-Centered Design. *Applied Measurement in Education*, *23*(4), 325–341. doi:10.1080/08957347.2010.510959

Fairclough, N. (1992). Discourse and text: Linguistic and intertextual analysis within discourse analysis. *Discourse & Society*, *3*(2), 193–217. doi:10.1177/0957926592003002004

Farkas, M. (2018). Beyond fake news: Determining what sources to trust. *American Libraries*, 1.

Fazio, L. (2020, February 18). Out-of-context photos are a powerful low-tech form of misinformation. *PBS.* https://www.pbs.org/newshour/science/out-of-context-photos-are-a-powerful-low-tech-form-of-misinformation

Ferrara, S., & Lai, E. (2016). Documentation to support test score interpretation and use. In S. Lane, M. R. Raymond, & T. M. Haladyna (Eds.), *Handbook of test development* (2nd ed., pp. 603–623). Routledge.

Ferrara, S., Lai, E., Reilly, A., & Nicols, P. D. (2016). Principled Approaches to assessment design, development, and implementation. In A. A. Rupp & J. P. Leighton (Eds.), *The handbook of cognition and assessment: Frameworks, methodologies, and applications* (pp. 41–74). Wiley. doi:10.1002/9781118956588.ch3

Figueira, A., & Oliveria, L. (2017). The Current State of Fake News: Challenges and Opportunities. *Procedia Computer Science*, *121*, 817–825. doi:10.1016/j.procs.2017.11.106

Fingar, K. R., & Jolls, T. (2014). Evaluation of a school-based violence prevention media literacy curriculum. *Injury Prevention*, *20*(3), 1–8. doi:10.1136/injuryprev-2013-040815 PMID:23956370

Finley, W., McGowan, B., & Kluever, J. (2017). Fake news: An opportunity for real librarianship. *ILA Reporter, 35*(3), 8-12.

Fleming, D. (2019). Fear of persuasion in the English language arts. *College English*, *81*(6), 508–541.

Fletcher, J. (2018). Deepfakes, Artificial Intelligence, and Some Kind of Dystopia: The New Faces of Online Post-Fact Performance. *Theatre Journal*, *70*(4), 455–471. doi:10.1353/tj.2018.0097

Floridi, L. (2018). Artificial Intelligence, Deepfakes and a Future of Ectypes. *Philosophy & Technology*, *31*(3), 317–321. doi:10.100713347-018-0325-3

Flynn, D. J., Nyhan, B., & Reifler, J. (2017). The Nature and Origins of Misperceptions: Understanding False and Unsupported Beliefs About Politics. *Political Psychology*, *38*, 127–150. doi:10.1111/pops.12394

Fontichiaro, K., & Oehrli, J. A. (2016). Why data literacy matters. *Knowledge Quest*, *44*(5), 21–27.

Forster, M., Bestelmeyer, S., Baez-Rodriguez, N., Berkowitz, A., Caplan, B., Esposito, R., Grace, E., & McGee, S. (2018). Data Jams. *Science Teacher (Normal, Ill.)*, *86*(2), 48–53.

Forsyth, S., & Liu, C. J. (2019). Designing tactile picture books: Critical making in libraries to broaden participation in STEM education and careers. Paper from AERA '19: Leveraging Education Research in a "Post-Truth" Era: Multimodal Narratives to Democratize Evidence, Toronto, Canada.

Forzani, E. (2018). How well can students evaluate online science information? Contributions of prior knowledge, gender, socioeconomic status, and offline reading ability. *Reading Research Quarterly*, *53*(4), 385–390. doi:10.1002/rrq.218

Fox, J. (2020). 'Fake news' – The perfect storm: Historical perspectives. *Historical Research*, *93*(259), 172–187. doi:10.1093/hisres/htz011

Frenda, S. J., Knowles, E. D., Saletan, W., & Loftus, E. F. (2013). False Memories of Fabricated Political Events. *Journal of Experimental Social Psychology*, *49*(2), 280–286. doi:10.1016/j.jesp.2012.10.013

Gallagher, B. (2016). *What impact does fake news have on the real world?* Mary Jane. https://merryjane.com/culture/fake-news-internetimpact

Gandhi & Jain. (2020). *Adversarial perturbations fool deepfake detectors.* arXiv preprint arXiv:2003.10596.

Gee, J.-P., & Esteban-Guitart, M. (2019). Designing for deep learning in the context of digital and social media. *Media Education Research Journal*, *58*(27), 9–17. doi:10.3916/C58-2019-01

Ghosn-Chelala, M. (2019). Exploring Sustainable Learning and Practice of Digital Citizenship: Education and Place-based Challenges, Education. *Citizenship and Social Justice*, *14*(1), 40–56. doi:10.1177/1746197918759155

Gil de Zúñiga, H., Jung, N., & Valenzuela, S. (2012). Social media use for news and individuals' social capital, civic engagement and political participation. *Journal of Computer-Mediated Communication*, *17*(3), 319–336. doi:10.1111/j.1083-6101.2012.01574.x

Gleason, B., & Gillern, S. V. (2018). Digital Citizenship with Social Media: Participatory Practices of Teaching and Learning in Secondary Education. *Journal of Educational Technology & Society*, *21*(1), 200–212.

Gleason, B., & von Gillern, S. (2018). Digital citizenship with social media: Participatory practices of teaching and learning in secondary education. *Journal of Educational Technology & Society*, *21*(1), 200–212.

Godowski, J. P. (2015). Out of the shadows and into the light: Liberation through education. *The Vermont Connection*, *36*(8), 50-57. https://scholarworks.uvm.edu/cgi/viewcontent.cgi?article=1007&context=tvc

Goel, S., Anderson, A., Hofman, J., & Watts, D. J. (2015). The Structural Virality of Online Diffusion. *Management Science*, *62*(1), 180–196.

Gordon, E., Elwood, S., & Mitchell, K. (2016). Critical spatial learning: Participatory mapping, spatial histories, and youth civic engagement. *Children's Geographies*, *14*(5), 1–15. doi:10.1080/14733285.2015.1136736

Gould, R. (2017). Data literacy is statistical literacy. *Statistics Education Research Journal*, *16*(1), 22–25.

Grady, C. (2015). Institutional review boards: Purpose and challenges. *Chest*, *148*(5), 1148–1155. doi:10.1378/chest.15-0706 PMID:26042632

Granjo, M., Castro Silva, J., & Peixoto, F. (2021). Teacher identity: Can ethical orientation be related to perceived competence, psychological needs satisfaction, commitment and global self-esteem? *European Journal of Teacher Education*, *44*(2), 158–179. doi:10.1080/02619768.2020.1748004

Graves, L., & Wells, C. (2019). From information availability to factual accountability. In J. Katz & K. K. Mays (Eds.), *Journalism and truth in an age of social media* (pp. 39–57). Oxford University Press. doi:10.1093/oso/9780190900250.003.0004

Grazulis, A., & Rogers, R. (2021). Ridiculous and untrue – Fake news!: The impact of labeling fake news. In *Research anthology on fake news, political warfare, and combatting the spread of misinformation* (pp. 25–38). IGI Global. doi:10.4018/978-1-7998-7291-7.ch002

Greenberg, D. (2018). A half century of 'liberal media bias'. *The Wall Street Journal*. Retrieved https://www.wsj.com/articles/a-half-century-of-liberal-media-bias-1535034293

Greenberg, D. (2008). The idea of "the liberal media" and its roots in the civil rights movement. A Journal of History. *Política y Cultura*, *1*(2), 167–186. doi:10.1080/17541320802457111

Green, D., Karafa, K., & Wilson, S. (2020). Art Therapy with Grieving Children: Effect on Affect in the Dual-Process Model. *Art Therapy: Journal of the American Art Therapy Association*, •••, 1–5. doi:10.1080/07421656.2020.1823197

Grinberg, N., Kenneth, J., Friedland, L., Swire-Thompson, B., & Lazer, D. (2019). Fake News on Twitter During the 2016 US Presidential Election. *Science*, *363*(6425), 374–378. doi:10.1126cience.aau2706 PMID:30679368

Groeling, T. (2013). Media bias by the numbers: Challenges and opportunities in the empirical study of partisan news. *Annual Review of Political Science*, *16*(1), 129–151. doi:10.1146/annurev-polisci-040811-115123

Groth, R. (2015). Research commentary: Working at the boundaries of mathematics education and statistics education communities of practice. *Journal for Research in Mathematics Education*, *46*(1), 4–16. doi:10.5951/jresematheduc.46.1.0004

Guardian. (2019). *Singapore fake news law a 'disaster' for freedom of speech, says rights group.* https://www.theguardian.com/world/2019/may/09/singapore-fake-news-law-a-disaster-for-freedom-of-speech-says-rights-group

Guera, D., & Delp, E. J. (2018, November). Deepfake video detection using recurrent neural networks. In *2018 15th IEEE International Conference on Advanced Video and Signal Based Surveillance (AVSS)* (pp. 1-6). IEEE. 10.1109/AVSS.2018.8639163

Guess, A. M., Lerner, M., Lyons, B., Montgomery, J. M., Nyhan, B., Reifler, J., & Sircar, N. (2020). A digital media literacy intervention increases discernment between mainstream and false news in the United States and India. *Proceedings of the National Academy of Sciences of the United States of America*, *117*(27), 15536–15545. doi:10.1073/pnas.1920498117 PMID:32571950

Gulrajani, Ahmed, Arjovsky, Dumoulin, & Courville. (2017). Improved training of wasserstein gans. *Advances in Neural Information Processing Systems*, 5767–5777.

Gunter, G. A. (2007). Building student data literacy: An essential critical-thinking skill for the 21st Century. *MultiMedia & Internet @ Schools, 14*(3), 24–28.

Haag, M., & Salam, M. (2017). Gunman in pizzagate shooting is sentenced to 4 years in prison. *The New York Times, 23*.https://www.nytimes.com/2017/06/22/us/pizzagate-attack-sentence.html

Haertel, E. H. (2006). Reliability. In R. L. Brennan (Ed.), *Educational measurement* (4th ed., pp. 65–110). Rowman & Littlefield.

Haigh, M., Haigh, T., & Matychak, T. (2019). Information literacy vs. Fake news: The sase of Ukraine. *Open Information Science*, *3*(1), 154–165. doi:10.1515/opis-2019-0011

Hajam, M. A. (2017). Users' information literacy competencies: A study with reference to scholarly community of Kashmir University. *DESIDOC Journal of Library and Information Technology*, *37*(3), 153–157. doi:10.14429/djlit.37.3.9739

Haladyna, T. M. (2006). Roles and importance of validity studies in test development. In S. M. Downing & T. M. Haladyna (Eds.), *Handbook of test development* (pp. 739–755). Lawrence Erlbaum.

Hallam, C., & Zanella, G. (2017). Online Self-Disclosure: The Privacy Paradox Explained as a Temporally Discounted Balance Between Concerns and Rewards. *Computers in Human Behavior*, *68*, 217–227. doi:10.1016/j.chb.2016.11.033

Hall, G., & Loucks, S. (1978). Teacher concerns as a basis for facilitating and personalizing staff development. *Teachers College Record*, *80*(1), 36–53.

Hall, G., Loucks, S., Rutherford, W., & Newlove, B. (1975). Levels of use of the innovation: A framework for analyzing innovation adoption. *Journal of Teacher Education*, *26*(1), 52–56. doi:10.1177/002248717502600114

Hansen, E. G., & Mislevy, R. J. (2004, April). *Toward a unified validity framework for ensuring access to assessments by individuals with disabilities and English language learners*. In The Annual Meeting of the National Council on Measurement in Education, San Diego, CA.

Harvey, L. (2020). Researching the real world. *Quality Research International*. Retrieved 27/07/2020, from https://www.qualityresearchinternational.com/methodology/RRW8pt2pt2Positivismandsurveys.php

Harvey, L., & Palese, E. (2018). #NeverthelessMemesPersisted: Building critical memetic literacy in the classroom. *Journal of Adolescent & Adult Literacy*, *62*(3), 259–270. doi:10.1002/jaal.898

Hasan, H. R., & Salah, K. (2019). Combating Deepfake Videos Using Blockchain and Smart Contracts. *IEEE Access: Practical Innovations, Open Solutions*, *7*, 41596–41606. doi:10.1109/ACCESS.2019.2905689

Hassell, H. J. G., Holbein, J. B., & Miles, M. R. (2020). There is no liberal media bias in which news stories political journalists choose to cover. *Science Advances*, *6*(14), eaay9344. Advance online publication. doi:10.1126ciadv.aay9344 PMID:32270038

Hattwig, D., Bussert, K., Medaille, A., & Burgess, J. (2013). Visual literacy standards in higher education: New opportunities for libraries and student learning. *Portal (Baltimore, Md.)*, *13*(1), 61–89. doi:10.1353/pla.2013.0008

Hayes, D., Christie, P., Mills, M., & Lingard, B. (2020). *Teachers and schooling making a difference: Productive pedagogies, assessment and performance*. Routledge., doi:10.4324/9781003117643

Head, A., & Eisenberg, M. (2011). How college students use the web for everyday life research. *First Monday*, *16*(4). Advance online publication. doi:10.5210/fm.v16i4.3484

Heinrichs, J. (2020). *Thank you for arguing: What Aristotle, Lincoln and Homer Simpson can teach us about the art of persuasion* (4th ed.). Broadway Books.

Helfand, D. (2013). Watering the roots of knowledge through collaborative learning. *The Chronicle of Higher Education*. Retrieved from October 28, 2014, from http://chronicle.com/article/Watering-the-Roots-of/140135/

Henzel, V., & Håkansson, A. (2021). Hooked on virtual social life: Problematic social media use and associations with mental distress and addictive disorders. *PLoS One*, *16*(4), e0248406. doi:10.1371/journal.pone.0248406 PMID:33831023

Hern, A. (2020). Fake coronavirus tweets spread as other sites take harder stance. *The Guardian*. https://www.theguardian.com/world/2020/mar/04/fake-coronavirus-tweets-spread-as-other-sites-take-harder-stance

He, Z., Zuo, W., Kan, M., Shan, S., & Chen, X. (2019). Attgan: Facial attribute editing by only changing what you want. *IEEE Transactions on Image Processing*, *28*(11), 5464–5478. doi:10.1109/TIP.2019.2916751 PMID:31107649

Hinton, P. (2017). Implicit stereotypes and the predictive brain: Cognition and culture in "biased" person perception. *Palgrave Communications*, *3*(17086), 17086. doi:10.1057/palcomms.2017.86

Hintz, A., Dencik, L., & Wahl-Jorgensen, K. (2017). Digital Citizenship and Surveillance Society. *International Journal of Communication*, *11*, 731–739.

Hobbs, R. (2004). A review of school-based initiatives in media literacy education. *The American Behavioral Scientist*, *48*(1), 42–59. doi:10.1177/0002764204267250

Hobbs, R. (2020). Propaganda in an age of algorithmic personalization: Expanding literacy research and practice. *Reading Research Quarterly*, *55*(3), 521–533. doi:10.1002/rrq.301

Hobbs, R., & Mcgee, S. (2008). Teaching about propaganda: An examination of the historical roots of media literacy. *The Journal of Media Literacy Education*, *6*(62), 56–67. www.jmle.org

Hockly, N. (2020). Five things you always wanted to know about data literacy (but were too afraid to ask). *English Teaching Professional*, *128*, 54.

Hollandsworth, R., Donovan, J., & Welch, M. (2017). Digital Citizenship: You Can't Go Home Again. *TechTrends*, *61*(6), 524–530. doi:10.100711528-017-0190-4

Holt, T. J., Brewer, R., & Goldsmith, A. (2019). Digital Drift and the "Sense of Injustice". *Counter-Productive Policing of Youth Cybercrime*, *40*(9), 1144–1156.

Houtman, E., & Wall, M. (2019). *Information disorder: Helping students to think critically about the news*. http://hdl.handle.net/1807/94747

Howel, L. (2013). *Digital wildfires in a hyperconnected world. Global Risks Report*. http://www3.weforum.org/docs/WEF_GlobalRisks_Report_2013.pdf

Hsu, C. C., Zhuang, Y. X., & Lee, C. Y. (2019). Deep fake image detection based on pairwise learning. Preprints, 2019050013.

Hsu, Lee, & Zhuang. (2018). They are learning to detect fake face images in the wild. In *2018 International Symposium on Computer, Consumer and Control (IS3C)* (pp. 388–391). IEEE.

Hsu, C.-C., Zhuang, Y.-X., & Lee, C.-Y. (2020). Deep fake image detection based on pairwise learning. *Applied Sciences (Basel, Switzerland)*, *10*(1), 370. doi:10.3390/app10010370

Hua, J., & Shaw, R. (2020). Corona Virus (COVID-19) "Infodemic" and Emerging Issues through a Data Lens: The Case of China. *International Journal of Environmental Research and Public Health*, *17*(7), 2309. doi:10.3390/ijerph17072309 PMID:32235433

Izaguirre, J. G. III. (2015). Prophets, gurus, and pundits: Rhetorical styles and public engagement. *The Quarterly Journal of Speech*, *101*(4), 673–677. doi:10.1080/00335630.2015.1128052

Jackson, J. E. (2014). Sensationalism in the newsroom: Its yellow beginnings, the nineteenth century legal transformation, and the current seizure of the American press. *Notre Dame Journal of Law, Ethics & Public Policy*, *19*(2), 789–816. https://scholarship.law.nd.edu/cgi/viewcontent.cgi?article=1232&context=ndjlepp

Jacobson, L. (2017). The smell test: Educators can counteract fake news with information literacy. Here's how. *School Library Journal*. https://www.slj.com/?detailStory=the-smell-test-educators-can-counter-fake-news-withinformation-literacy-heres-how

Jeffries, S., Kroondyk, J., Paolini, F., & Radisauskas, C. (2017). Says who? Librarians tackle fake news. *College & Research Libraries News*, *78*(10), 538–545. doi:10.5860/crln.78.10.538

Jiao, H. (2020). Module 10: Reliability and validity. In EDMS626: Instrumentation: Spring 2020. Academic Press.

Johnson, B. (2019, Mar. 25). Deepfakes are Solvable-But Don't Forget That Shallowfakes are Already Pervasive. *MIT Technology Review*.

Johnson, K. E. (1997). Comments on Karen E. Johnson's "The role of theory in L2 teacher education": The author responds. *TESOL Quarterly*, *31*(4), 779–782. doi:10.2307/3587761

Johnson, M. (2018). Fighting "fake news": How we overhauled our website evaluationlessons. *Knowledge Quest*, *47*(1), 32–36.

Jolls, T., & Thoman, E. (2008). *MediaLitKit: Literacy for the 21st Century* (2nd ed.). Centre for Media Literacy.

Jones-Kavalier, B., & Flannigan, S. (2006). Connecting the digital dots: literacy of the 21st century. *Educause Review*. Retrieved from: http://www.educause.edu/ero/article/connecting-digital-dots-literacy-21st-century

Jones, L. M., & Mitchell, K. J. (2016). Defining and Measuring Youth Digital Citizenship. *New Media & Society*, *18*(9), 2063–2079. doi:10.1177/1461444815577797

Jones, V. (2020). Artificial Intelligence Enabled Deepfake Technology: The Emergence of a New Threat, Utica College. *ProQuest Dissertations Publishing*, *2020*, 27962429.

Jowell, G. S., & O'Donnell, V. (2015). *Propaganda and persuasion* (6th ed.). Sage Publishing.

Kamarck, E. (2018). *Malevolent soft power, AI, and the threat to democracy*. Brookings. https://www.brookings.edu/research/malevolent-soft-power-ai-and-the-threat-to-democracy/

Kane, M. (2006). Content-related validity evidence in test development. In S. M. Downing & T. M. Haladyna (Eds.), *Handbook of test development* (pp. 131–153). Lawrence Erlbaum.

Kanuka, H., & Anderson, T. (1999). Using constructivism in technology-mediated learning: Constructing order out of the chaos in the literature. *Radical Pedagogy*, *1*, 1–12. Retrieved March 4, 2008, from https://radicalpedagogy.icaap.org/content/issue1_2/02kanuka1_2.html

Kaplan, A. (1997). Work, leisure, and the tasks of schooling. *Curriculum Inquiry*, *27*(4), 423–451. doi:10.1080/03626784.1997.11075501

Kaplan, A. (2015). Social media. In D. T. Cook & J. M. Ryan (Eds.), *The Wiley Blackwell Encyclopedia of Consumption and Consumer Studies* (pp. 519–523). Wiley Blackwell.

Kaplan, A. (2017). Academia goes social media, MOOC, SPOC, SMOC and SSOC: The digital transformation of higher education institutions and universities. In B. Rishi & S. Bandyopadhyay (Eds.), *Contemporary Issues in Social Media Marketing* (pp. 20–30). Routledge. doi:10.4324/9781315563312-2

Kaplan, A. (2018). A school is a building that has 4 walls – with tomorrow inside: Toward the reinvention of the business school. *Business Horizons, 61*(4), 599–608. doi:10.1016/j.bushor.2018.03.010

Kaplan, A., & Haenlein, M. (2009). The fairyland of *Second Life*: About virtual social worlds and how to use them. *Business Horizons, 52*(6), 563–572. doi:10.1016/j.bushor.2009.07.002

Kaplan, A., & Haenlein, M. (2010). Users of the world, unite! The challenges and opportunities of social media. *Business Horizons, 53*(1), 59–68. doi:10.1016/j.bushor.2009.09.003

Kaplan, A., & Haenlein, M. (2016). Higher education and the Digital Revolution: About MOOCs, SPOCs, social media, and the Cookie Monster. *Business Horizons, 59*(4), 441–450. doi:10.1016/j.bushor.2016.03.008

Kapoor, K. K., Tamilmani, K., Rana, N. P., Patil, P., Dwivedi, Y. K., & Nerur, S. (2018). Advances in social media research: Past, present and future. *Information Systems Frontiers, 20*(3), 531–558. doi:10.100710796-017-9810-y

Karras, T., Aila, T., Laine, S., & Lehtinen, J. (2017). *Progressive growing of gans for improved quality, stability, and variation.* arXiv preprint arXiv:1710.10196.

Karras, T., Laine, S., & Aila, T. (2019). A style-based generator architecture for generative adversarial networks. *Proceedings of the IEEE conference on computer vision and pattern recognition*, 4401–4410. 10.1109/CVPR.2019.00453

Karras, T., Laine, S., Aittala, M., Hellsten, J., Lehtinen, J., & Aila, T. (2020). Analyzing and improving the image quality of stylegan. *Proceedings of the IEEE/CVF Conference on Computer Vision and Pattern Recognition*, 8110–8119.

Kennedy, C., Blumenthal, M., Clement, S., Clinton, J. D., Durand, C., Franklin, C., McGeeney, K., Miringoff, L., Olson, K., Rivers, D., Saad, L., Witt, G. E., & Wlezien, C. (2018). An Evaluation of the 2016 Election Polls in the United States. *Public Opinion Quarterly, 82*(1), 1–33. doi:10.1093/poq/nfx047

Kenyon, T., & Beaulac, G. (2014). Critical thinking education and debiasing. *Informal Logic, 34*(4), 341–363. doi:10.22329/il.v34i4.4203

Kim, M., & Choi, D. (2018). Development of Youth Digital Citizenship Scale and Implication for Educational Setting. *Journal of Educational Technology & Society, 21*(1), 155–171.

Koehler, M. J., & Mishra, P. (2009). What is technological pedagogical content knowledge? *Contemporary Issues in Technology & Teacher Education, 9*(1), 60–70. doi:10.4324/9781315771328

Kong, S. C. (2014). Developing Information Literacy and Critical Thinking Skills Through Domain Knowledge Learning in Digital Classrooms: An Experience of Practicing Flipped Classroom Strategy. *Computers & Education, 78*, 160–173. doi:10.1016/j.compedu.2014.05.009

Konold, C., & Higgins, T. L. (2003). Reasoning about data. In J. Kilpatrick, W. G. Martin, & D. Schifter (Eds.), *A research companion to principles and standards for school mathematics* (pp. 193–215). National Council of Teachers of Mathematics.

Koopman, M., Rodriguez, A. M., & Geradts, Z. (2018). Detection of deepfake video manipulation. In *The 20th Irish Machine Vision and Image Processing Conference (IMVIP)* (pp. 133-136). Academic Press.

Korobkov, A. (2019). Donald Trump and the Evolving U. S. -Russia Relationship. *Perceptions, 24*(1), 39–58.

Korshunova, I., Shi, W., Dambre, J., & Theis, L. (2017). Fast faceswap using convolutional neural networks. *Proceedings of the IEEE International Conference on Computer Vision*, 3677–3685.

Kozyreva, A., Lewandowsky, S., & Hertwig, R. (2020). Citizens versus the internet: Confronting digital challenges with cognitive tools. *Psychological Science in the Public Interest, 21*(3), 103–156. doi:10.1177/1529100620946707 PMID:33325331

Kucharski, A. (2016). Post-truth: Study epidemiology of fake news. *Nature, 540*(7634), 525. doi:10.1038/540525a PMID:30905947

Kwok, A. O. J., & Sharon, G. M. K. (2020). Deepfake: A Social Construction of Technology Perspective. *Current Issues in Tourism*, 1–5. doi:10.1080/13683500.2020.1738357

Laar, E. V., Deursen, A. J. A. M. V., Dijk, J. A. G. M. V., & Haan, J. D. (2017). The Relation Between 21st-Century Skills and Digital Skills: A Systematic Literature Review. *Computers in Human Behavior, 72*, 577–588. doi:10.1016/j.chb.2017.03.010

LaMarco, N. (2018). Mainstream vs. alternative media. *Small Business Advertising & Marketing/ Media. Chron.* https://smallbusiness.chron.com/mainstream-vs-alternative-media-21113.html

Lantolf, J. P., & Thorne, S. L. (2006). *Sociocultural theory and the genesis of second language development.* Oxford University Press. doi:10.1093/applin/amm027

Lantolf, J. P., & Thorne, S. L. (2007). Sociocultural theory and second language learning. In B. VanPatten & J. Williams (Eds.), *Theories in second language acquisition* (pp. 201–224). Lawrence Erlbaum.

Leetaru, K. (2019). A Reminder That 'Fake News' Is An Information Literacy Problem—Not A Technology Problem. *Forbes.* https://www.forbes.com/sites/kalevleetaru/2019/07/07/a-reminder-that-fake-newsis-an-information-literacy-problem-not-a-technology-problem/

Lee, Y. H. (2021). Scaffolding university students' epistemic cognition during multimodal multiple-document reading: The effects of the epistemic prompting and the automated reflection report. *The Internet and Higher Education, 49*, 100777. doi:10.1016/j.iheduc.2020.100777

Lefkowitz, M. (2017). Library tackles fake news with workshops, resources, advice. *Cornell University Library*. https://www.library.cornell.edu/about/news/archive/library-tackles-fake-news-workshops-resources-advice

Lenker, M. (2016). Motivated reasoning, political information, and information literacyeducation. *portal. Portal (Baltimore, Md.)*, *16*(3), 511–528.

Letukas, L. (2012). *The ascent of punditry: Media and the news construction of cable news* (Doctoral dissertation). Available from ProQuest Dissertations and Theses database. (UMI No. 3526446)

Leu, D., Kulikowich, J., Sedransk, N., Coiro, J., Cui, W., Forzani, E., Kennedy, C., & Maykel, C. (2014, April 4). *The ORCA Project: Designing technology-based assessments for online research, comprehension, and communication*. Paper presented at the American Educational Research Conference, Philadelphia, PA.

Leu, D. J., Forzani, E., Rhoads, C., Maykel, C., Kennedy, C., & Timbrell, N. (2015). The new literacies of online research and comprehension: Rethinking the reading achievement Gap. *Reading Research Quarterly*, *50*(1), 37–59. doi:10.1002/rrq.85

Leu, D. J., Kinzer, C. K., Coiro, J. L., & Cammack, D. W. (2004). Toward a theory of new literacies emerging from the Internet and other information and communication technologies. In R. B. Ruddell & N. J. Unrau (Eds.), *Theoretical models and processes of reading* (5th ed., pp. 1570–1613). International Reading Association.

Leu, D. J., Kinzer, C. K., Coiro, J., Castek, J., & Henry, L. A. (2013). New literacies: A dual level theory of the changing nature of literacy, instruction, and assessment. In N. Unrau & D. Alvermann (Eds.), *Theoretical models and processes of reading* (6th ed., pp. 1150–1181). International Reading Association. doi:10.1598/0710.42

Lewandowsky, S., Ecker, U. K., & Cook, J. (2017). Beyond misinformation: Understanding and coping with the "post-truth" era. *Journal of Applied Research in Memory and Cognition*, *6*(4), 353–369. Advance online publication. doi:10.1016/j.jarmac.2017.07.008

LFW. (n.d.). http://vis-www.cs.umass. edu/lfw/

Li, X., Lang, Y., Chen, Y., Mao, X., He, Y., Wang, S., Xue, H., & Lu, Q. (2020). *Sharp Multiple Instance Learning for DeepFake Video Detection*. In MM '20, Seattle, WA.

Light, A. (2019). *Operation Mockingbird: A third of the CIA budget went to media propaganda operations*. Humans are Free. https://humansarefree.com/2019/10/operation-mockingbird-a-third-of-the-cia-budget-went-to-media-propaganda-operations.html

Limaye, R. J., Sauer, M., Ali, J., Bernstein, J., Wahl, B., Barnhill, A., & Labrique, A. (2020). Building trust while influencing online COVID-19 content in the social media world. *The Lancet. Digital Health*, *2*(6), e277–e278. doi:10.1016/S2589-7500(20)30084-4 PMID:32322814

Lim, V., Deahl, E., Rubel, L., & Williams, S. (2014). Local Lotto: Mathematics and mobile technology to study the lottery. In D. Polly (Ed.), *Cases on technology integration in mathematics education* (pp. 43–67). IGI Global.

Lingard, B. (2003). Where to in gender policy in education after recuperative masculinity politics? *International Journal of Inclusive Education*, *7*(1), 33–56. doi:10.1080/13603110210143626

Lingard, B., Hayes, D., & Mills, M. (2003). *Leading learning: Making hope practical in schools: Making hope practical in schools*. McGraw-Hill Education.

Lin, H. (2019). The Existential Threat from Cyber-Enabled Information Warfare. *Bulletin of the Atomic Scientists*, *75*(4), 187–196. doi:10.1080/00963402.2019.1629574

Litschka, M. (2019). The political economy of media capabilities: The capability approach in media policy. *Journal of Information Policy*, *9*, 63–94. doi:10.5325/jinfopoli.9.2019.0063

Liu, Z., Luo, P., Wang, X., & Tang, X. (2015). Deep learning face attributes in the wild. *Proceedings of the IEEE international conference on computer vision*, 3730–3738. 10.1109/ICCV.2015.425

Livingstone, S., Olafsson, K., Helsper, E. J., Lupinaz-Villanueva, F., Veltri, G. A., & Folkvord, F. (2017). Maximizing Opportunities and Minimizing Risks for Children Online: The Role of Digital Skills in Emerging Strategies of Parental Mediation. *Journal of Communication*, *67*(1), 1–24. doi:10.1111/jcom.12277

Li, Y., Chang, M. C., & Lyu, S. (2018). In ictu oculi: Exposing AI created fake videos by detecting eye blinking. In 2018 *IEEE International Workshop on Information Forensics and Security (WIFS)* (pp. 1-7). IEEE. 10.1109/WIFS.2018.8630787

Li, Y., & Lyu, S. (2019). Exposing deepfake videos by detecting face warping artifacts. In *Proceedings of the IEEE Conference on Computer Vision and Pattern Recognition Workshops* (pp. 46-52). IEEE.

Louise, M. (n.d.). *Operation mockingbird: CIA media manipulation*. Prison-Planet.com. https://www.scribd.com/document/6381980/Operation-Mockingbird-CIA-Media-Manipulation-by-Mary-Louise

Low, D., & Pandya, J. Z. (2019). Issues of validity, subjectivity, and reflexivity in multimodal literacy research and analysis. *Journal of Language & Literacy Education*, *15*(1), 1–22.

Luecht, R. M. (2013). Assessment Engineering task model maps, task models and templates as a new way to develop and implement test specification. *Journal of Applied Testing Technology*, *14*(4), 1–38. http://www.jattjournal.com/index.php/atp/article/view/45254

Lupyan, G. (2017). How reliable is perception? *Philosophical Topics*, *45*(1), 81–106. doi:10.5840/philtopics20174515

Luria, A. R. (1976). *Cognitive development: Its cultural and social foundations*. Harvard University Press.

Lyon, D. (2017). Surveillance Culture: Engagement, Exposure, and Ethics in Digital Modernity. *International Journal of Communication*, *11*, 824–842.

Lysonski, S., & Durvasula, S. (2008). Digital Piracy of MP3s: Consumer and Ethical Predispositions. *Journal of Consumer Marketing*, *25*(3), 167–178. doi:10.1108/07363760810870662

MacKenzie, A., & Bhatt, I. (2019). Opposing the power of lies, bullshit and fake news: The value of truth. *Postdigital Science and Education*, *2020*(2), 217–232. doi:10.100742438-019-00087-2

Mackenzie, A., & Bhatt, I. (2020). Lies, Bullshit, and Fake News: Some Epistemological Concerns, Postdigital. *Science and Education*, *2*, 9–13.

Mackey, T. P., & Jacobson, T. E. (2011). Reframing information literacy as a metaliteracy. *College & Research Libraries*, *72*(1), 62–78. doi:10.5860/crl-76r1

Mann, A., Nguyen, K., & Gregory, K. (2019). Emperor Cottrell': Accused Christchurch shooter had celebrated rise of the Australian far-right. *ABC News*, (March), 23.

Manzanero, N. M., & Ramírez, M. Y. (2018). Diálogos sobre educación democrática: Mirada intercultural de la formación de ciudadanos latinoamericanos. *Telos: Revista de Estudios Interdisciplinarios en Ciencias Sociales*, *20*(1), 101–128. doi:10.36390/telos201.06

Mao, X., Li, Q., Xie, H., & Raymond, Y. K. (2017). Least squares generative adversarial networks. *Proceedings of the IEEE international conference on computer vision*, 2794–2802.

Maras, M. H., & Alexandrou, A. (2019). Determining Authenticity of Video Evidence in the Age of Artificial Intelligence and the Wake of Deepfake Videos. *International Journal of Evidence & Proof*, *23*(3), 255–262. doi:10.1177/1365712718807226

Markham, A. N. (2020). Taking data literacy to the streets: Critical pedagogy in the public sphere. *Qualitative Inquiry*, *26*(2), 227–237. doi:10.1177/1077800419859024

Marr, B. (2019, January 21). Chinese social credit score: Utopian Big Data – Bliss? Or black mirror on steroids? *Forbes*. https://www.forbes.com/sites/bernardmarr/2019/01/21/chinese-social-credit-score-utopian-big-data-bliss-or-black-mirror-on-steroids/#139759c648b8

Marra, F., Gragnaniello, D., Cozzolino, D., & Verdoliva, L. (2018). Detection of gan-generated fake images over social networks. In *2018 IEEE Conference on Multimedia Information Processing and Retrieval (MIPR)* (pp. 384–389). IEEE. 10.1109/MIPR.2018.00084

Marra, F., Saltori, C., Boato, G., & Verdoliva, L. (2019). Incremental Learning for the Detection and Classification of GAN-Generated Images. *Proc. IEEE International Workshop on Information Forensics and Security*. 10.1109/WIFS47025.2019.9035099

Martiniello, M. (2008). Language and the performance of English-language learners in math word problems. *Harvard Educational Review*, *78*(2), 333–368. doi:10.17763/haer.78.2.70783570r1111t32

Matern, F., Riess, C., & Stamminger, M. (2019, January). Exploiting visual artifacts to expose deepfakes and face manipulations. In *2019 IEEE Winter Applications of Computer Vision Workshops (WACVW)* (pp. 83-92). IEEE.

Maurer, U. M. (2000). Authentication theory and hypothesis testing. *IEEE Transactions on Information Theory*, *46*(4), 1350–1356. doi:10.1109/18.850674

Maxmen, A. (2009). Taking risks to transform science. *Cell*, *139*(1), 13–15. doi:10.1016/j.cell.2009.09.019 PMID:19804745

McCloud, S. (1994). *Understanding comics: The Invisible art*. Harper Collins.

McGuire, W. J. (1964). Some contemporary approaches. *Advances in Experimental Social Psychology*, *1*, 191–229.

McQuail, D. (2010). *McQuail's Mass Communication Theory* (6th ed.). Sage.

Mena, P. (2020). Cleaning up social media: The effect of warning labels on likelihood of sharing false news on Facebook. *Policy and Internet*, *12*(2), 165–183. doi:10.1002/poi3.214

Mesquita, C. T., Oliveira, A., Seixas, F. L., & Paes, A. (2020). Infodemia, fake news and medicine: Science and the quest for truth. *International Journal of Cardiovascular Sciences*, *33*(3), 203–205. doi:10.36660/ijcs.20200073

Messick, S. (1995). The interplay of evidence and consequences in the validation of performance assessments. *Educational Researcher*, *23*(2), 13–23. doi:10.3102/0013189X023002013

Mihailidis, P., & Viotty, S. (2017). Spreadable spectacle in digital culture: Civic expression, fake news, and the role of media literacies in "post-fact" society. *The American Behavioral Scientist*, *61*(4), 441–454. doi:10.1177/0002764217701217

Miller, C. R., & Edwards, V. (1936). The Intelligent Teacher's guide through campaign propaganda. *The Clearing House: A Journal of Educational Strategies, Issues and Ideas*, *11*(2), 69–77. doi: 10.1080/00098655.1936.11474219

Mills, K. A. (2010). A review of the "Digital Turn" in the new literacy studies. *Review of Educational Research*, *80*(2), 246–271. doi:10.3102/0034654310364401

Milyakina, A. (2018). Rethinking literary education in the digital age. *Sign Systems Studies*, *46*(4), 569–589. doi:10.12697/SSS.2018.46.4.08

Mishra, P., & Koehler, M. J. (2006). Technological Pedagogical Content Knowledge: A new framework for teacher knowledge. *Teachers College Record*, *108*(6), 1017–1054. doi:10.1111/j.1467-9620.2006.00684.x

Mislevy, R. J. (2013). Evidence-Centered Design for simulation-based assessment. *Military Medicine*, *178*(10), 107–114. doi:10.7205/MILMED-D-13-00213 PMID:24084311

Mislevy, R. J., Almond, R. G., & Lukas, J. F. (2003). A brief introduction to evidence-centered design. *ETS Research Report Series*, *2003*(1), i–29. doi:10.1002/j.2333-8504.2003.tb01908.x

Miyato, T., Kataoka, T., Koyama, M., & Yoshida, Y. (2018). *Spectral normalization for generative adversarial networks*. arXiv preprint arXiv:1802.05957.

Mohamed, I. I., Khalifa Ahmad, H. E., Hassaan, S. H., & Hassan, S. M. (2020). Assessment of anxiety and depression among substance use disorder patients: A case-control study. *Middle East Current Psychiatry*, *27*(22), 22. Advance online publication. doi:10.118643045-020-00029-w

Molina, M. D., Shyam Sundar, S., Le, T., & Lee, D. (2019). "Fake news" is not simply false information: A concept explication and taxonomy of online content. *The American Behavioral Scientist*, *65*(2), 180–212. doi:10.1177/0002764219878224

Mossberger, K., Tolbert, C. J., & McNeal, R. S. (2008). *Digital Citizenship: The Internet*. Society and Participation, The MIT Press USA.

Mosseri, A. (2016). News feed FYI: addressing hoaxes and fake news. *Facebook Newsroom*. Retrieved on 3/08/2020, from https://newsroom.fb.com/news/2016/12/news-feed-fyi-addressing-hoaxes-and-fake-news/

Mulligan, D. L. (2021). Dangerous decisions: The precarity of real-world research-A provocation. In D. L. Mulligan & P. A. Danaher (Eds.), *Researchers at risk: Precarity, jeopardy and uncertainty in academia* (pp. 311–325). Palgrave Macmillan. doi:10.1007/978-3-030-53857-6_20

Musgrove, A. T., Powers, J. R., Rebar, L. C., & Musgrove, G. J. (2018). Real or fake?Resources for teaching college students how to identify fake news. *College & Undergraduate Libraries*, *25*(3), 243–260. doi:10.1080/10691316.2018.1480444

Nations, D. (2018). *What is social media? Take a clear look at what social media is really all about*. https://www.lifewire.com/

Naughton, J. (2020). *Fake news about Covid-19 can be as dangerous as the virus*. Retrieved on 17/07/2020, from https://www.theguardian.com/commentisfree/2020/mar/14/fake-news-about-covid-19-can-be-as-dangerous-as-the-virus

Neely-Sardon, A., & Tignor, M. (2018). Focus on the facts: A news and information literacyinstructional program. *The Reference Librarian*, *59*(3), 108–121. doi:10.1080/02763877.2018.1468849

Nelson, J. L., & Taneja, H. (2018). The small, disloyal fake news audience: The role of audience availability in fake news consumption. *New Media & Society*, *20*(10), 1–18. doi:10.1177/1461444818758715

Newman, E. J., Garry, M., Unkelbach, C., Bernstein, D. M., Lindsay, D., & Nash, R. A. (2015). Truthiness and Falsiness of Trivia Claims Depend on Judgmental Contexts. *Journal of Experimental Psychology. Learning, Memory, and Cognition*, *41*(5), 1337–1348. doi:10.1037/xlm0000099 PMID:25822783

Newton, P. M., & Miah, M. (2017). Evidence-based higher education – Is the learning styles 'myth' important? *Frontiers in Psychology*, *8*, 444. doi:10.3389/fpsyg.2017.00444 PMID:28396647

Ngai, E. W., Moon, K. L. K., Lam, S. S., Chin, E. S., & Tao, S. S. (2015). Social media models, technologies, and applications. *Industrial Management & Data Systems*, *115*(5), 769–802. doi:10.1108/IMDS-03-2015-0075

Nguyen, H. H., Yamagishi, J., & Echizen, I. (2019, May). Capsule-forensics: Using capsule networks to detect forged images and videos. In *2019 IEEE International Conference on Acoustics, Speech and Signal Processing (ICASSP)* (pp. 2307-2311). IEEE. 10.1109/ICASSP.2019.8682602

Nichols, P. D., Kobrin, J. L., Lai, E., & Koepfler, J. (2016). The role of theories of learning and cognition in assessment design and development. In A. Rupp & J. P. Leighton (Eds.), *The handbook of cognition and assessment* (pp. 13–40). Wiley & Sons. doi:10.1002/9781118956588.ch2

Ni, Z., & Yun, Q. (2008). Robust lossless image data hiding designed for semi-fragile image authentication. *IEEE Transactions on Circuits and Systems for Video Technology*, *18*(4), 497–509. doi:10.1109/TCSVT.2008.918761

Norberg, P. A., Horne, D. R., & Horne, D. A. (2007). The Privacy Paradox: Personal Information Disclosure Intentions Versus Behaviors. *The Journal of Consumer Affairs*, *41*(1), 100–126. doi:10.1111/j.1745-6606.2006.00070.x

Oceans of Data Institute. (2015). *Building global interest in data literacy: A dialogue*. Educational Development Center. Retrieved from oceansofdata.org/ourwork/building-global-interest-data-literacy-dialogue-workshop-report

Oddo, J. (2013). Discourse-Based methods across texts and semiotic modes: Three tools for micro-rhetorical analysis. *Written Communication*, *30*(3), 236–275. doi:10.1177/0741088313488071

Ohleiser, A. (2016). *This is how Facebook's fake-news writers make money*. Academic Press.

Ohler, J. (2011). Digital Citizenship Means Character Education for the Digital Age. *Kappa Delta Pi Record*, *47*(1), 25–27. doi:10.1080/00228958.2011.10516720

Öhman, C. (2020). Introducing the pervert's dilemma: A contribution to the critique of deepfake pornography. *Ethics and Information Technology*, *22*(2), 133–140. doi:10.100710676-019-09522-1

Omolayo, O. (2017). *Who fears social media?* https://techpoint.ng/2017/07/25/social-media-regulation-nigeria/

Pan American Health Organisation and World Health Organisation. (2020). *Understanding The Infodemic and Misinformation in the Fight Against Covid-19 Factsheet N.5*. Department of Evidence and Intelligence for Action in Health Office of the Assistant Director. Retrieved on 27/07/2020, from https://iris.paho.org/bitstream/handle/10665.2/52052/Factsheet-infodemic_eng.pdf?sequence=14

Pancer, E., & Poole, M. (2016). The Popularity and Virality of Political Social Media: Hashtags, Mentions, and Links Predict Likes and Retweets of 2016 US Presidential Nominees' Tweets. *Social Influence*, *11*(4), 259–270. doi:10.1080/15534510.2016.1265582

Panther & Siegel. (2021). *"I want to use my voice": Virtual Literacy Instruction Using Critical Memetic Analysis* [Manuscript submitted for publication]. Tift College of Education, Mercer University.

Papageorgis, D., & McGuire, W. J. (1961). The generality of immunity to persuasion produced by pre-exposure to weakened counterarguments. *Journal of Abnormal and Social Psychology, 62*(3), 475–481. doi:10.1037/h0048430 PMID:14483679

Parker, G. E. (2016). A framework for navigating institutional review board (IRB) oversight in the complicated zone of research. *Cureus, 8*(10), e844. doi:10.7759/cureus.844 PMID:27909632

Parshall, C. G., Harmes, J. C., Davey, T., & Pashley, P. (2010). Innovative items for computerized testing. In W. J. van der Linden & C. A. W. Glas (Eds.), *Computerized adaptive testing: Theory and practice* (2nd ed.). Kluwer Academic Publishers.

Parvin, S. (2019). *Essence of Learning "Metaliteracy" in the Age of Fake News*. https://www.daily-sun.com/arcprint/details/404947/Essence-of-Learning-%E2%80%9CMetaliteracy%E2%80%9D-in-the-Age-of-Fake-News-/2019-07-06

Patrikarakos, D. (2017). *Social media networks are the handmaiden to dangerous propaganda*. https://time.com/5008076/nyc-terror-attack-isis-facebook-russia/

Pelletier, K., Brown, M., Christopher, B., McCormack, M., Reeves, J., Arbino, N., Bozkurt, A., Crawford, S., Czerniewicz, L., Gibson, R., Linder, K., Mason, J., & Mondelli, V. (2021). *2021 EDUCAUSE Horizon Report: Teaching and Learning Edition*. EDUCAUSE. Retrieved from https://library.educause.edu/-/media/files/library/2021/4/2021hrteachinglearning.pdf?#page=4&la=en&hash=64CACBDA4DAC0F6158951941AD2A8952A9A81100

Peña, M. (2017). Vista de Democracia representativa y participación ciudadana en Venezuela (1958-2015). *Telos Revista de Estudios Interdisciplinarios En Ciencias Sociales., 19*(1), 3–26.

Pennycook, G., Epstein, Z., Mosleh, M., Arechar, A. A., Eckles, D., & Rand, D. G. (2021). Shifting attention to accuracy can reduce misinformation online. *Nature, 592*(7855), 590–595. doi:10.103841586-021-03344-2 PMID:33731933

Pennycook, G., McPhetres, J., Zhang, Y., Lu, J. G., & Rand, D. G. (2020). Fighting COVID-19 misinformation on social media: Experimental evidence for a scalable accuracy-nudge intervention. *Psychological Science, 31*(7), 770–780. doi:10.1177/0956797620939054 PMID:32603243

Petrina, S., Feng, F., & Kim, J. (2008). Researching cognition and technology: How we learn across the lifespan. *International Journal of Technology and Design Education, 18*(4), 375–396. doi:10.100710798-007-9033-5

Petsko, G. A. (2010). Shadows on the wall. *Genome Biology, 11*(9), 136. doi:10.1186/gb-2010-11-9-136 PMID:20863416

Philip, T. M., Olivares-Pasillas, M. C., & Rocha, J. (2016). Becoming racially literate about data and data-literate about race: Data visualizations in the classroom as a site of racial-ideological micro-contestations. *Cognition and Instruction, 34*(4), 361–388. doi:10.1080/07370008.2016.1210418

Prensky, M. (2013). Our brains extended. *Educational Leadership, 70*(6), 22–27.

Prensky, M. R. (2010). *Teaching digital natives: Partnering for real learning*. Corwin press.

Privitera, C., & Campbell, M. A. (2009). Cyberbullying: The new face of workplace bullying? *Cyberpsychology & Behavior*, *12*(4), 395–400. doi:10.1089/cpb.2009.0025 PMID:19594381

Pucciarelli, F., & Kaplan, A. (2016). Competition and strategy in higher education: Managing complexity and uncertainty. *Business Horizons*, *59*(3), 311–320. doi:10.1016/j.bushor.2016.01.003

Puddephat, A. (2011). *The importance of self-regulation of the media in upholding freedom of expression*. http://www.unesco.org/new/en/communication-and-information/resources/

Punnappurath & Brown. (2019). Learning raw image reconstruction-aware deep image compressors. *IEEE Transactions on Pattern Analysis and Machine Intelligence*, *42*(4), 1013–1019. PMID:30843804

Puyana, J. C., Puyana, J. C. J., Rubiano, A. M., Montenegro, J. H., Estebanez, G. O., Sanchez, A. I., & Vega-Rivera, F. (2017). Drugs, violence, and trauma in Mexico and the USA. *Medical Principles and Practice*, *26*(4), 309–315. doi:10.1159/000471853 PMID:28329741

Qian, Y., Dong, J., Wang, W., & Tan, T. (2015, March). Deep learning for steganalysis via convolutional neural networks. In *Media Watermarking* (Vol. 9409). Security, and Forensics.

Quach, T.-T. (2014). Extracting hidden messages in steganographic images. *Digital Investigation*, *11*, S40–S45. doi:10.1016/j.diin.2014.05.003

Quayyum, A., Quadir, J., Janjua, M. U., & Sher, F. (2019). Using Blockchain to Rein in the New Post-Truth World and Check the Spead of Fake News. *IT Professional*, *21*(4), 16–24. doi:10.1109/MITP.2019.2910503

Quellmalz, E. S., & Kozma, R. (2003). Designing assessments of learning with technology. *Assessment in Education: Principles, Policy & Practice*, *10*(3), 389–407. doi:10.1080/0969594032000148208

Radford, A., Metz, L., & Chintala, S. (2015). *Unsupervised representation learning with deep convolutional generative adversarial networks*. arXiv preprint arXiv:1511.06434.

Rainie, H., Anderson, J. Q., & Albright, J. (2017). *The future of free speech, trolls, anonymity and fake news online*. Pew Research Center.

Rampersad, G., & Althiyabi, T. (2020). Fake news: Acceptance by demographics and culture on social media. *Journal of Information Technology & Politics*, *17*(1), 1–11. doi:10.1080/19331681.2019.1686676

Redmiles, E. M., Kross, S., & Mazurek, M. L. (2016). How I Learned to be Secure: A Census-Representative Survey of Security Advice Sources and Behavior. *CCS*, *16*(October), 24–28. doi:10.1145/2976749.2978307

Redmond, T. (2016). Media literacy as mindful practice for democratic education. *Democracy & Education, 24*(2), 1-5. https://democracyeducationjournal.org/cgi/viewcontent.cgi?article=1261&context=home

Report, H. (2021). *The New Media Consortium.* Retrieved from https://library.educause.edu/resources/2021/4/2021-educause-horizon-report-teaching-and-learning-edition

Ribble, M. (2012). Digital Citizenship for Educational Change. *Kappa Delta Pi Record, 48*(4), 148–151. doi:10.1080/00228958.2012.734015

Ribble, M. S., & Bailey, G. D. (2004). Digital Citizenship Focus Questions for Implementation. *Learning and Leading with Technology, 32*(2), 12–15.

Ribble, M., & Miller, T. N. (2013). Educational Leadership in an Online World: Connecting Students to Technology Responsibly, Safely, and Ethically. *Journal of Asynchronous Learning Networks, 17*(1), 137–145. doi:10.24059/olj.v17i1.310

Ridgway, J. (2019, December). Data literacy. *International Statistical Literacy Project Newsletter, 1*(11), 10–13.

Ridsdale, C., Rothwell, J., Smit, M., Ali-Hassan, H., Bliemel, M., Irvine, D., Kelley, D., Matwin, S., & Wuetherick, B. (2016). *Strategies and best practices for data literacy education: Knowledge synthesis report.* Dalhousie University.

Ríos, R. (2017). *Teacher Agency for Equity: A Framework for Conscientious Engagement.* Taylor & Francis., doi:10.4324/9781315178646

Roberts, J. A., & David, M. E. (2016). ve David M. E. (2015). My Life has Become a Major Distraction from my Cell Phone: Partner Phubbing and Relationship Satisfaction Among Romantic Partners. *Computers in Human Behavior, 54*, 134–141. doi:10.1016/j.chb.2015.07.058

Rochlin, N. (2017). Fake news: Belief in post-truth. *Library Hi Tech, 35*(3), 386–392. doi:10.1108/LHT-03-2017-0062

Rosenblatt, L. M. (1976). *Literature as exploration* (3rd ed.). Noble and Noble. (Original work published 1938)

Rosen, L. (2010). *Rewired: Understanding the igeneration and the way we learn.* Palgrave Macmillan.

Ross, D. B., & Sasso, M. T. (2017). *The art of synthesizing: A masterpiece in the making.* Fischler College of Education: Faculty Articles. https://works.bepress.com/david-ross/90/

Ross, D. B., Louis, R., & Sasso, M. T. (2019). The increase of how mass media coverage manipulates our minds. In A. Starcevic (Ed.), *Chronic stress and its effect on brain structure and connectivity* (pp. 188–222). IGI Global. doi:10.4018/978-1-5225-7513-9.ch010

Ross, D. B., Peyton, G. L., Nethi, V., & Sasso, M. T. (2021). The need to be a leader of research in the United States: Take the risk and move beyond your opponents. In D. L. Mulligan & P. A. Danaher (Eds.), *Researchers at risk: Precarity, jeopardy and uncertainty in academia* (pp. 147–161). Palgrave Macmillan. doi:10.1007/978-3-030-53857-6_10

Ross, D. B., Peyton, G. L., Sasso, M. T., Matteson, R. W., & Matteson, C. E. (2020). The biased media and their utilization of propaganda: The true obstructionists of world events and our minds. In S. Kavoğlu & M. Salar (Eds.), *Political propaganda, advertising, and public relations: Emerging research and opportunities* (pp. 89–113). IGI Global. doi:10.4018/978-1-7998-1734-5.ch004

Rusdi, F., & Rusdi, Z. (2020). The role of online media gatekeeper in the era of digital media. *Advances in Social Science, Education and Humanities Research, 439*. https://www.atlantis-press.com/article/125940615.pdf

Russakovsky, O., Deng, J., Su, H., Krause, J., Satheesh, S., Ma, S., Huang, Z., Karpathy, A., Khosla, A., Bernstein, M., Berg, A. C., & Fei-Fei, L. (2015). Imagenet large scale visual recognition challenge. *International Journal of Computer Vision, 115*(3), 211–252. doi:10.100711263-015-0816-y

Sabir, E., Cheng, J., & Jaiswal, A. (2019). Recurrent convolutional strategies for face manipulation detection in videos. In *Proceedings of the IEEE Conference on Computer Vision and Pattern Recognition Workshops* (pp. 80-87). IEEE.

Sasso, M. T. (2017). *How narcissists cannot hold an organization together: A mixed method approach to a fictitious puzzle factory*. Academic Press.

Saunders, L., Gans-Boriskin, R., & Hinchliffe, L. (2018). *Know news: Engaging across allied professions to combat misinformation*. Simmons College. https://slis.simmons.edu/blogs/disinformation/files/2018/05/White-Paper-Final-Draft-1.pdf

Sauter, V. G. (2020). The 'liberal leaning' media has passed its tipping point. *The Wall Street Journal*. Retrieved from https://www.wsj.com/articles/the-liberal-leaning-media-has-passed-its-tipping-point-11590430876

Savage, C., Schmitt, E., Fandos, N., & Goldman, A. (2020, June 30). Trump got written briefing in February on possible Russian bounties, officials say. *New York Times*, A1.

Scheufele, D. A., & Krause, N. M. (2019). Science audiences, misinformation, and fake news. *Proceedings of the National Academy of Sciences of the United States of America, 116*(16), 7662–7669. doi:10.1073/pnas.1805871115 PMID:30642953

Schindler, L. A., Burkholder, G. J., Morad, O. A., & Marsh, C. (2017). Computer-based technology and student engagement: A critical review of the literature. *International Journal of Educational Technology in Higher Education, 14*(25), 25. Advance online publication. doi:10.118641239-017-0063-0

Schmidt, A., & Wiegand, M. (2017, April). A survey on hate speech detection using natural language processing. In *Proceedings of the fifth international workshop on natural language processing for social media* (pp. 1-10). 10.18653/v1/W17-1101

Schmitt, J. B., Reiger, D., Ernst, J., & Roth, H.-J. (2019). Critical media literacy and Islamist online propaganda: The feasibility, applicability and impact of three learning arrangements. *International Journal of Conflict and Violence*, *12*(0), 1–19. doi:10.4119/UNIBI/ijcv.642

Schuelke-Leech, B. A. (2018). A Model for Understanding the Orders of Magnitude of Disruptive Technologies. *Technological Forecasting and Social Change*, *129*, 261–274. doi:10.1016/j.techfore.2017.09.033

Schüler-Meyer, A., Prediger, S., Kuzu, T., Wessel, L., & Redder, A. (2019). Is formal language proficiency in the home language required to profit from a bilingual teaching intervention in mathematics? A mixed methods study on fostering multilingual students' conceptual understanding. *International Journal of Science and Mathematics Education*, *17*(2), 317–339. doi:10.100710763-017-9857-8

Schwartz, D. L., & Arena, D. (2013). *Measuring what matters most: Choice-based assessments for the digital age*. MIT Press. doi:10.7551/mitpress/9430.001.0001

Schwarzenegger, C. (2020). Personal epistemologies of the media: Selective criticality, pragmatic trust, and competence–confidence in navigating media repertoires in the digital age. *New Media & Society*, *22*(2), 361–377. doi:10.1177/1461444819856919

SCONUL. (2018). *Seven pillars of information literacy*. SCONUL. https://www.sconul.ac.uk/page/seven-pillars-of-information-literacy

Seroff, J. (2017). Using data in the research process. In K. Fontichiaro, J. A. Oehrli, & A. Lennex (Eds.), *Creating data literate students*. Michigan Publishing.

Share, J., Mamikonyan, T., & Lopez, E. (2019). Critical media literacy in teacher education, theory, and practice. Oxford Research Encyclopedia of Education, 1–30. doi:10.1093/acrefore/9780190264093.013.1404

Shaughnessy, J. M., Garfield, J., & Greer, B. (1996). Data handling. In A. J. Bishop, K. Clements, C. Keitel, J. Kilpatrick, & C. Laborde (Eds.), *International handbook of mathematics education* (pp. 205–237). Kluwer. doi:10.1007/978-94-009-1465-0_8

Shaw, G. B. (1903). Man and superman: A comedy and a philosophy. In Maxims for Revolutionists. Brentano's.

Shields, P., & Rangarajan, N. (2013). *A Playbook for Research Methods: Integrating Conceptual Frameworks and Project Management*. New Forums Press.

Shoffner, M., de Oliveira, L. C., & Angus, R. (2010). Multiliteracies in the secondary English classroom: Becoming literate in the 21st Century. *English Teaching*, *9*(3), 75–89.

Shreiner, T. L. (2019). Students' use of data visualizations in historical reasoning: A think-aloud investigation with elementary, middle, and high school students. *Journal of Social Studies Research, 43*(4), 389–404. doi:10.1016/j.jssr.2018.11.001

Shulman, L. S. (1986). Those who understand: A conception of teacher knowledge. *American Educator, 10*(1). Advance online publication. doi:10.3102/0013189X015002004

Siegel, M. A. (2005). *Assessing English learners in middle school science.* Paper presented at the annual meeting of the American Educational Research Association, Montreal, Canada.

Siegel, M. A. (2007). Striving for equitable classroom assessments for linguistic minorities: Strategies for and effects of revising life science items. *Journal of Research in Science Teaching, 44*(6), 864–881. doi:10.1002/tea.20176

Smagorinsky, P. (1995). The social construction of data: Methodological problems of investigating learning in the zone of proximal development. *Review of Educational Research, 65*(3), 191–212. doi:10.3102/00346543065003191

Smith & Comiskey. (1996). Modulation and information hiding in images. In *International Workshop on Information Hiding*, (pp. 207–226). Springer.

Solano-Flores, G., & Trumbull, E. (2003). Examining language in context: The need for new research and practice paradigms in the testing of English language learners. *Educational Researcher, 32*(2), 3–13. doi:10.3102/0013189X032002003

Soltaninejad, K. (2020). Methanol mass poisoning outbreak, a consequence of COVID-19 pandemic and misleading messages on social media. *The International Journal of Occupational and Environmental Medicine, 11*(3), 148–150. doi:10.34172/ijoem.2020.1983 PMID:32225177

Sparby, E. M. (2017). Digital social media and aggression: Memetic rhetoric in 4chan's collective identity. *Computers and Composition, 45*, 85–97. doi:10.1016/j.compcom.2017.06.006

Spencer, T., & Hertzog, L. (2014). Community Explorers. *Young Children, 69*(5), 66–71.

Spivak, R. (2019). Deepfakes: The Newest Way to Commit One of the Oldest Crimes, The Georgetown Law. *Technology Review, 3*(2), 339–400.

Spohr, D. (2017). Fake news and ideological polarisation: Filter bubbles and selective exposure on social media. *Business Information Review, 34*(3), 150–160. doi:10.1177/0266382117722446

Stoltz-Loike, M. (2013). Incentives and training. *Inside Higher Ed.* Retrieved October 28, 2014 from https://www.insidehighered.com/advice/2013/12/18/essay-incentives-and-training-teaching-online

Subrahmanyam, K., & Greenfied, P. (2008). Online Communication and Adolescent Relationships. *The Future of Children, 18*(1), 119–148. doi:10.1353/foc.0.0006 PMID:21338008

Sullivan, M. (2019). Libraries and fake news: What's the problem? What's the plan? *Communications in Information Literacy, 13*(1). Advance online publication. doi:10.15760/comminfolit.2019.13.1.7

Suwajanakorn, S., Seitz, S., & Kemelmacher-Shlizerman, I. (2017). Synthesizing Obama: 1355 Learning Lip Sync From Audio. *ACM Transactions on Graphics*, *36*(4), 1–13. doi:10.1145/3072959.3073640

Tacchini, E., Ballarin, G., Della Vedova, M. L., Moret, S., & de Alfaro, L. (2017). Some like it hoax: Automated fake news detection in social networks. *Human-Computer Interaction.*

Tandoc, E. C., Ling, R., Westlund, O., Duffy, A., Goh, D., & Wei, Z. L. (2018). Audiences' acts of authentication in the age of fake news: A conceptual framework. *New Media & Society*, *20*(8), 2745–2763. https://doi-org.jproxy.nuim.ie/10.1177/1461444817731756

Tandoc, E. C. Jr, Lim, Z. W., & Ling, R. (2018). Defining "fake news". *Digital Journalism*, *6*(2), 137–153. doi:10.1080/21670811.2017.1360143

Tarran, B. (2017). Why facts are not enough in the fight against fake news. *Significance*, *14*(5), 6–7. doi:10.1111/j.1740-9713.2017.01066.x

Temir, E. (2020). Deepfake: New Era in The Age of Disinformation & End of Reliable Journalism. *Selçuk Communication*, *13*(2), 1009–1024.

Thamarai Selvi, V. T., Gayathri, R., & Vishnu Priya, V. (2019). Teens and technology addiction - A survey. *Drug Invention Today*, *11*(3), 663–665.

The New London Group. (1996). A pedagogy of multiliteracies: Designing social futures. *Harvard Educational Review*, *66*(1), 1–31.

Thies, J., Zollhofer, M., Stamminger, M., Theobalt, C., & Niesner, M. (2018). Face2Face: Real-Time Face Capture and Reenactment of RGB Videos. *Communications of the ACM*, *62*(1), 96–104. doi:10.1145/3292039

Trout, J. D. (2009). *The empathy gap: Building bridges to the good life and the good society.* Penguin.

Tsfati, Y., Boomgaarden, H. G., Strömbäck, J., Vliegenthart, R., Damstra, A., & Lindgren, E. (2020). Causes and consequences of mainstream media dissemination of fake news: Literature review and synthesis. *Annals of the International Communication Association*, *44*(2), 157–173. doi:10.1080/23808985.2020.1759443

Turton, W., & Martin, A. (2020, January 5). How deepfakes make disinformation more real than ever. *Bloomberg*. https://www.bloomberg.com/news/articles/2020-01-06/how-deepfakes-make-disinformation-more-real-than-ever-quicktake

Tusikov, N. (2017). *Regulate social media platforms before it's too late*. Retrieved from: https://theconversation.com/

Twidale, M. B., Blake, C., & Gant, J. (2013). Towards a Data Literate Citizenry. In Proceedings of iConference 2013 (pp. 247–257). doi:10.9776/13189

U.S. Department of Health & Human Services. (1979). *The Belmont report: Office of the Secretary*. Retrieved from https://www.hhs.gov/ohrp/regulations-and-policy/belmont-report/read-the-belmont-report/index.html

U.S. Department of Health & Human Services. (2021). *Office for Human Research Protections*. Retrieved from https://www.hhs.gov/ohrp/

United Nations Educational, Scientific and Cultural Organization. (2020). *During this coronavirus pandemic, 'fake news' is putting lives at risk: UNESCO*. Retrieved at 06/05/2020, from https://news.un.org/en/story/2020/04/1061592

Ünsal, Z., Jakobson, B., Molander, B.-O., & Wickman, P.-O. (2018). Language Use in a Multilingual Class: A Study of the Relation Between Bilingual Students' Languages and Their Meaning-Making in Science. *Research in Science Education, 48*(5), 1027–1048. doi:10.100711165-016-9597-8

Unsworth, L. (2006). Towards a metalanguage for multiliteracies education: Describing the meaning - making resources of language-image interaction. *English Teaching, 5*(1), 55–76.

US Department Of State. (2020). *GEC Special Report : Pillars of Russia's Disinformation and Propaganda Ecosystem August 2020 Table of Contents*. Issue August.

Vaccari, C., & Chadwick, A. (2020). Deepfakes and Disinformation: Exploring the Impact of Synthetic Political Video on Deception, Uncertainty, and Trust in News. *Social Media + Society, 6*(1), 1–13. doi:10.1177/2056305120903408

Vahey, P., Rafanan, K., Patton, C., Swan, K., Hooft, M., Kratcoski, A., & Stanford, T. (2012). A cross-disciplinary approach to teaching data literacy and proportionality. *Educational Studies in Mathematics, 81*(2), 179–205. doi:10.100710649-012-9392-z

van 't Hooft, M., Swan, K., Cook, D., Stanford, T., Vahey, P., Kratcoski, A., Rafanan, K., & Yarnall, L. (2012). A cross-curricular approach to the development of data literacy in the middle grades: The Thinking with Data Project. *Middle Grades Research Journal, 7*(3), 19–33.

Van Bavel, J. J., Harris, E. A., Pärnamets, P., Rathje, S., Doell, K. C., & Tucker, J. A. (2021). Political psychology in the digital (mis) information age: A model of news belief and sharing. *Social Issues and Policy Review, 15*(1), 84–113. doi:10.1111ipr.12077

van der Linden, S. (2015). The conspiracy-effect: Exposure to conspiracy theories (about global warming) decreases pro-social behavior and science acceptance. *Personality and Individual Differences, 87*, 171–173. doi:10.1016/j.paid.2015.07.045

van der Linden, S., Panagopoulos, C., & Roozenbeck, J. (2020). You are fake news: Political bias in perceptions of fake news. *Media Culture & Society, 42*(3), 60–470. doi:10.1177/0163443720906992

Van Duyn, E., & Collier, J. (2018). Priming and Fake News: The Effects of Elite Discourse on Evaluations of News Media. *Mass Communication & Society, 22*(1), 29–48. doi:10.1080/15205436.2018.1511807

Vorhaus, M. (2020). *People Increasingly Turn To Social Media For News*. Retrieved on 1/08/2020, from https://www.forbes.com/sites/mikevorhaus/2020/06/24/people-increasingly-turn-to-social-media-for-news/#3a5763f43bcc

Vosoughi, S., Roy, D., & Aral, S. (2018). The Spread of True and False News Online. *Science*, *359*(6380), 1146–1151. doi:10.1126cience.aap9559 PMID:29590045

Vromen, A. (2017). Digital Citizenship and Political Engagement. In *Digital Citizenship and Political Engagement*. Interest Groups, Advocacy and Democracy Series. Palgrave Macmillan.

Vygostky, L. S. (1978). Interaction between learning and development. In L. S. Vygotsky, M. Cole, V. John-Steiner, S. Scribner, & E. Souberman (Eds.), *Mind in Society: The development of higher psychological processes* (pp. 79–91). Harvard University Press.

Vygotsky, L. S. (1978). Socio-cultural theory. *Mind & Society*, *6*, 52–58. doi:10.5040/9781472541437.ch-003

Wade, S., & Hornick, J. (2018). Stop! Don't share that story! Designing a pop-up undergraduate workshop on fake news. *The Reference Librarian*, *59*(4), 188–194. doi:10.1080/02763877.2018.1498430

Wagner, T. L., & Blewer, A. (2019). The World Real Is No Longer Real: Deepfakes, Gender, and Challenges of AI-Altered Video. *Open Information Science*, *3*(1), 32–46. doi:10.1515/opis-2019-0003

Walters, M. G., Gee, D., & Mohammed, S. (2019). A Literature Review: Digital Citizenship and The Elementary Educator. *International Journal of Technology in Education*, *2*(1), 1–21.

Wang, S.-Y. (2020). Cnn-generated images are surprisingly easy to spot... for now. *Proceedings of the IEEE Conference on Computer Vision and Pattern Recognition*, 7.

Wang, W. Y. (2017). Liar, liar pants on fire. A New Benchmark Dataset for Fake News Detection. *Computation and Language.*, 422–426. doi:10.18653/v1/P17-2067

Wang, X., Thome, N., & Cord, M. (2016). Gaze latent support vector machine for image classification. In *2016 IEEE International Conference on Image Processing (ICIP)*, (pp. 236–240). IEEE. 10.1109/ICIP.2016.7532354

Wardle, C. (2017). Fake news. It's complicated. *First Draft*. https://firstdraftnews.org/fake-news-complicated/

Watson, C. A. (2018). Digital literacy: Detecting fake news in a post-truth era. *Continuing Legal Education Presentations, 8*. https://digitalcommons.law.uga.edu/cle/2018/schedule/8

Watson, J. M., & English, L. D. (2015). Introducing the practice of statistics: Are we environmentally friendly? *Mathematics Education Research Journal*, *27*(4), 585–613. doi:10.100713394-015-0153-z

Watts, C. (2018). *Terrorism and social media: Is big tech doing enough?* https://www.fpri.org/article/2018/01/terrorism-social-media-big-tech-enough/

Waycott, J., Bennett, S., Kennedy, G., Dalgarno, B., & Gray, K. (2010). Digital divides? Student and staff perceptions of information and communication technologies. *Computers & Education*, *54*(4), 1202–1211. doi:10.1016/j.compedu.2009.11.006

Weaver, T. (2020). The Socratic Method: How to think for yourself. *Orion Philosophy*. Retrieved from https://www.orionphilosophy.com/stoic-blog/the-socratic-method

Webber, H., Nelson, S. J., Weatherbee, R., Zoellick, B., & Schauffler, M. (2014). The graph choice chart. *Science Teacher (Normal, Ill.)*, *81*(8), 37–43. doi:10.2505/4/tst14_081_08_37

Welbers, K., van Atteveldt, W., Kleinnijenhuis, J., & Ruigrok, N. (2018). A gatekeeper among gatekeepers. *Journalism Studies*, *19*(3), 315–333. doi:10.1080/1461670X.2016.1190663

Wendling, M. (2018). *The (almost) complete history of 'fake news'*. BBC News Services. https://www.bbc.com/news/blogs-trending-42724320

Wenzel, A. (2019). To Verify or to Disengage: Coping with "Fake News" and Ambiguity. *International Journal of Communication*, *13*, 19.

Wertsch, J. V. (1985). *Vygotsky and the social formation of mind*. Harvard University Press.

West, D. (2017, December 18). *How to combat fake news and disinformation*. The Brookings Institution. https://www.brookings.edu/research/how-to-combat-fake-news-and-disinformation/

Westerlund, M. (2019). The emergence of deepfake technology: A review. *Technology Innovation Management Review*, *9*(11), 39–52. doi:10.22215/timreview/1282

Whyte, C. (2020). Deepfake News: AI-enabled disinformation as a Multi-Level Public Policy Challenge. *Journal of Cyber-Policy*, 199-217.

Wilson, C., Grizzle, A., Tuazon, R., Akyempong, K., & Cheunj, C. K. (2011). *Media and information literacy curriculum for teachers*. UNESCO Digital Library. https://unesdoc.unesco.org/ark:/48223/pf0000192971

Wineburg, S., McGrew, S., Breakstone, J., & Ortega, T. (2016, November 22). *Evaluating information: The cornerstone of civic online reasoning*. Stanford History Education Group. https://purl.stanford.edu/fv751yt5934

Wojewidka, J. (2020). *The Deepfake Threat to Face Biometrics*. Academic Press.

Wolff, A., Gooch, D., Cavero Montaner, J. J., Rashid, U., & Kortuem, G. (2016). Creating an understanding of data literacy for a data-driven society. *The Journal of Community Informatics*, *12*(3), 9–26. doi:10.15353/joci.v12i3.3275

World Health Organisation. (2020). *Novel Coronavirus(2019-nCoV) Situation Report – 13*. Retrieved on 27/03/2020, from https://www.who.int/docs/default-source/coronaviruse/situation-reports/20200202-sitrep-13-ncov-v3.pdf

Xuan, X., Peng, B., Wang, W., & Dong, J. (2019). On the generalization of gan image forensics. In *Chinese Conference on Biometric Recognition*, (pp. 134–141). Springer. 10.1007/978-3-030-31456-9_15

Xu, S., Yang, H. H., MacLeod, J., & Zhu, S. (2019). Social Media Competence and Digital Citizenship Among College Students. *Convergence (London)*, *24*(4), 735–752. doi:10.1177/1354856517751390

Yadlin-Segal, A., & Oppenheim, Y. (2020). Whose Dystopia Is It Anyway? Deepfakes and Social Media Regulation. *Convergence (London)*, •••, 1–16.

Yang, P., Ni, R., & Zhao, Y. (2016). Recapture image forensics based on laplacian convolutional neural networks. In *International Workshop on Digital Watermarking*, (pp. 119–128). Springer.

Yang, P., Ni, R., & Zhao, Y. (2016, September). Recapture image forensics based on Laplacian convolutional neural networks. In *International Workshop on Digital Watermarking* (pp. 119-128). Springer.

Yang, X., Li, Y., & Lyu, S. (2019, May). Exposing deep fakes using inconsistent head poses. In *2019 IEEE International Conference on Acoustics, Speech and Signal Processing (ICASSP)* (pp. 8261-8265). IEEE. 10.1109/ICASSP.2019.8683164

Yaraghi, N. (2019). *How should social media platforms combat misinformation and hate speech*. Retrieved on 27/07/2020, from https://www.brookings.edu/blog/techtank/2019/04/09/how-should-social-media-platforms-combat-misinformation-and-hate-speech/

Yoon, S. (2008). Using memes and memetic processes to explain social and conceptual influences on student understanding about complex socio-scientific issues. *Journal of Research in Science Teaching*, *45*(8), 900–921. doi:10.1002/tea.20256

Yue, A., Nekmat, E., & Beta, A. R. (2019). Digital Literacy Through Digital Citizenship: Online Civic Participation and Public Opinion Evaluation of Youth Minorities in Southeast Asia. *Media and Communication*, *7*(2), 100–114.

Zalles, D. (2005). *Designs for assessing foundational data literacy*. Retrieved from http://serc.carleton.edu/files/NAGTWorkshops/assess/ZallesEssay3.pdf

Zannettou, S., Sirivianos, M., Blackburn, J., & Kourtellis, N. (2019). The Web of Fake Information: Rumors, Fake News, Hoaxes, Clickbait, and Various Other Shenanigans. *Journal of Data and Information Quality*, *1*(3), 1–37.

Zarocostas, J. (2020). How to fight an infodemic. *The Lancet, World report*. Retrieved on 27/07/2020, from https://www.thelancet.com/action/showPdf?pii=S0140-6736%2820%2930461-X

Zembylas, M. (2003). Emotions and teacher identity: A poststructural perspective. *Teachers and Teaching*, *9*(3), 213–238. doi:10.1080/13540600309378

Zenner, E., & Geeraerts, D. (2018). One does not simply process memes: Image macros as multimodal constructions. In Cultures and Traditions of Wordplay and Wordplay Research (pp. 167–194). doi:10.1515/9783110586374-008

Zhang, Goodfellow, Metaxas, & Odena. (2019). Selfattention generative adversarial networks. In *International conference on machine learning*, (pp. 7354–7363). PMLR.

Zhang, Y., Zheng, L., & Thing, V. L. (2017, August). Automated face swapping and its detection. In *2017 IEEE 2nd International Conference on Signal and Image Processing (ICSIP)* (pp. 15-19). IEEE. 10.1109/SIPROCESS.2017.8124497

Zhang, Y., Zheng, L., & Vrizlynn, L. L. (2017). Automated face swapping and its detection. In *2017 IEEE 2nd International Conference on Signal and Image Processing (ICSIP),* (pp. 15–19). IEEE.

Zheng, L., Duffner, S., Idrissi, K., Garcia, C., & Baskurt, A. (2016). Siamese multi-layer perceptrons for dimensionality reduction and face identification. *Multimedia Tools and Applications, 75*(9), 5055–5073. doi:10.100711042-015-2847-3

Zhou, P., Han, X., Morariu, V., & Davis, L. (2017). Two-Stream Neural Networks for Tampered Face Detection. *Proc. IEEE/CVF Conference on Computer Vision and Pattern Recognition Workshops*. 10.1109/CVPRW.2017.229

Zieky, M. J. (2006). Fairness review in assessment. In S. M. Downing & T. M. Haladyna (Eds.), *Handbook of test development* (pp. 359–376). Lawrence Erlbaum.

Zieky, M. J. (2014). An introduction to the use of evidence-centered design in test development. *Psicologia dell'Educazione, 20*(2), 79–87. doi:10.1016/j.pse.2014.11.003

Zimdars, M. (2016). *False, misleading, clickbait-y, and satirical news sources*. Creative Commons. https://docs.google.com/document/d/10eA5-mCZLSS4MQY5QGb5ewC3VAL6pLkT53V_81Z yitM/mobilebasic

Zimdars, M. (2016, November 18). My "fake news list" went viral. But made-up stories are only part of the problem. *The Washington Post*. https://www.washingtonpost.com/posteverything/wp/2016/11/18/my-fake-news-list-went-viral-but-made-up-storiesare-only-part-of-theproblem/?noredirect=on&utm_term=.d19fa7c1f621

Zinn, J. O. (2016). The meaning of risk-taking – Key concepts and dimensions. *Journal of Risk Research, 22*(1), 1–15. Advance online publication. doi:10.1080/13669877.2017.1351465

Zoe, T. (2020). *WHO says fake coronavirus claims causing 'infodemic'*. British Broadcasting Corporation. Retrieved on 17/07/2020, from https://www.bbc.com/news/technology-51497800

Zoellick, B., Schauffler, M., Flubacher, M., Weatherbee, R., & Webber, H. (2016, April). *Data Literacy: Assessing Student Understanding of Variability in Data*. Paper presented at the Annual Meeting of the National Association for Research in Science Teaching, Baltimore, MD.

Zsila, A., G'abor, O., & Kir'aly, O. (2018). Psychoactive substance use and problematic internet use as predictors of bullying and cyberbullying victimization. *International Journal of Mental Health and Addiction, 16*(2), 466–479. doi:10.100711469-017-9809-0 PMID:29670501

Zubiaga, A., Aker, A., Bontcheva, K., Liakata, M., & Procter, R. (2018). Detection and resolution of rumours in social media: A survey. *ACM Computing Surveys, 51*(2), 1–36. doi:10.1145/3161603

Related References

To continue our tradition of advancing academic research, we have compiled a list of recommended IGI Global readings. These references will provide additional information and guidance to further enrich your knowledge and assist you with your own research and future publications.

Aburezeq, I. M., & Dweikat, F. F. (2017). Cloud Applications in Language Teaching: Examining Pre-Service Teachers' Expertise, Perceptions and Integration. *International Journal of Distance Education Technologies, 15*(4), 39–60. doi:10.4018/IJDET.2017100103

Adera, B. (2017). Supporting Language and Literacy Development for English Language Learners. In J. Keengwe (Ed.), *Handbook of Research on Promoting Cross-Cultural Competence and Social Justice in Teacher Education* (pp. 339–354). Hershey, PA: IGI Global. doi:10.4018/978-1-5225-0897-7.ch018

Ahamer, G. (2011). How Technologies Can Localize Learners in Multicultural Space: A Newly Developed "Global Studies" Curriculum. *International Journal of Technology and Educational Marketing, 1*(2), 1–24. doi:10.4018/ijtem.2011070101

Ahamer, G. (2015). Conclusions from Social Dynamics in Collaborative Environmental Didactics. *International Journal of Technology and Educational Marketing, 5*(2), 68–92. doi:10.4018/IJTEM.2015070105

Ahamer, G. (2015). Designing and Analyzing Social Dynamics for Collaborative: Environmental Didactics. *International Journal of Technology and Educational Marketing, 5*(2), 46–67. doi:10.4018/IJTEM.2015070104

Ahamer, G. (2017). Quality Assurance for a Developmental "Global Studies" (GS) Curriculum. In I. Management Association (Ed.), Educational Leadership and Administration: Concepts, Methodologies, Tools, and Applications (pp. 438-477). Hershey, PA: IGI Global. doi:10.4018/978-1-5225-1624-8.ch023

Ahamer, G. (2017). Quality Assurance for a Developmental "Global Studies" (GS) Curriculum. In I. Management Association (Ed.), Educational Leadership and Administration: Concepts, Methodologies, Tools, and Applications (pp. 438-477). Hershey, PA: IGI Global. doi:10.4018/978-1-5225-1624-8.ch023

Alegre de la Rosa, O. M., & Angulo, L. M. (2017). Social Inclusion and Intercultural Values in a School of Education. In S. Mukerji & P. Tripathi (Eds.), *Handbook of Research on Administration, Policy, and Leadership in Higher Education* (pp. 518–531). Hershey, PA: IGI Global. doi:10.4018/978-1-5225-0672-0.ch020

Ambikairajah, E., Sethu, V., Eaton, R., & Sheng, M. (2014). Evolving Use of Educational Technologies: Enhancing Lectures. In F. Alam (Ed.), *Using Technology Tools to Innovate Assessment, Reporting, and Teaching Practices in Engineering Education* (pp. 241–258). Hershey, PA: IGI Global. doi:10.4018/978-1-4666-5011-4.ch018

Anderson, K. M. (2017). Preparing Teachers in the Age of Equity and Inclusion. In I. Management Association (Ed.), Medical Education and Ethics: Concepts, Methodologies, Tools, and Applications (pp. 1532-1554). Hershey, PA: IGI Global. doi:10.4018/978-1-5225-0978-3.ch069

Awdziej, M. (2017). Case Study as a Teaching Method in Marketing. In D. Latusek (Ed.), *Case Studies as a Teaching Tool in Management Education* (pp. 244–263). Hershey, PA: IGI Global. doi:10.4018/978-1-5225-0770-3.ch013

Bain, B. (2014). Exploring Assessment of Critical Thinking Learning Outcomes in Online Higher Education. In V. Wang (Ed.), *Handbook of Research on Education and Technology in a Changing Society* (pp. 1191–1202). Hershey, PA: IGI Global. doi:10.4018/978-1-4666-6046-5.ch089

Banas, J. R., & York, C. S. (2017). Pre-Service Teachers' Motivation to Use Technology and the Impact of Authentic Learning Exercises. In L. Tomei (Ed.), *Exploring the New Era of Technology-Infused Education* (pp. 121–140). Hershey, PA: IGI Global. doi:10.4018/978-1-5225-1709-2.ch008

Bariso, E. U. (2015). Educational Policy Analysis Debates and New Learning Technologies in England. In M. Khosrow-Pour (Ed.), *Encyclopedia of Information Science and Technology* (3rd ed.; pp. 2371–2378). Hershey, PA: IGI Global. doi:10.4018/978-1-4666-5888-2.ch230

Beycioglu, K., & Wildy, H. (2015). Principal Preparation: The Case of Novice Principals in Turkey. In K. Beycioglu & P. Pashiardis (Eds.), *Multidimensional Perspectives on Principal Leadership Effectiveness* (pp. 1–17). Hershey, PA: IGI Global. doi:10.4018/978-1-4666-6591-0.ch001

Beycioglu, K., & Wildy, H. (2017). Principal Preparation: The Case of Novice Principals in Turkey. In I. Management Association (Ed.), Educational Leadership and Administration: Concepts, Methodologies, Tools, and Applications (pp. 1152-1169). Hershey, PA: IGI Global. doi:10.4018/978-1-5225-1624-8.ch054

Bharwani, S., & Musunuri, D. (2018). Reflection as a Process From Theory to Practice. In M. Khosrow-Pour, D.B.A. (Ed.), Encyclopedia of Information Science and Technology, Fourth Edition (pp. 1529-1539). Hershey, PA: IGI Global. doi:10.4018/978-1-5225-2255-3.ch132

Bisschoff, T., & Rhodes, C. (2011). Transformation through Marketing: A Case of a Secondary School in South Africa. In P. Tripathi & S. Mukerji (Eds.), *Cases on Innovations in Educational Marketing: Transnational and Technological Strategies* (pp. 263–272). Hershey, PA: IGI Global. doi:10.4018/978-1-60960-599-5.ch016

Bodomo, A. B. (2010). Educational Technologies (WebCT): Creating Constructivist and Interactive Learning Communities. In A. Bodomo (Ed.), *Computer-Mediated Communication for Linguistics and Literacy: Technology and Natural Language Education* (pp. 252–290). Hershey, PA: IGI Global. doi:10.4018/978-1-60566-868-0.ch010

Bohjanen, S. L., Cameron-Standerford, A., & Meidl, T. D. (2018). Capacity Building Pedagogy for Diverse Learners. In J. Keengwe (Ed.), *Handbook of Research on Pedagogical Models for Next-Generation Teaching and Learning* (pp. 195–212). Hershey, PA: IGI Global. doi:10.4018/978-1-5225-3873-8.ch011

Brewer, J. C. (2018). Measuring Text Readability Using Reading Level. In M. Khosrow-Pour, D.B.A. (Ed.), Encyclopedia of Information Science and Technology, Fourth Edition (pp. 1499-1507). Hershey, PA: IGI Global. doi:10.4018/978-1-5225-2255-3.ch129

Brown, S. L. (2017). A Case Study of Strategic Leadership and Research in Practice: Principal Preparation Programs that Work – An Educational Administration Perspective of Best Practices for Master's Degree Programs for Principal Preparation. In V. Wang (Ed.), *Encyclopedia of Strategic Leadership and Management* (pp. 1226–1244). Hershey, PA: IGI Global. doi:10.4018/978-1-5225-1049-9.ch086

Brzozowski, M., & Ferster, I. (2017). Educational Management Leadership: High School Principal's Management Style and Parental Involvement in School Management in Israel. In V. Potocan, M. Üngan, & Z. Nedelko (Eds.), *Handbook of Research on Managerial Solutions in Non-Profit Organizations* (pp. 55–74). Hershey, PA: IGI Global. doi:10.4018/978-1-5225-0731-4.ch003

Cannaday, J. (2017). The Masking Effect: Hidden Gifts and Disabilities of 2e Students. In P. Dickenson, P. Keough, & J. Courduff (Eds.), *Preparing Pre-Service Teachers for the Inclusive Classroom* (pp. 220–231). Hershey, PA: IGI Global. doi:10.4018/978-1-5225-1753-5.ch011

Capobianco, B. M., & Lehman, J. D. (2010). Fostering Educational Technology Integration in Science Teacher Education: Issues of Teacher Identity Development. In J. Yamamoto, J. Kush, R. Lombard, & C. Hertzog (Eds.), *Technology Implementation and Teacher Education: Reflective Models* (pp. 245–257). Hershey, PA: IGI Global. doi:10.4018/978-1-61520-897-5.ch014

Chao, G. H., Hsu, M. K., & Scovotti, C. (2013). Predicting Donations from a Cohort Group of Donors to Charities: A Direct Marketing Case Study. In J. Wang (Ed.), *Optimizing, Innovating, and Capitalizing on Information Systems for Operations* (pp. 196–214). Hershey, PA: IGI Global. doi:10.4018/978-1-4666-2925-7.ch010

Chauhan, A. (2015). Beyond the Phenomenon: Assessment in Massive Open Online Courses (MOOCs). In E. McKay & J. Lenarcic (Eds.), *Macro-Level Learning through Massive Open Online Courses (MOOCs): Strategies and Predictions for the Future* (pp. 119–140). Hershey, PA: IGI Global. doi:10.4018/978-1-4666-8324-2.ch007

Coffman, T. L., & Klinger, M. B. (2013). Managing Quality in Online Education. In G. Kurubacak & T. Yuzer (Eds.), *Project Management Approaches for Online Learning Design* (pp. 220–233). Hershey, PA: IGI Global. doi:10.4018/978-1-4666-2830-4.ch011

Contreras, E. C., & Contreras, I. I. (2018). Development of Communication Skills through Auditory Training Software in Special Education. In M. Khosrow-Pour, D.B.A. (Ed.), Encyclopedia of Information Science and Technology, Fourth Edition (pp. 2431-2441). Hershey, PA: IGI Global. doi:10.4018/978-1-5225-2255-3.ch212

Cook, R. G. (2011). Educational Marketing: Coming Down from the Cloud Using Landing Gear. In U. Demiray & S. Sever (Eds.), *Marketing Online Education Programs: Frameworks for Promotion and Communication* (pp. 26–31). Hershey, PA: IGI Global. doi:10.4018/978-1-60960-074-7.ch003

Cook, R. G., & Ley, K. (2015). Past, Future and Presents: Meeting New Online Challenges with Primal Marketing Solutions. *International Journal of Technology and Educational Marketing*, *5*(2), 19–33. doi:10.4018/IJTEM.2015070102

Cooley, D., & Whitten, E. (2017). Special Education Leadership and the Implementation of Response to Intervention. In F. Topor (Ed.), *Handbook of Research on Individualism and Identity in the Globalized Digital Age* (pp. 265–286). Hershey, PA: IGI Global. doi:10.4018/978-1-5225-0522-8.ch012

Cosner, S., Tozer, S., & Zavitkovsky, P. (2017). Enacting a Cycle of Inquiry Capstone Research Project in Doctoral-Level Leadership Preparation. In I. Management Association (Ed.), Educational Leadership and Administration: Concepts, Methodologies, Tools, and Applications (pp. 1460-1481). Hershey, PA: IGI Global. doi:10.4018/978-1-5225-1624-8.ch067

Crawford, C. M. (2018). Instructional Real World Community Engagement. In M. Khosrow-Pour, D.B.A. (Ed.), Encyclopedia of Information Science and Technology, Fourth Edition (pp. 1474-1486). Hershey, PA: IGI Global. doi:10.4018/978-1-5225-2255-3.ch127

Crosby-Cooper, T., & Pacis, D. (2017). Implementing Effective Student Support Teams. In P. Dickenson, P. Keough, & J. Courduff (Eds.), *Preparing Pre-Service Teachers for the Inclusive Classroom* (pp. 248–262). Hershey, PA: IGI Global. doi:10.4018/978-1-5225-1753-5.ch013

Curran, C. M., & Hawbaker, B. W. (2017). Cultivating Communities of Inclusive Practice: Professional Development for Educators – Research and Practice. In C. Curran & A. Petersen (Eds.), *Handbook of Research on Classroom Diversity and Inclusive Education Practice* (pp. 120–153). Hershey, PA: IGI Global. doi:10.4018/978-1-5225-2520-2.ch006

Dass, S., & Dabbagh, N. (2018). Faculty Adoption of 3D Avatar-Based Virtual World Learning Environments: An Exploratory Case Study. In I. Management Association (Ed.), Technology Adoption and Social Issues: Concepts, Methodologies, Tools, and Applications (pp. 1000-1033). Hershey, PA: IGI Global. doi:10.4018/978-1-5225-5201-7.ch045

Davison, A. M., & Scholl, K. G. (2017). Inclusive Recreation as Part of the IEP Process. In C. Curran & A. Petersen (Eds.), *Handbook of Research on Classroom Diversity and Inclusive Education Practice* (pp. 311–330). Hershey, PA: IGI Global. doi:10.4018/978-1-5225-2520-2.ch013

DeCoito, I. (2018). Addressing Digital Competencies, Curriculum Development, and Instructional Design in Science Teacher Education. In M. Khosrow-Pour, D.B.A. (Ed.), Encyclopedia of Information Science and Technology, Fourth Edition (pp. 1420-1431). Hershey, PA: IGI Global. doi:10.4018/978-1-5225-2255-3.ch122

DeCoito, I., & Richardson, T. (2017). Beyond Angry Birds™: Using Web-Based Tools to Engage Learners and Promote Inquiry in STEM Learning. In I. Levin & D. Tsybulsky (Eds.), *Digital Tools and Solutions for Inquiry-Based STEM Learning* (pp. 166–196). Hershey, PA: IGI Global. doi:10.4018/978-1-5225-2525-7.ch007

Delmas, P. M. (2017). Research-Based Leadership for Next-Generation Leaders. In R. Styron Jr & J. Styron (Eds.), *Comprehensive Problem-Solving and Skill Development for Next-Generation Leaders* (pp. 1–39). Hershey, PA: IGI Global. doi:10.4018/978-1-5225-1968-3.ch001

Demiray, U., & Ekren, G. (2018). Administrative-Related Evaluation for Distance Education Institutions in Turkey. In K. Buyuk, S. Kocdar, & A. Bozkurt (Eds.), *Administrative Leadership in Open and Distance Learning Programs* (pp. 263–288). Hershey, PA: IGI Global. doi:10.4018/978-1-5225-2645-2.ch011

Dickenson, P. (2017). What do we Know and Where Can We Grow?: Teachers Preparation for the Inclusive Classroom. In P. Dickenson, P. Keough, & J. Courduff (Eds.), *Preparing Pre-Service Teachers for the Inclusive Classroom* (pp. 1–22). Hershey, PA: IGI Global. doi:10.4018/978-1-5225-1753-5.ch001

Dickerson, J., & Coleman, H. V. (2012). Technology, E-Leadership and Educational Administration in Schools: Integrating Standards with Context and Guiding Questions. In V. Wang (Ed.), *Encyclopedia of E-Leadership, Counseling and Training* (pp. 408–422). Hershey, PA: IGI Global. doi:10.4018/978-1-61350-068-2.ch030

Dickerson, J., Coleman, H. V., & Geer, G. (2012). Thinking like a School Technology Leader. In V. Wang (Ed.), *Technology and Its Impact on Educational Leadership: Innovation and Change* (pp. 53–63). Hershey, PA: IGI Global. doi:10.4018/978-1-4666-0062-1.ch005

Donne, V., & Hansen, M. (2017). Teachers' Use of Assistive Technologies in Education. In L. Tomei (Ed.), *Exploring the New Era of Technology-Infused Education* (pp. 86–101). Hershey, PA: IGI Global. doi:10.4018/978-1-5225-1709-2.ch006

Donne, V., & Hansen, M. A. (2018). Business and Technology Educators: Practices for Inclusion. In I. Management Association (Ed.), Business Education and Ethics: Concepts, Methodologies, Tools, and Applications (pp. 471-484). Hershey, PA: IGI Global. doi:10.4018/978-1-5225-3153-1.ch026

Dreon, O., Shettel, J., & Bower, K. M. (2017). Preparing Next Generation Elementary Teachers for the Tools of Tomorrow. In M. Grassetti & S. Brookby (Eds.), *Advancing Next-Generation Teacher Education through Digital Tools and Applications* (pp. 143–159). Hershey, PA: IGI Global. doi:10.4018/978-1-5225-0965-3.ch008

Drinka, D., Voge, K., & Yen, M. Y. (2005). From Principles to Practice: Analyzing a Student Learning Outcomes Assessment System. *Journal of Cases on Information Technology*, *7*(3), 37–56. doi:10.4018/jcit.2005070103

Durak, H. Y., & Güyer, T. (2018). Design and Development of an Instructional Program for Teaching Programming Processes to Gifted Students Using Scratch. In J. Cannaday (Ed.), *Curriculum Development for Gifted Education Programs* (pp. 61–99). Hershey, PA: IGI Global. doi:10.4018/978-1-5225-3041-1.ch004

Egorkina, E., Ivanov, M., & Valyavskiy, A. Y. (2018). Students' Research Competence Formation of the Quality of Open and Distance Learning. In V. Mkrttchian & L. Belyanina (Eds.), *Handbook of Research on Students' Research Competence in Modern Educational Contexts* (pp. 364–384). Hershey, PA: IGI Global. doi:10.4018/978-1-5225-3485-3.ch019

Ekren, G., Karataş, S., & Demiray, U. (2017). Understanding of Leadership in Distance Education Management. In I. Management Association (Ed.), Educational Leadership and Administration: Concepts, Methodologies, Tools, and Applications (pp. 34-50). Hershey, PA: IGI Global. doi:10.4018/978-1-5225-1624-8.ch003

Elmore, W. M., Young, J. K., Harris, S., & Mason, D. (2017). The Relationship between Individual Student Attributes and Online Course Completion. In K. Shelton & K. Pedersen (Eds.), *Handbook of Research on Building, Growing, and Sustaining Quality E-Learning Programs* (pp. 151–173). Hershey, PA: IGI Global. doi:10.4018/978-1-5225-0877-9.ch008

Ercegovac, I. R., Alfirević, N., & Koludrović, M. (2017). School Principals' Communication and Co-Operation Assessment: The Croatian Experience. In I. Management Association (Ed.), Educational Leadership and Administration: Concepts, Methodologies, Tools, and Applications (pp. 1568-1589). Hershey, PA: IGI Global. doi:10.4018/978-1-5225-1624-8.ch072

Everhart, D., & Seymour, D. M. (2017). Challenges and Opportunities in the Currency of Higher Education. In K. Rasmussen, P. Northrup, & R. Colson (Eds.), *Handbook of Research on Competency-Based Education in University Settings* (pp. 41–65). Hershey, PA: IGI Global. doi:10.4018/978-1-5225-0932-5.ch003

Farmer, L. S. (2017). Managing Portable Technologies for Special Education. In V. Wang (Ed.), *Encyclopedia of Strategic Leadership and Management* (pp. 977–987). Hershey, PA: IGI Global. doi:10.4018/978-1-5225-1049-9.ch068

Farmer, L. S. (2018). Optimizing OERs for Optimal ICT Literacy in Higher Education. In J. Keengwe (Ed.), *Handbook of Research on Mobile Technology, Constructivism, and Meaningful Learning* (pp. 366–390). Hershey, PA: IGI Global. doi:10.4018/978-1-5225-3949-0.ch020

Fındık, L. Y. (2017). Self-Assessment of Principals Based on Leadership in Complexity. In I. Management Association (Ed.), Educational Leadership and Administration: Concepts, Methodologies, Tools, and Applications (pp. 978-991). Hershey, PA: IGI Global. doi:10.4018/978-1-5225-1624-8.ch047

Flor, A. G., & Gonzalez-Flor, B. (2018). Dysfunctional Digital Demeanors: Tales From (and Policy Implications of) eLearning's Dark Side. In I. Management Association (Ed.), The Dark Web: Breakthroughs in Research and Practice (pp. 37-50). Hershey, PA: IGI Global. doi:10.4018/978-1-5225-3163-0.ch003

Floyd, K. K., & Shambaugh, N. (2017). Instructional Design for Simulations in Special Education Virtual Learning Spaces. In T. Kidd & L. Morris Jr., (Eds.), *Handbook of Research on Instructional Systems and Educational Technology* (pp. 202–215). Hershey, PA: IGI Global. doi:10.4018/978-1-5225-2399-4.ch018

Giovannini, J. M. (2017). Technology Integration in Preservice Teacher Education Programs: Research-based Recommendations. In M. Grassetti & S. Brookby (Eds.), *Advancing Next-Generation Teacher Education through Digital Tools and Applications* (pp. 82–102). Hershey, PA: IGI Global. doi:10.4018/978-1-5225-0965-3.ch005

Good, S., & Clarke, V. B. (2017). An Integral Analysis of One Urban School System's Efforts to Support Student-Centered Teaching. In J. Keengwe & G. Onchwari (Eds.), *Handbook of Research on Learner-Centered Pedagogy in Teacher Education and Professional Development* (pp. 45–68). Hershey, PA: IGI Global. doi:10.4018/978-1-5225-0892-2.ch003

Grobler, B. (2015). The Relationship between Emotional Competence and Instructional Leadership and Their Association with Learner Achievement. In K. Beycioglu & P. Pashiardis (Eds.), *Multidimensional Perspectives on Principal Leadership Effectiveness* (pp. 373–407). Hershey, PA: IGI Global. doi:10.4018/978-1-4666-6591-0.ch017

Hamidi, F., Owuor, P. M., Hynie, M., Baljko, M., & McGrath, S. (2017). Potentials of Digital Assistive Technology and Special Education in Kenya. In C. Ayo & V. Mbarika (Eds.), *Sustainable ICT Adoption and Integration for Socio-Economic Development* (pp. 125–151). Hershey, PA: IGI Global. doi:10.4018/978-1-5225-2565-3.ch006

Heavin, C., & Neville, K. (2015). Addressing the Learning Needs of Future IS Security Professionals through Social Media Technology. In M. Khosrow-Pour (Ed.), *Encyclopedia of Information Science and Technology* (3rd ed.; pp. 4766–4775). Hershey, PA: IGI Global. doi:10.4018/978-1-4666-5888-2.ch468

Henderson, L. K. (2017). Meltdown at Fukushima: Global Catastrophic Events, Visual Literacy, and Art Education. In R. Shin (Ed.), *Convergence of Contemporary Art, Visual Culture, and Global Civic Engagement* (pp. 80–99). Hershey, PA: IGI Global. doi:10.4018/978-1-5225-1665-1.ch005

Hismanoglu, M. (2012). Important Issues in Online Education: E-Pedagogy and Marketing. In I. Management Association (Ed.), E-Marketing: Concepts, Methodologies, Tools, and Applications (pp. 676-701). Hershey, PA: IGI Global. doi:10.4018/978-1-4666-1598-4.ch041

Howard, B. C. (2008). Common Features and Design Principles Found in Exemplary Educational Technologies. *International Journal of Information and Communication Technology Education*, *4*(4), 31–52. doi:10.4018/jicte.2008100104

Howard, B. C., & Tomei, L. A. (2008). The Classroom of the Future and Emerging Educational Technologies: Introduction to the Special Issue. *International Journal of Information and Communication Technology Education*, *4*(4), 1–8. doi:10.4018/jicte.2008100101

Hudgins, T., & Holland, J. L. (2018). Digital Badges: Tracking Knowledge Acquisition Within an Innovation Framework. In I. Management Association (Ed.), Wearable Technologies: Concepts, Methodologies, Tools, and Applications (pp. 1118-1132). Hershey, PA: IGI Global. doi:10.4018/978-1-5225-5484-4.ch051

Ion, G., Tomàs, M., Castro, D., & Salat, E. (2015). Analysis of the Tasks of School Principals in Secondary Education in Catalonia: Case Study. In K. Beycioglu & P. Pashiardis (Eds.), *Multidimensional Perspectives on Principal Leadership Effectiveness* (pp. 39–58). Hershey, PA: IGI Global. doi:10.4018/978-1-4666-6591-0.ch003

Janus, M., & Siddiqua, A. (2018). Challenges for Children With Special Health Needs at the Time of Transition to School. In I. Management Association (Ed.), Autism Spectrum Disorders: Breakthroughs in Research and Practice (pp. 339-371). Hershey, PA: IGI Global. doi:10.4018/978-1-5225-3827-1.ch018

Jesus, R. A. (2018). Screencasts and Learning Styles. In M. Khosrow-Pour, D.B.A. (Ed.), Encyclopedia of Information Science and Technology, Fourth Edition (pp. 1548-1558). Hershey, PA: IGI Global. doi:10.4018/978-1-5225-2255-3.ch134

Kaplan-Rakowski, R., & Rakowski, D. (2011). Educational Technologies for the Neomillennial Generation. In E. Dunkels, G. Franberg, & C. Hallgren (Eds.), *Interactive Media Use and Youth: Learning, Knowledge Exchange and Behavior* (pp. 12–31). Hershey, PA: IGI Global. doi:10.4018/978-1-60960-206-2.ch002

Karpinski, A. C., D'Agostino, J. V., Williams, A. K., Highland, S. A., & Mellott, J. A. (2018). The Relationship Between Online Formative Assessment and State Test Scores Using Multilevel Modeling. In M. Khosrow-Pour, D.B.A. (Ed.), Encyclopedia of Information Science and Technology, Fourth Edition (pp. 5183-5192). Hershey, PA: IGI Global. doi:10.4018/978-1-5225-2255-3.ch450

Kats, Y. (2017). Educational Leadership and Integrated Support for Students with Autism Spectrum Disorders. In I. Management Association (Ed.), Educational Leadership and Administration: Concepts, Methodologies, Tools, and Applications (pp. 101-114). Hershey, PA: IGI Global. doi:10.4018/978-1-5225-1624-8.ch007

Kaya, G., & Altun, A. (2018). Educational Ontology Development. In M. Khosrow-Pour, D.B.A. (Ed.), Encyclopedia of Information Science and Technology, Fourth Edition (pp. 1441-1450). Hershey, PA: IGI Global. doi:10.4018/978-1-5225-2255-3.ch124

Keough, P. D., & Pacis, D. (2017). Best Practices Implementing Special Education Curriculum and Common Core State Standards using UDL. In P. Dickenson, P. Keough, & J. Courduff (Eds.), *Preparing Pre-Service Teachers for the Inclusive Classroom* (pp. 107–123). Hershey, PA: IGI Global. doi:10.4018/978-1-5225-1753-5.ch006

Kilburn, M., Henckell, M., & Starrett, D. (2018). Factors Contributing to the Effectiveness of Online Students and Instructors. In M. Khosrow-Pour, D.B.A. (Ed.), Encyclopedia of Information Science and Technology, Fourth Edition (pp. 1451-1462). Hershey, PA: IGI Global. doi:10.4018/978-1-5225-2255-3.ch125

Konecny, L. T. (2017). Hybrid, Online, and Flipped Classrooms in Health Science: Enhanced Learning Environments. In I. Management Association (Ed.), Flipped Instruction: Breakthroughs in Research and Practice (pp. 355-370). Hershey, PA: IGI Global. doi:10.4018/978-1-5225-1803-7.ch020

Kowch, E. G. (2013). Towards Leading Diverse, Smarter and More Adaptable Organizations that Learn. In J. Lewis, A. Green, & D. Surry (Eds.), *Technology as a Tool for Diversity Leadership: Implementation and Future Implications* (pp. 11–34). Hershey, PA: IGI Global. doi:10.4018/978-1-4666-2668-3.ch002

Krezmien, M., Powell, W., Bosch, C., Hall, T., & Nieswandt, M. (2017). The Use of Tablet Technology to Support Inquiry Science for Students Incarcerated in Juvenile Justice Settings. In I. Levin & D. Tsybulsky (Eds.), *Optimizing STEM Education With Advanced ICTs and Simulations* (pp. 267–295). Hershey, PA: IGI Global. doi:10.4018/978-1-5225-2528-8.ch011

Leach, L. F., Winn, P., Erwin, S., & Benedict, L. P. (2015). What 21st Century Students Want: Factors that Influence Student Selection of Educational Leadership Graduate Programs. *International Journal of Technology and Educational Marketing*, *5*(1), 15–28. doi:10.4018/ijtem.2015010102

Leng, H. K. (2014). An Update on the Use of Facebook as a Marketing Tool by Private Educational Institutions in Singapore. In I. Lee (Ed.), *Trends in E-Business, E-Services, and E-Commerce: Impact of Technology on Goods, Services, and Business Transactions* (pp. 191–205). Hershey, PA: IGI Global. doi:10.4018/978-1-4666-4510-3.ch011

Leone, S. (2018). An Open Learning Format for Lifelong Learners' Empowerment. In M. Khosrow-Pour, D.B.A. (Ed.), Encyclopedia of Information Science and Technology, Fourth Edition (pp. 1517-1528). Hershey, PA: IGI Global. doi:10.4018/978-1-5225-2255-3.ch131

Ley, K., & Gannon-Cook, R. (2010). Marketing a Blended University Program: An Action Research Case Study. In S. Mukerji & P. Tripathi (Eds.), *Cases on Technology Enhanced Learning through Collaborative Opportunities* (pp. 73–90). Hershey, PA: IGI Global. doi:10.4018/978-1-61520-751-0.ch005

Loose, W., & Marcos, T. (2016). Instructional Design for Millennials: Instructor Efficiency in Streamlining Content, Assignments, and Assessments. In P. Dickenson & J. Jaurez (Eds.), *Increasing Productivity and Efficiency in Online Teaching* (pp. 1–25). Hershey, PA: IGI Global. doi:10.4018/978-1-5225-0347-7.ch001

Lovell, K. L. (2017). Development and Evaluation of Neuroscience Computer-Based Modules for Medical Students: Instructional Design Principles and Effectiveness. In J. Stefaniak (Ed.), *Advancing Medical Education Through Strategic Instructional Design* (pp. 262–276). Hershey, PA: IGI Global. doi:10.4018/978-1-5225-2098-6.ch013

Manuel, N. N. (2016). Angolan Higher Education, Policy, and Leadership: Towards Transformative Leadership for Social Justice. In N. Ololube (Ed.), *Handbook of Research on Organizational Justice and Culture in Higher Education Institutions* (pp. 164–188). Hershey, PA: IGI Global. doi:10.4018/978-1-4666-9850-5.ch007

Marouchou, D. V. (2015). The Impact of Academic Beliefs on Student Learning. In M. Khosrow-Pour (Ed.), *Encyclopedia of Information Science and Technology* (3rd ed.; pp. 4796–4804). Hershey, PA: IGI Global. doi:10.4018/978-1-4666-5888-2.ch471

McCormack, V. F., Stauffer, M., Fishley, K., Hohenbrink, J., Mascazine, J. R., & Zigler, T. (2018). Designing a Dual Licensure Path for Middle Childhood and Special Education Teacher Candidates. In D. Polly, M. Putman, T. Petty, & A. Good (Eds.), *Innovative Practices in Teacher Preparation and Graduate-Level Teacher Education Programs* (pp. 21–36). Hershey, PA: IGI Global. doi:10.4018/978-1-5225-3068-8.ch002

McDaniel, R. (2017). Strategic Leadership in Instructional Design: Applying the Principles of Instructional Design through the Lens of Strategic Leadership to Distance Education. In V. Wang (Ed.), *Encyclopedia of Strategic Leadership and Management* (pp. 1570–1584). Hershey, PA: IGI Global. doi:10.4018/978-1-5225-1049-9.ch109

Memon, R. N., Ahmad, R., & Salim, S. S. (2018). Critical Issues in Requirements Engineering Education. In I. Management Association (Ed.), Computer Systems and Software Engineering: Concepts, Methodologies, Tools, and Applications (pp. 1953-1976). Hershey, PA: IGI Global. doi:10.4018/978-1-5225-3923-0.ch081

Mendenhall, R. (2017). Western Governors University: CBE Innovator and National Model. In K. Rasmussen, P. Northrup, & R. Colson (Eds.), *Handbook of Research on Competency-Based Education in University Settings* (pp. 379–400). Hershey, PA: IGI Global. doi:10.4018/978-1-5225-0932-5.ch019

Mense, E. G., Griggs, D. M., & Shanks, J. N. (2018). School Leaders in a Time of Accountability and Data Use: Preparing Our Future School Leaders in Leadership Preparation Programs. In E. Mense & M. Crain-Dorough (Eds.), *Data Leadership for K-12 Schools in a Time of Accountability* (pp. 235–259). Hershey, PA: IGI Global. doi:10.4018/978-1-5225-3188-3.ch012

Mense, E. G., Griggs, D. M., & Shanks, J. N. (2018). School Leaders in a Time of Accountability and Data Use: Preparing Our Future School Leaders in Leadership Preparation Programs. In E. Mense & M. Crain-Dorough (Eds.), *Data Leadership for K-12 Schools in a Time of Accountability* (pp. 235–259). Hershey, PA: IGI Global. doi:10.4018/978-1-5225-3188-3.ch012

Mestry, R., & Naicker, S. R. (2017). Exploring Distributive Leadership in South African Public Primary Schools in the Soweto Region. In I. Management Association (Ed.), Educational Leadership and Administration: Concepts, Methodologies, Tools, and Applications (pp. 1041-1064). Hershey, PA: IGI Global. doi:10.4018/978-1-5225-1624-8.ch050

Monaghan, C. H., & Boboc, M. (2017). (Re) Defining Leadership in Higher Education in the U.S. In V. Wang (Ed.), *Encyclopedia of Strategic Leadership and Management* (pp. 567–579). Hershey, PA: IGI Global. doi:10.4018/978-1-5225-1049-9.ch040

Muthee, J. M., & Murungi, C. G. (2018). Relationship Among Intelligence, Achievement Motivation, Type of School, and Academic Performance of Kenyan Urban Primary School Pupils. In M. Khosrow-Pour, D.B.A. (Ed.), Encyclopedia of Information Science and Technology, Fourth Edition (pp. 1540-1547). Hershey, PA: IGI Global. doi:10.4018/978-1-5225-2255-3.ch133

Naranjo, J. (2018). Meeting the Need for Inclusive Educators Online: Teacher Education in Inclusive Special Education and Dual-Certification. In D. Polly, M. Putman, T. Petty, & A. Good (Eds.), *Innovative Practices in Teacher Preparation and Graduate-Level Teacher Education Programs* (pp. 106–122). Hershey, PA: IGI Global. doi:10.4018/978-1-5225-3068-8.ch007

Nkabinde, Z. P. (2017). Multiculturalism in Special Education: Perspectives of Minority Children in Urban Schools. In J. Keengwe (Ed.), *Handbook of Research on Promoting Cross-Cultural Competence and Social Justice in Teacher Education* (pp. 382–397). Hershey, PA: IGI Global. doi:10.4018/978-1-5225-0897-7.ch020

Nkabinde, Z. P. (2018). Online Instruction: Is the Quality the Same as Face-to-Face Instruction? In J. Keengwe (Ed.), *Handbook of Research on Digital Content, Mobile Learning, and Technology Integration Models in Teacher Education* (pp. 300–314). Hershey, PA: IGI Global. doi:10.4018/978-1-5225-2953-8.ch016

O'Connor, J. R. Jr, & Jackson, K. N. (2017). The Use of iPad® Devices and "Apps" for ASD Students in Special Education and Speech Therapy. In Y. Kats (Ed.), *Supporting the Education of Children with Autism Spectrum Disorders* (pp. 267–283). Hershey, PA: IGI Global. doi:10.4018/978-1-5225-0816-8.ch014

Okolie, U. C., & Yasin, A. M. (2017). TVET in Developing Nations and Human Development. In U. Okolie & A. Yasin (Eds.), *Technical Education and Vocational Training in Developing Nations* (pp. 1–25). Hershey, PA: IGI Global. doi:10.4018/978-1-5225-1811-2.ch001

Paciga, K. A., & Hoffman, J. L. (2015). Realizing the Potential of e-Books in Early Education. In M. Khosrow-Pour (Ed.), *Encyclopedia of Information Science and Technology* (3rd ed.; pp. 4787–4795). Hershey, PA: IGI Global. doi:10.4018/978-1-4666-5888-2.ch470

Paulson, E. N. (2017). Adapting and Advocating for an Online EdD Program in Changing Times and "Sacred" Cultures. In I. Management Association (Ed.), Educational Leadership and Administration: Concepts, Methodologies, Tools, and Applications (pp. 1849-1876). Hershey, PA: IGI Global. doi:10.4018/978-1-5225-1624-8.ch085

Petersen, A. J., Elser, C. F., Al Nassir, M. N., Stakey, J., & Everson, K. (2017). The Year of Teaching Inclusively: Building an Elementary Classroom for All Students. In C. Curran & A. Petersen (Eds.), *Handbook of Research on Classroom Diversity and Inclusive Education Practice* (pp. 332–348). Hershey, PA: IGI Global. doi:10.4018/978-1-5225-2520-2.ch014

Pfannenstiel, K. H., & Sanders, J. (2017). Characteristics and Instructional Strategies for Students With Mathematical Difficulties: In the Inclusive Classroom. In C. Curran & A. Petersen (Eds.), *Handbook of Research on Classroom Diversity and Inclusive Education Practice* (pp. 250–281). Hershey, PA: IGI Global. doi:10.4018/978-1-5225-2520-2.ch011

Preast, J. L., Bowman, N., & Rose, C. A. (2017). Creating Inclusive Classroom Communities Through Social and Emotional Learning to Reduce Social Marginalization Among Students. In C. Curran & A. Petersen (Eds.), *Handbook of Research on Classroom Diversity and Inclusive Education Practice* (pp. 183–200). Hershey, PA: IGI Global. doi:10.4018/978-1-5225-2520-2.ch008

Randolph, K. M., & Brady, M. P. (2018). Evolution of Covert Coaching as an Evidence-Based Practice in Professional Development and Preparation of Teachers. In V. Bryan, A. Musgrove, & J. Powers (Eds.), *Handbook of Research on Human Development in the Digital Age* (pp. 281–299). Hershey, PA: IGI Global. doi:10.4018/978-1-5225-2838-8.ch013

Rawlins, P., & Kehrwald, B. (2010). Education Technology in Teacher Education: Overcoming Challenges, Realizing Opportunities. In R. Luppicini & A. Haghi (Eds.), *Cases on Digital Technologies in Higher Education: Issues and Challenges* (pp. 50–63). Hershey, PA: IGI Global. doi:10.4018/978-1-61520-869-2.ch004

Rell, A. B., Puig, R. A., Roll, F., Valles, V., Espinoza, M., & Duque, A. L. (2017). Addressing Cultural Diversity and Global Competence: The Dual Language Framework. In L. Leavitt, S. Wisdom, & K. Leavitt (Eds.), *Cultural Awareness and Competency Development in Higher Education* (pp. 111–131). Hershey, PA: IGI Global. doi:10.4018/978-1-5225-2145-7.ch007

Riel, J., Lawless, K. A., & Brown, S. W. (2017). Defining and Designing Responsive Online Professional Development (ROPD): A Framework to Support Curriculum Implementation. In T. Kidd & L. Morris Jr., (Eds.), *Handbook of Research on Instructional Systems and Educational Technology* (pp. 104–115). Hershey, PA: IGI Global. doi:10.4018/978-1-5225-2399-4.ch010

Roberts, C. (2017). Advancing Women Leaders in Academe: Creating a Culture of Inclusion. In S. Mukerji & P. Tripathi (Eds.), *Handbook of Research on Administration, Policy, and Leadership in Higher Education* (pp. 256–273). Hershey, PA: IGI Global. doi:10.4018/978-1-5225-0672-0.ch012

Rodgers, W. J., Kennedy, M. J., Alves, K. D., & Romig, J. E. (2017). A Multimedia Tool for Teacher Education and Professional Development. In C. Martin & D. Polly (Eds.), *Handbook of Research on Teacher Education and Professional Development* (pp. 285–296). Hershey, PA: IGI Global. doi:10.4018/978-1-5225-1067-3.ch015

Romanowski, M. H. (2017). Qatar's Educational Reform: Critical Issues Facing Principals. In I. Management Association (Ed.), Educational Leadership and Administration: Concepts, Methodologies, Tools, and Applications (pp. 1758-1773). Hershey, PA: IGI Global. doi:10.4018/978-1-5225-1624-8.ch080

Ruffin, T. R., Hawkins, D. P., & Lee, D. I. (2018). Increasing Student Engagement and Participation Through Course Methodology. In M. Khosrow-Pour, D.B.A. (Ed.), Encyclopedia of Information Science and Technology, Fourth Edition (pp. 1463-1473). Hershey, PA: IGI Global. doi:10.4018/978-1-5225-2255-3.ch126

Rutaisire, J. (2011). Innovations in Technology for Educational Marketing: Stakeholder Perceptions and Implications for Examinations System in Rwanda. In P. Tripathi & S. Mukerji (Eds.), *Cases on Innovations in Educational Marketing: Transnational and Technological Strategies* (pp. 214–233). Hershey, PA: IGI Global. doi:10.4018/978-1-60960-599-5.ch013

Sabina, L. L., Curry, K. A., Harris, E. L., Krumm, B. L., & Vencill, V. (2017). Assessing the Performance of a Cohort-Based Model Using Domestic and International Practices. In I. Management Association (Ed.), Educational Leadership and Administration: Concepts, Methodologies, Tools, and Applications(pp. 913-929). Hershey, PA: IGI Global. doi:10.4018/978-1-5225-1624-8.ch044

Santamaría, A. P., Webber, M., & Santamaría, L. J. (2017). Effective School Leadership for Māori Achievement: Building Capacity through Indigenous, National, and International Cross-Cultural Collaboration. In I. Management Association (Ed.), Educational Leadership and Administration: Concepts, Methodologies, Tools, and Applications (pp. 1547-1567). Hershey, PA: IGI Global. doi:10.4018/978-1-5225-1624-8.ch071

Santamaría, L. J. (2017). Culturally Responsive Educational Leadership in Cross-Cultural International Contexts. In I. Management Association (Ed.), Educational Leadership and Administration: Concepts, Methodologies, Tools, and Applications (pp. 1380-1400). Hershey, PA: IGI Global. doi:10.4018/978-1-5225-1624-8.ch064

Sarafidou, J., & Xafakos, E. (2015). Transformational Leadership and Principals' Innovativeness: Are They the "Keys" for the Research and Innovation Oriented School? In K. Beycioglu & P. Pashiardis (Eds.), *Multidimensional Perspectives on Principal Leadership Effectiveness* (pp. 324–348). Hershey, PA: IGI Global. doi:10.4018/978-1-4666-6591-0.ch015

Segredo, M. R., Cistone, P. J., & Reio, T. G. (2017). Relationships Between Emotional Intelligence, Leadership Style, and School Culture. *International Journal of Adult Vocational Education and Technology*, *8*(3), 25–43. doi:10.4018/IJAVET.2017070103

Shaik, N., & Ritter, S. (2012). Social Media Based Relationship Marketing. In I. Management Association (Ed.), E-Marketing: Concepts, Methodologies, Tools, and Applications (pp. 88-110). Hershey, PA: IGI Global. doi:10.4018/978-1-4666-1598-4.ch006

Shalev, N. (2017). Empathy and Leadership From the Organizational Perspective. In Z. Nedelko & M. Brzozowski (Eds.), *Exploring the Influence of Personal Values and Cultures in the Workplace* (pp. 348–363). Hershey, PA: IGI Global. doi:10.4018/978-1-5225-2480-9.ch018

Siamak, M., Fathi, S., & Isfandyari-Moghaddam, A. (2018). Assessment and Measurement of Education Programs of Information Literacy. In R. Bhardwaj (Ed.), *Digitizing the Modern Library and the Transition From Print to Electronic* (pp. 164–192). Hershey, PA: IGI Global. doi:10.4018/978-1-5225-2119-8.ch007

Siozos, P. D., & Palaigeorgiou, G. E. (2008). Educational Technologies and the Emergence of E-Learning 2.0. In D. Politis (Ed.), *E-Learning Methodologies and Computer Applications in Archaeology* (pp. 1–17). Hershey, PA: IGI Global. doi:10.4018/978-1-59904-759-1.ch001

Siu, K. W., & García, G. J. (2017). Disruptive Technologies and Education: Is There Any Disruption After All? In I. Management Association (Ed.), Educational Leadership and Administration: Concepts, Methodologies, Tools, and Applications (pp. 757-778). Hershey, PA: IGI Global. doi:10.4018/978-1-5225-1624-8.ch037

Skibba, K., Moore, D., & Herman, J. H. (2013). Pedagogical and Technological Considerations Designing Collaborative Learning Using Educational Technologies. In J. Keengwe (Ed.), *Research Perspectives and Best Practices in Educational Technology Integration* (pp. 1–27). Hershey, PA: IGI Global. doi:10.4018/978-1-4666-2988-2.ch001

Slagter van Tryon, P. J. (2017). The Nurse Educator's Role in Designing Instruction and Instructional Strategies for Academic and Clinical Settings. In J. Stefaniak (Ed.), *Advancing Medical Education Through Strategic Instructional Design* (pp. 133–149). Hershey, PA: IGI Global. doi:10.4018/978-1-5225-2098-6.ch006

Slattery, C. A. (2018). Literacy Intervention and the Differentiated Plan of Instruction. In *Developing Effective Literacy Intervention Strategies: Emerging Research and Opportunities* (pp. 41–62). Hershey, PA: IGI Global. doi:10.4018/978-1-5225-5007-5.ch003

Smith, A. R. (2017). Ensuring Quality: The Faculty Role in Online Higher Education. In K. Shelton & K. Pedersen (Eds.), *Handbook of Research on Building, Growing, and Sustaining Quality E-Learning Programs* (pp. 210–231). Hershey, PA: IGI Global. doi:10.4018/978-1-5225-0877-9.ch011

Souders, T. M. (2017). Understanding Your Learner: Conducting a Learner Analysis. In J. Stefaniak (Ed.), *Advancing Medical Education Through Strategic Instructional Design* (pp. 1–29). Hershey, PA: IGI Global. doi:10.4018/978-1-5225-2098-6.ch001

Spring, K. J., Graham, C. R., & Ikahihifo, T. B. (2018). Learner Engagement in Blended Learning. In M. Khosrow-Pour, D.B.A. (Ed.), Encyclopedia of Information Science and Technology, Fourth Edition (pp. 1487-1498). Hershey, PA: IGI Global. doi:10.4018/978-1-5225-2255-3.ch128

Stocklin, S. (2015). Building Capacity by Managing a Mission. In J. Feng, S. Stocklin, & W. Wang (Eds.), *Educational Strategies for the Next Generation Leaders in Hotel Management* (pp. 115–139). Hershey, PA: IGI Global. doi:10.4018/978-1-4666-8565-9.ch005

Storey, V. A., Anthony, A. K., & Wahid, P. (2017). Gender-Based Leadership Barriers: Advancement of Female Faculty to Leadership Positions in Higher Education. In V. Wang (Ed.), *Encyclopedia of Strategic Leadership and Management* (pp. 244–258). Hershey, PA: IGI Global. doi:10.4018/978-1-5225-1049-9.ch018

Stottlemyer, D. (2018). Develop a Teaching Model Plan for a Differentiated Learning Approach. In *Differentiated Instructional Design for Multicultural Environments: Emerging Research and Opportunities* (pp. 106–130). Hershey, PA: IGI Global. doi:10.4018/978-1-5225-5106-5.ch005

Stottlemyer, D. (2018). Developing a Multicultural Environment. In *Differentiated Instructional Design for Multicultural Environments: Emerging Research and Opportunities* (pp. 1–27). Hershey, PA: IGI Global. doi:10.4018/978-1-5225-5106-5.ch001

Swami, B. N., Gobona, T., & Tsimako, J. J. (2017). Academic Leadership: A Case Study of the University of Botswana. In N. Baporikar (Ed.), *Innovation and Shifting Perspectives in Management Education* (pp. 1–32). Hershey, PA: IGI Global. doi:10.4018/978-1-5225-1019-2.ch001

Swanson, K. W., & Collins, G. (2018). Designing Engaging Instruction for the Adult Learners. In M. Khosrow-Pour, D.B.A. (Ed.), Encyclopedia of Information Science and Technology, Fourth Edition (pp. 1432-1440). Hershey, PA: IGI Global. doi:10.4018/978-1-5225-2255-3.ch123

Swartz, B. A., Lynch, J. M., & Lynch, S. D. (2018). Embedding Elementary Teacher Education Coursework in Local Classrooms: Examples in Mathematics and Special Education. In D. Polly, M. Putman, T. Petty, & A. Good (Eds.), *Innovative Practices in Teacher Preparation and Graduate-Level Teacher Education Programs* (pp. 262–292). Hershey, PA: IGI Global. doi:10.4018/978-1-5225-3068-8.ch015

Taliadorou, N., & Pashiardis, P. (2015). Emotional Intelligence and Political Skill Really Matter in Educational Leadership. In K. Beycioglu & P. Pashiardis (Eds.), *Multidimensional Perspectives on Principal Leadership Effectiveness* (pp. 228–256). Hershey, PA: IGI Global. doi:10.4018/978-1-4666-6591-0.ch011

Taliadorou, N., & Pashiardis, P. (2017). Emotional Intelligence and Political Skill Really Matter in Educational Leadership. In I. Management Association (Ed.), Educational Leadership and Administration: Concepts, Methodologies, Tools, and Applications (pp. 1274-1303). Hershey, PA: IGI Global. doi:10.4018/978-1-5225-1624-8.ch060

Tam, F. W., & Kwan, P. Y. (2011). School Images, School Identity, and How Parents Select Schools for Their Children: The Case of Hong Kong. In P. Tripathi & S. Mukerji (Eds.), *Cases on Innovations in Educational Marketing: Transnational and Technological Strategies* (pp. 87–103). Hershey, PA: IGI Global. doi:10.4018/978-1-60960-599-5.ch005

Tandoh, K. A., & Ebe-Arthur, J. E. (2018). Effective Educational Leadership in the Digital Age: An Examination of Professional Qualities and Best Practices. In J. Keengwe (Ed.), *Handbook of Research on Digital Content, Mobile Learning, and Technology Integration Models in Teacher Education* (pp. 244–265). Hershey, PA: IGI Global. doi:10.4018/978-1-5225-2953-8.ch013

Tinoca, L., Pereira, A., & Oliveira, I. (2014). A Conceptual Framework for E-Assessment in Higher Education: Authenticity, Consistency, Transparency, and Practicability. In S. Mukerji & P. Tripathi (Eds.), *Handbook of Research on Transnational Higher Education* (pp. 652–673). Hershey, PA: IGI Global. doi:10.4018/978-1-4666-4458-8.ch033

Tobin, M. T. (2018). Multimodal Literacy. In M. Khosrow-Pour, D.B.A. (Ed.), Encyclopedia of Information Science and Technology, Fourth Edition (pp. 1508-1516). Hershey, PA: IGI Global. doi:10.4018/978-1-5225-2255-3.ch130

Torres, M. L., & Ramos, V. J. (2018). Music Therapy: A Pedagogical Alternative for ASD and ID Students in Regular Classrooms. In P. Epler (Ed.), *Instructional Strategies in General Education and Putting the Individuals With Disabilities Act (IDEA) Into Practice* (pp. 222–244). Hershey, PA: IGI Global. doi:10.4018/978-1-5225-3111-1.ch008

Toulassi, B. (2017). Educational Administration and Leadership in Francophone Africa: 5 Dynamics to Change Education. In S. Mukerji & P. Tripathi (Eds.), *Handbook of Research on Administration, Policy, and Leadership in Higher Education* (pp. 20–45). Hershey, PA: IGI Global. doi:10.4018/978-1-5225-0672-0.ch002

Umair, S., & Sharif, M. M. (2018). Predicting Students Grades Using Artificial Neural Networks and Support Vector Machine. In M. Khosrow-Pour, D.B.A. (Ed.), Encyclopedia of Information Science and Technology, Fourth Edition (pp. 5169-5182). Hershey, PA: IGI Global. doi:10.4018/978-1-5225-2255-3.ch449

Usman, L. M. (2011). Adult Education and Sustainable Learning Outcome of Rural Widows of Central Northern Nigeria. *International Journal of Adult Vocational Education and Technology*, *2*(2), 25–41. doi:10.4018/javet.2011040103

Vettraino, L., Castello, V., Guspini, M., & Guglielman, E. (2018). Self-Awareness and Motivation Contrasting ESL and NEET Using the SAVE System. In M. Khosrow-Pour, D.B.A. (Ed.), Encyclopedia of Information Science and Technology, Fourth Edition (pp. 1559-1568). Hershey, PA: IGI Global. doi:10.4018/978-1-5225-2255-3.ch135

Wang, V. C. (2013). Marketing Educational Programs through Technology and the Right Philosophies. In P. Tripathi & S. Mukerji (Eds.), *Marketing Strategies for Higher Education Institutions: Technological Considerations and Practices* (pp. 15–24). Hershey, PA: IGI Global. doi:10.4018/978-1-4666-4014-6.ch002

Wiemelt, J. (2017). Critical Bilingual Leadership for Emergent Bilingual Students. In I. Management Association (Ed.), Educational Leadership and Administration: Concepts, Methodologies, Tools, and Applications (pp. 1606-1631). Hershey, PA: IGI Global. doi:10.4018/978-1-5225-1624-8.ch074

Williams, D. D. (2006). Measurement and Assessment Supporting Evaluation in Online Settings. In D. Williams, M. Hricko, & S. Howell (Eds.), *Online Assessment, Measurement and Evaluation: Emerging Practices* (pp. 1–9). Hershey, PA: IGI Global. doi:10.4018/978-1-59140-747-8.ch001

Wolf, F., Seyfarth, F. C., & Pflaum, E. (2018). Scalable Capacity-Building for Geographically Dispersed Learners: Designing the MOOC "Sustainable Energy in Small Island Developing States (SIDS)". In U. Pandey & V. Indrakanti (Eds.), *Open and Distance Learning Initiatives for Sustainable Development* (pp. 58–83). Hershey, PA: IGI Global. doi:10.4018/978-1-5225-2621-6.ch003

Woodley, X. M., Mucundanyi, G., & Lockard, M. (2017). Designing Counter-Narratives: Constructing Culturally Responsive Curriculum Online. *International Journal of Online Pedagogy and Course Design*, *7*(1), 43–56. doi:10.4018/IJOPCD.2017010104

Woods, P. A., & Woods, G. J. (2011). Lighting the Fires of Entrepreneurialism?: Constructions of Meaning in an English Inner City Academy. *International Journal of Technology and Educational Marketing*, *1*(1), 1–24. doi:10.4018/ijtem.2011010101

Yell, M. L., & Christle, C. A. (2017). The Foundation of Inclusion in Federal Legislation and Litigation. In C. Curran & A. Petersen (Eds.), *Handbook of Research on Classroom Diversity and Inclusive Education Practice* (pp. 27–52). Hershey, PA: IGI Global. doi:10.4018/978-1-5225-2520-2.ch002

Zhao, J. (2011). China Special Education: The Perspective of Information Technologies. In P. Ordóñez de Pablos, J. Zhao, & R. Tennyson (Eds.), *Technology Enhanced Learning for People with Disabilities: Approaches and Applications* (pp. 34–43). Hershey, PA: IGI Global. doi:10.4018/978-1-61520-923-1.ch003

Zinger, D. (2016). Developing Instructional Leadership and Communication Skills through Online Professional Development: Focusing on Rural and Urban Principals. In A. Normore, L. Long, & M. Javidi (Eds.), *Handbook of Research on Effective Communication, Leadership, and Conflict Resolution* (pp. 354–370). Hershey, PA: IGI Global. doi:10.4018/978-1-4666-9970-0.ch019

Zutshi, A., Pogrebnaya, M., & Fermelis, J. (2014). Wellness Programs in Higher Education: An Australian Case. In N. Baporikar (Ed.), *Handbook of Research on Higher Education in the MENA Region: Policy and Practice* (pp. 391–419). Hershey, PA: IGI Global. doi:10.4018/978-1-4666-6198-1.ch017

About the Contributors

Rebecca J. Blankenship is an Associate Professor and Director of TESOL programs in the Elementary Education Department at Florida A&M University's CAEP nationally accredited College of Education. Dr. Blankenship has over 16 years of public school teaching experience in both the states of Tennessee and Florida. She earned her Ph.D. from the University of South Florida in Second Language Acquisition and Instructional Technology (SLA/IT) with an emphasis in teaching English to Speakers of Other Languages (ESOL) and virtual/simulated professional development for pre-service teacher candidates. She holds a Master of Science in Secondary Education and Master of Arts in Political Science from the University of Tennessee where she also completed her undergraduate degree with a double major in Pre-Law and Spanish. She was a member of the Inaugural Provost's Digital Learning Initiative in 2017 and currently serves as a DLI Ambassador. She also serves as an Association of Teacher Educators (ATE) Clinical Educator Fellow as well as an Association of Colleges and Universities (ACUE) Effective Teaching Practices Nationally Certified recipient in Effective Teaching Practices (2021). Dr. Blankenship's research interests include the development of virtual training environments for pre-service teacher candidates, the digital agency and literacy development of pre-service teachers and university faculty, and the effects of politics and social media on the teaching profession. She has committed herself through her university teaching, supervision of interns, and faculty service to provide the most salient experiences for pre-service teacher candidates, particularly those representing marginalized populations, to ensure they are well prepared to enter the teaching profession. Her list of accomplishments and publications in addition to her university, state, national, and international service demonstrates her ongoing commitment to the preparation of this nation's future minority teaching corps. A native of Tennessee, she has lived in Florida for 20 years where she presently resides in the Tampa Bay area with her husband and two beagles. She is an avid reader, lover of classic movies, runner, and dedicated shell seeker.

* * *

Adebowale Jeremy Adetayo is an academic staff of Adeleke University. His research interest is Library Science, Social media, Knowledge Management, and Business Information Management. He has published many articles in reputable journals and currently working on projects relating to pandemics, vaccines and virtual learning. He is a graduate of Babcock University.

Collence Chisita is a Research Fellow based at the University of South Africa. Chisita completed PHD in Information Sciences focusing on library consortium models for Zimbabwe. Chisita is a renowned writer and speaker who has presented papers at various fora including Euro Africa Partnership for Research in ICT's, Promoting African European Research Infrastructure Partnerships (PAERIP), IFLA, among others. Chisita has published a number of journal articles in internationally renowned journals, book chapters and books. He has collaborated with local, regional and international authors. His research interests covers Information Science, Digital technologies, forensic bibliographic control, intellectual genealogy and the evolving digital libraries.

Tinyiko Vivian Dube is working at the University of South Africa (Unisa) Library as an Information Resource Request Processor. This is her 10th year working in an academic library. Her core duties are to assist remote clients in Africa to have access to information resources from the main Unisa Library. Previously, Tinyiko worked at public libraries until 2010 when she decided to advance her career by joining the team of Information Resource Request Processors at the Unisa Library. Tinyiko holds a degree in Master of Arts in Information Science and currently pursuing a degree of Doctor of Philosophy and Literature in Information Science.

Oluwole O. Durodolu is a Post-Doctoral fellow of the Department of Information Science at the University of South Africa. He holds a PhD in library and information science from the University of Zululand, South Africa in 2016. A Certified Librarian of Nigeria and a member of the Association for Southern African Indexers and Bibliographers. He has published articles on information literacy, ICT4D, informetrics, information communication technology.

Gina L. Peyton, an Associate Professor at Nova Southeastern University, USA, teaches doctoral level courses in organizational and higher education leadership, and master level leadership courses. Dr Peyton earned her Doctor of Education in organizational leadership, specializing in higher education leadership, her Master of Science degree in reading and her Bachelor of Science degree in psychology from Nova Southeastern University. With over 25 years of higher education experience, Dr Peyton has extensive knowledge of leadership theories and practice, ethical leadership, strategic leadership, leading and managing organizational change, education and research. Dr Peyton is a dissertation chair and serves on numerous leadership committees.

David B. Ross, a professor at Nova Southeastern University, teaches doctoral level courses in educational, organizational, and higher educational leadership. Learning from many perspectives and philosophies from mentors while attending Northern Illinois University, the University of Alabama, and Florida Atlantic University, has assisted him in guiding students in the learning process. Dr. Ross earned his Doctorate in Educational Leadership, Master of Justice Policy Management with an Executive Certificate in Public Management at Florida Atlantic University, and his Bachelor of Science Degree in Computer Science at Northern Illinois University. Dr. Ross regularly speaks at conferences and provides consultation and training in the areas of leadership and management, policy issues, critical thinking, risk-taking in research, professional development, academic writing, education, and behavior management. He has written articles and book chapters on leadership, power, narcissism, organizational stress, academic integrity, plagiarism and fraud, entitlement, mainstream media, mobbing/bullying, Gerontechnology, policy development, professional development, and areas of homeland security. Dr. Ross is a co-editor of a book titled Higher Education Challenges for Migrant and Refugee Students in a Global World. Dr. Ross is a dissertation chair and a reviewer for the university's Institutional Review Board. Dr. Ross was named Professor of the Year 2015-2016 for the Abraham S. Fischler College of Education. Dr. Ross is a retired Criminal Investigator/Agent with extensive-applied supervisory and field operations experience involving complex federal, state, local, and international crime; covert-clandestine operative and worked with informants; smuggling, profiling and drug interdiction; public order crime; asset forfeiture, money laundering, and conspiracy; wire and mail fraud; development of evidence for use in sworn affidavits, arrest and search and seizure warrants, pen registers; public and political corruption, technical operations including wire-oral intercepts, high technical human, stationary and aircraft/marine surveillance; intelligence-led programs, and RICO Act crimes.

Paul Siegel is a doctoral candidate at Mercer University. His work has focused on the intersection between digital multimodal media and literacy. He has also taught high school English for the last decade in the public schools of Georgia.

Seda Gökçe Turan received her B.S. degree from METU, department of Early Childhood Education in 2005. Then she received master degree Gazi University department of Child Development in 2012 and PhD degree in 2016 from Marmara University department of Informatics. As her professional career she is studying about child abuse, online abuse, cyber-bullying, justification of cyber-harassment and digital media literacy. Since 2011 she is working as lecturer at Bahçeşehir University, Department of Child Development.

Semi Yeom is a doctoral candidate at the University of Maryland. Her research interests include data literacy education, fair assessments for diverse students, and English learners' sense of belonging. Her doctoral dissertation aims to devise a data literacy assessment that serves both English speakers and English learners. She has worked with schools in D.C. and Maryland using quantitative and qualitative research methods.

Index

G

I

K

L

M

O

P

R

S

T

V

Y

Z

www.ingramcontent.com/pod-product-compliance
Lightning Source LLC
LaVergne TN
LVHW061538290926
849162LV00004B/832